TULSA CITY-COUNTY LIBRARY

PLEASE RETURN THIS ITEM
BY THE DUE DATE TO ANY
TULSA CITY-COUNTY LIBRARY.

FINES ARE 5¢ PER DAY; A
MAXIMUM OF $1.00 PER ITEM.

SEP 25 1996

Oklahoma's First Ladies

OKLAHOMA'S FIRST LADIES

By
LU CELIA WISE

Acknowledgements

We wish to acknowledge the invaluable assistance and encouragement of the following:

Governor George Nigh and his staff
Lieutenant Governor Spencer Bernard and his staff
    The first ladies who gave personal interviews and provided biographical information:
        Mrs. Raymond (Emma) Gary
        Mrs. J. Howard (Jeannette) Edmondson
        Mrs. Henry (Shirley) Bellmon
        Mrs. Dewey (Ann) Bartlett
        Mrs. Janna Boren Robbins
        Mrs. David (Molly) Boren
        Mrs. George (Donna) Nigh

Mrs. Jack (Lillian) Russell, Oklahoma City Fashion Group, originator of the First Ladies Gown Collection Project.

Mrs. Elizabeth Niblack Melton of Wagoner, Oklahoma, granddaughter of Mrs. Lillian Haskell, for supplying information and picture.

Mrs. Mary B. Stidham of Checotah, Oklahoma, sister of Mrs. J. Howard Edmondson, for supplying information and picture.

Mrs. M. E. Trapp, Jr. of Oklahoma City, Oklahoma, for a private interview furnishing information about former Governor and Mrs. M. E. Trapp and for her personal support.

Mrs. Jimmie Cook, Department of English, Oklahoma State University, Stillwater, Oklahoma, and her students in Honors English who researched some of the first ladies:

        Kyle Godsey   Lyde Marland
        Vanissa Smith   Mary Alice Murray
        Katie Mnich   Willie Murray
        Sarah West   Jeannette Edmondson
        Tisha Lee   Grayce Breene Kerr
        Jennifer Jacob   Donna Nigh

Sheila Rodgers Hayden, additional research

Dr. LeRoy H. Fischer, Oppenheim Regents Professor of History, Oklahoma State University, Stillwater, Oklahoma

Gilcrease Museum Library Staff, Tulsa, Oklahoma

Dr. Bob L. Blackburn and the library staff, Oklahoma Historical Society, Oklahoma City, Oklahoma

Mr. Jim Standard, Managing Editor, The Oklahoma Publishing Company

Text and photographs on Governors of Oklahoma courtesy of The Oklahoma Department of Libraries, DIRECTORY OF OKLAHOMA 1983, Copyright 1983.

Betty J. Brown, Oklahoma Research Librarian, Oklahoma Department of Libraries, Oklahoma City, Oklahoma

State Department of Education
        Dr. Leslie Fisher, State Superintendent of Public Instruction
        Dr. John Folks, Associate Deputy Superintendent, Department Administrators and Education Specialists
        Rita Geiger, Social Studies Specialist, State Department of Education

Copyright 1983 Evans Publications
P. O. Box 520
Perkins, Oklahoma 74059
December 1983

Printed in the United States of America
Library of Congress Catalog Card Number
83-82947
International Standard Book Number:
0-934188-10-6

Introduction

The story of Oklahoma's first ladies is a study in contrasts. It points up a wide range of personalities, tastes, and physical appearances. Several of these ladies were more interested in their homes and families than in the social and political activities of their husbands.

In contrast, some were politically ambitious. One of the wives, Willie Murray, ran for governor after her husband, Johnston, completed his term of office. Another first lady, Jeannette Edmondson, became Oklahoma's Secretary of State. Molly Shi was a judge before she married Governor Boren.

Physically, the ladies were certainly a varied lot. Janna Boren was very small—little more than five feet tall—while Grayce Kerr was a statuesque five feet ten and one-half inches.

Their backgrounds were also very different. Several of these women were very proud to consider themselves country girls. Others lived in relative luxury before their husbands became governor. Lillian Haskell lived in a twenty-three room house in Ohio before the Haskells moved to Muskogee and her husband became Oklahoma's first governor. Mrs. Haskell and the six Haskell children—including three from his first marriage—spent the winters in San Antonio, Texas with a governess. Each spring, they rode back to their home in Ohio in a private railroad car. This was not the background one might expect from a pioneer lady in Indian Territory.

The ages of the first ladies differed by many years. Several were matrons with grown children. Others were very young. Lydie Marland was the beautiful young wife of the tenth governor. In fact, her marriage to E. W. Marland had been the subject of state-wide and even national publicity. She was 28 and he was fifty-four at the time of their marriage. She had been adopted by her aunt, the first Mrs. Marland, and E. W. when she was ten years old. After the death of his wife, Marland had the adoption set aside so that he could marry Lydie.

It is hard to establish a firm count of Oklahoma's first ladies. Chickie LeFlore, wife of the second governor, Lee Cruce, died before he became governor. Robert Lee Williams, the third governor, never married. Therefore, when the sixth governor, Martin Trapp, took office there had been five governors but only three first ladies. Furthermore, his immediate predecessor, Jack Walton, had been impeached, and Governor Trapp had no formal inauguration ceremony. Governor Trapp's successor Henry S. Johnston, the seventh governor, was impeached also. William J. Holloway, the eighth governor, had no inauguration when he replaced the impeached Governor Johnston.

For several succeeding terms, things seemed to work out on a regular one-governor-one-first-lady basis and no other governors were impeached. However, George Nigh was not married when he became the 17th governor, serving the last nine days of Governor Howard Edmondson's term. Governor David Boren was married to Janna Lou Little and later Molly Shi while serving as governor. George Nigh was married at the time he served the last five days of Governor Boren's term. He came Oklahoma's 22nd governor, and Donna became the 20th first lady.

To add to the confusion, on January 10, 1983, George Nigh was sworn in for a history-making second term. Oklahoma has actually had twenty women serve as first lady and twenty-one men who have served as governor.

In spite of the differences, Oklahoma's first ladies seem to have had at least one thing in common: a desire to make a contribution, each in her own way, to her husband's success as governor.

The gowns of Oklahoma's First Ladies reflect the changing life styles of our state and the world. Fashion books tell us that styles in clothing change very little in twenty-five to fifty year periods. In most cases we are looking at examples of a four year period for each First Lady and we find drastic changes in those intervals.

Hattie Tingle Bentley described those early changes in her 1938 thesis:

> Contrary to expectation in a state that was only the day before a territory, women appeared at the very first inaugural ball very handsomely gowned in fashionable materials of crepe de chine, lace and net showing the French influence in their colors and lines. These long, clinging diaphanous gowns were replaced at the next inaugural ball by simple trainless affairs in velvets and satin brocades heavily embroidered and beaded.
>
> In 1915 there was a complete change in the silhouette, the most radical change being in the flaring full circular skirts. Out of the perplexing economic conditions here and the war in Europe grew the American fashion of wearing cotton. Its influence was reflected in the 1915 silhouette which was similar to the one of 1830 when cottons had previously been at their height.
>
> Four years later, in 1919, with economic conditions improved the pendulum of fashion swung toward all important materials replacing the less elegant ones of the previous inaugural ball. The bodices with high backs and modest openings in front became extremely low both in front and back.
>
> In 1923 the classic Grecian line predominated in combinations of fabrics and colors. Trailing trains of 1919 remained fashionable for diplomatic and great state functions.
>
> The fashion of 1927 showed the most drastic change since statehood in its penciled silhouette with skirts rising two inches above the knees and the waist line dropped below the hips.
>
> The unsettled condition of our country was reflected in the gowns of 1931. The mode, that of self-expression, made the women more important than her gown. Many gowns that year were reminiscent of the periods of the First Empire, the French Revolution, Medieval Times, the romantic 1830's and of Egypt each employing a material characteristic of the period from which it gained its inspiration.
>
> With conditions improved in 1935 the fashionable evening silhouettes were confined to the slim sheath gained through use of stiff fabric, usually taffeta, and the robe de style gained through use of soft clinging materials.
>
> Looking back over the illustrations of the typical styles that appeared at these four-year intervals it is obvious that they reflect the fluctuating economic conditions, change and development in the textile industry, growth and increasing importance of American centers of fashion design and the cultural development of our times and state.

In the next fifty years we see a continuation of world conditions reflected in dress. Wars, depressions, television and other scientific innovations even our moral values are apparent in the changing views of what is considered good taste in what we wear.

The oil crunch of the seventies brought cotton and wool back to replace to some extent the use of practical polyester as a favorite material. Blue jeans showed up everywhere from ballgames to balls all over the world. In direct contrast, hats and gloves also returned to favor. The pendulum swings very quickly from one extreme to the other to express the ever changing conditions of our world.

Lu Celia Wise

Contents

Lillian Gallup Haskell — 8
    November 16, 1907 to January 9, 1911

Isabelle Butler Robertson — 12
    January 13, 1919 to January 8, 1923

Madeleine Orrick Walton — 16
    January 8, 1923 to November 19, 1923

Lula C. (Lou) Strang Trapp — 20
    November 19, 1923 to January 10, 1927

Ethel L. Littleton Johnston — 24
    January 10, 1927 to March 20, 1929

Amy Arnold Holloway — 28
    March 20, 1929 to January 12, 1931

Mary Alice Hearrell Murray — 32
    January 12, 1931 to January 14, 1935

Lydie Roberts Marland — 36
    January 14, 1935 to January 9, 1939

Myrtle Ellenberger Phillips — 40
    January 9, 1939 to January 11, 1943

Grayce Breene Kerr — 44
    January 13, 1943 to January 13, 1947

Jessica Grimm Turner — 48
    January 13, 1947 to January 8, 1951

Willie Emerson Murray — 52
    January 8, 1951 to January 10, 1955

Emma Mae Purser Gary — 56
    January 10, 1955 to January 12, 1959

Jeannette Bartleson Edmondson — 60
    January 12, 1959 to January 6, 1963

Shirley Osborn Bellmon — 64
    January 14, 1963 to January 9, 1967

Ann Smith Bartlett — 68
    January 9, 1967 to January 11, 1971

Jo Evans Hall — 72
    January 11, 1971 to January 13, 1975

Janna Lou Little Boren — 76
    January 13, 1975 to October 23, 1975

Molly Shi Boren — 80
    November 27, 1977 to January 3, 1979

Donna Skinner Nigh — 84
    January 3, 1979 to present

(Photo Courtesy Oklahoma Historical Society)

Charles Nathaniel Haskell, Oklahoma's first State Governor, was born March 13, 1860, in Putman County, Ohio. He was educated as a lawyer, admitted to the Ohio Bar in 1881, and began practice in Ottawa, Ohio. In 1901, he moved to Muskogee, Indian Territory, where he added to his law practice the promotion of railroads. He was a leader in the Oklahoma Constitutional Convention in 1906. After his term as Governor, from November 16, 1907, to January 9, 1911, he engaged in the oil business. He died on July 5, 1933, and is buried in Muskogee, Oklahoma.

Text and Photograph courtesy Oklahoma Department of Libraries

Lillian Elizabeth Gallup Haskell

Lillian Elizabeth Gallup married Charles N. Haskell in September 1889. The Gallup family had come to America in 1630 from Dorset, England. Lillian was born in Ottawa, Ohio, in 1863. Haskell's first wife, Lucie Pomeroy, had died in March 1888, leaving him with three children: Norman, Murray, and Lucie. He and Lillian had three more children: Frances, Jane, and Joseph.

Although the Haskells maintained a twenty-three room house in Ottawa, Ohio, they spent much of the 1890s in other parts of the country. Each winter Lillian, the six Haskell children, and a governess traveled to San Antonio, Texas. They lived at the Menger Hotel until spring. At that time, they returned to Ohio in the Haskells' private railroad car. Charles Haskell's primary business was railroad construction.

In the early 1900s the Haskell family moved to Muskogee, Indian Territory. Early in 1901, Haskell had agreed to construct a railroad from Fayetteville, Arkansas, to Muskogee. He quickly became one of the town's leading citizens. He was given an engraved silver tea service by "grateful citizens of Muskogee." His prominence in Muskogee soon spread throughout Indian Territory. He became a very influential member of both the Sequoyah and Oklahoma constitutional conventions. Charles Nathaniel Haskell was elected Oklahoma's first governor on September 17, 1907.

On November 16, 1907, Lillian and the Haskell children joined Charles Haskell on the steps of the Guthrie Public Library for his inauguration as governor of the new state of Oklahoma—the 46th state of the Union.

The city of Guthrie made great preparation for its first "statehood day." Crowds of people from all parts of the two territories came by train, wagons, buggies, carriages, horseback, and on foot to join in the celebration. "Crying babies, eager excited children, tired-faced farm women, rough bearded pioneers, well-dressed business men, and fashionably attired society matrons, all helped to make up the throngs that crowded the streets of the capital city." The National Guard with their uniforms and shouldered guns added a military touch to the proceedings.

Page 8 - Oklahoma's First Ladies

(Photo Courtesy Oklahoma Historical Society)
(Inlay photo courtesy of Mrs. Elizabeth Niblack Melton)

First Lady Lillian Haskell, Nov. 6, 1907 to Jan. 9, 1911

Mrs. Haskell's elaborate inaugural ball gown was a Parisian import of white crepe de chine with a rather low, round neckline and elbow-length sleeves. It was embroidered in pastel shades with lace medallion insets and five thousand French knots. Bands of lace made the circular flounce around the lower part of the skirt which extended into a train. Diamond jewelry added an elegant touch.

As part of the inagural ceremony, a mock wedding was performed joining Miss Indian Territory and Mr. Oklahoma Territory. A beautiful Indian woman, Mrs. Leo Bennett of Muskogee, acted as Miss Indian Territory; C. G. Jones of Oklahoma City, dressed as a cowboy, represented Oklahoma Territory.

Approximately 10,000 people enjoyed a huge barbecue at the city park. All afternoon the milling crowd swarmed the streets enjoying the holiday spirit of the occasion. Late in the afternoon, a large part of the crowd began to disperse.

The evening was given over to a state ball attended by two thousand people. At 10:05 the grand march began, led by Governor and Mrs. Haskell. The clock was turned back and dancing continued until the morning hours. The great ballroom was brilliantly lighted by myriads of electric globes, half-hidden in encircling vines. The governor, his wife and daughters, and other members of the receiving party stood against a background of palms and tall chrysanthemums.

The ladies were handsomely gowned. Mrs. Haskell wore a beautiful Paris gown of white crepe de chine with low neck and elbow sleeves embroidered in pastel shades and 5,000 French knots. Lace medallions were set in, and bands of lace made the circular flounce around the lower part of the skirt extending into the train. Her ornaments were diamonds.

According to Elizabeth Niblack Melton, the Haskell's granddaughter, Mrs. Haskell purchased her dress in St. Louis at the World's Fair in 1904. She paid $350 for the Paris designed gown—an exorbitant price at the time. It was originally intended as a robe. Mrs. Haskell had a dressmaker convert it into an elaborate dress with a flowing train.

The elaborate grand ball was described by Hattie Tingle Bentley in **A Study of Fashions as Portrayed Through Costumes of Governors' Wives**:

> Miss Lucie Haskell, eldest daughter of Governor Haskell, was charming in a frock of yellow net over crepe de chine with an armful of big yellow "mums."
>
> Miss Frances Haskell, second daughter, beautiful and vivacious, was gowned in white net, gold spangled, trimmed with roses of pink panne velvet. Her costume was the most striking in the ballroom.
>
> Miss Jane Haskell, the schoolgirl daughter, wore a blue net frock, lace trimmed over a blue silk slip.
>
> Mrs. Leo Bennett, who took the bride's part of Miss Indian Territory in the symbolic marriage ceremony earlier in the day, looked regal in a Greek key design lace princess style dress. The high necked, long sleeved gown had a small train. At her throat, she wore a platinum brooch in an exquisite leaf design, studded with fifty small diamonds.
>
> The richness and value of many of the costumes and much of the jewelry may appear remarkable beside the territorial people they adorned but it should be remembered that many of these people who attended the inaugural ball had been in Indian Territory only two or three years, having come from older states bringing their wealth and tradition with them. In spite of the fact that Oklahoma was the newest state, the first inaugural ball surpassed many of its older sister states in gorgeous costumes and elegant appointments.
>
> It is worthy of note that, although during the day people from every walk of life appeared in all types of costumes, in the evening no inaugural ball could have given evidence of greater beauty, sophistication and wealth than did the first inaugural ball of Oklahoma.

Charles N. Haskell was born in Leipsic, Ohio, on March 13, 1860. His father, George Haskell, a cooper by trade, died of pneumonia before Charles was three years old. His mother, left with five children and no income, struggled against almost insurmountable odds to support her family. At one time only an animal skin over the door kept out the old winter wind. Charles started early working outside the home. He studied at night, eventually taught school, and was admitted to the Ohio bar on December 6, 1880. One of his cases involved a railroad right-of-way. He became a successful railroad promoter, while also involving himself in Ohio politics.

After the Haskells moved to Muskogee, Indian Territory, where he continued to promote and build railroads, he also pursued other ventures. He built the Turner Hotel, an opera house, and an office building, and rebuilt the town's street railway system. He owned interest in a local bank, began the publication of a weekly newspaper, the **New State Tribune,** and attempted to reopen navigation of the Arkansas River.

During his term as Oklahoma's first governor, Haskell strove to upgrade and promote public schools and higher education. He considered the comprehensive banking system established during his administration his greatest contribution to state development. Haskell's most noted action as governor, however, was the removal of the state capital from Guthrie to Oklahoma City.

Governor Haskell had many political and legal problems during his term in office. He became involved in national politics, rising in prominence in the Democratic party. He had a long running feud with President Theodore Roosevelt. Eventually, he gained the president's respect, and they became good friends.

Mrs. Haskell held an unusual place in her husband's esteem, serving as his most trusted adviser. She earned a reputation for being as much at ease in his office as in her home. When he returned to private business, she was constantly at his side. After his death on July 5, 1933, she moved to San Antonio, Texas. She died in 1940 and was buried in Muskogee beside her husband.

James Brooks Ayers Robertson was born March 15, 1871, in Keokuk County, Iowa, and was educated in the public schools. In 1893, he moved to Oklahoma and was admitted to the Oklahoma Bar in 1898. He held the following political offices: Lincoln County Attorney, 1900–1902; Judge of the Tenth Judicial District of Oklahoma, 1909–1910; Member of the State Capitol Commission, 1911; Member of the Supreme Court Commission, 1911–1914; Governor of Oklahoma, January 13, 1919, to January 8, 1923; Democratic Presidential Elector-at-Large, 1932. He died at his home in Oklahoma City on March 7, 1938.

Text and Photograph courtesy Oklahoma Department of Libraries

Copyright 1930-78, The Oklahoma Publishing Co. From the Oklahoman & Times 1930-1978

Isabelle Butler Robertson

Miss Isabelle Butler met James B. A. Robertson through one of his law clients. They were married on November 28, 1917. Robertson's first wife, Olive Stubblefield, had died three years earlier.

James Brooks Ayers Robertson, Oklahoma's fourth governor, was inaugurated on January 13, 1919. He was the first governor to be elected from the Oklahoma Territory side of the state and the first governor to be sworn in at the new state capitol. The actual construction of the building had not begun until July 1914. His inaugural address dealt with the many problems the state would face as an aftermath of World War I.

Governor and Mrs. Robertson gave a reception for the public in the state room of the Capitol from four to six in the afternoon in which all state officials and their wives took part. The inaugural ball on the legislative floor at the state house concluded the day, with Governor and Mrs. Robertson heading the grand march. Oklahoma's first lady wore a magnificent costume of gold and black brocade in bold leaf design, handsomely trimmed in jet, decollette with a court train.

The ball was well remembered by all of those attending because of the failure of the lighting system. Hattie Tingle Bentley describes the event in detail:

> At exactly nine-thirty, when all the state officials and dignitaries were going "over the top" of the grand stairway leading to the fourth floor, all lights were shut off.
>
> The most remarkable thing about the occurrence was the poise and cheerfulness of hundreds of men and women who moved right on just as though nothing at all had happened.
>
> In a moment, a few men began to strike matches which flashed like fire-flies on a dark night. Then a flashlight in one of the balconies was produced which relieved the dense darkness in the corridors and rotunda until somebody, finding a lone candle, stuck it in one of the beautiful bronze pedestals with their cluster lights that refused to burn.
>
> The band, deprived of its dance scores, played old familiar tunes and the guests danced about in the dusk. The women on the stairway settled there as

(Photo Courtesy Oklahoma Historical Society)

First Lady Isabelle Robertson, Jan. 13, 1919 to Jan. 8, 1923

Mrs. Robertson's magnificent costume for their inaugural ball was of gold and black brocade in a bold leaf design. The long torso top was covered with jet "ropes" attached at the shoulders hanging loose until they were fastened at the hipline.

comfortably as they could, taking handkerchiefs and spreading them on the steps as a protection to their delicate gowns before sitting down.

Those who arrived after the lights had failed danced in their tall hats, some of them in their overcoats. At eleven o'clock everyone was still waiting for the lights when Captain N. C. Jewett announced that there was no prospect of more lights and that those who wished might go home. At eleven thirty-five when a third of the guests had gone home, the lights suddenly flashed on and those remaining enjoyed the beauty that had been arranged with so much care by the ball committee.

The turbulent times of early statehood continued into Governor Robertson's term. He escaped impeachment by one vote; two of his successors, John C. Walton and Henry S. Johnston, were impeached. He had to deal with lynchings, the Tulsa race riot, and the Ku Klux Klan, which grew to a membership of several thousand in Oklahoma immediately after World War I. The national coal miners' strike closed the mines of eastern Oklahoma and stopped railway service—closing many businesses for lack of fuel. All this unsettling activity caused Robertson to use the military power of the governor's office to suppress the disturbances by calling out the National Guard on numerous occasions. Highway construction became a major issue.

Jimmie L. White, Jr., in **Oklahoma's Governors, 1907-1929**, describes what he considers one of Governor Robertson's finer achievements—granting suffrage to women in Oklahoma:

> Governor Robertson believed that many unjust laws needed to be changed to provide more equality and freedom for the state's citizens. During the November election of 1918, the men of Oklahoma gave their approval for the legislature to ratify the Nineteenth Amendment to the United States Constitution, which gave women the right to vote. Governor Robertson asked for legislative action, but the 1919 legislature adjourned without considering the bill. Then he called the legislature into special session between February 23-28, 1920, to ratify the Nineteenth Amendment. This task was accomplished, and Oklahoma's women were franchised.

The Robertsons continued to live in Oklahoma City following his term in office. After having graciously received Oklahoma's distinguished visitors during World War I, Mrs. Robertson enjoyed a quiet life in the family's rather unpretentious home at 1416 West 16th Street in Oklahoma City. She and the former governor spent many hours reading about the on-going political battles in Oklahoma. In fact, he ran unsuccessfully for a United States Senate seat and for the Oklahoma Supreme Court. In 1935 he became the attorney for the Oklahoma Corporation Commission, a position he retained until his death in March 1938.

(Photo Courtesy Oklahoma Historical Society)

Another view of Mrs. Robertson in her magnificent costume for the inaugural ball.

Jack Callaway Walton was born March 6, 1881, on a farm near Indianapolis, Indiana. After a ten-year stay in Lincoln, Nebraska, he joined the Army in 1897. Although he saw no foreign service during the Spanish-American War, he did live in Mexico before coming to Oklahoma City in 1903, as a sales engineer. He was Commissioner of Public Works in 1917; Mayor of Oklahoma City, 1919–23; elected Governor in 1922, and impeached within the year, serving from January 8, to November 19, 1923; served in the State Corporation Commission from 1932, until 1939, when he retired to enter private law practice. He died November 25, 1949, and is buried in the Rose Hill Cemetery in Oklahoma City.

Text and Photograph courtesy Oklahoma Department of Libraries

Copyright 1930-78, The Oklahoma Publishing Co. From the Oklahoman & Times 1930-1978

Madeleine Orrick Walton

Madeleine Orrick was married to "Jack" Walton three weeks after he had divorced his first wife. They evidently had a harmonious family life with their two daughters. Her Catholic background and humanitarian beliefs were a stabilizing influence on Walton's later life.

According to a description by Hattie Tingle Bentley, the inauguration of John Callaway "Jack" Walton, the fifth governor, was one of the most colorful and dramatic of any Oklahoma inaugural. He took office on January 8, 1923. The oath of office was administered by Chief Justice of the Oklahoma Supreme Court John T. Johnson—the same judge who would preside at Walton's impeachment ten months later.

In his campaign Walton had stated that he wanted to represent the common man. He declared that there would be "no inaugural ball and there will not be a **tea dansant**." He intended to give an "old fashioned square dance and barbecue—a party for all the people." He kept his promise about the party; however, the celebration lasted three days and ended with an inaugural ball. The parade and barbecue were made extremely colorful because of the mixture of people in such wildly diverse dress.

Bentley described the exciting event in the following manner:

> Among the guests was Buck Garrett neatly attired in a salt and pepper business suit and wearing a white doe-skin vest nattily slashed with scarlet at the edges.
> Major Gordon Lillie (Pawnee Bill) who was dressed in his native costume. Indian war bonnets and gorgeous hued blankets mingled with silk hats and other habiliments of statecraft; farmers' wives with babes in arms held even place with society matrons and their sisters of wealth.
> Out of the past rode Zack Mulhall, marshal of the parade, booted and spurred and topped with a sweeping sombrero, who led the multitude of paraders and spectators to the barbecue. Streaming endlessly through the fifteen serving units, rich men, poor men, women with sealskin coats and diamonds, farm wives and children swelled the total fed to 60,000. Governor Walton was dressed in a plain business suit and Mrs. Walton in a neat street suit. There

(Photo Courtesy Oklahoma Historical Society)

First Lady Madeleine Walton, Jan. 8, 1923 to Nov. 19, 1923

Mrs. Walton's gown was a stately one of white satin with a court train. The long waist, with its bateau neckline, was fitted at the hips. It was heavily beaded with crystal beads in large floral designs. The skirt was ankle length showing silver cloth evening shoes. Graceful draping on the sides extended into a train.

was no affectation of pomp displayed by any member of the receiving line.

On Wednesday, January 10, the occasion that ended the three day festivities, which had ushered J. C. Walton into office, was the inaugural ball.

Workers in overalls and the elite in costly furs and dress suits mingled in dancing throngs at the brilliantly lighted state capitol building. Elderly square dancers contrasted with younger couples who whirled in modern steps to old rhythms.

National guard staff officers and private soldiers in military costume paraded together with girls dressed in red and white silk riding costumes. Indians wearing showy head dresses danced with capital stenographers, a slow step which they taught each girl with whom they danced.

Several bands were placed on the various floors of the building. Separate dance centers formed around each, on the various floors in the corridors, in offices, in the stately senate chamber and in the halls of the house of representatives.

Indian women of the Arapaho, Creek, and Osage tribes were there. Mingled with them were pioneer women, ineffaceably marked with the signs of times through which they struggled, and society leaders, wives of oil magnates, and daughters of old time cowmen. Picturesque characters of early days lent color to the crowds thronging the capitol building for the inaugural ball but they did not detract from the elegance of the gowns of the women of the official families and many other women who were there. Mrs. Walton was not without her inaugural ball gown even if Governor Walton did wear a business suit of navy blue.

Mrs. Walton's gown was a stately one of white satin with a court train. The long waist with bateau neckline rested upon the hips. It was heavily beaded with crystal beads in large floral designs. The skirt was ankle length with graceful draping on the side that extended into a train, showing silver cloth slippers.

Governor Walton's short term in office was one of the stormiest in the history of the state. He constantly changed positions on many issues. He was elected by the largest majority of any of his predecessors. During his campaign he had appealed to the common man in all of his speeches. It seems, however, that immediately after taking office he became enamored with the good life. He was playing the same old political game of building up a political power base at the expense of the common people.

He also changed positions on the Ku Klux Klan—or "Kluckers" as he called them. He fought them in his campaign; as governor he secretly became a member and later repudiated them. It is said that Mrs. Walton, with her Catholic background, influenced the governor to finally turn away from the Klan.

Walton was the first Oklahoma governor to be impeached. Mrs. Walton was with him during the various removal proceedings. His term as governor lasted little more than ten months. He later ran unsuccessfully for several public offices, including governor. In 1932 Walton finally staged a remarkable political comeback by being elected to the Oklahoma Corporation Commission.

Madeleine Walton died in 1947, having lived through all of her husband's hectic political life without ever flinching in her devotion.

Copyright 1930-78, The Oklahoma Publishing Co
From the Oklahoman & Times 1930-1978

Martin Edwin Trapp, born April 18, 1877, in Robinson, Kansas, was educated almost entirely by association and study with Mr. McDaniel, a neighbor. He served as County Clerk of Logan County, 1905–1907; State Auditor, 1907–1911; Lieutenant Governor, 1915–1927. After the impeachment of Governor Walton, he served as Governor of the State from November 19, 1923, until January 10, 1927. Following this he was a dealer in investment securities until his death on July 26, 1951, in Oklahoma City.

Text and Photograph courtesy Oklahoma Department of Libraries

Lula C. (Lou) Strang Trapp

Lula C. (Lou) Strang was the attractive daughter of Judge J. C. Strang, who had been the attorney general in the administrations of two Oklahoma territorial governors. The Strangs were of French Huguenot descent. The French spelling of the name was "Le Strange." In 1685 when the family immigrated to America, they settled on the Hudson River in New York. Lou Strang's great grandfather served in the Revolutionary War and was on General George Washington's staff.

Lou's father had moved from New York to Kansas in 1877. He had a very successful career in Kansas, becoming a state senator and, in 1881, a judge. He moved to Guthrie, Oklahoma Territory, in 1893. His success continued in Oklahoma, where he served as territorial attorney general.

Lou Strang and Martin Edwin Trapp married in 1907. Trapp was born in Kansas. His family arrived in Oklahoma Territory in 1889 and settled near Guthrie. Martin Trapp became a teacher and, later, a state auditor. He was elected lieutenant governor in 1914, 1918, and again in 1922. He was serving in that capacity when Governor Walton was impeached on October 23, 1923. Trapp became acting governor on that date.

The Trapps had been married seventeen years when he became governor. Their son, Edwin, was eight years old. Mrs. Trapp's main interests were her son, her home, and her husband. She once remarked: "Public Life? I don't like it at all. I'd rather have my husband at home."

According to a newspaper report, Mrs. Trapp did not feel that women should be active in politics. She voted against the proposition to give women the right to hold important executive positions. She felt that women could assume a more important role in reforming politics through their position of power in the home. She felt that if a woman made her home pleasant for her family, wielded an influence for good with her husband, and raised her children to be honest, God-fearing men and women who would take a stand for the right things, then she had exercised her influence in politics and the world in general.

Page 20 - Oklahoma's First Ladies

Courtesy Oklahoma Historical Society, Hattie Tingle Bentley Thesis

First Lady Lula (Lou) Trapp, Nov. 19, 1923 to Jan. 10, 1927

Mrs. Trapp wore a French costume of embroidered black grosgrain silk to the Johnston inaugural. The skirt was trimmed in bands of green, blue and gold. Her corsage was of cerise ostrich feathers.

Despite her feelings about politics, she did travel to some campaign meetings in later years. During a visit by Mrs. Trapp to the family's former home in Muskogee, an observer noted that, although the governor's wife did not make public speeches, she excelled as a listener and an observer.

Lou Trapp was not an exponent of women's suffrage but, after it was granted, she considered it her duty to vote. She believed there were women whose ideals were not of the highest that never failed to vote. She was convinced that it was the duty of women who believed that honesty and right should prevail to go to the polls and cast their ballot.

Mrs. Trapp was not active in social organizations. She belonged to only one club in Oklahoma City. The Alcorn Club was made up originally of people who had moved to Oklahoma City from Guthrie, but later broadened into a study club with limited membership. Mrs. Trapp was an associate member.

When asked about her hobbies, Mrs. Trapp responded that her son was her only hobby. She was sure that she bored some of her friends with her talk about him. The Trapps were married eight years before Edwin, their only child, was born. She admitted that their whole existence centered around him.

Governor Trapp planned to run again after filling out the impeached Governor Walton's term. The law stated that a governor could not succeed himself, but because he had never taken the official oath of office, Trapp believed he was still eligible. He had taken no part in the controversy over Walton's impeachment. One district court judge ruled that Trapp had only been acting governor and thus could run. The Oklahoma Supreme Court later reversed the ruling, and he was not allowed to attempt another term. Governor Trapp had used his quiet political skills to bring many needed reforms. He was referred to as the "Sphinx of Oklahoma."

The former governor accepted the turn of events and concentrated his efforts on his business interests. He eventually founded Trapp Enterprises, which became a leader in the construction and oil and gas industries in Oklahoma and Texas. He and Mrs. Trapp enjoyed their family and success.

Copyright 1930-78, The Oklahoma Publishing Co. From the Oklahoman & Times 1930-1978

First Lady Lula (Lou) Trapp

Oklahoma's First Ladies - Page 23

Copyright 1930-78, The Oklahoma Publishing Co. From the Oklahoman & Times 1930-1978

Henry Simpson Johnston, born December 30, 1867, near Evansville, Indiana, migrated to Colorado at the age of twenty-four where he studied law and was admitted to the Colorado Bar in 1891. Later he came to Perry, Oklahoma to practice. He was a member, and Temporary Presiding Officer of the Constitutional Convention in 1906. His term as Governor which began January 10, 1927, was terminated March 20, 1929, after his impeachment. He practiced law in his home town of Perry, Oklahoma until his death on January 7, 1965.

Text and Photograph courtesy Oklahoma Department of Libraries

Ethel Littleton Johnston

Ethel Littleton was a court reporter during the first session of the Oklahoma State Legislature. The attractive brunette reporter caught the eye of Henry S. Johnston, president pro tempore of the senate. They were married soon afterward.

The spotlight shone on the Perry lawyer on January 10, 1927, when he became Oklahoma's seventh governor. Loud speakers and radio equipment carried the proceedings to a vast audience for the first time at an inaugural ceremony in Oklahoma.

In the afternoon a general reception was held in the Blue Room adjoining the executive offices in the Capitol. Governor and Mrs. Johnston, along with ex-Governor and Mrs. Trapp and other officials, received a huge crowd. The public had been invited to attend the reception and the inaugural ball that followed.

At this point attention shifted to the governor's wife, Ethel Littleton Johnston. Slender and very style conscious, she wore her dark hair in a "short bob." Her inaugural ball gown was a striking Parisian import. The short skirt with its uneven hemline was a dramatic change from the inaugural gowns of earlier years.

A huge crowd was wedged into the Capitol as the Governor and Mrs. Johnston made their way from the second to the fourth floor of the building. Very few of the packed struggling masses were able to see Mrs. Johnston—but they all seemed to have come for that purpose. There were men in full dress suits, tuxedoes, business suits, and even boots and spurs.

The women were dressed in everything from the plainest street dresses to flamboyant evening clothes. The ball was colorful and gay, with prominent women from all over the state dressed in their finest, paying homage to Oklahoma's first lady. Short dresses and bright colors predominated and helped to create an unusually youthful appearance. The raised hemlines showed off a new trend toward elaborate evening slippers of many colors. The hose matched exactly or were a neutral flesh color. Black satin pumps with huge rhinestone buckles were also very popular.

(Photo Courtesy Oklahoma Historical Society)

First Lady Ethel Johnston, Jan. 10, 1927 to Mar. 20, 1929

Mrs. Johnston's inaugural gown followed the elegant trend set by her predecessors except that her dress had the short uneven hemline so popular in the twenties. The dress was designed and made in Paris. It was made of dull Roman gold colored beads and sequins on a filmy silk net over self-color satin. The dress weighed two and one-half pounds. The shoulder scarf was of flame colored georgette with gold and silver embroidery. Her shoes were of gold brocade.

Henry Johnston was born in Evansville, Indiana, in 1870. His family moved to Kansas, where he received most of his education. He later moved to Colorado, where he studied law. He was admitted to the bar in Denver in 1891. Some two years later he took advantage of the opening of the Cherokee Outlet in Oklahoma Territory. He settled in Perry and practiced law there for the rest of his life, except for his short term as governor. He was active in the politics of the territory and served as presiding officer of the organizational phase of the Oklahoma Constitutional Convention. William H. "Alfalfa Bill" Murray, the convention chairman, termed Johnston the "smoothest and best parliamentarian" in the group.

Johnston's term as governor did not go smoothly from the very first. Excerpts from **Oklahoma's Governors, 1907-1929: Turbulent Politics** give details of his problems:

> A matter that caused friction between Johnston's office and the legislature, as well as with many outside of the state government, was the appointment of Mrs. O. O. (Mayme) Hammonds as the confidential secretary to the governor. Mrs. Hammonds was a former worker in the women's division of the state Ku Klux Klan and the Democratic Party. She had met Johnston during the election effort. Mrs. Hammonds first found opposition in the legislature when she urged Johnston not to return to the senate the first slate of names for appointment to the Oklahoma Highway Commission. She soon became known as the one who guarded the governor from those who wanted to use him for their own interests, but at the same time many legislators, who believed that they had important business with the governor, were often kept waiting unannounced by Mrs. Hammonds. Toward the end of the 1927 legislative session, one of Johnston's strongest supporters, Senator Jess Pullen, introduced a resolution asking that she be removed from the governor's staff....
>
> The most bizarre of the stories was one written by Aldrich Blake, a former member of the Walton administration, who charged that Johnston belonged to the Rosicrucian philosophical group, that Mrs. Hammonds was supposed to travel through space to investigate the character of applicants for public office while still physically at her desk, and that Judge Armstrong was restored to health by a guru from India. Blake also charged that Johnston signed legislative bills by the signs of the zodiac and enlisted the aid of Mrs. Hammonds to consult with the dead. All of the charges were denied by Johnston, but his credibility was severely damaged by the story.
>
> Would the governor discharge Mrs. Hammonds, a major target of the disgruntled legislators, in order to fend off the investigation? Johnston replied in a manner characteristic of his wide reading in religious literature and indicative of his stubborn personality: "Suppose you had 1,000 sheep and one little ewe lamb.... Would you put the ewe with the sheep to be slaughtered even though it might save you from destruction?" Johnston said that to discharge Mrs. Hammonds now would not only be "base and venal," but would also be "hiding behind a woman's skirts."
>
> By refusing to sacrifice Mrs. Hammonds to the will of a group of legislators, Governor Johnston paved the way for the beginning of one of the most unusual episodes in Oklahoma history, the "ewe lamb rebellion." Led by the so-called "Four Horsemen" of the Oklahoma House of Representatives, the revolt, though centered around Mrs. Hammonds, went much deeper than Governor Johnston's confidential secretary. It was doubtful that any sacrifice on the part of Johnston could save him from the events that were to come. These developments would soon see the state's seventh governor impeached after only two years in office.
>
> The senate agreed that there was no criminal intent on the part of the governor, and on March 20, 1929, found Johnston not guilty of all the charges except the one charge of incompetency.

Johnston, therefore, became the second Oklahoma governor to be removed from office by impeachment. Johnston returned to Perry, where he was met by a large crowd of townspeople, friends, and supporters throughout the state, including the same band that appeared at his inauguration two years earlier. Johnston remained in Perry for the rest of his life, but he did not retire, for he remained active in the practice of law well into his nineties.

In 1932 he placed the name of his friend and fellow delegate to the Oklahoma Constitutional Convention, William H. "Alfalfa Bill" Murray, in nomination for President of the United States before the Democratic National Convention. That same year, Johnston was elected to the Oklahoma Senate, where he served with many of the same men who had voted to impeach him. Johnston remained active, meanwhile, in fraternal affairs and continued to practice law. He was the principal lawyer for the noted 101 Ranch during the years of its receivership and bankruptcy.

Although ninety-four years of age, Johnston's death was unexpected when he died at the family table at noon on January 7, 1965. His death came only one day after a proposal was submitted to the Oklahoma Legislature to soften the stigma of his impeachment. His body laid in state in the Oklahoma Capitol Building, and then funeral services were held in the First Christian Church in Perry. . . .

After the Johnstons returned to Perry, they were received as if they had only been away on a trip for two years. They reopened their home, and Mrs. Johnston resumed her work in her community's civic affairs. She still had a trim figure which she helped to maintain by long walks and horseback riding. During their long marriage, the Johnstons adopted four children.

William Judson Holloway, who succeeded Governor Johnston in office and completed the term to January 12, 1931, was a native of Arkadelphia, Arkansas, born December 15, 1888. After graduation from Ouachita College in 1910, he attended the University of Chicago for a time. While he was living in Hugo and working as a high school principal he began to read law. He later completed his course at Cumberland University and was admitted to the practice of law at Hugo. He was elected county attorney in 1916; was a State Senator from 1920 to 1924, serving as President Pro Tempore; in 1926, he was elected Lieutenant Governor and thus advanced to the Governor's office. He practiced law in Oklahoma City until his death on January 28, 1970.

Text and Photograph courtesy Oklahoma Department of Libraries

Amy Arnold Holloway

Copyright 1930-78, The Oklahoma Publishing Co. From the Oklahoman & Times 1930-1978

Amy Holloway served as Oklahoma's first lady for two years while her husband, William J. Holloway, filled out the unexpired term of impeached Governor Henry S. Johnston.

Mrs. Holloway was not especially anxious to assume the duties of the wife of a governor and accordingly, to change her lifestyle. She told a reporter as they prepared to move into the mansion, "We are just the same today as we were yesterday, and we'll be the same tomorrow."

Mrs. Holloway, the former Amy Arnold, was born in Paducah, Kentucky, and grew up in Arkadelphia, Arkansas. She was a graduate of Ouachita College at Arkadelphia. She was teaching school at Hugo (Oklahoma) High School when she met William Holloway, who had resigned as high school principal to open a law office in Hugo. They were married on June 16, 1917.

She once remarked that she preferred to leave the newsmaking to her husband. When asked why she never took part in political campaigns, she would reply, "I don't know anything about politics. My husband does not want it and I have all I can do to take care of my son." William Jr. was an active five-year-old when his father became governor.

William Holloway's political career began early when he was elected county attorney of Bryan County in 1916. He served two terms in the state senate. He also served as president pro tempore of that body and was elected lieutenant governor when Henry S. Johnston was elected governor in 1926.

After Johnston's impreachment, Holloway filled out his term in a quiet and unassuming manner. He conducted the state's affairs in a business-like fashion. The financial panic of 1929 and the depression that followed discouraged Holloway. He failed to erase the state's deficit as he had hoped. He did, however, make some changes in the Democrats' complete control of state government. He appointed a Republican, Lew Wentz of Ponca City, as chairman of the highway commission.

(Photograph courtesy Lieutenant Governor Spencer Bernard's office)

First Lady Amy Holloway, Mar. 20, 1929 to Jan. 12, 1931

Mrs. Holloway's family donated a favorite dress to the First Ladies Gown Collection, since she had no inaugural gown. It was warm beige colored crepe trimmed in wide bands and sleeves of black lace.

In the 1930 election, William H. "Alfalfa Bill" Murray returned from Bolivia and won the race for governor. Thomas P. Gore came out of a ten-year retirement to win a United States Senate seat. The state's political arena once more became the dramatic stage for colorful and controversial action. William Holloway did not find himself a leading part in this scenario.

Amy Holloway very quietly lived out the couple's 52 years of marriage. The Holloway's only child, William Judson Holloway Jr., became a judge of the Tenth United States Circuit Court of Appeals.

In addition to the pleasures of her family duties, Mrs. Holloway enjoyed a long membership in St. Luke's United Methodist Church in Oklahoma City. At one time she served as president of its Women's Society of Christian Service. She also served as president of the Wesley House Board. Her club memberships included the Blue Flower Garden Club and the Bookmark Club.

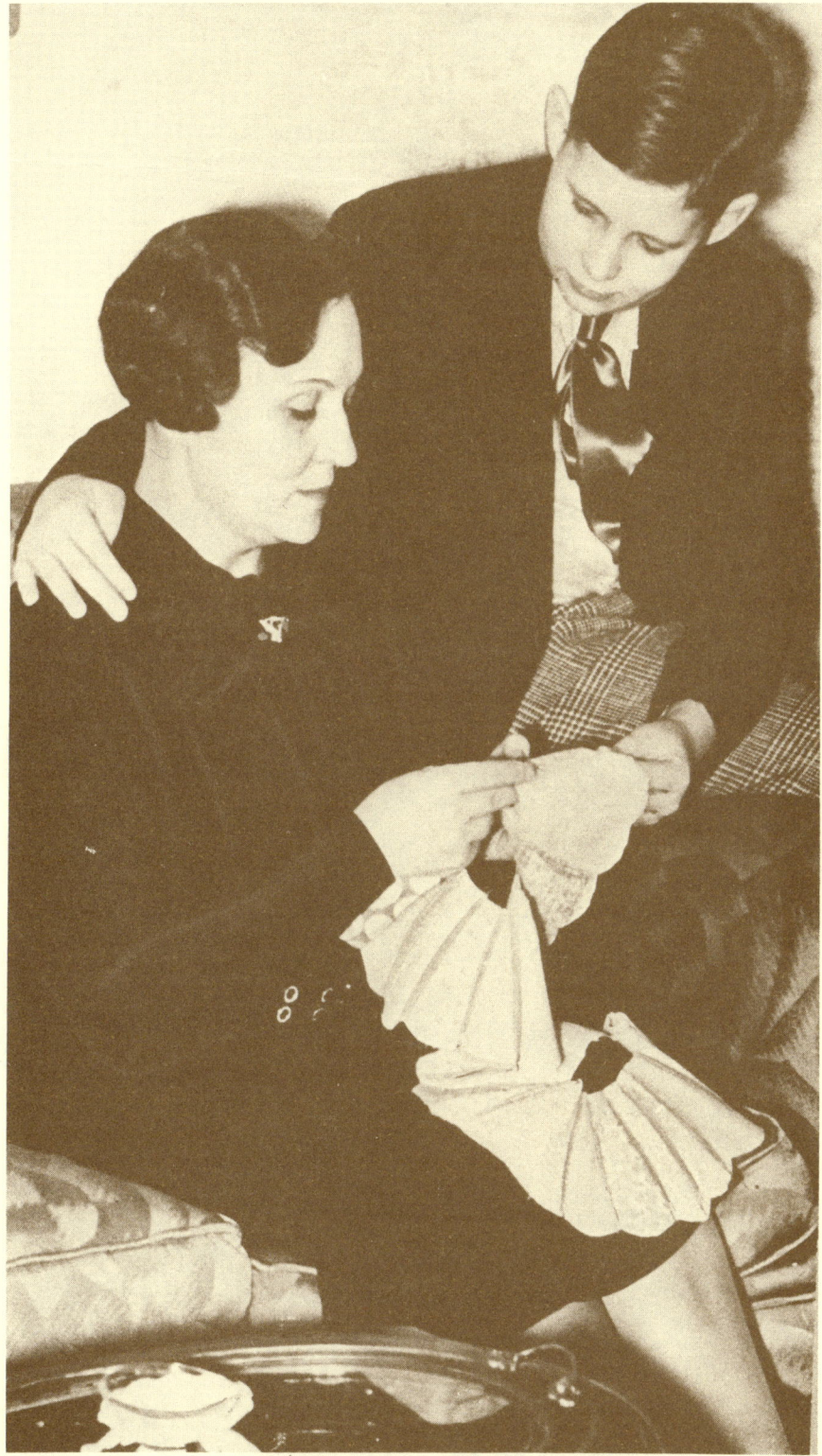

Copyright 1930-78, The Oklahoma Publishing Co. From the Oklahoman & Times 1930-1978

Mrs. Amy Holloway and her son, William Judson Holloway Jr., who became a judge of the Tenth U. S. Circuit Court of Appeals.

Oklahoma's First Ladies - Page 31

Copyright 1930-78, The Oklahoma Publishing Co.
From the Oklahoman & Times 1930-1978

William Henry Murray, probably Oklahoma's most colorful political figure, was born November 21, 1869, in Collinsville, Texas. At twenty years of age he graduated from College Hill Institute in Springtown, Texas. For the next six years he held various jobs, including day laborer, teacher, editor of a Dallas farm magazine, and of a Corsicana daily newspaper. Admitted to the bar in 1895, he Practiced at Fort Worth before moving to Tishomingo, Indian Territory, in 1898. There he became legal advisor to the Governor of the Chickasaw Nation. He was President of the Oklahoma Constitutional Convention in 1906; Speaker of the House of Representatives, 1907–1908; Member of the Sixty-third and Sixty-fourth United States Congresses; and Governor of the State from January 12, 1931, to January 15, 1935. His ranching interest spread from Oklahoma to Bolivia, South America, where he established a colony. He wrote articles and books, mostly dealing with constitutional rights, etc. His death occurred on October 15, 1956.

Text and Photograph courtesy Oklahoma Department of Libraries

Mary Alice Hearrell Murray

Mary Alice Hearrell was an accomplished young woman when she met her future husband. She was the talented, educated daughter of a Scotch-English father and a Chickasaw mother. After the death of her parents, she and her two sisters, Ada and Daisy, were reared by their uncle, Douglas Johnston, who at the time was president of the Bloomfield Seminary for Girls near Denison, Texas.

Mary Alice was very popular. She was attractive and studious, with a good sense of humor. After graduating from college in 1894, she accepted a teaching position at the seminary where she met a lanky, young lawyer from Texas. "Alfalfa Bill" Murray would eventually become the ninth, and probably the most controversial governor of Oklahoma.

Mary Alice and William H. Murray were married on July 19, 1899, in the home of her uncle in Emet, Oklahoma, near Tishomingo. An Indian Territory newspaper reported the event as the wedding of a "Prominent Young Attorney and a Chickasaw Queen." According to Keith L. Bryant Jr. in his book **Alfalfa Bill Murray**, "Five Chickasaw tribesmen gave the groom the necessary recommendations for marrying into the tribe and becoming one of its intermarried citizens."

Their first home was a 1,400-acre farm at Twelve Mile Prairie near Tishomingo. Bill loved farming and worked very hard to improve crop production. He was especially interested in alfalfa hay. He wrote and talked so much about it that a reporter referred to him as "Alfalfa Bill" in one of his articles. The name stuck so well that most people referred to him by that name long after his death.

Bill Murray loved the law and politics almost as much as he did farming. He became deeply involved with the legal problems of Indians in Indian Territory. Many Indian residents of the territory opposed unification of Indian and Oklahoma territories, and, instead, wanted to join the Union as a separate Indian state to be named Sequoyah. The Sequoyah Constitutional Convention was held to further that idea. Bill Murray attended the convention as a

Page 32 - Oklahoma's First Ladies

(Photo Courtesy Oklahoma Historical Society)

First Lady Mary Alice Murray, Jan. 12, 1931 to Jan. 14, 1935

Mrs. Murray's inaugural dress of black lace was very much in fashion in the early thirties. A touch of georgette and blonde lace outlined the deep V neckline. The skirt began at the normal waistline and widened from the hips down to the floor.

Oklahoma's First Ladies - Page 33

representative of Mary Alice's uncle, Douglas Johnston, who had become governor of the Chickasaw Nation.

The problem of statehood, however, was left to a vote of the people, resulting in a merging of the two territories to form the State of Oklahoma. Bill Murray was elected president of the Oklahoma Constitutional Convention. He used many ideas from the Sequoyah Convention in writing the constitution for the new state.

Mary Alice remained the same as her husband moved from one public office to another. The **Boston Sunday Globe** of February 8, 1914, described her as "quiet, dignified and intellectual—a descendant of Chickasaw chiefs." The article was written at the time the Murrays were moving to Washington, D. C., where Alfalfa Bill served two terms as representative-at-large from Oklahoma.

After two terms in Congress, Bill became disillusioned with life in the United States. He needed a new frontier. He became fascinated with the idea of living in South America, especially Bolivia. In 1919 he began a concentrated effort to establish an agricultural colony in that country. He worked for six years to iron out all the details with the governments of the United States and Bolivia and to sign up enough **people to begin his colony**. Finally, twenty-nine adults and forty-five children began an ordeal of rough primitive living on the undeveloped land in Bolivia. Mary Alice and Alfalfa Bill, their two youngest children, plus their two older sons and their families, struggled to make a success of the venture. It was doomed from the start. Insects, rain, and homesickness caused the colonists to return to their former homes.

Despite the colony's failure, Murray had received much national publicity because of the South American venture. The Murray family returned to Oklahoma, and Alfalfa Bill again entered politics. He was elected Oklahoma's ninth governor and inaugurated on January 12, 1931. An Indian prayer linking the white and Indian people was part of the ceremony.

A picture of Mary Alice with one of her paintings was carried in an Oklahoma City newspaper. Her early, white pioneer family background and her Indian ancestry were told in detail.

The next year, Alfalfa Bill was nominated for president of the United States at the Democratic National Convention. Will Rogers supposedly rode in the parade that followed the Murray nomination. Murray, whose slogan was "Bread, Butter, Bacon and Beans," became a lifelong enemy of Franklin D. Roosevelt over the battle of the Democratic presidential nomination. After Roosevelt was elected president, Murray fought the president's New Deal with all his remaining power. His vehement opposition to the popular Roosevelt contributed to the decline of his political career after he left the governor's office.

Mary Alice believed that being a good wife and mother were the two most important privileges that a woman could have. These were her top priorities throughout her hectic married life. She was the leveling agent for her family of five children and her flamboyant husband. Her personal lifestyle remained the same whether they were living at Twelve Mile Prairie near Tishomingo, in Washington, D. C., on an agricultural settlement in Bolivia, or in the Oklahoma governor's mansion. In addition to the time spent with her family, Mrs. Murray's painting and flowers filled her quiet hours.

Mary Alice's death in 1938 had a devastating effect on Bill Murray. He wrote a memorial to her and their thirty-nine years of marriage. He called her "the perfect wife." He said later that her perfect behavior had won her the respect of all the people even if he had never gained it. After her death, she was honored by being the first woman whose body laid in state in the Oklahoma State Capitol.

Johnston Murray, son of Bill and Mary Alice Murray, later became Oklahoma's fourteenth governor.

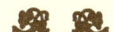

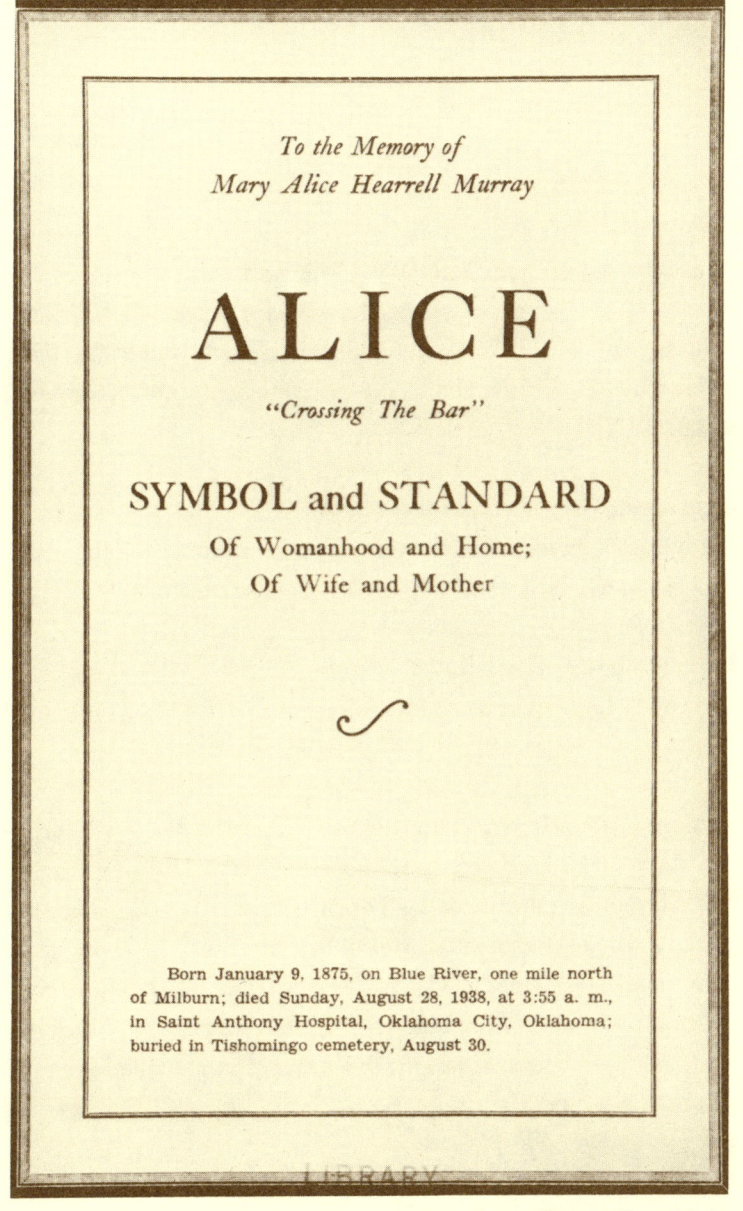

To the Memory of
Mary Alice Hearrell Murray

ALICE

"Crossing The Bar"

SYMBOL and STANDARD

Of Womanhood and Home;
Of Wife and Mother

Born January 9, 1875, on Blue River, one mile north of Milburn; died Sunday, August 28, 1938, at 3:55 a. m., in Saint Anthony Hospital, Oklahoma City, Oklahoma; buried in Tishomingo cemetery, August 30.

Courtesy Oklahoma Historical Society

Ernest Whitworth Marland, a native of Pittsburgh, Pennsylvania, was born May 8, 1874. He was educated at Park Institute of that City and received his LL.B. from the University of Michigan, in 1893. He began his law practice at Pittsburgh, but engaged in the oil production business after moving to Oklahoma. He was President of the Marland Oil Company until its consolidation; Member of the Seventy-third United States Congress from 1933 to 1935; Govenor of Oklahoma from January 15, 1935, to January 9, 1939. He died October 3, 1941. His civic contributions to Ponca City included the pioneer Woman Statue.

Text and Photograph courtesy Oklahoma Department of Libraries

(Photo Courtesy Oklahoma Historical Society)

Lydie Roberts Marland

Lyde, as she was usually called, and Ernest W. Marland were the direct opposites of their immediate predecessors in the governor's mansion, Mary Alice and "Alfalfa Bill" Murray. Lyde was young and beautiful, and E. W., much older, had made and lost at least two fortunes.

Lyde Roberts Marland lived an unusual and often mysterious life that could be divided into six very different stages:

- as the third child in an impoverished family;
- as the adopted daughter of an aunt and the aunt's multimillionaire husband;
- as the wife of a politician who became Oklahoma's tenth governor;
- as the widow of a pauper;
- as a missing person for many years;
- as a Ponca City recluse who helped with the project to turn the Marland mansion into a museum.

Lyde Roberts was born in Flourtown, Pennsylvania. Her parents, the George Roberts, were very poor. Her aunt, Mary Virginia Collins, had married E. W. Marland, the son of a wealthy iron mill owner. The Marlands had moved to Ponca City, a town in Oklahoma. E. W. soon became very successful in the oil business, forming the Marland Oil Company. The Marlands built a beautiful home and entertained lavishly. To help relieve the financial burden of the Roberts family in rearing their other two children, Virginia and E. W. Marland brought Lyde, who was ten years old, and her brother George, who was twelve, to Oklahoma to live with them. Later, they adopted both Lyde and George. Lyde was very shy; but George was outgoing and boisterous.

Their new father by adoption, E. W. Marland, held that there was more to life than making money. He believed that success should be shared with the employees who helped make it

Copyright 1930-78, The Oklahoma Publishing Co. From the Oklahoman & Times 1930-1978

First Lady Lydie Marland, Jan. 14, 1935 to Jan. 9, 1939

Mrs. Marland looked youthfully regal at the inaugural ball in a gown of white silk. The fitted body of the dress flared at the bottom of the skirt and flowed into a graceful train. Mrs. Marland stated that the dress was borrowed and could not go into the First Ladies' Gown Collection.

Oklahoma's First Ladies - Page 37

possible. His idea of caring and sharing was to open the doors to an earthly paradise by bringing polo, fox hunting, and classic horseback riding to the people of the plains. He encouraged his employees to play on his golf courses and swim in his pools. He awarded his favorite employees with stock in his company. He took money from the business when he needed it for any of these expenditures. After all, the wealth belonged to everyone. His dream was to bring happiness to everyone in Ponca City.

E. W. Marland was not just an idle dreamer; he practiced his largess everyday. He took his top aides with him on extensive trips on his yachts and his private railroad cars. Virginia and Lyde also accompanied him on many of these trips. They visited foreign countries, living in the grand style of the oil rich. Lyde soon became accustomed to a life of luxury. She developed a love for music and art, and they became her primary interests.

Close acquaintances claimed that Marland was very strict with Lyde. He insisted that she leave home to attend school in Long Island, New York, and St. Louis, Missouri—but her social life was limited. She spent most of her leisure time playing polo and fox hunting with Marland.

After his wife's death in 1926, Marland had Lyde's adoption set aside; they were married in 1928, causing a scandal that rocked the town of Ponca City and the entire state for years. E. W. was fifty-four years old and Lyde was twenty-eight when they married.

The newlyweds started building a fabulous estate that included a game reserve, polo fields, a golf course, several ponds, an enormous swimming pool, and lavish gardens. They spent millions on the mansion and had to start borrowing money from J. P. Morgan. When the debts could not be paid, Morgan's company, Continental Oil, took control of Marland Oil Company.

After losing his oil business, Marland entered politics and again achieved success; he won election as Oklahoma's tenth governor in 1934. Even as first lady, Lyde still did not participate in many social functions. The public referred to her as "Princess Lyde, the youngest first lady in history." She rarely visited the governor's office, and when she did she would approach the receptionist very timidly and ask if she might see her husband.

The Marlands returned to Ponca City after his term as governor. He made three unsuccessful attempts to be elected to Congress. He then established another oil company, but he died in 1941 and the business later failed.

After Marland's death, Lyde shut herself away in the art studio of the Marland estate, which was then owned by the Carmelite Fathers. She soon became old news, only to become front page news again through another affair of the heart and subsequent disappearance.

A lengthy article appeared in the November 22, 1958, issue of **Saturday Evening Post** under the heading "Where Is Lyde Marland?" It described her friendship with a Ponca City meter reader, former army sergeant Louis Cassel, as the reason for her disappearance. The article gave lurid details of the affair that began in 1950. It showed several pictures of Lyde, Governor Marland, and Cassel. There was also a picture of a woman claiming to be the illegitimate daughter of Lyde and E. W.

According to the article, Cassel was not a very stable person. He soon began asking Lyde for money, which she gave him. At one time, she gave him $5,000 with which to buy a farm. One year later he sold the farm for $6,000 and used part of the money to pay off back alimony and the rest to take off for Seattle, Washington. Cassel was so incensed over the article that he sued the **Post**, but the outcome of the suit was never revealed.

Mrs. Marland was very upset over Cassel's disappearance; in March of 1953, a few weeks after he left, she also disappeared. She was fifty-five years old at the time. She was seen leaving Ponca City in a 1949 Studebaker with the back seat full of paintings valued at more than $10,000. She supposedly took about the same amount of cash with her.

In addition to the **Post** article, there were others from time to time. Some indicated that Mrs. Marland had spent several weeks with a family in Missouri. No one heard from her directly for years. Her brother George requested an investigation, and she was declared a missing person in 1955. Shortly before she was to be declared legally dead, sufficient evidence was produced for Oklahoma investigators to declare her to be alive. The case was closed in December 1959.

In 1960 two reporters startled Mrs. Marland by tracing her to Arkansas City, Kansas, and approaching her near a supermarket. When they identified themselves, she ran into the market and hid among the canned goods until they left. She was not actually seen or heard from again, as far as the public knew, until she returned to Ponca City in 1975. She was then seventy-five years old. She continued to live as a recluse.

Leon Chase Phillips was born December 9, 1890, in Worth County Missouri, but moved to Oklahoma at an early age. While a student at Epworth University in Oklahoma City, he studied for the ministry, but changed to law and received his LL.B. from the University of Oklahoma in 1916. He was admitted to the State Bar in that year and to practice before the United States Supreme Court later. After service in World War I, he returned to Okemah where he practiced law. He was a memeber of the State Legislature from 1933 to 1938; Speaker of the House in 1935; Governor from January 9, 1939, to January 11, 1943. He was a practicing attorney in his old home of Okemah until his death on March 27, 1958. He is buried in Weleetka.

Text and Photograph courtesy Oklahoma Department of Libraries

Copyright 1930-78, The Oklahoma Publishing Co.
From the Oklahoman & Times 1930-1978

Myrtle Ellenberger Phillips

Myrtle Ellenberger met her future husband, Leon "Red" Phillips, in church when he was a law student at the University of Oklahoma. The Ellenberger family had moved from Iowa to a farm near Norman when Myrtle was young. She graduated from the university with a bachelor of arts degree in 1912.

The Phillipses moved to Okemah soon after their marriage. They adopted a four-week-old boy and a four-week-old girl. They named the boy, Robert Rowe, for Leon Phillips' law partner and the girl Lois Ann for Leon's sister and Myrtle's mother.

Robert Rowe was sixteen and Lois Ann was twelve when Phillips began talking about running for governor. His family was not enthusiastic about the idea. They were a close family, so a four member conference was held. It was obvious that the race meant a great deal to "Red" Phillips.

Mrs. Phillips had not gone to the courthouse while her husband was building his reputation as a lawyer. When he became a member of the state legislature, she stayed in Okemah and kept the children in school. After he became speaker of the house and could not come home on weekends, she did visit him in Oklahoma City.

Mrs. Phillips and the children knew how demanding the office of governor would be. Because Leon Phillips loved to play games and relax with his family, he weighed the pros and cons very carefully. Finally, they agreed that he should run. Robert Rowe was the last to accede, but he too finally capitulated.

When he was elected governor, Phillips remarked, "I think my wife and family are plain enough not to be affected by the glamour of the governorship or its difficulties."

Governor Phillips' term in office saw larger expenditures for farm-to-market roads, aid for weak schools, and other much needed programs. The governor had warned the legislature about deficit spending. In order to avoid this, taxes were raised on tobacco, cigarettes, and gasoline.

Copyright 1930-78, The Oklahoma Publishing Co. From the Oklahoman & Times 1930-1978

First Lady Myrtle Phillips, Jan. 9, 1939 to Jan. 11, 1943

Mrs. Phillips's long black lace dress was complimented by a small black hat and an orchid. Elbow length gloves and an evening bag completed the picture of an elegant first lady. Governor Phillips is shown with his favorite accompaniment—a cigar—as they began the grand march.

Oklahoma's First Ladies - Page 41

With the advent of World War II, a number of large military and naval training bases were established in Oklahoma. They included Tinker Air Field and Will Rogers Field at Oklahoma City, naval air stations at Clinton and Norman, a naval hospital at Norman, and air training centers at Miami and Ponca City.

Observers felt that a happy home life permitted Leon Phillips to follow a political career without being distracted by domestic difficulties. Myrtle and Leon Phillips seemed to have developed complete trust in and a deep respect for one another.

Copyright 1930-78, The Oklahoma Publishing Co. From the Oklahoman & Times 1930-1978

Mrs. Phillips with Lois Ann, 12, and Robert Rowe, 16, at the time they lived in the governor's mansion.

Oklahoma's First Ladies - Page 43

Robert Samuel Kerr, Oklahoma's first native born governor, was born near Ada, Indian Territory, on September 11, 1896. His college work was done at East Central Normal School, and Oklahoma Baptist University. He was admitted to the Oklahoma Bar in 1922, and practiced in Ada. Beginning as a drilling contractor in 1926, he built up a large oil producing company and at the time of his death was President of the Kerr-McGee Oil Industries, Inc. He served as Governor of Oklahoma from January 13, 1943 to January 13, 1947. He was elected U. S. Senator on November 2, 1948 and served until his death on January 1, 1963. He is buried at his birthplace near Ada, Oklahoma.

Text and Photograph courtesy Oklahoma Department of Libraries

Copyright 1930-78, The Oklahoma Publishing Co. From the Oklahoman & Times 1930-1978

Grayce Breene Kerr

Grayce Breene dreamed of going to Paris, studying voice and becoming a great singer. After that she planned to find the right person and get married. A visit to her sister in Ada, Oklahoma, changed that dream. While she was there, she was invited to sing at the local Lions Club. A big, young lawyer, Robert S. Kerr, was in charge of the program. Grayce sat next to him, and they became attracted to each other immediately.

A short time later, Grayce was invited to a house party in Fort Sill, Oklahoma, arranged by Bob Kerr. This occasion marked the beginning of a short courtship. They were married the day after Christmas in 1925.

Grayce was born in Jewett, Ohio, but moved to Independence, Kansas, at a very young age. Her father farmed and became involved in the development of the Mid-Continent Oil Field. Because of his interest in oil, the family moved to Bartlesville, Oklahoma, and later to Tulsa. Grayce and Bob Kerr were married in the Breene home.

The young couple began their married life in Ada, where they lived for nine years. Their four children—Robert Jr., Breene, Grayce Kay, and William Grayce—were born there.

Robert Samuel Kerr was born in a log cabin near Ada in Indian Territory in 1896. After returning from service in World War I, he suffered losses in several business ventures. He also lost his first wife, Reba Shelton, who died in childbirth.

Kerr had attended the East Central State Normal School in Ada, Oklahoma Baptist University at Shawnee, and the University of Oklahoma Law School. After he and Grayce were married, he practiced law and became involved in the oil business. Grayce's father, Harry Breene, insisted that Bob Kerr had all the qualifications for becoming a successful oil man. His faith was later justified.

In 1930 the Kerrs moved to a forty-acre farm near Oklahoma City. There they found plenty of room for the four Kerr children to play. Mrs. Kerr was an expert at home canning and enjoyed farm life. Bob Kerr became involved in drilling for oil in the Oklahoma City oil field on a

Page 44 - Oklahoma's First Ladies

Copyright 1930-78, The Oklahoma Publishing Co. From the Oklahoman & Times 1930-1978

First Lady Grayce Kerr, Jan. 13, 1943 to Jan. 13, 1947

Mrs. Kerr is shown in a dress she wore to a formal function later in the year that she became first lady. The dress was a handsome long black one with metallic gold midsection. The Kerrs did not have an inaugural ball.

Oklahoma's First Ladies - Page 45

percentage basis. In 1931, during the Depression, Kerr's interest in this field made the family wealthy.

The next ten years were eventful for Grayce Breene Kerr. She saw her husband rise from a small town lawyer to governor of the state of Oklahoma. He also became a partner in the Kerr-McGee Oil Company.

Problems of World War II and implementation of President Franklin Roosevelt's war policies in Oklahoma occupied Kerr's first two years in the governor's office. He became an effective public speaker, gaining national attention when Roosevelt chose him to make the keynote speech at the Democratic National Convention in 1944. Kerr was elected to the United States Senate in 1948 and had one of his most bitter campaign battles when he ran for reelection in 1954 against former governor Roy Turner. The **Tulsa Tribune** described the race as "two millionaire oil men squared off in the Democratic U. S. Senate Primary and as one reporter described it 'beat each other to death with money bags.' " Turner finally withdrew saying that he could not match the Kerr dollars. Kerr won his race and served in the Senate until his death on January 1, 1963. He became known as the "uncrowned king of the Senate." He fought and won the battle for the McClellan-Kerr Arkansas Navigation System, opening a waterway from Catoosa, Oklahoma, to the Gulf of Mexico. This inland water system had been a dream of many people since steamships carried furs and other trade goods over some of the same route a hundred years earlier.

Mrs. Kerr always loved their Black Angus ranch near Poteau, Oklahoma. Their home with the beautiful hilltop view was a source of great pleasure. Taking over the Black Angus Restaurant at Poteau in 1961 was her idea of a challenge. She stated that, while she was in the governor's mansion and in Washington, D. C., she managed a big household and planned dinners for twenty to thirty people. She didn't see much difference in that and pleasing people in a restaurant. Her motto was "keep people happy and keep out of the red"—the same as at home. She wanted to build a reputation for her chicken fried steaks, hot rolls, and pies.

According to an article prepared in the governor's office in 1946, Grayce and Bob Kerr had successfully united two different religious beliefs. Robert Kerr, like his parents, was a devout Baptist and gave of his time and support to that church. Mrs. Kerr was very active in the First Church of Christ, Scientist. Bob Kerr always referred to his wife as "my Grayce." When people congratulated him on being a self-made man, his answer was, "No, I'm a wife-made man."

After Kerr's death in 1963, Grayce married Olney Flynn, oil man and former mayor of Tulsa. In March 1965, she died at the age of sixty-four.

Copyright 1930-78, The Oklahoma Publishing Co. From the Oklahoman & Times 1930-1978

Mrs. Grayce Kerr, happy in the kitchen of her Black Angus restaurant.

Oklahoma's First Ladies - Page 47

Roy Joseph Turner, on November 6, 1894, was born in Lincoln County, Oklahoma Territory. Upon completion of his high school education, he attended Hill's Business College in Oklahoma City. He was a bookkeeper for Morris Packing Company in Oklahoma City from 1911–1915; a salesman for the Goodyear Tire and Rubber Company there and after his service in World War I, he was a dealer in real estate, principally in Oklahoma, Florida and Texas. By 1928 he had become an independent oil producer. In 1933, he established the Turner Ranch at Sulphur, but he maintained a residence in Oklahoma City where he served on the Board of Education from 1939 to 1946. His term as Governor of Oklahoma was from January 13, 1947, to January 8, 1951. He lived in Oklahoma City until his death June 11, 1973 and he is buried in Rose Hill Burial Park there.

Text and Photograph courtesy Oklahoma Department of Libraries

Copyright 1930-78, The Oklahoma Publishing Co. From the Oklahoman & Times 1930-1978

Jessica Grimm Turner

Jessica E. Grimm and Roy Turner, along with their teenage twins, Betty and Roy W. (Bill), were living the life of affluent ranchers at the time he became Oklahoma's thirteenth governor.

Roy Turner was the son of a homesteader in Lincoln County, Indian Territory. Roy was reared by hardworking parents who taught him the value of success through his own efforts. He attended Hill's Business College in Oklahoma City and began his career as a bookkeeper and later as a salesman. After World War I, he became active in the real estate business in Oklahoma, Texas, and Florida. He later became a partner in the Harper-Turner oil producing firm.

Turner's business ventures enabled the family to own a beautiful 10,000-acre ranch near Sulphur, Oklahoma. The famous Turner herds of purebred Hereford cattle were raised there. Jessica Turner and the twins enjoyed ranch life. The ranch gained national recognition through such magazines as **Life, Time,** and **Newsweek.** The prestigious magazines paid tribute to Turner's successful ranching operation. In 1940 the ranch became the site of an annual 4-H judging contest to encourage young people to raise better cattle. Governor Turner said later that the cattle and the members of the Future Farmers of America made the difference in his campaign for governor.

Turner had one embarrassing incident as a cattle raiser. He once sold a bull for $51,000, the highest price ever paid up to that time, and the bull was found to be impotent. The white-faced bull produced a red-faced Turner. The Turner Ranch was sold to Winthrop Rockefeller in 1963. Roy Turner was sixty-nine years old at that time.

The best known project of the Turner administration was the Turner Turnpike. The building of this, the first toll road west of the Mississippi, caused a bitter political battle. The turnpike authority bill passed the state senate by only one vote. Its eventual success set the stage for building other toll roads in Oklahoma, thus making superhighways possible. With the completion of the Cimarron Turnpike, the state had 489 miles of toll roads.

Page 48 - Oklahoma's First Ladies

Copyright 1930-78, The Oklahoma Publishing Co. From the Oklahoman & Times 1930-1978

First Lady Jessica Turner, Jan. 18, 1947 to Jan. 8, 1951

Mrs. Turner selected a gold, street-length dress for her inaugural. The material of the bodice and cuffs had a smocked effect. She wore a small, frilly hat and an orchid.

Oklahoma's First Ladies - Page 49

Copyright 1930-78, The Oklahoma Publishing Co. From the Oklahoman & Times 1930-1978

The Turner family enjoyed spending time on their 10,000-acre ranch that sprawled across Pontotoc, Murray, and Johnston counties. Turner developed a herd of purebred Hereford cattle on this ranch before selling it to Winthrop Rockefeller.

Although Roy Turner was proud of the Turner Turnpike, he was even prouder of the $36 million bond issue that he introduced for upgrading the care of mental patients and for colleges. He was also a leader in the television industry in Oklahoma and helped to bring the Cowboy Hall of Fame to Oklahoma City.

Jessica Turner was perfectly at ease living at the ranch, in the governor's mansion, or at the Skirvin Tower Hotel in Oklahoma City. The Turners lived at the hotel after Turner withdrew from the Senate race against Bob Kerr. One of Mrs. Turner's activities was serving as a member of the Library Board of Oklahoma City. She is pictured in everything from simple ranch clothes to fur coats and orchids.

Copyright 1930-78, The Oklahoma Publishing Co. From the Oklahoman & Times 1930-1978

Mrs. Kerr and the new first lady, Mrs. Roy Turner, appeared at the Turner inaugural ball in almost identical fur coats and orchid corsages. Both of these ladies were just as comfortable in ranch clothes.

Oklahoma's First Ladies - Page 51

Johnston Murray was born July 21, 1902, in the mansion of the Chickasaw Nation's Governor at Emet, Johnston County, Indian Territory. His early education was governed by the location of the work of his famous father, former Governor William H. Murray. After graduation from the Murray State School of Agriculture, in 1924, he went to Bolivia where he lived for four years trying to make a success of his father's colonization expedition there. He received his law degree in 1946, having studied and worked at other things for a number of years. He served as Governor from January 8, 1951, to January 1955. He served as an attorney with the State Department of Welfare until his death April 16, 1974. He is buried at Tishomingo along with his father.

Text and Photograph courtesy Oklahoma Department of Libraries

Courtesy of Mrs. E. W. Marland

Willie Emerson Murray

Willie Emerson was a very active and talented young woman. According to friends, she had red hair and a temper to match. She was a very good student, graduating from college at seventeen. Her father died when she was very young, leaving her mother and brother responsible for her upbringing.

Willie developed her talents as a pianist at an early age. In her hometown, she became well-known for her musical ability, becoming the youngest assistant to the head of the piano department at the college in Weatherford, Oklahoma.

Johnston Murray and Willie met in 1932 at a meeting of the state Democratic committee. Johnston's first marriage to Marion Draughon had ended in divorce in 1930. They had one son, Johnston Jr.

Johnston graduated in 1924 from Murray State School of Agriculture in Tishomingo and twenty-two years later earned a law degree at the University of Oklahoma. In 1924, after Johnston graduated from Murray, he left for Bolivia with his father, "Alfalfa Bill," and their families to try to establish an agricultural colony there. After his return to the United States in 1930, he became active in state politics. His work in the Democratic party led to his meeting with Willie. After their marriage in 1933, Willie became the motivating force behind Johnston's political ambitions.

Willie encouraged Johnston to run for governor and became very active in his campaign. She worked with W. C. Doenges, a Tulsa businessman, to set up billboards along the highway showing Johnston's picture with his slogan "Just Plain Folks." The truth of the matter was Johnston was a rather poised and easy going politician; in sharp contrast had been his father, "Alfalfa Bill," with his blunt and country-style manners. Although Willie and Doenges often disagreed on political tactics, they were successful in getting Johnston elected. He was sworn in as Oklahoma's fourteenth governor on January 8, 1951, by his eighty-one-year-old father. Even though Johnston had never held political office, he showed a natural ability to handle the duties

(Photo Courtesy Oklahoma Historical Society)

First Lady Willie Murray, Jan. 8, 1951 to Jan. 10, 1955

Mrs. Murray is shown in a delightful pose with Governor Johnston Murray as they wave to friends from their doorway. Mrs. Murray enjoyed wearing dramatic clothes—especially hats.

of governor and later filled many national positions as well.

Willie was a very busy first lady. She used many Oklahoma products to decorate and furnish the mansion. Her "traveling medicine show of Oklahoma products" became well known. Because an Oklahoma governor then could not succeed himself, Willie decided to run for the office. So did Bill Doenges. Their following was divided, and neither of them was elected. In fact, it brought on so much bad publicity that neither of them ever ran for office again.

Whether or not this situation influenced the breakup of the Murray marriage is a matter of conjecture. Johnston Murray filed for and was granted a divorce. It is said that Willie never recovered from the ending of her twenty-two-year marriage. She never stopped grieving for Johnston. Willie Emerson Murray died of cancer on April 4, 1963, at the age of fifty-four.

(Photo Courtesy Oklahoma Historical Society)

Mrs. Murray wore this exciting dress at the International Trade Fair in New Orleans. She was a great promoter of Oklahoma products.

Raymond Dancel Gary was the first Governor to be born in Oklahoma since statehood. His birthdate was January 21, 1908, and his birthplace, a farm midway between Madill and Kingston. He was educated in the local schools and Southeastern State College. After five years of teaching he was elected County Superintendent of Schools and served for four years. In 1936, he began his business career, first in school and office supplies, later as President of the Sooner Oil Company. He was a State Senator from 1941 until he became Governor on January 10, 1955, for a four-year term. Madill, Oklahoma, is his home.

Text and Photograph courtesy Oklahoma Department of Libraries

(Photograph Courtesy of Mrs. Raymond Gary)

Emma Mae Purser Gary

Emma Mae Purser and Raymond Gary attended school together at Madill (Oklahoma) High School. Soon after she graduated as valedictorian of her class, they were married. Emma Purser was the only girl that Raymond Gary ever dated.

While teaching school in Durant, Gary decided to enter state politics. At age twenty-four, he won election for county superintendent of schools.

Mrs. Gary's primary interests were her home, family, and church. She spent her time with the children, Mona Mae and Raymond Jerdy, and working with the Home Demonstration Club, Garden Club, Women's Federated Club, and Women's Missionary Union of the Kingston Baptist Church.

Gary served in the state senate beginning in 1940. He became a gubernatorial candidate while serving as president pro tempore of the senate. He won election to the governor's office in 1954, during a declining period of livestock and crop prices and reduced employment in manufacturing and transportation.

His term in office happened to occur at a time when the whole country experienced some degree of racial unrest. By 1950, Oklahoma colleges and universities were admitting blacks on an equal basis with white students. Gary and other officials upheld the Supreme Court's decision to end racial segregation in schools; he saw to it that peaceful integration was incorporated in Oklahoma's public schools. The governor also abolished other forms of racial segregation, such as separate rest rooms, drinking fountains, and parks.

As first lady, Emma Gary remained what one person described as "a sweet, motherly person, always putting her family first." Some of her special projects included fund-raising teas, opening the Indian Exposition at Lawton, and playing hostess for the Oklahoma Semi-centennial Celebration. However, her pet project was the mansion grounds. She assisted in the complete re-landscaping of the grounds and devoted special attention to the west rose garden, which is named in her honor, "The Emma Gary Rose Garden."

(Photograph Courtesy of Mrs. Raymond Gary)

First Lady Emma Gary, Jan. 10, 1955 to Jan. 12, 1959

Mrs. Gary did not have an inaugural ball gown as they had no inaugural ball. The dress shown here is one of her favorites. It is the gown she wore to the opening of the musical **Oklahoma** in New York City. The long brocade gown and long white gloves were very appropriate for the occasion.

After serving as governor and first lady, the Garys returned to their home in Madill, where they concentrated on their business, church, and community. In 1977, they presented a gift of land and money to the Baptist General Convention of Oklahoma for the founding of a children's home, which is named the Emma Gary Cottage. Since then, a Baptist retirement home has also been constructed on land donated by the Garys.

Photograph Courtesy, Department of Children, Baptist General Convention of Oklahoma

Former Governor Raymond Gary and Mrs. Gary donated land and a large monetary gift to Dr. Joe Ingram, executive secretary of the Baptist General Convention of Oklahoma, and Lowell Milburn of the BGCO's Child Care Department. The gifts of land provided the location for several brick cottages for children and a Baptist Retirement Center.

James Howard Edmondson, the youngest governor in the history of the State, was born in Muskogee, Oklahoma, on September 27, 1925. He attended elementary and secondary schools in that city and enrolled in the University of Oklahoma after high school graduation. He enlisted in the U.S. Air force in March, 1942, and served until December 5, 1945. He returned to the University and completed his law degree in August, 1948. After practicing law in Muskogee, he moved to Tulsa to become the chief prosecutor in the office of the county attorney of Tulsa County. He was elected county attorney of that county in 1954 and was re-relected in 1956. On January 8, 1959, J. Howard Edmondson was inaugurated Governor of Oklahoma, after having been elected to that post by the largest majority ever given a gubernatorial candidate in the state. On January 6, 1963, he resigned from the office of Governor and was appointed to the United States Senate to fill the position left vacant by the death of Robert S. Kerr. At the time of his death on November 17, 1971, he was a practicing attorney in Oklahoma City.

Text and Photograph courtesy Oklahoma Department of Libraries

Photograph Courtesy of Jeannette Edmondson

Jeannette Bartleson Edmondson

When Jeannette Bartleson married J. Howard Edmondson at her home in Muskogee in May 1946, they had known each other almost all their lives. According to Jeannette's younger sister, Mary Stidham, the couple seemed to start "going steady in about the first grade."

Their marriage was one of teamwork. After graduating from the University of Oklahoma, Jeannette taught French while Howard attended law school. While he was busy working in the Tulsa County attorney's office, Jeannette busied herself being mother to James H. Jr., Jeanne, and Patricia Lynn. During Edmondson's campaign for governor, Jeannette and her friends organized teas and coffees and busily made buttons that were cut from styrofoam in the shape of the State of Oklahoma and edged with red sequins. She also wrote campaign letters that were sent statewide each week to Edmondson volunteers.

The efforts paid off with Edmondson being elected governor by the largest majority of votes ever received by any candidate in Oklahoma's history. He was inaugurated on January 12, 1959. The inaugural ball, held at the fairgrounds building in Oklahoma City, was a formal occasion. The new first lady appeared in a white full-length, peau de soie evening gown; the governor dressed in white tie and tails. Later that year, Oklahoma's first lady modeled her inaugural gown and other clothes in a **Ladies Home Journal** feature article.

Governor Edmondson—at thirty-three, the state's youngest governor—was a popular official. Some of his reforms and objectives, however, were challenged by particular groups for reasons having nothing to do with party issues. One of the longest legislative sessions in the state's history ended on July 29, 1961, after failing to obtain equitable reapportionment of the legislature on the basis of population increases in the cities. One of his more successful endeavors was the establishment of a merit system for the selection of state employees.

During his term, the state constitution was changed to permit the sale of liquor in package stores. He also initiated a "Pride in Oklahoma" program to acquaint Oklahoma citizens with their state and its resources and to develop a unified spirit among them.

(Photograph Courtesy of Mrs. Mary B. Stidham)

First Lady Jeannette Edmondson, Jan. 12, 1959 to Jan. 6, 1963

Mrs. Edmondson's inaugural gown was a beautiful full length white peau de soie. With it, she wore rhinestone jewelry and long white gloves.

Governor Edmondson resigned on January 6, 1963, upon the death of United States Senator Robert Kerr. Lieutenant Governor George Nigh became acting governor and appointed Edmondson to Kerr's seat in the Senate.

As first lady, Jeannette Edmondson's special project became the renovation of the mansion. She commented upon moving in that the governor's house was a cross between a "chateau and a covered wagon." When the remodeling was complete, she gave a party for all the volunteers who had helped in any way.

After Howard Edmondson left the United States Senate, the family moved to Edmond, Oklahoma, so that Howard could be near his corporate law practice in Oklahoma City. Jeannette enjoyed their home life there and kept busy entertaining friends, puttering in the garden, and keeping their ten acres mowed with her little red tractor. After her husband died of a heart attack in 1971 at age forty-six, she obtained a real estate license and went to work.

Jeannette married E. E. Duffner, an Oklahoma City builder, on July 13, 1975. Although the marriage did not last, the couple remained friends. James Howard Jr., Jeannette's only son, died of cancer while she was married to Duffner.

Jeannette Edmondson was sworn in as secretary of state of Oklahoma in February 1979. Twenty years earlier, she had watched her husband's swearing in as governor. Edmondson was again the name of one of the state's top officeholders.

(Courtesy Mrs. Jeannette Edmondson)

Mrs. Jeannette Edmondson taking the oath of office of Secretary of State from Justice Robert Simms, while daughter Jeanne Watkins holds the Bible.

Oklahoma's First Ladies - Page 63

Henry Louis Bellmon, the first Republican Governor of the State of Oklahoma was born in Tonkawa, Oklahoma, September 3, 1921. He is the son of George and Edith Caskey Bellmon. He attended Colorado State University, later transferring to Oklahoma State University where he was granted the degree of Bachelor of Science in Agriculture. Henry Bellmon served with the U. S. Marine Corps from 1942 through 1946, received the Silver Star for action on Saipan and the Legion of Merit for action on Iwo Jima. He was a member of the Oklahoma House of Representatives during the Twenty-first Oklahoma Legislature in 1947. He was engaged in farming at Billings, Oklahoma, at the time of his election as Governor. He served from January 14, 1963 to January 9, 1967 and was elected U. S. Senator in 1967 and again in 1974. He chose not to run in 1980.

Text and Photograph courtesy Oklahoma Department of Libraries

Copyright 1930-78, The Oklahoma Publishing Co. From the Oklahoman & Times 1930-1978

Shirley Osborn Bellmon

Shirley Lee Osborn grew up in Billings, Oklahoma, a hometown that remained a haven to which she returned many times during her husband's career. After marrying Henry Bellmon of Tonkawa, they made their home in Billings and were wheat farming there when he was elected Oklahoma's first Republican governor in 1962. Bellmon's knowledge of the land, his easy-going manner, and his sweat-stained campaign hat—which had also served him atop a tractor in the wheat fields—appealed to Oklahomans in general, farmers in particular. The women who volunteered to work in his campaign were known as Bellmon Belles.

When the Bellmon family moved into the mansion, Shirley brought along her favorite hobby, sewing. She would rise at 5:30 a.m. to get in some sewing time. Her skill was such that she designed and made her own dress and matching coat for her husband's inaugural ball on January 14, 1963.

As first lady, she continued to sew for herself and three daughters, Patricia, Gail, and Ann. Very much a home and family person, Shirley conquered the big kitchen of the governor's mansion and found time occasionally to bake a homemade pie. Her duties as first lady, however, kept her busy; often on weekends, she accompanied the governor on trips to various parts of the state to meet people and shake hands. The experience was good for her because, after Bellmon's term as governor, he was elected United States senator in 1968 and 1974.

Once her obligations as first lady were passed on to the next candidate's wife, Shirley was back home in Billings starting her own dress-making business under the "Shir-Lee" label. She designed shirtwaist dress of 100 percent silk that were appliqued in bright colors with Oklahoma's state bird, the Scissortail Flycatcher. Some hometown friends opened shop with Shirley in the Bellmon basement.

Copyright 1930-78, The Oklahoma Publishing Co. From the Oklahoman & Times 1930-1978

First Lady Shirley Bellmon, Jan. 14, 1963 to Jan. 9, 1967

Mrs. Bellmon designed and made the short evening dress and matching coat she wore to the inaugural. The dress and coat were made of blue brocade. The dress had side draped pockets trimmed in tiny pearls. She wore blue shoes, a pearl necklace, and an orchid corsage.

Oklahoma's First Ladies - Page 65

When Bellmon decided not to run for reelection to the Senate in 1980, he returned to Billings to resume wheat farming. He was appointed to serve as acting head of the Oklahoma Department of Human Services, a post he agreed to hold for six months, from January to June 1983. In the fall of 1983, the former governor taught political science at Central State University in Edmond, Oklahoma. The family, however, continued to make its home at Billings.

Shirley Bellmon designed and made clothes for herself and her three daughters in the basement of her home in Billings, Oklahoma. That led to the Shir-Lee line of clothes she produced for several years.

Copyright 1930-78, The Oklahoma Publishing Co.
From the Oklahoman & Times 1930-1978

Mrs. Bellmon enjoyed using Oklahoma emblems in her designs. Oklahoma's state flower, Mistletoe, served as the motif for a distinctive square dance dress.

Copyright 1930-78, The Oklahoma Publishing Co.
From the Oklahoman & Times 1930-1978

Page 66 - Oklahoma's First Ladies

Copyright 1930-78, The Oklahoma Publishing Co. From the Oklahoman & Times 1930-1978

Oklahoma's state bird the Scissortail Flycatcher was the inspiration for one of the most popular Shir-Lee designs.

Oklahoma's First Ladies - Page 67

Dewey Follett Bartlett, the second Republican Governor of the State of Oklahoma, was born in Marietta, Ohio, March 28, 1919. He is the son of David A. and Jessie Follett Bartlett. He attended Princeton University where he was granted a B.S.E. degree in Geological Engineering. Dewey Bartlett served in the Marine Corps during World War II as a combat dive bomber pilot. He received the Air Medal. He was a partner in Keener Oil Company, one of Oklahoma's oldest, small independent oil companies. He currently owns a 200-acre farm in Tulsa county. He was first elected to the State Senate in 1962 and was re-elected in 1964. He served as Governor from January 9, 1967 to January 11, 1971, and was elected to the U. S. Senate on November 7, 1972. He died March 1, 1979.

Text and Photograph courtesy Oklahoma Department of Libraries

Copyright 1930-78, The Oklahoma Publishing Co. From the Oklahoman & Times 1930-1978

Ann Smith Bartlett

Ann Smith's future was to be thousands of miles away from her hometown of Seattle, Washington. Growing up there, she attended college at Seattle University and the University of Washington. While visiting her grandmother in Southern California during World War II, she met a young Princeton graduate at a USO dance. They dated three weeks before he was shipped to the South Pacific, where he served as a combat dive-bomber pilot. After exchanging letters on a daily basis, Ann and Dewey Follett Bartlett were married at San Juan Capistrano Mission in 1945.

Dewey, who grew up in Marietta, Ohio, was named for his relative, Admiral George Dewey, who commanded the American fleet at the Battle of Manila Bay in the Spanish-American War. Following World War II, the Bartletts made their home in Tulsa, Oklahoma. Dewey's background in geology led to his becoming a partner in one of Oklahoma's oldest independent oil companies. He was elected to Tulsa's lone seat in the Oklahoma Senate in 1962 and 1964. In 1966 he was the second consecutive Republican to be elected governor.

Ann helped with the campaign; she met people, shook hands, and passed out cards with her and Dewey's picture on one side and a recipe for coconut balls and Western casserole on the other side. An avid knitter, she even knitted a ski sweater for her daughter while on the campaign trail. As first lady, Ann was involved in various projects: the arts, state libraries, day care centers, and Indian arts and crafts. After a visit to Guatemala, she worked hard to raise money to build a Catholic hospital there. Before her husband became governor, Ann had been a director and secretary for the Tulsa Family and Children's Service. She continued to lend her support to that organization after she moved to the Governor's Mansion.

Although much of his gubernatorial platform pertained to education, Governor Bartlett was honored by the American Academy of Achievement for his efforts in bringing new industry to Oklahoma. His hometown's college, Marietta College, where his brother was on the board of trustees and where his father was memorialized with a building named for him, presented him

(Courtesy of Mrs. Ann Bartlett)

First Lady Ann Bartlett, Jan. 9, 1967 to Jan. 11, 1971

Mrs. Bartlett's inaugural gown was a pale pink silk with a graceful back drape of chiffon flowing from the shoulder line to the floor. An orchid corsage was fastened to her evening bag. Long white gloves and a pearl necklace completed the elegant picture.

with a Doctor of Laws degree. In a press release, the school cited several accomplishments by the governor:

He appointed Oklahoma's first black judge.

He traveled an estimated 100,000 miles and called upon 137 of America's top companies in search for new industry.

He appointed the first Youth Advisory Council to receive ideas from Oklahoma young people.

He helped improve Oklahoma's Vocational-Technical educational system.

He spearheaded a drive for voter approval of a $99.8 million building bond issue to provide additional mental health facilities.

Bartlett was the first Oklahoma governor who was eligible to run for a second consecutive term. He did run but was defeated by Democrat David Hall. The Bartletts went to their Delaware County farm to decide whether or not to run for the United States Senate. He was elected to the Senate in 1972, a post he held until his death on March 1, 1979.

Ann Bartlett candidly remarked in an interview for the **Daily Oklahoman** in 1974 that she preferred being the wife of a senator to that of governor. She was very open about her other thoughts:

"I think that women in and out of politics are becoming much more independent and many have decided that being a homemaker or housewife is not what they want.

"For those women, it's much better to find something they are interested in. I can't think of anything worse than being stuck in the house if you don't want to be," she said.

"Personally I've enjoyed homemaking so much because I have a husband who enjoys home so much. I guess if he didn't it would be a pretty dumb job," she said.

Mrs. Bartlett, who had a maid four days a week, thinks that one unfortunate aspect of the women's liberation movement is that it has caused some people to think homemaking is "not a respected thing to do" or is a "dreary job."

"I don't agree," she stated.

In Washington, she said, "I don't feel a part of the community so I have more time for myself that way," and she is called upon to do fewer things in connection with her husband's career—"which is just fine with me. You can leave me out any day," she said.

She said many of the women who have more problems with being a senatorial wife are wives of more senior members who "have more demands on them" and wives with small children.

She hopes for those with small children that the "educational advantages" and the knowledge that their parents "are doing something important" helps to compensate for the fact their parents are not around as often as is normal.

But she realizes, "When you're young, there's nothing as important as your own school play."

She does miss "the really terrific people" she saw and worked with in the Governor's Mansion, and she does miss the lifelong friends she has in Oklahoma.

"One of the main differences at home was I had a group of friends I had known since I was a bride, and we all knew each other. That's not true here—your friends might not even know each other," she said.

Mrs. Bartlett moved back to Tulsa after Senator Bartlett's death. Aside from spending time with her three grown children—Dewey, Joan and Michael—she continued her hobbies of reading and gardening and became active in the work of the American Cancer Society.

Pictured in their Tulsa home are members of the family of Dewey Bartlett who became Oklahoma's 19th governor. Shown are Mrs. Ann Bartlett, Gov. Bartlett, Joanie, 18, a student at Colorado State College; Dewey Jr., 19, a student at Regis College, Denver, and Mike 16, a student at Edison High School and the family's pet poodle and collies. He was Oklahoma's second Republican governor and the first governor eligible to succeed himself. [*Tribune Staff Photographer Lewis Jarrett*]

David Hall was born October 20, 1930 in Oklahoma City. He is the son of Mr. and Mrs. William A. "Red" Hall. He was Phi Beta Kappa at the University of Oklahoma where he received a Bachelor of Arts degree in 1952. David Hall served in the U.S. Air Force from 1952 to 1954. He continued his education at the University of Tulsa, where he received his law degree in 1959. He served as Assistant County Attorney of Tulsa County from 1959 to 1962 and as County Attorney from 1962 to 1966. In 1968 he returned to the University of Tulsa where he served as Professor of Law. He was inaugurated January 11, 1971 following the closest gubernatorial election in the state's history.

Text and Photograph courtesy Oklahoma Department of Libraries

Jo Evans Hall

Jo Evans was an attractive airline stewardess when she met her future husband, David Hall. On her second night in Tulsa, Oklahoma, after having been transferred from New York City, she had a blind date with the future governor. He was working his way through law school at the time. The date was in December 1955. They were married six months later.

Jo Evans grew up in the small town of Morrilton, in the central part of Arkansas. Her dark eyes and hair and her soft voice gave an indication of her Cherokee heritage.

David, the son of Mr. and Mrs. William "Red" Hall, was reared in Oklahoma City. He attended old Classen High School, where he played on the Classen football team that beat Tulsa Central for the state high school championship in 1948. He was also president of the student body that year.

After the Halls were married, Jo worked for the airline for two more years in an on-the-ground job, while David completed his law degree at the University of Tulsa. He worked at a full-time job in the land department of a major oil company while going to the university. He became involved in politics after receiving his law degree and eventually becoming district attorney in Tulsa.

Jo and David had been married fifteen years when he became governor. She had the same apprehensions that most home-loving wives have when their husbands take on top jobs in public life. Even when David had served as district attorney in Tulsa, their home life had been very quiet and orderly. Their three children led typical teenage lives. They made good grades and were involved in many school activities. Douglas liked sports. Nancy was a junior high school cheerleader. Julie loved their three dogs and a cat. The Halls had a cabin on a lake, played a lot of tennis, and entertained in their home. According to one reporter, they never would have been in the Hollywood tabloid sheets.

The Halls were a handsome family. The children had their mother's dark coloring. David was 6'2'' with a great smile and prematurely silver hair. When he ran for the office of governor, Jo

Page 72 - Oklahoma's First Ladies

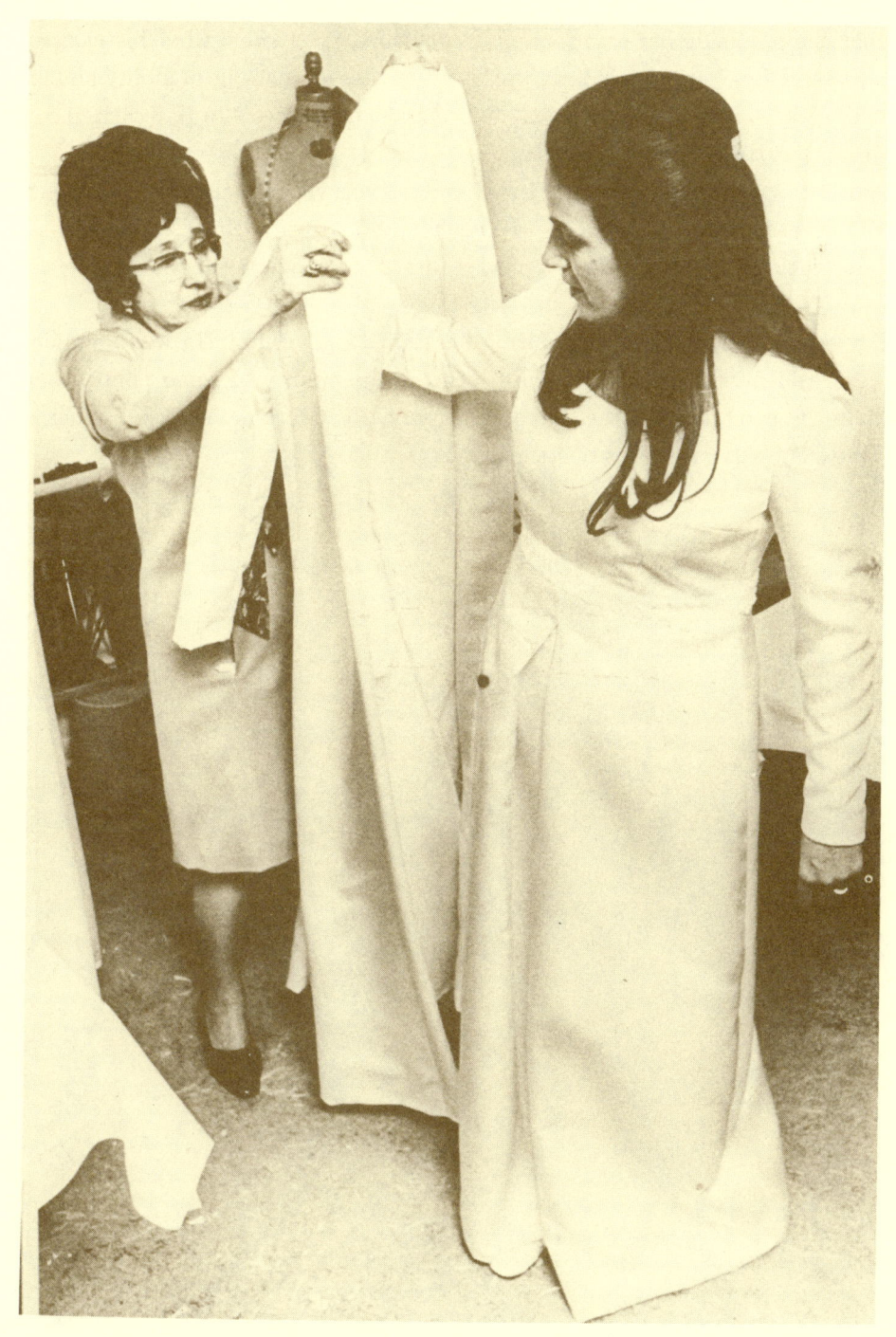

Copyright 1930-78, The Oklahoma Publishing Co. From the Oklahoman & Times 1930-1978

First Lady Jo Hall, Jan. 11, 1971 to Jan. 13, 1975

Mrs. Hall's inaugural gown and coat of white satin were designed and made especially for her and donated by a famous dressmaker, Mrs. Jennie Spagna of Oklahoma City, formerly of New York City with Christian Dior.

Oklahoma's First Ladies - Page 73

remarked that she put aside her own feelings of reluctance, "I knew what his campaign and governorship would do to our private little world. But he has a great gift of ability and integrity, and he's always felt so deeply that this was something he had to do." Jo Hall carried the love of home and family into the governor's mansion.

 The inaugural gown and coat worn by First Lady Hall was very special. Mrs. Jennie Spagna, a former Dior dressmaker, had moved to Oklahoma City from New York. She said that designing and making the inaugural costume for Mrs. Hall was just something she wanted to do.

 David Hall gained national attention during his term as governor. He was mentioned as a possible vice-presidential candidate. He also incurred the enmity of some political foes, who were determined to end his rise in the Democratic party. Jo Hall remained loyal to her husband throughout the troubled times of his political career.

World Staff Photo - Jim Tinkler - World Publishing Co.

Jo and David Hall pose with their children Nancy, Doug, and Julie just before he took office as governor.

Oklahoma's First Ladies - Page 75

David Lyle Boren was born in Washington, D.C., April 21, 1941, the son of Lyle H. and Christine McKown Boren. He graduated from Yale University Summa Cum Laude, receiving a B.A. degree in 1963, graduated with honors with a M.A. degree from Oxford University, England in 1965, and received his J.D. degree in 1968 from the University of Oklahoma where he was Class President of the College of Law. He was an outstanding law graduate and scholar and was selected as a Rhodes Scholar. In addition to his profession as an attorney, he was Chairman of the Division of Social Sciences and professor of political science at Oklahoma Baptist University. He was Company Commander, Oklahoma Army National Guard. He was elected to the House of Representatives in 1967 and served until his election as Governor in November, 1974. He was inaugurated on January 13, 1975. He is the father of two children, Carrie Christine and David Daniel. The governor made his home at Seminole before moving into the Governor's Mansion. He was elected to the U.S. Senate in 1978.

Text and Photograph courtesy Oklahoma Department of Libraries

Copyright 1930-78, The Oklahoma Publishing Co. From the Oklahoman & Times 1930-1978

Janna Lou Little Boren

Janna Lou Little was the daughter of a wealthy southern Oklahoma oilman and attorney, Reuel Little, former chairman of the American Party in Oklahoma. Janna received her secondary education from Hockaday, an elite private school in Dallas, Texas. She graduated from Boston College with a degree in communications, with a specialization in television direction.

In 1968 she married David Boren, a state legislator from Seminole, Oklahoma. When Boren decided to run for governor in 1976, the couple had two children—Carrie and Dan—and Janna was secure in her role as wife and mother. Boren had never had a political opponent prior to the gubernatorial election, so running for governor meant busy—and mostly separate—campaigning for both of them. Janna picked up her broom and went to work with "Boren's Broom Brigade," which traveled the state to tell people of Boren's goal to sweep dirty politics out of Oklahoma. Janna's private schooling, however, had not prepared her for such an experience. She later advised people to become involved in a political campaign if they really wanted an education.

Governor Boren, a graduate of Yale University and a Rhodes Scholar at Oxford University, was not new to political life. His father, Lyle Boren, had been an Oklahoma congressman for ten years. As a child, the governor spent time in the nation's capital, where he met such famous politicians as Presidents Franklin D. Roosevelt and Harry S. Truman and Speaker of the House Sam Rayburn.

Nine months after Boren's inauguration on January 13, 1975, the thirty-one-year-old first lady filed for divorce. Both she and the governor expressed deep regret over the decision but stated that irreconcilable differences had made the step necessary. Later, the governor stated that he accepted full responsibility for the marriage's failure.

In 1976 Janna met and married John Clinton Robbins, an oil producer and civic leader of Longview, Texas. The next year Governor Boren married Molly Shi of Ada, Oklahoma.

(Photo Courtesy Oklahoma Historical Society)

The Borens leading the inaugural ball at the Myriad January 13, 1975. Janna's dress was a long, pale blue silk.

Oklahoma's First Ladies - Page 77

Copyright 1930-78, The Oklahoma Publishing Co. From the Oklahoman & Times 1930-1978

Jo Hall, Oklahoma's seventeenth First Lady invited Janna Boren, Oklahoma's eighteenth First Lady for coffee and a preview of the Governor's Mansion.

Copyright 1930-78, The Oklahoma Publishing Co. From the Oklahoman & Times 1930-1978

Broom Brigade led by Mrs. David Boren, right, made a symbolic "sweep to clean up state government" as the brigade prepares to travel around the state on Boren's behalf in his race for the Democratic nomination for governor. The brigade members sold the brooms for "$10, $1 or whatever they wanted to give."

Oklahoma's First Ladies - Page 79

David Lyle Boren was born in Washington, D.C., April 21, 1941, the son of Lyle H. and Christine McKown Boren. He graduated from Yale University Summa Cum Laude, receiving a B.A. degree in 1963, graduated with honors with a M.A. degree from Oxford University, England in 1965, and received his J.D. degree in 1968 from the University of Oklahoma where he was Class President of the College of Law. He was an outstanding law graduate and scholar and was selected as a Rhodes Scholar. In addition to his profession as an attorney, he was Chairman of the Division of Social Sciences and professor of political science at Oklahoma Baptist University. He was Company Commander, Oklahoma Army National Guard. He was elected to the House of Representatives in 1967 and served until his election as Governor in November, 1974. He was inaugurated on January 13, 1975. He is the father of two children, Carrie Christine and David Daniel. The governor made his home at Seminole before moving into the Governor's Mansion. He was elected to the U.S. Senate in 1978.

Text and Photograph courtesy Oklahoma Department of Libraries

(Photo Courtesy of Micki Van Deventer)

Molly Shi Boren

Growing up as a country girl near Ada, Oklahoma, Molly Shi had strong Oklahoma roots. One of her grandfathers was an original settler of Stratford, Indian Territory—now Stratford, Oklahoma. He and his brother, a pioneer doctor at Blanchard, Oklahoma, put each other through medical school by working alternate years building the railroad. Her brother carried on the medical tradition by setting up his practice in Seminole, Oklahoma. Molly's mother taught school, and her father was a rancher.

Teaching was Molly's goal too when she majored in English at East Central State University at Ada. Before proceeding on her doctoral work, she decided to enter law school. Upon graduation from the University of Oklahoma College of Law, she opened her own law office in Ada. Later she was appointed special district judge of Pontotoc County, a position she held until 1977 when she married Governor David Boren and became Oklahoma's first lady.

The governor's family also had strong ties to Oklahoma. His father had been a United States Congressman, and his mother had taught elementary school in Hominy, Oklahoma. Among his other relatives were a variety of ministers and teachers. One uncle had been president of Southwestern Oklahoma State University at Weatherford. Governor Boren's sister worked as a research specialist in education at the Library of Congress. An aunt, Mae Boren Axton, had written an early Elvin Presley hit, "Heartbreak Hotel." Her son, Hoyt, became a country singer and television personality. John, another son and attorney, collaborated on songwriting.

When Molly turned in her judge's robe to become first lady, she became the second Mrs. Boren to fill that role. As she revealed in a newspaper interview soon after her marriage, "I don't think of myself as being the second. . . .I don't believe in competing in human relationships." She brought her own unique personality to the mansion. Raised on a farm, Molly remained an outdoors-type person. She and the governor liked to put on their jeans and spend the weekend at a cabin at Beaver's Bend State Park near Broken Bow, Oklahoma. The part Choctaw-Scottish first lady, however, equally enjoyed private moments with a good book or

(Photo Courtesy of Micki Van Deventer)

First Lady Molly Boren, Nov. 27, 1977 to Jan. 3, 1979

Mrs. Molly Boren has donated her wedding dress to the First Ladies Gown Collection. The dress and jacket of pale blue polyester were made by her sister, Mrs. Judy Connally.

Oklahoma's First Ladies - Page 81

her favorite music. She believed that, with the governor's hectic schedule, she needed such private time to function effectively in her role as first lady.

Molly Boren wanted the people of Oklahoma to know that the governor's mansion belonged to them. She gave teas that brought visitors from all over the state to see where the governor lived and sometimes worked. When people visited, they were also able to see works by Oklahoma artists that Molly had placed in the mansion.

Governor Boren was also committed to supporting Oklahoma arts. During his administration, a Summer Arts Institute was established for Oklahoma young people. Some of his other accomplishments included the repeal of the state inheritance tax on surviving spouses, the elimination of double taxation, the creation of state-funded programs for talented and gifted students, the establishment of a new trails and scenic river protection program, the extension of educational television coverage to rural areas, and the formation of new health care programs.

Boren remained true to the needs of Oklahomans as he took his seat in the United States Senate. He and Molly both had campaigned avidly for his election. In the Senate Boren has served on three committees that handle legislation of vital importance to Oklahoma: Agriculture, Finance, and Small Business.

While enjoying the excitement of congressional life in Washington, D.C., the Borens have retained close Oklahoma ties. When they leave their three-story Georgian townhouse in Arlington, Virginia, they return home to Seminole and a much less imposing white frame cottage located on a street where the senator played as a boy. Both Borens enjoy the comfortable, peaceful atmosphere of their Seminole house but laugh as they remember how it looked when they bought it. It was in such a state of disrepair that even their mothers encouraged them to look elsewhere. But the house was special to Senator Boren, who had been in it many times as a child, because he had settled the estate of the woman who lived there more than 30 years—it had been his first case as an attorney.

With their antiques and Molly's sense of decorating, the house was transformed. A picture of the interior of artist Claude Monet's home in France inspired Molly to select the pale yellow and blue color scheme. The result is a home where they can truly relax, watch the birds play in the yard, and feel in touch with Oklahomans.

(Photo Courtesy of Micki Van Deventer)

Mrs. Molly Boren in the dining room of the Boren's three-story Georgian townhouse in Arlington, Virginia where they live while in Washington, D. C.

Oklahoma's First Ladies - Page 83

George Patterson Nigh was born in McAlester, Oklahoma on June 9, 1927, son of Wilbur R. and Irene Crockett Nigh. He attended public schools in McAlester and Eastern Oklahoma Agricultural and Mechanical College at Wilburton, Oklahoma. From June 1945 through September 1946, he served in the U.S. Navy. He was granted a Bachelor of Arts degree from East Central State College, Ada, Oklahoma in 1950. From 1952 to 1958, he taught at McAlester High School. George Nigh served in the House of Representatives from the Twenty-third through the Twenty-sixth Oklahoma Legislatures. He was elected Lieutenant Governor, the youngest in the State's history in 1958, and was elected Lieutenant Governor again in 1966, 1970 and 1974. In 1963, Nigh became the 17th Governor of Oklahoma, filling an unexpired 9-day term following the resignation of Governor J. Howard Edmondson. He was elected November 7, 1978 as the 22nd Governor of Oklahoma. On January 3, 1979, Nigh became the 22nd Governor of Oklahoma serving five days to fill an unexpired term following the resignation of Governor David Boren. He was re-elected November 2, 1982.

On Monday, January 10, 1983, George Nigh was sworn in for a history-making second term, the first time any Oklahoma governor had succeeded himself.

Text and Photograph courtesy Oklahoma Department of Libraries

(Courtesy Gov. Nigh's Staff)

Donna Skinner Nigh

When Donna Faye Skinner of Morris, Oklahoma married George Patterson Nigh on October 19, 1963, he was known as "Oklahoma's most eligible bachelor." Governor Nigh has been known to tell what he refers to Donna's version of that title. That version points out that he had no job, no home, and no car when they married. She had all three. At the time neither of them had any idea that they would make Oklahoma history when Governor Nigh became the first man to be elected to two consecutive terms as governor. He was first inaugurated for a full term on January 3, 1979. His second inauguration took place on January 10, 1983. Earlier, as a lieutenant governor he had to complete the terms of two other governors. In 1963 he served out the last nine days of the administration of Governor Howard Edmondson. Sixteen years later, he completed the last five days of Governor David Boren's term.

Several aspects of Nigh's second inaugural stand out. The **Tulsa World** of Sunday, January 9, 1983, carried the headline: "Nigh to Make History When He Takes Oath." The writer described the event:

> The festivities actually got underway Saturday night in the Kirkpatrick Fine Arts Auditorium at Oklahoma City University, where Nigh presided over an Inaugural Arts Gala and at an Arts Gala Reception at an Oklahoma City bank.
>
> The gala—for the first time a part of the inaugural celebration—featured Oklahoma visual art, music and dance, with performances by Tulsa classical guitarist Ronald Radfaord, Norman folk music group Banish Misfortune and black artists Tyrone Wilkerson, Regina Johnson, Stacy McFarland, Al Bostic and Ballet Theatre's "Four Moons" ballet, Ballet Oklahoma's "A Mi Lado" and "The Long and the Short of It" and Oklahoma City University's Surrey Singers.
>
> A Sunday prayer service was scheduled at Nigh's church, the Council Road Baptist Church. A processional and recessional of inaugural guests was scheduled, along with a fellowship following the service.
>
> Nigh's inauguration as the 22nd governor of Oklahoma will take place at the Flag Plaza and the south steps of the Capitol at 1 p.m. Monday.

(Copyright 1982, The Oklahoma Publishing Co. from The Daily Oklahoman, April 5)

First Lady Donna Nigh, Jan. 3, 1979 to Present

Mrs. Nigh and Lillian Russell take a look at Mrs. Nigh's dark blue, full-length dress for the Nigh's first inaugural. The entire top of the dress was covered in dark blue sequins. The flowing skirt of sheer chiffon was belted at the waist.

The Piedmont High School Band and the 145th Army Band will play preludes, and the governor's honor guard, composed of elements of Oklahoma Air and Army National Guard units will participate.

Oklahoma City banker Jack Conn, president of the Oklahoma Historical Society and chairman of last year's Oklahoma Diamond Jubilee celebration will preside.

The inaugural procession, including Nigh, his wife, Donna, other state officials and members of the House and Senate, will take place at 2 p.m., with the oath of office to be administered afterward by Oklahoma Supreme Court Justice Ralph Hodges.

The oath will be administered to other elected state officials by Chief Justice Don Barnes, and Justice Marion Opala will swear in Lt. Governor Spencer Bernard.

Wendell R. Estep, pastor of the Council Road Baptist Church, will give the invocation.

Nigh will be introduced by Carl Albert, former speaker of the U. S. House of Representatives, and the governor's inaugural address is scheduled following the administering of the oath.

Former Speaker Carl Albert stated that when "Governor Nigh stopped teaching history, he started making it."

Although Mrs. Nigh has been supportive of the governor's programs and of her two children, Mike and Georgeann, she also enjoys working on special projects of her own. For the past fifteen years, Donna has promoted new and innovative programs for handicapped persons. She has been particularly interested in programs for the mentally retarded adults. In 1981 she garnered legislative approval and funding for a unique pilot program of group homes for mildly retarded adults. These homes are now being established in communities throughout the state. In addition, Mrs. Nigh, a former vice-president of the Oklahoma Association of Retarded Citizens, has been active in the fundraising activities for the Meadows, which will be the first private residential and vocational community in Oklahoma for adult, mentally retarded citizens. Donna Nigh has also been deeply involved with programs for children. She has appeared in television commercials to urge parents to buckle children in car seats while traveling.

Donna continued her tireless efforts in her civic and community activities in her second term as first lady just as she had in the first.

(Copyright 1983 Oklahoma Publishing Co. From "The Look" 11-16-83)

The gracefully curved staircase at the Governor's Mansion provides the backdrop for Mrs. Nigh's second inaugural gown, a soft flow of green sequins falling from a cowl neckline.

Bibliography

Allen, Robert B. "Lydie Marland: Veil of Mystery Tight." The Daily Oklahoman, 1 March 1976.

Bentley, Hattie Tingle. "A Study of Fashions in Oklahoma as Portrayed Through Costumes of Governor's Wives." Masters Thesis, Oklahoma Agricultural and Mechanical College, 1938.

Bryant, Keith L. Jr. Alfalfa Bill Murray. Norman: University of Oklahoma Press, 1968.

"Campaigning." The Sunday Oklahoman, 3 Nov. 1974.

Culver, Harry. "Borens Agree on Alimony." Oklahoma Journal, 24 Oct. 1975.

The Daily Oklahoman, 8 Jan. 1937, series of former First Ladies.

"The Democrat." The Daily Oklahoman, 17 Oct. 1958.

"Descended from Chickasaw Chiefs." The Boston Sunday Globe. 8 Feb. 1914.

Directory of Oklahoma 1983. Oklahoma City: The Oklahoma Department of Libraries.

Dyer, Kay. "Life Normal for the Bellmons—Almost." The Oklahoma City Times, 17 May 1963.

"Mrs. Edmondson Marries." The Daily Oklahoman, 22 July 1975.

Ervin, Chuck. "Nigh Urges Sooners to Help Neighbors." Tulsa World, 11 Jan. 1983, p. 1.

Forward Oklahoma, campaign pamphlet for Roy J. Turner, 1946.

Frey, Phil. "The Private World of Oklahoma's New Governor." Tulsa World, 10 Jan. 1971.

Gibson, Arrell M. The Oklahoma Story. Norman: The University of Oklahoma, 1978.

"The Governor and the Governor's Lady." Living for Young Homemakers, July 1960, p. 37.

Gregory, Bob. "The Marland Mystery." Oklahoma Monthly, Jan. 1981, p. 51.

History of Oklahoma at the Golden Anniversary of Statehood. Vol. III. New York: Lewis Historical Publishing Co., Inc., 1957.

"Illness Claims Former Oklahoma First Lady." Oklahoma City Times, 8 Sept. 1969, p. 1, 28.

"Janna Honeymooning." The Daily Oklahoman, 2 Sept. 1976.

Kobler, John. "Where is Lyde Marland?" The Saturday Evening Post, 22 Nov. 1958, pp. 19-20, 44, 47, 51, 52.

"The Life of a Governor." The Daily Oklahoman, 7 Jan. 1979, p. 2.

Matthews, John Joseph. Life and Death of an Oilman. Norman: The University of Oklahoma Press, 1951.

McReynolds, Edwin C. Oklahoma: A History of the Sooner State. Norman: The University of Oklahoma Press, 1954.

_____, Alice Marriott, Estelle Fairecover. Oklahoma: The Story of Its Past and Present. Norman: The University of Oklahoma Press, 1961.

Montgomery, Ed. "Now It's Secretary Edmondson." The Sunday Oklahoman, 18 Sept. 1966.

"'My Grayce' Kerr's Top Achievement." The Oklahoma City Times, 3 March 1965.

"Nigh to Make History When He Takes Oath." Tulsa World, 9 Jan. 1983, p. 1.

Oklahoma Election Board, Directory of Oklahoma 1982. Oklahoma City: Oklahoma Election Board, 1982.

Oklahomans for Boren Report, 1983-84.

Oklahoma's Governors 1907-1929: Turbulent Politics. ed. LeRoy H. Fischer. Oklahoma City: Oklahoma Historical Society, 1982.

"Oklahoma's New Governor." Creek County Democrat, 25 Oct. 1923. p. 1.

"Phone Calls Keep Her Busy." The Daily Oklahoman, 26 July 1950, p. 9.

"'Plain Folks' at First Thursday Open House." The Daily Oklahoman, 16 Nov. 1951, p. 1.

"Retirement Village Dedicated." Texoman, 27 August 1983.

Ritter, Cecil E. ed. "Roy J. Turner." Oklahoma Statehouse Reporter, 38, No. 8 (1969), p. 28.

Ruth, F. A. "Highlights in the Life of Jack Callaway Walton." unpublished manuscript.

"Sands of Time Don't Dull Willie Murray's Colorful but Busy Past." The Daily Oklahoman, 14 Dec. 1962, p. 19.

Sanger, Helen Ford. "Mrs. Bellmon Takes on Project." The Daily Oklahoman, 13 Aug. 1967.

"She's Again an Edmondson." The Daily Oklahoman, 1 June 1978.

Standard, Jim. "Lyde Marland Still Running." The Oklahoma City Times, 17 Nov. 1961.

Stanton, Joyce. Cimarron Family Legends. Vol. II. 1980, p. 326.

Sullivant, Otis. "State's New First Lady is Homemaker." The Daily Oklahoman, 21 Nov. 1938, p. 14.

_____. "Democratic Nominee Roy J. Turner." The Daily Oklahoman, 25 Aug. 1946.

"Trapp is Declared Governor." The Daily Oklahoman, 23 Oct. 1923, p. 1, 16.

Tulsa Sunday World, 11 May 1975.

Tulsa Tribune, 23 June 1982.

"Turner Well Known as Oil Man and Rancher." The Young Democrat, July 1946, p. 14.

Van Deventer, M. J. "Borens at Home." Oklahoma Home and Garden, January 1983.

"Vote Buying, Martial Law Marred Election." Tulsa Tribune, 7 July 1982, p. 5.

Walker, Elviretta. "Mrs. Edmondson Faces New Role as State's First Lady with Confidence." The Daily Oklahoman, 11 Jan. 1959, p. 2C, col. 8.

_____. "Mrs. Kerr is Restaurant Boss." The Daily Oklahoman, 2 Aug. 1961.

_____. Series of articles on Molly Shi Boren. Oklahoma Journal, January 1978.

"Willie Murray Dies." The Daily Oklahoman, 4 April 1963, p. 1.

"Willie Murray Praised in Senate." The Daily Oklahoman, 5 March 1963, p. 3.

FOREWORD

The scientific disciplines of ecology and environmental toxicology have not been communicating adequately with each other, to the detriment of both. Ecologists often fall short when it comes to applying the theory and findings of their relatively young science in useful practice to meet society's needs for assessment of the environmental impacts of toxic pollutants. Environmental toxicologists are increasingly having difficulty in trying to convince society's decision-makers what the results of their test methodologies in simple systems really mean in a complex, highly interactive ecological world.

This report takes a step toward marrying some of the concepts of these two scientific disciplines. At the request of the Environmental Protection Agency's Office of Toxic Substances, the Environmental Sciences Division of Oak Ridge National Laboratory has reviewed and evaluated potential techniques for studying ecological effects of toxic chemicals in systems that transcend the practicable but oversimplified conditions of most currently used toxicological test systems.

James J. Reisa
Associate Deputy Assistant Administrator
for Toxic Substances
U.S. Environmental Protection Agency

PREFACE

This report was prepared by the Environmental Sciences Division, Oak Ridge National Laboratory, under an Interagency Agreement between the Department of Energy and the Environmental Protection Agency.

The study was undertaken because of the need to examine the potential for development and standardization of tests for effects of chemical substances on selected ecological parameters that are indicative of interspecific interactions, community dynamics and ecosystem functions.

Aquatic and terrestrial laboratory methods for measuring the effects of chemicals on population interactions and ecosystem properties are discussed and evaluated for use in ecological hazard and risk assessment processes. The report is not intended to provide detailed descriptions of all suitable tests. Instead, it is intended to provide a critical review of useful or potentially useful ecological tests (i.e., those most amenable for laboratory test development) for consideration by various technical and administrative personnel responsible for implementing the Toxic Substances Control Act.

Although an extensive review of mathematical models was not included in the scope of this study, a general discussion of the roles of broad categories of models in ecotoxicology is provided. The document is a useful resource for ecologists, environmental toxicologists and scientists interested in the application of mathematical models to environmental hazard and risk assessments.

Anna S. Hammons

ABSTRACT

This report critically evaluates selected laboratory methods for measuring ecological effects and recommends tests considered most suitable for research and development for use in predicting the effects of chemical substances on interspecific interactions and ecosystem properties. The role of mathematical models in chemical hazard assessment is also discussed. About 450 references are cited. A bibliography of more than 700 references is provided.

The Office of Toxic Substances, U.S. Environmental Protection Agency (EPA) is responsible for implementing the Toxic Substances Control Act (TSCA). TSCA, promulgated in 1976, is comprehensive legislation designed to broadly protect human health and the environment from unreasonable risks resulting from the manufacture, processing, distribution, use and disposal of chemical substances.

Under TSCA, EPA is responsible for identifying and prescribing test standards to be used in developing the data necessary to predict the risks associated with chemical releases into the environment. To aid EPA in this endeavor, laboratory methods for measuring the effects of chemical substances on aquatic and terrestrial interspecific interactions and ecosystem processes were reviewed and evaluated for their potential for standardization for use in environmental hazard and risk assessment processes. The criteria used for these evaluation include whether or not the tests are: rapid, reproducible, relatively inexpensive, unequivocal, sensitive, socially relevant, predictive, generalizable and well-developed.

Approval of this document does not signify that the contents necessarily reflect the views and policies of the Environmental Protection Agency, nor does the mention of trade names or commercial products constitute endorsement or recommendation for use.

This report was submitted in partial fulfillment of Interagency Agreement No. EPA 78-D-X0387 between the Department of Energy and the U.S. Environmental Protection Agency.

Anna S. Hammons is a Research Associate in the Environmental Sciences Division of Oak Ridge National Laboratory (ORNL). She received her BS degree in biology from Cumberland College, Williamsburg, Kentucky, and is currently working toward a PhD degree in ecology at the University of Tennessee. Since joining the staff of ORNL in 1964, her activities have included research in the areas of immunology and inhalation carcinogenesis and development and direction of an information program on health and environmental studies. She is currently involved in research and development of ecotoxicological test methods for use in environmental hazard assessment.

Jeffrey M. Giddings is a Research Associate in the Environmental Sciences Division of Oak Ridge National Laboratory. He received a PhD in aquatic ecology and a BA in Biology from Cornell University. Since joining the staff of Oak Ridge National Laboratory in 1975, Dr. Giddings has been involved in a variety of research projects, including development of pond microcosms for studying chemical fate and effects, investigation of effects of organic compounds on algal photosynthesis and assessment of the environmental hazards of synthetic fuels. He currently directs research on the transport, fate, and effects of coal liquefaction product spills in aquatic and terrestrial ecosystems.

Glenn W. Suter, II is a Terrestrial Ecologist in the Environmental Sciences Division of Oak Ridge National Laboratory. He received a BS in biology from Virginia Polytechnic Institute and a PhD in ecology from the University of California-Davis. At ORNL he is co-principal investigator in the Environmental Sciences Division's Environmental Risk Assessment Project. Dr. Suter has published 18 technical papers and reports in the areas of soil ecology, ecological toxicology, environmental monitoring and environmental assessment and has also contributed to more than 20 environmental impact statements and assessments of nuclear, geothermal and synthetic fuels technologies.

Lawrence W. Barnthouse is a Research Associate in the Environmental Sciences Division of Oak Ridge National Laboratory. He earned a BA from Kenyon College and his PhD in biology from the University of Chicago. Since joining the ORNL staff in 1976, Dr. Barnthouse has participated in assessments of environmental impacts of synthetic fuels technologies and served as a technical advisor and expert witness for the U.S. Environmental Protection Agency in NPDES permit hearings. He is currently involved in research on applications of population dynamics theory to environmental impact assessment, the design of environmental monitoring programs and environmental risk assessment.

CONTENTS

Foreword iii
Preface iv
Abstract v
Tables xi
Figures xii
Acknowledgments xiii

1. **Introduction** 1

    1.1 Purpose 1
    1.2 Scope and Organization 3
    1.3 Constraints 4
    1.4 Criteria to Be Met for a Standardized Test 5
    1.5 References 7

2. **Conclusions and Recommendations** 9

    2.1 Aquatic Test Systems 9
        2.1.1 Available in the Near Future 9
            (1) Algal Competition 9
            (2) Predation by Fish 10
            (3) Mixed Flask Cultures 10
            (4) Periphyton Communities 10
            (5) Sediment Cores 11
            (6) Pond Microcosms 11
        2.1.2 Recommended for Research and Development 11
            (1) Zooplankton-Zooplankton Predation Tests . . 11
            (2) Fish-Zooplankton Predation Tests 12
            (3) Parasitism 12
            (4) Zooplankton-Algae Grazing Tests 12
            (5) Pelagic Microcosms 13
            (6) Model Streams 13
    2.2 Terrestrial Test Systems 13
        2.2.1 Available in the Near Future 14
            (1) Soil 14
            (2) Legume-Rhizobia 15
            (3) Mycorrhizae 15
        2.2.2 Recommended for Research and Development 15
            (1) Population Interactions 15
            (2) Ecosystems 16
    2.3 Mathematical Models 16
        2.3.1 Available in the Near Future 16
            (1) Ecosystem Simulation Models 16
            (2) Generalized Multipopulation Models 17
            (3) Loop Analysis and Time-Averaging 17
            (4) Input-Output Analysis 17
            (5) Population Genetics Models 17
        2.3.2 Recommended for Research and Development 17
            (1) Ecosystem Parameter Handbook 17
            (2) Model Validation Methods 18

		(3)	Theoretical Studies	18
		(4)	Strategy for Model Selection and Application	18
	2.4	References		19

3. Laboratory Tests for Chemical Effects on Aquatic Population Interactions and Ecosystem Properties, J. M. Giddings ... 23

3.1	Competition		26
	3.1.1	Algal Competition Experiments	26
	3.1.2	Conclusions and Recommendations	28
3.2	Predation		28
	3.2.1	Protozoa-Protozoa	31
		(1) Population Dynamics Experiments	31
		(2) Mechanistic Studies	32
		(3) Evaluation	34
	3.2.2	Zooplankton-Zooplankton	34
		(1) High-Speed Photography Studies	35
		(2) Population Experiments	35
		(3) Evaluation	36
	3.2.3	Fish-Zooplankton	37
		(1) Reactive Distance	37
		(2) Prey Selection	39
		(3) Capture Success	40
		(4) Handling Time	41
		(5) Population Experiments	41
		(6) Evaluation	42
	3.2.4	Fish-Macroinvertebrates	43
		(1) Predation on Grass Shrimp	43
		(2) Predation on Crayfish	45
		(3) Evaluation	46
	3.2.5	Fish-Fish	46
		(1) Examples of Recent Research	46
		(2) Methodological Details	48
		(3) Evaluation	50
	3.2.6	Conclusions and Recommendations	51
3.3	Parasitism		53
3.4	Plant-Herbivore Interactions		54
3.5	Symbiosis		55
3.6	Ecosystem Properties		55
	3.6.1	Properties of Aquatic Ecosystems	55
	3.6.2	Realism and Generality	58
	3.6.3	Potentially Useful Model Ecosystems	61
		(1) Mixed Flask Cultures	61
		(2) Periphyton Communities	63
		(3) Sediment Cores	65
		(4) Pelagic Microcosms	67
		(5) Pond Microcosms	70
		(6) Model Streams	71
	3.6.4	Conclusions and Recommendations	72
3.7	References		75

4. **Laboratory Tests for Chemical Effects on Terrestrial Population Interactions and Ecosystem Properties, G. W. Suter, II** 93

    4.1 Population Interactions 97
        4.1.1 Competition 98
            (1) Microbial Competition 99
            (2) Plant Competition 101
            (3) Arthropod Competition 102
                (a) Drosophila 102
                (b) Other Flies 103
                (c) Tribolium 104
                (d) Other Grain Insects 104
                (e) Soil Arthropods 105
            (4) Other Animals 105
        4.1.2 Herbivore-Plant 105
            (1) Sucking Insect-Plant 107
                (a) Aphid-Alfalfa 107
                (b) Aphid-Grain 107
                (c) Whitefly-Plant 107
                (d) Scale-Plant 108
            (2) Chewing Insect-Plant 108
        4.1.3 Predator-Prey 109
            (1) Microbe-Microbe 109
            (2) Arthropod-Predators 110
                (a) Parasitoid-Gall Midge 110
                (b) Parasitoid-Whitefly 111
                (c) Parasitoid-Aphid 111
                (d) Predator-Aphid 112
                (e) Parasitoid-Grain Moth 112
                (f) Parasitoid-Bean Weevil 113
                (g) Parasitoid-Fly 113
                (h) Ground-Dwelling Beetle-Prey .. 113
                (i) Spider-Prey 114
                (j) Mite-Mite 114
            (3) Vertebrate Predators 116
        4.1.4 Host-Parasite 116
        4.1.5 Symbiosis 117
            (1) Lichens 117
            (2) Rhizobium-Legume 117
            (3) Mycorrhizae 118
        4.1.6 Community Composition 121
        4.1.7 Summary 122
    4.2 Ecosystem Properties 123
        4.2.1 Parameters 123
            (1) Primary Productivity 123
            (2) Nutrient Cycling 124
            (3) Community Metabolism 126
            (4) Summary 127
        4.2.2 Test Components 128
        4.2.3 Soil Type 131
        4.2.4 Size 132

```
            4.2.5  Synthetic Systems . . . . . . . . . . . . . . . 132
                   (1)  Soil Systems . . . . . . . . . . . . . . . 132
                   (2)  Litter . . . . . . . . . . . . . . . . . . 133
                   (3)  Soil-Litter  . . . . . . . . . . . . . . . 133
                   (4)  Gnotobiotic Soil . . . . . . . . . . . . . 134
                   (5)  Soil-Plant . . . . . . . . . . . . . . . . 134
                        (a)  Pot . . . . . . . . . . . . . . . . . 134
                        (b)  Lichtenstein  . . . . . . . . . . . . 134
                        (c)  Agroecosystem Chamber . . . . . . . . 134
                        (d)  Summary . . . . . . . . . . . . . . . 134
                   (6)  Soil, Litter, Plant, and Animal  . . . . . 135
                        (a)  Odum  . . . . . . . . . . . . . . . . 135
                        (b)  Witkamp . . . . . . . . . . . . . . . 135
                        (c)  Metcalf . . . . . . . . . . . . . . . 135
                        (d)  Terrestrial Microcosm Chamber (TMC) . 136
            4.2.6  Excised System . . . . . . . . . . . . . . . . . 136
                   (1)  Soil Core  . . . . . . . . . . . . . . . . 136
                   (2)  Grassland Core . . . . . . . . . . . . . . 137
                   (3)  Sod  . . . . . . . . . . . . . . . . . . . 137
                   (4)  Treecosm . . . . . . . . . . . . . . . . . 137
                   (5)  Outcrops . . . . . . . . . . . . . . . . . 138
            4.2.7  Summary  . . . . . . . . . . . . . . . . . . . . 139
     4.3  References . . . . . . . . . . . . . . . . . . . . . . . 140
```

5. Mathematical Models Useful in Chemical Hazard Assessment, L. W. Barnthouse 155

```
     5.1  Available Models and Modeling Methodology  . . . . . . . 158
            5.1.1  Ecosystem Simulation Models  . . . . . . . . . . 158
                   (1)  Terrestrial Simulation Models  . . . . . . 159
                   (2)  Aquatic Simulation Models  . . . . . . . . 160
            5.1.2  Generalized Multipopulation Models . . . . . . . 160
            5.1.3  Alternative Methodologies  . . . . . . . . . . . 161
                   (1)  Loop Analysis  . . . . . . . . . . . . . . 161
                   (2)  Time-Averaging . . . . . . . . . . . . . . 162
                   (3)  Input-Output Analysis  . . . . . . . . . . 162
                   (4)  Population Genetics Models . . . . . . . . 162
     5.2  Criteria for Evaluating and Selecting Models . . . . . . 163
     5.3  References . . . . . . . . . . . . . . . . . . . . . . . 166
```

APPENDIXES
A. Summary Table of Aquatic Test Systems 169
B. Summary Table of Terrestrial Test Systems 179
C. Alphabetical Bibliography 189
D. Bibliography Arranged by Sections 249

TABLES

3.1	Characteristics of model ecosystems	73
4.1	Laboratory studies of mite-mite predation	115
4.2	Relative frequency of significant responses by parameters of the rhizobium-legume symbiosis to toxic chemicals	119
4.3	Relative frequency of significant responses by ecosystem process parameters to toxic chemicals in laboratory systems	129

FIGURES

4.1 Ratio diagram: I_1/I_2 = the ratio of the input frequencies of species 1 and 2 and O_1/O_2 = the ratio of output frequencies 100

5.1 Scheme for selecting appropriate models for use in hazard assessments 165

ACKNOWLEDGMENTS

We wish to express our appreciation to the following scientists in the Environmental Sciences Divison (ESD), Oak Ridge National Laboratory (ORNL), who reviewed sections of this report and offered valuable comments and suggestions: B. G. Blaylock, R. B Craig, C. W. Gehrs, S. B. Gough, F. W. Harris, H. H. Shugart, B. P. Spalding, W. Van Winkle, B. T. Walton, J. B. Waide, and J. W. Webb. We also appreciate the comments provided by the National Academy of Sciences Committee to Review Methods for Ecotoxicology.

In addition, gratitude is expressed to J. Vincent Nabholz, Project Officer, Environmental Protection Agency (EPA), James J. Reisa, Associate Deputy Assistant Administrator for the EPA Office of Toxic Substances, and David E. Reichle, ESD Associate Director, ORNL, for their advice and continuing support throughout the preparation of this report.

We also wish to thank members of the Information Division, ORNL, for obtaining the references reviewed for this report and members of the Technical Information Department, Science Applications, Inc., Oak Ridge for preparing the manuscript for publication. The services of Betty Cornett (ORNL) and Bonnie Winsbro and Judy Mason (SAI) are especially acknowledged.

SECTION 1

INTRODUCTION

1.1 Purpose

The voluminous production of chemicals since World War II has significantly increased the potential for exposing the general public to toxic substances. More than 44,000 chemicals have been listed in the Toxic Substances Control Act Chemical Substances Inventory: Initial Inventory, published in May 1979 by the Environmental Protection Agency (EPA 1979a), and new chemicals are added to the market at the rate of several hundred per year. Sources of exposure range from foods and other consumer products to waste disposal sites and polluted air and water. Increasing concern about the effects of such exposure led to the development of deliberate and comprehensive legislation, the Toxic Substances Control Act (TSCA), which was promulgated in 1976. The Office of Toxic Substances, EPA, is responsible for implementing TSCA.

Other laws have been enacted that give the federal government authority to regulate chemical substances. Some agencies responsible for such regulation include the Food and Drug Administration, Consumer Products Safety Commission, Occupational Safety and Health Administration, U.S. Department of Agriculture, and the U.S. Department of Transportation. For the first time, TSCA subjects the entire chemical industry in the United States to federal regulation that broadly protects human health and the environment from unreasonable risks resulting from the manufacture, processing, distribution, use, and disposal of a chemical substance. Requirements under this law include testing of chemicals identified as possible risks and controlling chemicals proven to present a risk. The most significant aspect of TSCA is that regulatory action can be taken before widespread exposure and possible serious damage have occurred. Therefore, justification for such action must be based on the predicted effects of specific chemicals on human health and the environment.

Under TSCA, EPA is responsible for identifying and prescribing test standards to be used in developing data necessary to predict the human health and ecological risks associated with releases of chemical substances into the environment. EPA has recognized a set of standard toxicity testing procedures for assessing the environmental hazards of chemicals (U.S. EPA 1979). These procedures are simple, rapid, inexpensive, and easily applied to large numbers of chemicals in laboratories throughout the country. Each test measures a direct toxic response (usually death) of an organism or group of organisms of a single species. The primary objective of such tests is to screen or compare chemicals and to rank them according to their relative toxicity. Chemicals ranking low in toxicity are presumed to pose no ecological hazard; chemicals ranking high in toxicity are subjected to further testing. The success of a hazard assessment program depends (1) on the ability of the screening tests to correctly identify potentially hazardous chemicals and (2) on the availability of advanced test methods to confirm and refine the results of screening tests and to define the suspected environmental hazards more precisely.

There is substantial evidence that some chemicals can produce effects on organisms that do not result in death in single-species toxicity tests, but that nevertheless impair the ability of the organism to survive under actual ecological conditions. For example, polychlorinated biphenyls (PCBs) in concentrations well below the lethal levels alter the behavior of grass shrimp to such an extent that the shrimp become more vulnerable to predation by fish; this effect is not readily detectable unless the fish are present (Tagatz 1976; Farr 1977). The same compounds impair the nutrient uptake capability of some marine diatoms, an effect that becomes apparent only when the diatoms are competing with other algal species for nutrients (Fisher et al. 1974). Effects such as these, which depend on interactions between populations for their manifestation, can be just as significant in a realistic ecological context as the more easily measured direct toxic effects.

A suitable scheme for identifying and evaluating hazards to environmental systems should include tests for predicting effects on events and processes occurring above the single-species level. Therefore, EPA is investigating the potential for developing test protocols which predict the effects of chemical substances on selected ecological parameters, indicative of interspecific interactions, community dynamics, and ecosystem functions. Streamlined protocols are necessary if consistent results are to be expected among different laboratories. Unfortunately, the state of the art of ecotoxicology does not allow the choice of appropriate tests to be made easily. As a result, EPA has enlisted the aid of the Environmental Sciences Division (ESD), Oak Ridge National Laboratory (ORNL); the Council on Environmental Quality (CEQ); and the National Research Council (NRC) in its effort to determine the importance of including such tests in hazard assessment processes and to identify suitable extant tests and those most amenable to laboratory test development.

Three major efforts comprise the investigation initiated by EPA: (1) a review of laboratory test methods that predict ecological effects on interspecific interactions and ecosystem properties and of ecological parameters most amenable for laboratory test development; (2) an evaluation of their potential utility to the hazard identification and risk assessment processes of TSCA; and (3) development of recommendations and criteria that might be used to advance the state of applied ecological science in toxicological assessment. The CEQ contracted the NRC to establish a National Academy of Sciences (NAS) Committee of experts to perform the last task. The first two tasks have been performed by ESD, ORNL, under an Interagency Agreement between EPA and the Department of Energy (DOE). Results of the ORNL review and evaluation are contained in this report. The NAS report (NAS 1981) will be available in early 1981.

1.2 Scope and Organization

This report provides a review of tests for measuring aquatic and terrestrial population interactions and ecosystem properties in laboratory systems. Little information is available on techniques developed or used specifically to predict the effects of chemicals on ecological systems. Nevertheless, tests that might be considered are discussed in terms of their potential for use in this area. The criteria used to evaluate this potential include whether or not the tests are simple, rapid, reproducible, relatively inexpensive, un-equivocal, sensitive, socially and economically relevant, and predictive. The extent of experience with and development of each test as well as the generalizability of test results were also considered. These criteria, which are necessary considerations for effective implementation of TSCA testing requirements, are defined in Section 1.4.

The general problems encountered in toxicology testing processes (i.e., selecting the appropriate dose, interpreting dose response, or choosing the best test species) intentionally are not discussed in this report. These problems are not unique to multispecies test procedures. Choices will depend to some extent on the environmental characteristics of each chemical, the expected release to the environment, and the potential for exposure. Criteria for evaluating these issues must be determined and established while tests are being developed and standardized.

Many resources were used to gather information, including the ORNL Ecological Sciences Information Center, workshops, and ESD staff scientists. The review of testing protocols was initiated by machine and manual searching for information published in scientific literature on (1) procedures used to measure changes in population dynamics such as competition, predation, parasitism, herbivory, and symbiosis and (2) ecosystem processes such as primary production, nutrient cycling, community metabolism, and litter decomposition. In addition, a series of six workshops on ecotoxicological test systems was conducted by the ESD staff to bring together investigators presently working with aquatic or terrestrial laboratory test systems. The intent of these workshops was to ensure that every available test potentially usable in a standardized ecological effects testing scheme would be identified and considered. The topics of the workshops were: Assessment and Policy Requirements of Ecological Toxicity Testing Protocols, Mathematical Models Useful in Toxicity Assessment, Methods for Measuring Effects of Chemicals on Terrestrial Ecosystem Properties, Methods for Measuring Effects of Chemicals on Aquatic Ecosystem Properties, Methods for Measuring Effects of Chemicals on

Terrestrial Population Interactions, and Methods for Measuring Effects of Chemicals on Aquatic Population Interactions. The results of these workshops will be published as a single ORNL/EPA report (Hammons, 1981). Other valuable resources were the many scientists at ORNL who were available for consultation, document review, and workshop participation and whose data files were made available for our perusal.

This report is organized into three sections: (1) aquatic population interactions and ecosystem properties, (2) terrestrial population interactions and ecosystem properties, and (3) mathematical models. A brief discussion of categories of models is included because models are recognized as potential tools for identifying and assessing environmental hazards.

Many published documents describing laboratory test systems were reviewed by the authors, and many investigators were contacted personally, but to minimize the time required to complete this project, no attempt was made to provide detailed methodologies or discussions of the results of all the tests considered. Nevertheless, examples of the different types of tests discussed in this report are cited throughout the text, and a complete bibliography is attached (Appendixes C and D) for the reader who is interested in obtaining more detailed information. Summary tables (Appendixes A and B) are also used to present additional details about the most significant aspects of specific tests.

1.3 Constraints

As expected, relatively few laboratory tests for predicting the effects of chemicals on interspecific interactions, community dynamics, or ecosystem properties exist. In addition, the understanding of community and ecosystem responses to perturbations is limited. This limited knowledge in basic ecology makes it impossible at present to recommend with certainty tests useful for successfully predicting adverse ecological effects resulting from exposure to chemical substances. It is important for the development of adequate hazard assessment tools to establish by continued research into the mechanisms of communities and ecosystems: (1) the limits to which these systems can be taken before recovery is no longer possible, (2) the measurable parameters or "symptoms" indicative of adverse effects, and (3) the generality of these symptoms among other communities and ecosystems.

The tests recommended in this report are considered to have the best potential for use under the TSCA based on the present state of the knowledge of ecotoxicological testing. As indicated throughout this report, more information is needed in many areas of ecological science before unequivocal conclusions can be reached concerning appropriate laboratory tests for predicting the ecological effects of chemical substances.

1.4 Criteria to Be Met for a Standardized Test

This report was prepared in the context of a general, tiered testing scheme for hazard assessment. Such a scheme provides for different levels or stages of testing which progressively become more complex and more definitive as positive results from one level trigger decisions to proceed to the next higher level.

Several criteria were determined by EPA and ESD to be important in selecting ecotoxicological tests for development and standardization for use in a hazard assessment scheme. These criteria were applied to the test systems reviewed for this report in a qualitative manner based on the scientific judgment of the authors and the input received from the many researchers who participated in the workshop series. Several of the criteria were applied differently, depending on the level of testing that was considered. For example, although cost should always be minimized, it would be expected to increase with increasing complexity of the test system used. Sufficient information was not always available to apply all of the criteria to all of the tests.

The following list provides definitions of the criteria as they were used in evaluating the tests selected for inclusion in this report:

Cost per Test - The total cost of completing a test for a single chemical assuming that the facilities are already available.

Documentation - The extent to which the behavior of a laboratory system (not necessarily toxicological) has been investigated and reported.

Generality - The usefulness of the test in predicting the responses of a variety of interspecific interactions or ecosystems and their major components.

Rapidity - The total amount of time required to complete a test assuming that facilities already exist.

Realism - The ability to unambiguously interpret the response of the test system in terms of responses of real ecosystems.

Rejection Standards - Defined criteria for rejecting test results--ranging from informal or common-sense criteria (e.g., many controls die) to a complete and well-defined set of criteria (e.g., more than 10% of controls fail to achieve a weight of 20 g).

Replicability - The variance in response within an experiment among individual units of a test system.

Reproducibility - The ability of a test to produce common results in
    different laboratories.

Sensitivity - The ability of a test to produce measurable responses
    at low doses of test chemicals.

Social Relevance - The value to society, direct or indirect, of the
    response measured. The value may be economic, aesthetic, or
    indirectly related to human health and welfare.

Standardization - The definition of conditions and components of a
    test system to allow different laboratories to obtain similar
    results from a test.

Statistical Basis - Accepted statistical criteria for detecting and
    interpreting responses of the test system.

Training-Expertise Requirements - The extent to which use of a test
    may be limited by requirements for higher education, specialized
    training, or expertise.

Validity - The extent to which the responses of a test system are
    known to reflect responses in the field.

1.5 References

Farr, J. A. 1977. Impairment of antipredator behavior in *Palaemonetes pugio* by exposure to sublethal doses of parathion. Trans Am. Fish. Soc. 106:287-290.

Fisher, N. S., E. J. Carpenter, C. C. Remsen, and C. F. Wurster. 1974. Effects of PCB on interspecific competition in natural and gnotobiotic phytoplankton communities in continuous and batch cultures. Microbial Ecol. 1:39-50.

Hammons, Anna S. 1981. Ecotoxicological Test Systems: Proceedings of a Series of Workshops, ORNL-5709; EPA 560/6-81-004, Oak Ridge National Laboratory, Oak Ridge, Tennessee.

National Academy of Sciences. 1981. Testing effects of chemicals on ecosystems. A report by the Committee to Review Methods for Ecotoxicology. National Academy of Sciences, Washington, D.C.

Tagatz, M. E. 1976. Effects of mirex on predator-prey interaction in an experimental estuarine ecosystem. Trans. Am. Fish. Soc. 105:546-549.

U.S. Environmental Protection Agency. 1979a. Toxic Substances Control Act chemical substances inventory: Initial inventory. Office of Toxic Substances.

U.S. Environmental Protection Agency. 1979b. Toxic Substances Control Act premanufacture testing of new chemical substances (OTS-050003; FRL-1069-1), Fed. Regist. 44(53): 16240-16292.

SECTION 2

CONCLUSIONS AND RECOMMENDATIONS

2.1 Aquatic Test Systems

We have surveyed the recent ecological and toxicological literature for reports of laboratory techniques for measuring the effects of chemicals on interactions between aquatic organisms. Interactions considered in this survey included interspecific competition, predation, parasitism, grazing (herbivory), and symbiosis. We found few relevant studies pertaining to parasitism, grazing, or symbiosis. However, a variety of techniques are available for testing chemical effects on competition and predation. A few of these techniques appear to be quite amenable for standardization and routine use--that is, they are relatively simple, rapid, economical, and reproducible.

We have also surveyed test methods for chemical effects on whole ecosystems. Ecosystem-level phenomena, such as energy flow, nutrient cycling, and homeostasis, result from interactions among ecosystem components, but the mechanisms involved are not completely understood. Effects of chemicals on ecosystem properties are therefore not predictable from results of single-species toxicity tests. Very little is known about the sensitivity of ecosystem properties to toxic chemicals. Furthermore, the complex network of interactions occurring in an ecosystem can cause chemical effects on one species to affect other ecosystem components in unpredictable ways. Because all populations in nature are parts of whole ecosystems, there is a clear need for methods of testing chemicals for ecosystem-level effects.

Very few aquatic multispecies test systems have been developed specifically for chemical hazard assessment, but several have been refined to the point that protocols could be formulated and tested with a variety of chemical types (Sect. 2.1.1). Other aquatic test systems are potentially usable for chemical hazard assessment, but require further research before standard procedures can be specified (Sect. 2.1.2). The true merits, if any, of all of these systems will be revealed only through practical experience. Moreover, effective use of laboratory test systems to predict chemical effects on aquatic population interactions and ecosystem properties will depend on advances in our basic understanding of the structure and function of aquatic ecosystems. Until such advances are forthcoming, no hazard assessment protocol at any level of biological organization can be considered truly "validated."

2.1.1 Available in the Near Future

(1) <u>Algal competition</u>. Algae are more sensitive to toxic chemicals when competitors are present than in pure culture (Fielding

and Russell 1976; Fisher et al. 1974; Kindig 1979; Mosser et al. 1972). Algal competition tests such as those of Mosser et al. (1972) and Fisher et al. (1974) are simple, inexpensive, rapid (1 to 2 weeks), easily standardized, and ecologically meaningful. Developmental needs include selection of appropriate species pairs, comparison of batch vs. continuous culture techniques, and standardization of experimental conditions. The ecological significance of alterations in phytoplankton community structure must be documented. Algal competition experiments are discussed in Section 3.1.1.

(2) Predation by fish. Predator-prey systems incorporating fish as predators and either fish or shrimp as prey are ready for standardization as hazard assessment protocols. Various options for the design of fish predation tests are discussed in Sections 3.2.4 and 3.2.5. Several experimental approaches have been used for measuring chemical effects, but without comparative data on specific compounds in different test systems, it is impossible to recommend any particular system for further development. Rather, the effects of major design options on the sensitivity, reproducibility, and efficiency of chemical effects tests should be investigated.

(3) Mixed flask cultures. Mixed cultures of bacteria, algae, protozoa, and zooplankton have been found to exhibit certain characteristics common to all ecosystems and could be used as ecosystem-level "white rats" for screening purposes. These abstract model ecosystems are small, easily replicated, and technically simple to operate. The major questions remaining to be resolved are: (a) are ecosystem-level properties more sensitive to chemicals than conventional bioassay organisms, and (b) are rankings generated by these systems different from rankings produced by conventional tests? If the answer to either question is affirmative, then mixed flask cultures should be included early in the chemical hazard assessment testing sequence. Factors to be considered in the design of these systems are discussed in Section 3.6.3 (1).

(4) Periphyton communities. Periphyton communities, which are found in nearly every aquatic habitat, exhibit all the major ecosystem functions. These communities grow well in laboratory systems; they are stable, replicable, biologically complex, and easily handled. Periphyton community structure has been widely used as an indicator of aquatic pollution, and chemical effects on periphyton community function have been observed in chronic experiments (Rodgers et al. 1980). Unlike the other test systems recommended for development in the near future, standardization of periphyton systems for chemical hazard assessment has not been attempted. However, the reviewer sees no serious methodological obstacles to the development of a periphyton community assay and recommends that research be initiated towards that objective [Section 3.6.3 (2)].

(5) _Sediment cores_. The technique of extracting sediment cores overlaid with water for study in the laboratory has been widely used by ecologists. If cores are maintained at ambient temperatures, with aeration and mixing of the water to simulate natural conditions, ecological processes and effects of chemicals can be examined over extended periods of time. The approach is essentially identical for studies in hypolimnetic, littoral, or coastal marine environments. The sediment core technique could be applied at almost any level of a hazard assessment scheme. Simple static systems are amenable to short-term tests of chemical effects, whereas more complex semi-continuous flow systems are suitable for long-term studies. An outline for a chemical testing protocol using sediment cores was formulated at the Workshop on Methods for Measuring Effects of Chemicals on Aquatic Ecosystem Properties held in conjunction with this project (Giddings 1981). This protocol, or one like it, should be refined and tested with a variety of chemicals. Relevant features of sediment core systems are discussed in Section 3.6.3(3).

(6) _Pond microcosms_. Naturally derived pond microcosms are structurally and functionally realistic representations of natural ponds. These model ecosystems are quite simple to assemble and to use for chemical effects studies, and a proposed pond microcosm protocol has been published (Harris et al. 1980). The next step in the development of these systems for chemical testing should be identification of the most sensitive and informative responses to be measured. The best use of pond microcosms in hazard assessment would be for confirmation and refinement of predictions based on simpler laboratory tests. At least one major chemical manufacturer (Monsanto) includes pond microcosms in the advanced stages of its hazard assessment program (Gledhill and Saeger 1979). Pond microcosm research is reviewed in Section 3.6.3(5).

2.1.2 Recommended for Research and Development

(1) _Zooplankton-zooplankton predation tests_. Most predator-prey studies with zooplankton have used the population approach in which groups of prey animals are exposed to a predator for a specified period of time, and the survivors of the prey population are counted. These experiments are simple and rapid and could easily be adapted to toxicity testing. Many zooplankton species are easily cultured, and large reproductive populations can be maintained in static aquaria. Predation tests can be conducted in small, static systems. Experiments can be completed in 8 h or less, and the surviving prey can be preserved to be enumerated later. Because zooplankton are nonvisual predators, lighting is not a critical factor, and experiments can be conducted in darkness. Learning, social interactions, and disturbances caused by observers are much less important in zooplankton-zooplankton systems than in fish systems. The sensitivity of zooplankton predation to chemicals is unknown. Replicability of zooplankton-zooplankton systems is probably good. These systems are discussed in Section 3.2.2.

(2) <u>Fish-zooplankton predation tests</u>. Many fish are obligate or facultative planktivores during at least part of their lives. The quality and quantity of available prey and the ability of fish to locate and capture food organisms are important factors in controlling fish productivity and in determining which fish species will succeed in a particular environment. Field studies have shown that selective predation by planktivorous fish can dramatically alter the species composition of the zooplankton community.

Fish-zooplankton predation tests are more complicated than tests with zooplankton predators. Fish cultures require more space than zooplankton cultures, and continuous flow systems are necessary for most species. Likewise, predation studies involving fish generally require large volumes and/or continuous flow. Lighting conditions and background must be carefully controlled to ensure repeatable results with these visual predators. Effects of learning, social behavior, and unintentional disturbances are more likely to occur with fish than with zooplankton predators. All of these factors imply that fish-zooplankton systems would be less amenable to chemical hazard assessment than zooplankton-zooplankton systems. However, experiments with fish might be faster than zooplankton predation tests since fish consume more prey in a given time than do zooplankton.

Because of the social and economic importance of many planktivorous fish, an attempt should be made to develop an efficient fish-zooplankton test system. The problems discussed above and in Section 3.2.3 indicate that test procedures would have to be specified in considerable detail, but the problems are not insurmountable in developing a protocol.

(3) <u>Parasitism</u>. It is widely recognized that the incidence of parasitism or disease in a population is determined partially by the physiological state of the host organism and that various environmental stressing agents can reduce the host's resistance to infection (Snieszko 1974; Wedemeyer 1970). However, only one example was found of an experiment specifically designed to measure chemically induced susceptibility to parasitism (Couch and Courtney 1977). Since the effects of chemicals (in this case, drugs) on parasitism and disease are the subjects of clinical parasitology, it is recommended that the literature of this field be surveyed to evaluate the possibility of developing a hazard assessment protocol.

(4) <u>Zooplankton-algae grazing tests</u>. Grazing by zooplankton on phytoplankton is recognized as an important component of ecosystem energy flow and nutrient cycling and as a possible determinant of plankton community structure, but it has received little attention in environmental toxicology. One reason for this is that methods for measuring plankton grazing rates, either in situ or in the laboratory, are still poorly developed. A phytoplankton-zooplankton hazard assessment test would be essentially a single-species bioassay, with zooplankton grazing rate as the measured response. Inert particles

could be (and often are) substituted for algae in this type of test without changing the nature of the experiment significantly. The sensitivity of zooplankton grazing to chemical stress is not known and should be investigated.

(5) <u>Pelagic microcosms</u>. Simulation of marine and freshwater pelagic (open-water) ecosystems in laboratory microcosms has been attempted at the EPA Environmental Research Laboratory at Narragansett, Rhode Island (Perez et al. 1977) and at the Lawrence Berkeley Laboratory (Harte et al. 1978, 1980). Pelagic ecosystems are dominated by physical processes such as turbulence and advection that are difficult to scale down to a laboratory system. However, by directing careful attention to simulation of natural physical conditions, it is possible to reproduce many features of pelagic ecosystems in the laboratory. In their current state of development, pelagic microcosms are useful tools for basic research and some special applications, but they are not yet ready for standardization as TSCA hazard assessment protocols. Further research should concentrate on measurements of ecosystem properties rather than taxonomic structure of pelagic systems. Given several more years of research, it is possible that a streamlined protocol will emerge for chemical hazard assessment. Pelagic microcosms are discussed in detail in Section 3.6.3 (4).

(6) <u>Model streams</u>. Streams are, in the opinion of Warren and Davis (1971), "among the most difficult freshwater systems to model." Participants in the Workshop on Methods for Measuring Effects of Chemicals on Aquatic Ecosystem Properties (Giddings 1981) concluded that simple laboratory recirculating streams come closest to satisfying the <u>operational</u> criteria (simplicity, rapidity, reproducibility, low expense) for a TSCA hazard assessment tool. However, the same systems that are most amenable for routine chemical hazard assessment may be the least generalizable to natural ecosystems. Small recirculating model streams lack the openness that is the distinctive feature of stream ecosystems; only larger, open systems are enough like natural streams to permit reliable predictions. Even with larger model streams, doubts about ecological realism were expressed by the participants in the Workshop (Giddings 1980). While potentially useful in many areas of applied and basic ecological research, model streams are not yet suitable for chemical hazard assessment under TSCA. With further refinement, they might be used in advanced stages of testing when transport and fate have been fully characterized and probable ecological effects have been carefully defined. Model streams are discussed in Section 3.6.3 (6).

2.2 <u>Terrestrial Test Systems</u>

Multispecies test systems are needed to test effects on system properties that are not present in single species systems because (1) emergent and collective properties of ecosystems cannot be tested in single species systems, (2) single organisms and populations do not necessarily respond realistically in isolation, and (3) the properties of chemicals can be changed by various ecosystem components. However, terrestrial ecotoxicology has been largely concerned with the transport, accumulation, and degradation of toxicants; this activity generates estimates of environmental concentrations, the results of which are interpreted according to the responses of single species. Ecosystem-level responses have been studied much less commonly, and most of this work has been done with systems that only include soil and associated microbiota. Only these systems are sufficiently developed for use in testing effects on ecosystem properties. The responses of more complex "microcosms" are not yet interpretable in terms of either their internal responses or their relevance to field responses, but results are sufficiently promising to justify further research and development.

Little work has been done on the toxicology of population interactions. It is not clear whether (1) species associations respond to chemicals as a unit, (2) the effects of chemicals on a species are qualitatively affected in any regular way by the presence of a second species, or (3) the presence of a second species simply has a quantitative effect on the response of the first species. A second major issue is generality--for example, which responses, if any, of a test system using predation by the parasitoid Encarsia formosa on the whitefly Trialeurodes vaporariorum are generally applicable to hymenopteran predators and homopteran prey, insect predators and prey, or to all predation. Answers to these types of questions are central to the design of a test program for population interactions because they indicate what parameters should be measured and which and how many species associations must be tested.

2.2.1 Available in the Near Future

Because terrestrial ecological toxicology has been a relatively neglected field, only a few potential test systems are available for use in the near future. In addition to the problems identified for each test, there are some common developmental problems. First, a set of standard reference test chemicals must be identified and used in test development and as positive controls for test use. Second, the responses of a test protocol must be validated by field experiments. Third, the ability of a test protocol to give consistent results must be confirmed by use in several laboratories.

(1) Soil. The best developed multispecies test system is a simple test for CO_2 production and nitrogen mineralization by natural soil microbial communities [Sect. 4.2.5(1)]. This type of test is relatively rapid, inexpensive, and easily performed. A tentative protocol for this test, similar to the one developed by the ORNL workshop participants (Suter 1981b), should undergo confirmatory testing to determine the effects of soil type and substrate amendments on standard reference chemicals. Studies to determine the optimum number of replicates, amount of soil per replicate, and sampling

schedule could be conducted concurrently. Because this system, as proposed, requires 2 weeks and is not apparently sensitive [Sect. 4.2.1(4)], it does not appear to be useful as a screening test, but it could be used relatively early in the hazard assessment process.

(2) <u>Legume-rhizobia</u>. A test for effects on this symbiotic relationship should be developed using a domestic legume, commercial innoculum, and greenhouse conditions [Sect. 4.1.5(2) and Suter 1980a]. Test development should include examination of the effects of soil type, legume and <u>Rhizobium</u> species, and parameters measured on test performance. This test should be easy to perform, relatively inexpensive, and require less than a month to complete. While it does not appear suitable for screening, it could be used early in the testing scheme.

(3) <u>Mycorrhizae</u>. Tests for effects of chemicals on the symbiosis of flowering plants with endo-and ectomycorrhizae should be developed [Sect. 4.1.5(3)]. Test development should include examination of the effects on test performance of soil type, plant and fungus species, and parameters measured. While these tests appear to be reasonably inexpensive and easy to perform, they would probably not be used early in a testing scheme because they require approximately 3 months for completion.

2.2.2 Recommended for Research and Development

(1) <u>Population interactions</u>. Because of the absence of toxicological experience with population interactions other than the two already listed (Sect. 2.2.1), there is no strong basis for selecting specific systems or even for prescribing the necessary number of categories of tests. However, on the basis of perceived importance, feasibility, and ability to represent real systems, we consider the following potential test systems to be good candidates:

Grass-legume competition [Sect. 4.1.1(2)]
Homopteran-plant herbivory [Sect. 4.1.2(1)]
Lepidopteran-plant herbivory [Sect. 4.1.2(2)]
Parasitoid-homopteran predation [Sect. 4.1.3(2)]
Ladybird-homopteran predation [Sect. 4.1.3(2)]
Mite-mite predation [Sect. 4.1.3(2)]

Other systems are highly developed and easily implemented, but are not felt to be realistic or representative. These systems can aid in the development of population interaction tests by providing relatively quick and inexpensive checks of the generality of responses observed in the more realistic test systems. This category includes:

Drosophila competition [4.1.1(3)]
Tribolium competition [4.1.1(3)]
Housefly-blowfly competition [4.1.1(3)]
Parasitoid-grain moth predation [4.1.3(2)]
Parasitoid-fly predation [4.1.3(2)]

Because there is no empirical or theoretical basis for ranking systems within these groups, ranking should be conducted on the basis of the interests and qualifications of responding researchers.

(2) Ecosystems. More research and development should be performed on medium-sized soil core microcosms with soil covers of litter, herbaceous vegetation, and seedling trees (Sect. 4.2.5 and 4.2.6). These studies are needed to elucidate the importance of the different physical and biotic components to system response (Sect. 4.2.2) and the importance and representativeness of parameters measured in microcosms relative to whole-ecosystem responses (Sect. 4.2.1).

2.3 Mathematical Models

A variety of mathematical models and modeling methodologies appear potentially useful in hazard assessments conducted under TSCA. Possible uses include both predicting the effects of chemical substances on multipopulation systems and ecosystems and interpreting the results of microcosm experiments in terms of causal pathways. Most of these models and methodologies were developed as research tools and have never had practical applications. All require substantial development and testing before they can be reliably used in hazard assessments. Additional research above and beyond the development of specific models is required because of the fundamental differences between mathematical models and laboratory test systems. The number and identity of components included in a model, as well as the detail with which each component is modeled, can be designed to fit the specific needs of the problem at hand. Strategies for efficiently utilizing this versatility in hazard assessments need to be developed. Similar, and equally plausible, models of the same system can yield radically different predictions about the effects of chemical substances. For this reason, it is essential that efficient methods for evaluating the validity of model predictions and for selecting between alternative models be developed.

2.3.1 Available in the Near Future

(1) Ecosystem simulation models. A variety of ecosystem simulation models exist that could, with varying degrees of modification, be used to make predictions about the effects of chemical substances on ecosystems. Because of their relatively realistic representations of ecological processes, forest succession

models (Botkin et al. 1972; Shugart and West 1977), IBP biome models (e.g., Innis 1972; Park et al. 1975), and pesticide fate-and-effects models (e.g., Falco and Mulkey 1976) appear to be especially appropriate candidates.

(2) _Generalized multipopulation models._ These are simple, highly generalized models that can be rapidly and inexpensively tailored to fit any system of interacting populations, aquatic or terrestrial. Because physical, chemical, and biological processes are not represented in realistic detail, these models are thought to be more appropriate for screening of substances for potential effects than for detailed toxicant- or site-specific assessments (as might be required in connection with regulatory actions).

(3) _Loop analysis and time-averaging._ Loop analysis (Levins 1974; Lane and Levins 1977) and time-averaging (Levins 1979) are methods of analyzing the qualitative behavior of systems of coupled differential equations such as those employed in generalized multipopulation models. In addition to predicting responses of multipopulation systems to chemical substances, these methods can be used (a) to identify critical parameters that should be measured, (b) to identify system properties that enhance or reduce impacts, and (c) to analyze data obtained from microcosm experiments.

(4) _Input-output analysis._ Input-output analysis (Finn 1976; Hannon 1973; Lettenmaier and Richey 1978) is a method of econometric analysis that has been modefied for use in analyzing material budgets in ecosystems. Presently, its primary use is in deriving descriptive indices that summarize complex data relating to material cycling patterns. Changes in these indices may indicate system dysfunction caused by stress. Input-output analysis requires further development and testing before it can be used for predictive purposes.

(5) _Population genetics models._ The very large body of theory on population genetics can be applied to predicting the evolutionary responses of populations to chemical substances. Such applications have great potential value because populations in nature frequently evolve in response to exposure to chemical substances (e.g., pesticides and antibiotics). No other kind of model can predict these effects.

2.3.2 Recommended for Research and Development

(1) _Ecosystem parameter handbook._ Standard ecosystem simulation models, specially tailored for predicting the effects of chemical substances, and standard data sets are needed for representative terrestrial and aquatic environments. As an aid to model development, an ecosystem parameter handbook should be compiled. This handbook would include definitions and standard notations for parameters that are used in ecosystem models. It would also include a codification of

properties of ecosystems relevant to modeling (e.g., numbers of trophic levels and functional groups in different ecosystem types, relationships between primary and secondary production, and average numbers of prey species fed on by various predators).

(2) <u>Model validation methods</u>. Research on model validation methods is urgently needed to support the use of mathematical models in hazard assessments. Clearly, it is necessary to evaluate the reliability of any model that will be used as part of the basis for regulatory actions. Equally important, efficient methods for determining the relative merits of alternative models must be developed, because decision makers in contested proceedings are likely to be presented with different models, sponsored by different contesting parties, that make radically different predictions because radically different predictions can be made using different models. The technical basis for recommending the specific research projects necessary for developing operational model validation protocols does not presently exist. It is recommended that EPA develop contacts with researchers actively engaged in model validation studies to enlist their aid in developing a research program. A national or international conference on model validation would be a valuable first step.

(3) <u>Theoretical studies</u>. Theoretical studies using generalized multipopulation models, loop analysis, input-output analysis, and any other similar analytical methodologies should be performed to define the possible responses of systems to chemical substances. Examples of the kinds of results that could be obtained are the identification of (a) system properties that confer resilience or vulnerability to chemical substances and (b) conditions under which sublethal exposures to chemical substances can cause destabilization of competitive or predator-prey systems. Results of such studies, which can be conducted relatively rapidly and inexpensively, would suggest processes that should be incorporated in more complex models and hypotheses that should be tested using ecosystem simulation models, microcosm studies, and field studies.

(4) <u>Strategy for model selection and application</u>. Regardless of how many and what kinds of models are available, an overall strategy for selecting and applying models will be required to use models productively as part of the hazard assessment process. As part of this strategy, a flowchart decision tree should be developed as an aid in identifying the best model(s) for any given assessment problem. Because development of this strategy will require intimate knowledge of the hazard assessment process and the overall procedures for implementing TSCA, active participation by the Office of Toxic Substances will be necessary.

2.4 REFERENCES

Botkin, D. B., J. F. Janak, and J. R. Wallis. 1972. Some ecological consequences of a computer model of forest growth. J. Ecol. 60:849-872.

Couch, J. A., and L. Courtney. 1977. Interaction of chemical pollutants and virus in a crustacean: A novel bioassay system. Annals N.Y. Acad. Sci. 298:497-504.

Falco, J. W., and L. A. Mulkey. 1976. Modeling the effect of pesticide loading on riverine ecosystems. IN Ott, W. R. (ed.), Environmental Modeling and Simulation. EPA-600/9-76-016/.

Fielding, A. H., and G. Russell. 1976. The effect of copper on competition between marine algae. J. Ecol. 64:871-876.

Finn, J. T. 1976. Measures of ecosystem structure and function derived from analysis of flows. J. Theor. Biol. 56:363-380.

Fisher, N. S., E. J. Carpenter, C. C. Remsen, and C. F. Wurster. 1974. Effects of PCB on interspecific competition in natural and gnotobiotic phytoplankton communities in continuous and batch cultures. Microbial. Ecol. 1:39-50.

Giddings, J. M. 1981. Methods for measuring effects of chemicals on aquatic ecosystem properties. IN Hammons, Anna S. (ed.), Ecotoxicological Test Systems: Proceedings of a Series of Workshops, ORNL 5709; EPA 560/6-81-004, Oak Ridge National Laboratory, Oak Ridge, Tennessee.

Gledhill, W. E., and V. W. Saeger. 1979. Microbial degradation in the environmental hazard evaluation process. pp. 434-442. IN Bourquin, A. W., and P. H. Pritchard (eds.), Microbial Degradation of Pollutants in Marine Environments. EPA-600/9-79-012.

Hannon, B. 1973. The structure of ecosystems. J. Theor. Biol. 41:535-646.

Harris, W. F., B. S. Ausmus, G. K. Eddlemon, S. J. Draggan, J. M. Giddings, D. R. Jackson, R. J. Luxmoore, E. G. O'Neill, R. V. O'Neill, M. Ross-Todd, and P. Van Voris. 1980. Microcosms as potential screening tools for evaluating transport and effects of toxic substances. EPA-600/3-80-042.

Harte, J., D. Levy, E. Lapan, A. Jassby, M. Dudzik, and J. Rees. 1978. Aquatic microcosms for assessment of effluent effects. Electrical Power Research Institute EA-936.

Harte, J., D. Levy, J. Rees, and E. Saegebarth. 1980. Making microcosms an effective assessment tool. IN Giesy, J. P. (ed.), Microcosms in Ecological Research (in press).

Innis, G. S. 1972. Simulation models of grassland and grazing lands. Prep. No. 35, Grassland Biome, Natural Resource Ecology Laboratory, Colorada State University, Fort Collins.

Kindig, A. 1979. Investigations for streptomycin-induced algal competitive dominance reversals. Experimental Report ME25, FDA Contract No. 223-76-8348, University of Washington.

Lane, P. A., and R. Levins. 1977. The dynamics of aquatic ecosystems 2. The effects of nutrient enrichment on model plankton communities. Limnol. Oceanogr. 22(3):454-471.

Lettenmaier, D. P., and J. E. Richey. 1978. Ecosystem modeling: A structural approach. J. Environ. Eng. Dive., Proc. Am. Soc. Civ. Eng. 104:1015-1021.

Levins, R. 1974. The Qualitative analysis of partially specified systems. Ann. N.Y. Acad. Sci. 231:123-138.

Levins, R. 1979. Coexistence in a variable environment. Am. Nat. 114:765-783.

Mosser, J. L., N. S. Fisher, and C. F. Wurster. 1972. Polychlorinated biphenyls and DDT alter species composition in mixed cultures of algae. Science 176:533-535.

Park, R., et al. 1975. A generalized model for simulating lake ecosystems. Contribution No. 152, Eastern Deciduous Forest Biome, U. S. International Biological Program. Simulation Councils, Inc.

Perez, K. T., G. M. Morrison, N. F. Lackie, C. A. Oviatt, and S. W. Nixon. 1977. The importance of physical and biotic scaling to the experimental simulation of a coastal marine ecosystem. Helgol. Wiss. Meersunters. 30:144-162.

Rodgers, J. H., Jr., J. R. Clark, K. L. Dickson, and J. Cairns, Jr. 1980. Nontaxonomic analyses of structure and function of aufwuchs communities in lotic microcosms. IN Giesy, J. P. (ed.), Microcosms in Ecological Research (in press).

Shugart, H. H., and D. C. West. 1980. Forest succession models. BioScience. 30:308-313.

Snieszko, S. F. 1974. The effects of environmental stress on outbreaks of infectious diseases of fishes. J. Fish. Biol. 6:197-208.

Suter, G. W. 1981a. Methods for measuring effects of chemicals on terrestrial population interaction. IN Hammons, Anna S. (ed.), Ecotoxicological Test Systems: Proceedings of a Series of Workshops, ORNL-5709; EPA 560/6-81-004, Oak Ridge National Laboratory.

Suter, G. W. 1981b. Methods for measuring effects of chemicals on terrestrial ecosystem properties. IN Hammons, Anna S. (ed.), Ecotoxicological Test Systems: Proceedings of a Series of Workshops, ORNL-5709; EPA 560/6-81-004, Oak Ridge National Laboratory.

Wedemeyer, G. 1970. The role of stress in disease resistance of fishes. pp. 30-35. IN Snieszko, S. F. (ed.), A Symposium on Diseases of Fishes and Shellfishes. Amer. Fish. Soc., Washington, D.C.

LABORATORY TESTS FOR CHEMICAL EFFECTS ON AQUATIC POPULATION INTERACTIONS AND ECOSYSTEM PROPERTIES

J. M. Giddings
Environmental Sciences Division
Oak Ridge National Laboratory

SECTION 3

LABORATORY TESTS FOR CHEMICAL EFFECTS ON AQUATIC POPULATION INTERACTIONS AND ECOSYSTEM PROPERTIES

This section presents the results of a survey to identify methods for measuring chemical effects on aquatic population interactions and whole ecosystems. These methods are evaluated in the context of a tiered hazard assessment scheme (Cairns 1980; Hushon et al. 1979). In such a scheme, chemicals are first subjected to a battery of simple, rapid tests aimed at identifying those chemicals that might be hazardous to the environment. Chemicals that are indicated to be potentially hazardous are tested further to better define the effects that might occur and to establish the concentration ranges likely to produce those effects. If the concentration that produces adverse effects is close to the expected environmental concentration, the chemical is tested under more realistic conditions to confirm the earlier results and to predict the ecological impacts in as much detail as possible.

Tests to be used early in the assessment process must be highly sensitive, since the objective is to produce no false negatives (Hushon et al. 1979). Because these early tests will be applied to hundreds or thousands of chemicals, they must also be rapid, inexpensive, replicable, and readily standardized for use by different laboratories. Tests for confirmation and prediction can be more expensive and time-consuming, since few chemicals will reach this stage of the assessment scheme; however, these tests must include as much ecological realism as possible so that actual effects may be reliably predicted. Tests used in the intermediate stages of the assessment scheme are designed to compromise between realism on the one hand and sensitivity, rapidity, replicability, low cost, and standardizability on the other. Most of the tests reviewed are most suitable for the intermediate and advanced stages of hazard assessment, but a few might be incorporated into the initial battery.

Few aquatic multispecies test systems have yet been developed or adapted for chemical hazard assessment. Without a great deal more practical experience with chemical effects testing above the population level, it will be impossible to determine which types of tests will be most useful. Development of chemical hazard assessment protocols should draw on the entire body of ecological experience rather than focusing too narrowly on a particular published procedure. Therefore, this review can only indicate general approaches that appear to be fruitful, without recommending specific procedures to be followed. Where alternative strategies exist for conducting a given type of experiment, major issues are discussed which must be resolved before a standard method can be selected.

3.1 Competition

Competition has been defined as an interaction between two species in which each population adversely affects the other in the struggle for limiting resources (Odum 1971). Competition is not a series of discrete events, like predation, but rather is manifested over generations in the history of a population. Therefore, laboratory studies of competition are usually conducted with short-lived organisms such as bacteria, algae, and zooplankton.

Many organisms are more sensitive to toxic chemicals when competitors are present than in pure cultures (Fielding and Russell 1976; Fisher et al. 1974; Kindig 1979; Mosser et al. 1972). Chemical effects on competition are generally interpreted as effects on the abilities of organisms to take up, assimilate, or store a limiting resource. If competing species are affected by a chemical in different degrees, the normal competitive dominance under a given set of conditions may be altered or reversed. On a community level, this results in changes in the relative abundance of species, with or without a change in the total biomass or overall activity of the community (May 1973; O'Neill and Giddings 1979).

The effects of a chemical on a group of competing species depend on the environmental conditions and on which species are present (Fielding and Russell 1976). The behavior of any species, including its abundance and distribution in space and time, can vary tremendously in the presence of different competitors (O'Neill and Giddings 1979). Thus, the results of a competition experiment with two species do not indicate what would have occurred if a third species had been involved. Competition experiments have been used primarily to elucidate the mechanisms of competition and to validate ecological theories, rather than to predict the course of events in nature.

Because they are (1) extremely sensitive and (2) nonpredictive, competition experiments are most applicable in the first or intermediate levels of the hazard assessment sequence. Zooplankton competition experiments reported in literature range from 6 to 100 weeks in duration, so their utility for testing large numbers of chemicals is doubtful. Experiments with algae can be completed in as little as 4 days, and bacterial experiments may be even shorter. Because only one example of a bacterial competition experiment (Hansen and Hubbell 1980) was found in our literature review, we have focused on algae as logical subjects of tests for chemical effects on competition.

3.1.1 Algal Competition Experiments

Competition can be extremely important in structuring algal communities (O'Neill and Giddings 1979). Shifts in algal dominance may have repercussions on the quality and abundance of animal life in an aquatic ecosystem because some algal species are not easily ingested or are of greater nutritional value to consumers than are others (see references cited in Mosser et al. 1972). Assessment of the true ecological significance of alterations in algal community structure should be an objective of future research.

Of all the numerous published studies of algal competition (Appendix A), those by Mosser et al. (1972) and Fisher et al. (1974) are perhaps the best demonstrations of the ability of algal systems to reveal effects at very low chemical concentrations. These experiments involved the marine diatom Thalassiosira pseudonana and the marine green alga Dunaliella tertiolecta. The growth of T. pseudonana in pure batch culture was inhibited by polychlorinated biphenyl (PCB) at 25 µg/L, but not at 10 µg/L or less. D. tertiolecta in pure culture was unaffected by 25 µg/L. When grown together in batch culture with no PCB, T. pseudonana attained densities 8 or 9 times as high as D. tertiolecta. However, when PCB at 1 µg/L was included in the medium, the growth of T. pseudonana was slightly reduced and that of D. tertiolecta was substantially increased, resulting in T. pseudonana to D. tertiolecta cell ratios of only about 2 to 1 (Mosser et al. 1972). The authors concluded that the diatom normally stripped the nutrients from the medium before the green alga could achieve much growth. PCB impaired the diatom's nutrient uptake capacity and thus permitted the green alga, which was unaffected, to reach higher population densities.

In a subsequent study, Fisher et al. (1974) compared the effects of PCB in batch and continuous cultures of the same two species. PCB at 0.1 µg/L did not affect the outcome of competition in mixed batch cultures, nor did it affect either species growing alone in continuous culture. In mixed continuous culture, PCB reduced the proportion of T. pseudonana to 50% of the total cells, as compared to control proportions of over 90%. When natural phytoplankton communities dominated by T. pseudonana and two other diatom species were tested in similar continuous culture experiments, the same effect on T. pseudonana was observed as in the two-species experiments. The PCB concentration of 0.1 µg/L that produced this effect was at least two orders of magnitude below the concentration that inhibited pure batch cultures of T. pseudonana.

Continuous cultures are appropriate for algal competition experiments for several reasons (Fisher et al. 1974). In a continuous culture, resources are always limiting; therefore, competition is always occurring. Batch cultures, however, do not become nutrient-limited until they reach the senescent phase. Continuous cultures can be maintained in the active growth phase for longer periods than batch cultures, thus allowing competitive displacement to take place. The greater sensitivity of continuous cultures, compared to batch cultures, derives from these two factors. Continuous cultures are certainly more representative of most natural growth situations. On the other hand, batch cultures are technically simpler (although analytically more complex) than continuous cultures. An effort should be made to assess the relative cost, efficiency, and sensitivity to chemicals of these two kinds of competition tests.

3.1.2 Conclusions and Recommendations

The studies of Fisher et al. (1974) and Mosser et al. (1972) are examples of how algal competition experiments could be applied in chemical hazard assessment. Other competition experiments are described in Appendix A. <u>Because these systems are relatively simple and extremely sensitive to chemicals, they should be developed into a TSCA hazard assessment protocol.</u> A systematic search for suitable species pairs (freshwater and marine) should be undertaken, basing the final selection on ease of culture, predictability of response, sensitivity to chemicals, and ecological relevance. Optimal experimental conditions can then be established, and the system can undergo the validation and interlaboratory testing sequence necessary for all standard methods.

3.2 <u>Predation</u>

The principal mechanism by which chemicals (and other types of stress) have been observed to influence predator-prey interactions is through behavioral alterations in the prey. These behavioral changes often make the prey more conspicuous to predators (e.g., increased activity, erratic movement, failure to seek shelter) or reduce their ability to avoid capture once detected (e.g., sluggishness, slowed swimming speed, reduced stamina). Most published experiments on chemical effects on predator-prey interactions, therefore, have been essentially behavioral studies.

Behavioral effects of chemicals are generally the most sensitive type of sublethal response. Furthermore, natural predators are frequently capable of discerning behavioral abnormalities in their prey even when the abnormalities are not obvious to a human observer. Therefore, predator-prey interactions should be affected by chemicals at lower concentrations than many biological responses measured in conventional toxicity tests. Indeed, many of the studies reviewed in this section demonstrated predator-prey effects at concentrations orders of magnitude below the lethal level. The apparent sensitivity of predator-prey interactions is the major justification for their inclusion in a hazard assessment program.

However, because chemical effects on predation derive primarily from behavioral alterations in the prey, the response of any particular predator-prey combination may not be readily generalizable to other species pairs. For example, stress-induced hyperactivity can make mosquito fish more susceptible to predation by largemouth bass (Goodyear 1972), but less susceptible to predation by bowfin, which prefer slow-moving prey (Herting and Witt 1967). Current knowledge of critical factors in predator-prey interactions does not allow us to select a small set of species pairs upon which to base general conclusions about chemical effects on predation. An effect observed in one situation serves only to indicate the <u>potential</u> for effects on other predator-prey interactions, but the magnitude, direction, or even occurrence of effects on other species pairs cannot be accurately predicted.

Effects observed in most laboratory predator-prey experiments are of no more value in predicting actual events in nature than conventional bioassay results. A multitude of physical, chemical, and ecological factors other than predation influence the distribution, abundance, and activities of species in natural ecosystems. As an obvious example, a population whose density is limited by intraspecific competition may be totally unaffected by changes in predation rates. To predict the effect of a chemical on natural populations from results of a predator-prey experiment, detailed information on the population dynamics of both species and on the trophic structure of the ecosystem would be needed at the very least.

High sensitivity, poor generalizability, and poor predictive power of predator-prey tests imply that they would be most useful in the early stages of a hazard assessment scheme. Methods used early in the testing sequence must be simple, inexpensive, and rapid since they will be applied to a large number of chemicals; they must also be well standardized so that consistent results can be achieved by different laboratories. Therefore, the experimental approaches evaluated below were selected from the many published techniques because of their efficiency and ease of standardization.

Many studies of predation are designed to measure specific components of a predator-prey interaction such as reactive distance, handling time, or capture success. An alternative approach is to enclose a predator with a population of prey and count the survivors. These two types of experiments can be labeled the "mechanistic approach" and the "population approach," respectively, for lack of better terms. It must be presumed that at least some mechanisms are more sensitive to chemical stress than the net survivorship of the population because various factors may compensate for changes in particular components of the interaction. To choose a hypothetical example, a chemical that produces hyperactivity in the prey might reduce the searching time of the predator, but may simultaneously make the prey more difficult to capture. The net effect on the predation rate might be small. Effects of chemicals on mechanisms might also be more generalizable to other species than effects on net population survival. To extend the above example, a chemical causing hyperactivity in one species would probably produce the same effects on related species, but the compensating effect (decreased capture success) would depend on specific behavioral characteristics of the predator and the prey; hence, the net outcome might be different with different species pairs. Focusing on a single component of the predator-prey interaction might make a test more sensitive and more generalizable, but omission of potential compensating effects would reduce the predictive power of the test compared to a test using the population approach.

The mechanistic and population approaches impose different demands on the investigator. Population experiments under reasonably realistic conditions take at least several hours and sometimes days or weeks. Mechanistic measurements are often completed in seconds or minutes. However, mechanistic measurements must be repeated many times to generate enough data for statistical analysis, while a carefully controlled population experiment might need to be performed only once or twice to achieve the same level of statistical confidence. Most mechanistic approaches require that an observer monitor the experiment continuously (e.g., to count attacks or captures or to measure handling time or reactive distance). A population experiment can be designed in such a way that only one count of surviving prey is necessary. Depending on the organisms involved, the survivors may even be preserved to be counted at the convenience of the experimenter. Therefore, one experimenter can conduct a number of population experiments at once, but mechanistic experiments have to be run separately. <u>Because experience is lacking with either approach to chemical testing, neither is clearly preferable in every case</u>.

In the population approach, treated and control prey may be offered to the predator simultaneously or in separate trials. Either strategy has certain advantages and disadvantages, as discussed in Sect. 3.2.5(2). With simultaneous exposure of two prey groups to the predator, some means of differentially marking the groups is necessary; this may be impossible with zooplankton. The experimental results are complicated by the continuously changing ratios of the two prey groups. The possibility of treated prey affecting the performance of control prey cannot be discounted, especially in experiments with schooling fish. However, when prey groups are presented separately, differences in predator performance may obscure treatment effects. Ideally, the same predator or group of predators should be tested with both treated and control prey so that variations among predators do not influence the results. Even with this precaution, the order in which prey groups are presented may be significant; learning in one trial may affect the outcome of the next. [This is possible even in protozoa (G. W. Salt, personal communication).] Another disadvantage of separate presentation is that more trials are required than when prey groups are presented simultaneously. A systematic investigation of these factors should be conducted before selecting either experimental design for chemical hazard assessment. It should be pointed out, however, that mixed groups of exposed and unexposed prey are probably unusual in nature.

3.2.1 Protozoa-Protozoa

Protozoa have been popular subjects for predation studies since the early experiments of Gause (1934; Gause et al. 1936). Salt (1967) offered two reasons why protozoa are well suited for such research: (1) "if there are any universal characteristics of predation they should be present in the simplest animals;" and (2) such characteristics should be more easily discernable in protozoa than in animals with sexes, life stages, and other complicating factors. Protozoa have therefore been used as model predators; the publications reviewed here did not consider the ecological significance, if any, of protozoan predation.

(1) *Population dynamics experiments*. The ciliates *Didinium nasutum* (a predator) and *Paramecium aurelia* or *P. caudatum* (prey) were selected by Gause (1934), and many of those who followed him, in studying predator-prey interactions among protozoa. Gause found that mixed cultures of these species were invariably short-lived. Growth of *Paramecium* populations allowed *Didinium* to increase. *Didinium* then drove the prey to extinction and subsequently starved. This simple predator-prey oscillation leading to extinction of prey was also observed by Luckinbill (1973, 1974) and by Veilleux (1979). As Salt (1974) pointed out, this phenomenon is "precisely what does not occur in nature." A great deal of theoretical and experimental work, including the studies reviewed below, has been directed towards identifying the critical factors permitting stable coexistence of protozoan predators and their prey.

Luckinbill (1973) reasoned that the predator-prey interaction might be stabilized if the frequency of predator-prey encounters could be reduced. He cultured *Didinium* and *Paramecium* together in a medium to which methyl cellulose had been added to slow the movements of both species. The medium was enriched with Cerophyl, a bacterial growth medium, inoculated with *Aerobacter aerogenes* as food for *Paramecium*. The cultures were started with 35 predators and 90 prey in 6 ml of medium. All the animals were removed and placed in fresh medium every 2 days. Without methyl cellulose, these cultures went through a typical predator-prey oscillation terminating in less than 10 h with the extinction of *Paramecium*. Methyl cellulose prolonged the interation; the cultures persisted through two to three oscillations over 16 days, and *Didinium* was the first to become extinct. Luckinbill found that the oscillations could be perpetuated by reducing the food supply to the prey (by reducing the Cerophyl concentration). With fewer bacteria, the *Paramecium* were undernourished at the peaks of their population density. *Didinium* feeding on these undernourished *Paramecium* reproduced more slowly than when feeding on healthy prey and were unable to completely eliminate the prey. These cultures (with methyl cellulose) went through seven stable oscillations in 32 days and were terminated voluntarily. Luckinbill concluded that coexistence of predator and prey was possible if two conditions were met: (1) the prey were able to reach low enough densities that the predator could not find them all, while still maintaining numbers that ensured the survival of the population; and (2) the prey were restricted in their growth by something other than predation (in this case, food).

Veilleux's (1979) methods were nearly identical to Luckinbill's method, with the following exceptions: (1) rather than transferring all the animals to fresh medium every 2 days, Veilleux replaced half the culture volume with fresh medium and did not remove any ciliates; and (2) the cultures were started with 15 Didinium and 45 Paramecium. Without methyl cellulose, these cultures became extinct without oscillations. With methyl cellulose in the medium, the experimental outcome depended on the Cerophyl concentration. At high Cerophyl concentrations, the prey eventually became extinct after a series of oscillations of increasing amplitude. At slightly lower Cerophyl concentrations, the predator became extinct. With still lower Cerophyl levels, the cultures reached stable oscillations. At the lowest Cerophyl concentrations, the Paramecium did not support the nutritional requirements of Didinium, and the latter became extinct. The conditions resulting in stable oscillations were the same as those in Luckinbill's study (1973).

Luckinbill (1974) attempted to produce stable cultures without methyl cellulose by increasing the culture volume. He reasoned that with a relatively large "arena" for the predator-prey interaction, the prey could reach low enough population densities to avoid capture by the predator while still maintaining an absolute population size sufficient to ensure their survival. He established cultures ranging from 0.1 mL to 1000 mL, each with initial densities of 20 Paramecium and 10 Didinium per milliliter. The cultures were observed under a dissecting microscope at 20-min intervals until no Paramecium could be found. None of the cultures attained stable oscillations, but their persistence increased from 2.8 h at 0.1 mL to 82 h at 1000 mL. Reducing the Cerophyl concentration prolonged the existence of large cultures, but did not stabilize them. In nature, the almost infinitely large "arena," coupled with possible food limitation of prey, may permit the coexistence of protozoan predators and prey (Luckinbill 1974). In the laboratory, coexistence has been achieved only in cultures with methyl cellulose.

(2) Mechanistic studies. Salt (1967, 1968, 1969, 1974) and Veilleux (1979) devised experiments to measure several other aspects of the predator-prey interaction among protozoa. Unlike the experiments described above, these mechanistic studies were not intended to perpetuate a predator-prey system, but rather to measure various components of the interaction over short time intervals. The experiments were conducted in 0.1-mL cultures, covered by a layer of paraffin oil to prevent evaporation (Salt 1967). Salt (1967) devised an automated system to photograph entire 0.1-mL drops periodically. The numbers of animals and, in some cases, their metabolic state could be determined with good accuracy by examining the film record under a

dissecting microscope. Salt's basic technique was to start a culture with two predators (Didinium nasutum, Amoeba proteus, or Woodruffia metabolica) and about 200 prey (Paramecium aurelia). No food was provided for the prey; prey were added to the cultures as needed to maintain the desired densities throughout an experiment. Each experiment was terminated when the predators reached a preselected density. Based on the counts derived from the film record, Salt calculated the generation times, feeding rates, and other characteristics of the predator. His primary objective was to examine variations in these parameters as a function of predator and prey densities. Veilleux (1979) used similar methods (generally in shorter experiments) to investigate the effects of methyl cellulose and Cerophyl concentrations.

The generation times of Woodruffia (Salt 1967), Amoeba (Salt 1968), and Didinium (Salt 1974; Veilleux 1979) were independent of predator and prey densities. The generation time of Didinium, however, was increased when the animals were feeding on undernourished Paramecium (Veilleux 1979). According to Salt (1969), Woodruffia cultured in the laboratory for 1000 to 1500 generations had longer generation times than members of the same species freshly collected from the field. He inferred that the animals had undergone genetic changes in the laboratory cultures and cautioned against using data from laboratory stocks to make quantitative predictions about wild populations.

The rate of food consumption by Didinium was shown to vary with the density of prey (Salt 1974; Veilleux 1979). The maximum feeding rate in Salt's experiments was about two prey per predator per hour; Veilleux (1979) measured up to 12 prey per predator per day. The discrepancy may reflect differences in Cerophyl concentrations in the cultures of Paramecium fed to the predators or the Didinium cultures used by the two investigators may have been genetically different. Because both authors omitted certain relevant information in their descriptions of methods, the discrepancy remains unresolved.

Another quantity measured in several of these studies was the number of prey consumed by one predator before fission occurred. Salt found this number to decrease with increasing predator density in cultures of Woodruffia (Salt 1967) and Amoeba (Salt 1968) and later concluded that the metabolic efficiency of these predators was greater at high densities (Salt 1979). Veilleux (1979) measured a three-fold variation in prey consumed per fission in Didinium over a range of Cerophyl concentrations.

For the most part, the connection between these mechanistic studies and the population dynamics experiments has not been made. In particular, the density-dependence of some components of the predator-prey interaction have yet to be assimilated into mechanistic population models.

(3) _Evaluation_. The social significance of nonpathogenic protozoa is nil, and the ecological significance of protozoan predators is not well known. The major advantages of protozoa as subjects for chemical effects tests are their small size and ease of culture. Protozoa tests are probably easier to standardize than tests with higher organisms, and no special equipment or skills are required. Counting protozoan populations, however, is tedious and could limit the number of tests that could be run in a given period of time. The suggestion that protozoa, by virtue of their simplicity, exhibit the essential features of all predator-prey phenomena (Salt 1967) is not entirely logical, and there is little evidence to support it. <u>Protozoan predator-prey systems have little utility for chemical hazard assessment in their present state of development.</u>

3.2.2 Zooplankton-Zooplankton*

The impact of predation on the composition of freshwater zooplankton communities has been extensively studied over the past two decades in field observations and laboratory experiments (Hall et al. 1976). The primary emphasis has been on vertebrate predators (see Sect. 3.2.3). Only recently have studies focused on the effects of invertebrate predators on zooplankton communities. Brooks and Dodson (1965) originally hypothesized that when vertebrate predation was low, the dominance of large zooplankton species was due to their ability to outcompete smaller species for a limited food supply. However, efforts to verify this hypothesis were inconclusive (Hall et al. 1976). Dodson (1974a) later proposed that small zooplankton are selectively reduced by invertebrate predators. Supportive evidence for this hypothesis has come from numerous field studies (Allan 1973; Anderson 1970; Confer and Cooley 1977; Dodson 1970, 1972; Lynch 1979; McQueen 1969; Sprules 1972). Other field studies have suggested that under the constant stress of invertebrate predation, individuals of the stressed populations undergo morphological changes (Dodson 1974b; Kerfoot 1975; O'Brien and Vinyard 1978; O'Brien and Schmidt 1979; O'Brien et al. 1979) or reproductive changes (Kerfoot 1974, 1977a) to reduce this predation. Laboratory studies that have attempted to test these hypotheses are the focus of this section. Although these studies were designed to examine individual predator-prey interactions, the techniques could be adapted for the testing of chemical substances for environmental effects.

Invertebrate predators such as the cladocerans <u>Leptodora</u> and <u>Polyphemus</u>, cyclopoid copepods, and certain calanoid copepods, and the phantom midge larvae <u>Chaoborus</u> are primarily nonvisual, grasping predators that depend to some extent on random contact for prey capture (Zaret 1975). Gerritsen and Strickler (1977) recognized four

---

*This section was contributed by John D. Cooney, University of Tennessee.

progressive stages of interaction for this type of predation: encounter, attack, capture, and ingestion. However, because of the small size of the animals, very little detailed information is available on these various stages.

(1) <u>High-speed photography studies</u>. Through the use of high-speed photography and constant observation under a dissecting microscope, Kerfoot (1977b, 1978) was able to document the predator-prey interaction between cyclopoid copepods of the genus <u>Cyclops</u> and the cladoceran <u>Bosmina longirostris</u>. Kerfoot found that cyclopoids can perceive objects at a distance of about 2 to 3 body lengths and that most attacks on prey occur within a single body length (about 1 to 2 mm). Zooplankton swimming speeds have also been measured by high-speed photography (Gerritsen 1978; Strickler 1977). Different instars and sexes of the same species may swim at different speeds. This is important because the probability of a planktonic animal encountering an invertebrate predator is determined in part by the animal's swimming speed. Acridine, a nitrogen-containing aromatic compound, has been observed to reduce the swimming speed of copepods (J.D. Cooney, unpublished data).

High-speed photography has also revealed that the predator's hunting strategy is important in determining the probability of encountering prey. Ambush predators, such as phantom midge larvae (<u>Chaoborus</u>), rest motionless in the water column and attack passing prey. For these animals, encounter probability is a function of prey speed. With predators that swim continuously, such as the calanoid copepod <u>Epischura</u>, encounter probability is relatively constant (Gerritsen 1978).

Studies such as these have provided useful information on predator-prey interactions. However, high-speed photography techniques are highly specialized and are not readily adaptable to general toxicity testing.

(2) <u>Population experiments</u>. Most predator-prey studies with zooplankton have used the population approach in which prey animals (or groups of prey of different sizes or species) are exposed to a predator for a specified period of time, and the survivors of the prey population are counted. Groups of prey without predators are sometimes included in these experiments as controls. Experiments may be as short as 6 to 8 h (Mullin 1979), or they may continue for several days with new prey added daily (Brandl and Fernando 1974; Confer 1971). The length of the experiments should be shorter than the reproductive period for the test animals because many predators eat their own young, which would bias the results. Many species of predators and prey have been studied. Cyclopoid copepods (e.g., <u>Mesocyclops</u> and <u>Cyclops</u>) are the most common predators, and cladocerans (e.g., <u>Bosmina</u> and <u>Ceriodaphnia</u>) or calanoid copepods (e.g., <u>Acartia</u> or <u>Diaptomus</u>) are typical experimental prey. A few studies (Brandl and Fernando 1978; Li and Li 1979) have used natural

prey communities. Similar techniques have been used to study predation by insect larvae (Akre and Johnson 1979; Gerritsen 1978; Thompson 1978).

In most of these studies, the experimental animals were obtained directly from field collections and then sorted in the laboratory, either by using a dissecting microscope or by passing the plankton sample through a series of sieves of various mesh sizes. These procedures are tedious and may injure the animals. Brandl and Fernando (1978) used a sieve to remove predators and then used a plankton splitter to subdivide the prey animals into control and test groups. Predators were then reintroduced at varying densities, and prey numbers were compared with control groups after 24 h.

Acclimation periods for experimental animals ranged from 6 h (Confer 1971) to one week (Kerfoot 1977). Standard acclimation periods are important to ensure the same nutritional status for predators in each test. Some investigators recommend starving predators for 24 h before testing (Akre and Johnson 1979; Gerritsen 1978; Kerfoot 1977; Li and Li 1979).

Containers most frequently used in testing were glass beakers, ranging in size from 50 to 4000 mL (Brandl and Fernando 1979; Confer 1971; Kerfoot 1977; Landry 1978; Mullin 1978). Li and Li (1979) used small Petri dishes, which facilitated observations under a dissecting microscope. Kerfoot (1977) found rectangular 10 L aquaria to be inadequate because prey animals would remain in the corners, where predators have difficulty feeding.

Studies that use field collections as a means of obtaining experimental animals are severely limited by temporal abundance of suitable predators and prey. Using zooplankton species for which culture methods have already been determined and life history parameters measured in the laboratory (e.g., _Diaptomus clavipes_, _Bosmina longirostris_, _Cyclops bicuspidatus thomasi_, _Cyclops versalis_) would be more efficient and would provide an abundance of experimental animals of the required sizes throughout the year. The use of laboratory animals would also reduce the inherent variability of results obtained using field-collected animals because laboratory populations could be homogeneous with respect to nutritional status.

(3) _Evaluation_. Zooplankton predator-prey experiments are simple and rapid and could be easily adapted to toxicity testing. Many zooplankton species are easily cultured, and large reproductive populations can be maintained in static aquaria. Their short lifespans and small size make it possible for many experiments to be conducted in limited space and time. Experiments can be completed in 8 h or less, and the surviving prey can be preserved to be enumerated later. Because zooplankton are nonvisual predators, lighting is not a critical factor, and experiments can be conducted in darkness. Learning, social interactions, and disturbances caused by observers

are much less important in zooplankton predation tests than in tests with fish (see Sects. 3.2.3, 3.2.4, and 3.2.5). Replicability of zooplankton-zooplankton systems is probably good. There are no reports of chemical effects studies on zooplankton predator-prey interactions.

3.2.3 Fish-Zooplankton

Many fish are obligate or facultative planktivores during at least part of their lives. The quality and quantity of available prey and the ability of fish to locate and capture food organisms are important factors in controlling fish productivity and in determining which fish species will succeed in a particular environment. Furthermore, several field studies have shown (Brooks and Dodson 1965; Dodson 1970; Galbraith 1967; Green 1967; Hall et al. 1970; Warshaw 1972; Wells 1970) that selective predation by planktivorous fish can dramatically alter the species composition of the zooplankton community. Brooks and Dodson (1965) hypothesized that fish alter zooplankton communities by preferentially consuming larger individuals. This suggestion prompted many investigations into the selective feeding habits of planktivorous fish and the mechanisms responsible for the observed food preferences. Effects of toxic chemicals or other environmental stresses have not been examined in this context, but some of the experimental techniques used to study fish-zooplankton interactions in the laboratory could be adapted for chemical hazard evaluation.

(1) <u>Reactive distance</u>. In a recent analysis of fish predation on zooplankton, O'Brien (1979) distinguished four phases of the interaction: location of prey by fish, followed by pursuit, attack, and capture. Because prey are small relative to predators, location of prey is usually the critical step in feeding. Most planktivorous fish are visual predators, and their ability to locate prey is influenced by prey size (Confer and Blades 1975a, b; Confer et al. 1978; Eggers 1977; Vinyard and O'Brien 1976; Ware 1972, 1973; Werner and Hall 1974), prey pigmentation (Confer et al. 1978; Eggers 1977; Ware 1973; Zaret 1972; Zaret and Kerfoot 1975), prey movement (Confer and Blades 1975a; Eggers 1977; Ware 1973), predator hunger (Confer et al. 1978), and light intensity (Confer et al. 1978; Eggers 1977; Vinyard and O'Brien 1976; Ware 1973).

The ability of a fish to locate zooplankton prey is commonly expressed in terms of reactive distance (RD)--the distance between predator and prey when the predator begins pursuit. Reactive distances have been measured in the laboratory by Confer and Blades (1975a, b), Confer et al. (1978), Vinyard and O'Brien (1976), Ware (1972, 1973), and Werner and Hall (1974). The methods used in these various experiments have much in common. In each case a starved fish is placed at one end of a long, narrow aquarium, and a prey is introduced at a distance beyond the fish's visual range. The point at which the fish begins to pursue the prey is observed, and the distance from that point to the prey is measured by a scale along one side of the aquarium. Distinguishing active pursuit from random searching is not always possible; Confer and Blades (1975a) reported discarding one-third of their observations for this reason, and the problem has undoubtedly occurred with other workers who simply did not report it.

A long, narrow aquarium is necessary so that RD can be accurately determined from the positions of predator and prey along one dimension. This introduces some artificiality into the predator-prey interaction since fish need only search in one direction. Confer et al. (1978) used a large aquarium and three observers to determine RD in three dimensions for lake trout (Salvelinus namaycush). They discovered that fish searching in three dimensions are not 100% efficient--that is, they overlook some prey within their visual range. These authors concluded that the actual volume searched by this fish is 50 to 70% less than would be estimated from the RD measured in a long, narrow tank. This factor would not affect comparisons of relative RD, but it would have to be considered in predicting absolute predation rates in nature.

The reactive distance of fish decreases as they become satiated (Confer et al. 1978). To eliminate this variable from experiments, fish are usually starved for at least 24 h before feeding trials. A single fish can be used for a number of trials in one experiment before satiation begins to reduce the RD. Bluegill (Lepomis macrochirus) 6.5 cm in length can consume more than 25 large Daphnia magna without affecting RD (Vinyard and O'Brien 1976), and 11-cm lake trout (Salvelinus namaycush) can eat 65 D. magna before RD begins to decline (Confer et al. 1978). A fish can be used for more than one experiment if a starvation period is allowed between experiments.

Not all fish are amenable to laboratory experimentation. Zaret (1972; Zaret and Kerfoot 1975) found that Melaniris chagresi, a planktivore from Gatun Lake, Panama, were extremely nervous in aquaria and could not be held in captivity for more than 10 days. Vinyard and O'Brien (1975) reported terminating some feeding sessions with bluegill (Lepomis macrochirus) when the fish became excited or distressed. Any fish used in predation studies must be conditioned to find and capture prey under experimental conditions. Introducing the prey without attracting or disturbing the fish may be difficult. Vinyard and O'Brien (1976) waited until the fish was facing the opposite direction before placing the prey into the aquarium. In other studies (O'Brien et al. 1976; Ware 1973), the aquarium was partitioned into a holding compartment and a feeding compartment. After the fish was placed in the holding compartment and activity normalized, the prey was positioned in the feeding compartment. Then the fish was released by removing the partition. Pre-experimental conditioning and isolation of the fish during prey introduction are useful practices for reducing extraneous factors that could influence the behavior of the fish.

Measurements of RD appear to be replicable within and between experiments. Werner and Hall (1974) reported standard errors equivalent to 3 to 5% of the mean in experiments with two bluegill (Lepomis macrochirus). In 9 to 28 trials with two rainbow trout (Salmo gairdneri) feeding on five size classes of prey, standard errors were less than 10% of the mean RD (Ware 1972). Confer et al. (1978) found no significant differences among lake trout (Salvelinus namaycush) of similar sizes. Among a group of eight pumpkinseed (Lepomis gibbosus), the responses of six were statistically indistinguishable (Confer and Blades 1975b). O'Brien (1979) compiled RD vs prey size data from several sources and found a good agreement between experiments.

(2) Prey selection. Reactive distance is incorporated into many mathematical models of fish predation on zooplankton (Confer and Blades 1975a; Confer et al. 1978; Eggers 1977; O'Brien et al. 1976; Ware 1973; Werner and Hall 1974). These models consistently indicate that the probability of encountering prey (a function of RD) is of primary importance in determining the diet of fish at low prey densities. At higher densities, a fish may see more than one prey at once, and the fish's diet will then depend partially on which prey is selected. This conclusion was supported by the experiments of Werner and Hall (1974). O'Brien and his co-workers have used two methods to examine prey selection by bluegill (Lepomis macrochirus). One method (O'Brien et al. 1976) was an extension of the RD experiments described above. The fish was held behind a screen while two Daphnia magna of the same or different sizes were positioned in the aquarium; the fish was then allowed to swim through an opening in the screen. The experimenters noted which prey was selected and the distances of both prey from the fish when pursuit began. They determined that bluegill select the prey with the largest apparent size, regardless of the actual size of the individuals offered. Thus, a small D. magna close to the fish might be selected over a larger individual at a greater distance. The authors determined that the data of Werner and Hall (1974) were consistent with the apparent-size-selection hypothesis.

The other method used for determining prey preference was the "tilt box" (Vinyard and O'Brien 1975). This technique was based on the following aspects of bluegill behavior: (a) bluegill will orient their dorsal surface toward light; (b) they will orient their ventral surface toward gravity; and (c) the actual position of the fish is a compromise between the light response and the gravity response, with the light response taking on greater importance when the fish sees a prey of interest. The tilt box was a 50- by 15- by 15-cm plexiglas chamber illuminated from the side by a reflector flood lamp. Water was passed through the box with a current speed of 2 to 6 cm/s, which ensured that the fish faced the appropriate direction. A 2- by 1- by 14-cm presentation chamber was located 10 cm in front of the fish. Test fish were placed in the chamber for 1 to 2 h per day for a week to familiarize them with the environment. In each experiment, a starved fish was placed in the box in dim light for 1/2 to 1 h. The light was then turned on full, and the tilt of the fish was measured against a protractor on the rear wall of the chamber. A prey was placed in the presentation chamber, and the change in tilt of the fish was measured. The change in tilt was found to be proportional to the length of the prey, ranging from about 1° for small prey to 7° for large prey. No change in tilt occurred when prey were not presented. Small bluegill (which are entirely planktivorous) responded more than large bluegill (which eat other prey besides zooplankton).

Recently, Fisher et al. (1980) used the tilt box to measure the effect of hydrazine on bluegill (Lepomis macrochirus). Artificial prey (a piece of commercial fish food glued to a microscope slide) was used instead of live zooplankton. Individual fish were placed in the box, acclimated for 5 min in the dark, and then illuminated from the side. After 1 to 6 min the tilt was measured. A screen in front of the prey was then removed and the tilt was measured again. Each fish was used in only one experiment and was exposed to the hydrazine only during the time that it was in the tilt box (10 to 15 min). Hydrazine had no effect on the tilt before the prey was exposed, but it significantly reduced the change in tilt when the screen was removed. The chemical effect in the tilt box occurred at 0.1 mg/L; the static 96-h LC_{50} for this species was determined to be 1.08 mg/L. The authors cautioned that "drawing ecological implications from this study would be inappropriate because both the prey used and lateral light sources are not natural aspects of the bluegill's habitat. Yet, as a sensitive technique to assess toxicant stress, the dorsal light response offers a new approach for behavioral bioassay studies." As the authors point out, more information on the natural predatory behavior of the bluegill is needed before the biological significance of the dorsal light response can be determined.

(3) Capture success. Planktivorous fish are very successful in capturing most prey they pursue. Pumpkinseed (Lepomis gibbosus) were 100% successful at capturing Daphnia magna and D. pulex in RD experiments (Confer and Blades 1975a), and rainbow trout (Salmo gairdneri) were 84 to 91% successful at capturing amphipods (Ware 1972). The capture success of L. gibbosus for copepods averaged 80%, with daily variances possibly due to learning by the fish. The copepods became sluggish after 36 h in the laboratory, which added to the variability in capture success (Confer and Blades 1975a). Copepods are stronger, faster swimmers than cladocerans; they are also negatively rheotactic and, therefore, swim away from the suction currents produced by planktivorous fish (Janssen 1976). Drenner et al. (1978) constructed an artificial suction device to test the avoidance capabilities of various zooplankton species. The capture frequency for Ceriodaphnia reticulata and Daphnia galeata mendotae was the same as for neutrally buoyant bubbles and heat-killed Daphnia; D. pulex escaped somewhat more successfully, and Cyclops sp., Mesocyclops sp., Diaptomus pallidus, and Chaoborus sp. avoided the suction strongly. Janssen (1976) used a similar device to demonstrate that

suction currents capture more Daphnia retrocurva than Diaptomus oregonensis. Brooks and Dodson (1965) suggested that the escape capabilities of Cyclops bicuspidatus thomasi were responsible for that species remaining in Crystal Lake, Connecticut, in the face of predation by the alewife (Alosa pseudoharengus), which had eliminated all other zooplankton of the same size. Evasion is a function of temperature; arctic grayling capture copepods more successfully at 5°C than at 15°C (O'Brien 1979). As noted by Drenner et al. (1978), the ability of zooplankton to avoid capture by fish has drawn little attention in predation studies despite the fact that this phenomenon is fairly easy to measure in the laboratory.

(4) Handling time. The interval between seizure of prey and swallowing is known as handling time. Werner (1974) measured handling times for bluegill (Lepomis macrochirus) and green sunfish (L. cyanellus) feeding on various types of prey. His method was exceedingly simple: a fish was fed prey one at a time while an observer with a stopwatch measured the time between seizure and swallowing. Handling time was relatively constant, approximately 1 s, for small prey and rose steeply for prey nearly as large as the mouth of the fish. Handling time for a given prey size increased gradually as the fish continued eating because satiated fish swallowed prey 2½ to 3 times more slowly than hungry fish. Ware (1972) observed a similar effect with rainbow trout (Salmo gairdneri), noting that partially satiated fish often rejected a prey several times before swallowing. Handling time sets an upper limit to feeding rates at high prey densities (Ware 1972) and may restrict small fish to small prey under these conditions (Werner 1974), but this is not likely to be significant in most natural situations.

(5) Population experiments. All of the experiments just described involved close observation of mechanisms involved in individual predation events. The results of these studies were used to identify critical factors in the predator-prey interaction and formed the basis for many mechanistic models of fish predation on zooplankton. To test the predictions and implications of these models and, in some cases, to derive values for model parameters, a different experimental approach has been used in which fish are allowed to feed on a zooplankton population or community rather than one individual at a time. The outcome of such an experiment is determined by comparing the surviving prey population with the initial population or by analyzing the stomach contents of the fish. The objective is to assess the feeding selectivity of the predator without necessarily distinguishing the mechanisms of selection.

The work of Drenner et al. (1978) is typical of this approach. Experiments were conducted in plastic swimming pools containing 120 to 150 L of water. Gizzard shad (Dorosoma cepedianum) were placed in the pools (31 to 38 fish per pool), and a freshly collected zooplankton community was mixed into the water. The zooplankton were sampled periodically, and experiments lasted from 1 to 13.5 h. Cladocerans

(_Daphnia galeata mendotae_ and _Ceriodaphnia reticulata_) were consumed most rapidly, cyclopoids (_Cyclops_ sp. and _Mesocyclops_ sp.) less rapidly, and the calanoid _Diaptomus pallidus_ least rapidly. These results were consistent with conclusions reached in experiments with artificial suction feeders (Drenner et al. 1978; Janssen 1976).

Werner and Hall (1974) adopted a similar approach for experiments with bluegill (_Lepomis macrochirus_). Ten fish were acclimated in pools (1.3 to 1.7 m in diameter, 15 to 28 cm deep) for 24 h, and then _Daphnia magna_ were added at various densities and size class proportions. To avoid significant changes in the prey populations, the fish were allowed to feed for only 0.5 to 5 min and were then removed from the pool and their stomach contents analyzed. The results indicated that large prey were consumed in greater proportions than their proportions in the prey population. The authors analyzed the data in terms of a model based on foraging energetics. O'Brien et al. (1976) later demonstrated that the same data could be explained by an apparent-size-selection model (see above).

Zaret (1972) examined the relative preference of _Melaniris chagresi_ (a tropical planktivore) for two forms of _Ceriodaphnia cornutum_ by allowing two fish to feed for approximately 1 h on a mixture of the two forms and then analyzing the fish stomach contents. The feeding time was selected to permit the fish to consume 10 to 30% of the prey. As noted above, this fish was difficult to handle in the laboratory. Two to three fish were added to each 38-L aquarium the day before the experiment, and one fish had usually died by the time the experiment began. These experiments confirmed the preference of _M. chagresi_ for the more visible (larger eye pigmentation area) form of _C. cornutum_.

Ware (1972) measured the consumption rate of rainbow trout (_Salmo gairdneri_) on the amphipods _Crangonyx richmondensis_ and _Hyalella azteca_ at different prey densities and in the presence of different litter substrates. The amphipods were placed in the 90- by 45- by 45-cm aquarium 1 h before the experiment began to allow them to disperse and find cover. One fish was then added and observed for 50 min. Attacks and captures were recorded, and the number of surviving prey was determined at the end of the feeding period.

(6) _Evaluation_. Predation by fish on zooplankton is an important phenomenon in aquatic ecosystems. Interference with fish-zooplankton interactions could have significant economic consequences as well since the diet of many commercial and game fish consists mainly of zooplankton or planktivorous fish. Because hundreds of laboratories throughout the country are presently equipped to culture fish and zooplankton for single-species bioassays, the incorporation of predation tests into chemical hazard assessments would not require facilities or skills not already available.

The sensitivity of fish-zooplankton interactions to toxic chemicals is unknown. Effects on the visual acuity, swimming speed, agility, and behavior of the fish would probably have a greater influence on predation than any physiological or behavioral impairment of the zooplankton. Exposing the predator, instead of (or in addition to) the prey, to a test chemical would be a logical experimental approach. Of the various parameters measurable in mechanistic studies, reactive distance is most likely to be influenced by toxicants. The reactive distance of an individual fish for a given class of prey can be measured in a few hours, but the measurement is labor-intensive and replicates would have to be run sequentially rather than simultaneously. The population approach described above is a more efficient means of measuring effects on fish-zooplankton systems since experiments can be set up with many replicates at once, and surviving prey can be preserved and counted when convenient. The studies by Drenner et al. (1978) are good examples of the population approach to fish-zooplankton interactions.

Because light intensity, turbidity, and background all have significant effects on the ability of fish to locate zooplankton, experimental conditions must be carefully controlled in fish-zooplankton studies. Hunger and feeding experience of the fish are critical in any predation experiment. The age and size of both predators and prey must be specified, and other factors (configuration of the test chamber, timing of the experiments, and potential interference by the observer) can also influence the results. All these variables should be rigidly standardized among tests and among laboratories if consistent results are to be achieved.

The ecological and economic significance of fish predation on zooplankton and the widespread familiarity with these animals as subjects of bioassays justify incorporation of fish-zooplankton predation tests in the battery of hazard assessment methods. Studies should be undertaken to determine the sensitivity of fish-zooplankton interactions to toxic chemicals and to optimize the experimental procedure for routine testing.

3.2.4 Fish-Macroinvertebrates

A survey of the literature indicated that little laboratory research has been done on predation by fish upon macroinvertebrates. Two groups of studies are reviewed here: (1) a series of experiments on predation by estuarine fish on grass shrimp conducted at EPA's Gulf Breeze Environmental Research Laboratory (ERL) and (2) a group of studies concerning the interactions between smallmouth bass and crayfish. Grass shrimp and crayfish, both detritivores, are important components of the food webs of coastal ecosystems and lakes, respectively.

(1) Predation on grass shrimp. Tagatz (1976) reported the first of a series of predation experiments involving the grass shrimp,

Palaemonetes pugio. His experiments were performed in model ecosystems similar in concept to the terrestrial-freshwater microcosms of Metcalf et al. (1971). The model ecosystems consisted of 4 cm of sand and 160 L of artificial seawater in 180-L aquaria. Turtle grass (Thalassia testudinum) was planted over two-fifths of the bottom surface, and 75 grass shrimp were added. The systems were allowed to equilibrate for 4 to 6 days, and mirex was then added. There was no significant mortality of shrimp for 13 days in these systems compared to controls. After 13 days, two pinfish (Lagodon rhomboides) were introduced into each tank, and the numbers of surviving shrimp were determined after 1 to 3 days of predation. Predation was significantly higher in systems treated with mirex than in the controls. The author recognized that the results might have reflected effects of mirex on either the predator or the prey, but concluded on the basis of previous toxicity tests that only shrimp were affected. He stated that the concentration of mirex found to alter the predator-prey interaction (0.025 µg/L) was "the lowest concentration of mirex in water that has been reported to cause death of an estuarine animal." Death in this case was an indirect result of exposure to the toxicant.

Tagatz (1976) believed that the effects of mirex were caused by alterations in the behavior of the grass shrimp, but he reported no observations that would support this contention. Farr (1977) conducted experiments specifically designed to reveal behavioral alterations in shrimp exposed to toxicants. He conditioned Gulf killifish (Fundulus grandis) to feed on grass shrimp introduced into the aquarium with a dip net. Ten shrimp were presented to each fish daily, and the survivors were removed after a 3-h feeding period. When the fish had become accustomed to this procedure, Farr exposed groups of shrimp to methyl or ethyl parathion for 24 to 72 h and then fed them to the killifish as usual. He measured the time between the consumption of the first shrimp and the capture of the third and counted the survivors after 15 min and again after 3 h, when the remaining shrimp were removed. A single run consisted of one fish, which was fed control shrimp one day and treated shrimp the next; thus, each run included its own control. Farr found that parathion significantly reduced the time needed for the fish to capture the second and third shrimp and increased the number of shrimp consumed in 15 min. There were no effects on the total number of shrimp captured in 3 h (probably because there were few survivors even among controls). Treated shrimp were more active than controls and therefore presumably more conspicuous to the fish. Since parathion also decreased their physical endurance, the shrimp were easier for the fish to catch.

In a subsequent study, Farr (1978) examined prey selection by killifish which were offered grass shrimp and sheepshead minnows (Cyprinodon variegatus) simultaneously. Equal numbers of shrimp and minnows were placed in aquaria, and some were exposed to methyl parathion for 24 h. One killifish was then added to each tank, and prey survival was monitored for 5 days. In tanks without parathion, minnows were consumed more rapidly than shrimp. Parathion caused increased predation on both species, but shrimp were affected more strongly than minnows, and selection by the predator was apparently reversed for a time. This effect was more pronounced at higher parathion concentrations. Farr presented the results in three ways: (a) as percent survival of each species; (b) as the ratio of surviving shrimp to surviving minnows; and (c) as a capture coefficient equal to the ratio of prey species consumed, divided by the ratio of prey species available to the predator. Presentations (b) and (c) both indicated that parathion erased the predator's preference for minnows, but only (a) revealed that the survival of treated minnows averaged 61% of controls. Farr did not mention this latter result and omitted statistical treatment of the data in (a); therefore, the significance of the effect on minnows is unknown. The two-prey system (Farr 1978) may be an improvement over the one-prey experiments (Farr 1977), but inconsistencies in the 1978 paper make an objective evaluation impossible.

Experiments on predation on grass shrimp continued for a time after Farr's departure from the Gulf Breeze ERL, but have now been suspended; further research has been directed towards single-species behavioral bioassays (C. R. Cripe, personal communication).

(2) <u>Predation on crayfish</u>. Factors affecting predation on crayfish (<u>Orconectes propinquus</u>) by smallmouth bass (<u>Micropterus dolomieui</u>) were investigated by Stein and Magnuson (1976) and by Stein (1977). Experiments were conducted in flow-through aquaria with sand, pebble, or gravel substrates. In a typical experiment, equal numbers of four size classes of crayfish were placed in tanks with one bass; surviving crayfish were removed, counted, and returned to the tanks every 2 h (Stein 1977). (In other experiments, survivors were counted daily.) Variations on this experimental design were used to measure predation as a function of the sex, reproductive condition, and molting stage of the crayfish (Stein 1977) and as a function of substrate type (Stein and Magnuson 1976). These experiments lasted from 10 h to 7 days.

The handling time for bass feeding on crayfish was measured in another series of experiments (Stein 1977). An opaque tube was placed vertically in the water, and a crayfish was added. When the crayfish settled to the bottom of the tube, the tube was removed; the bass were trained to eat crayfish presented in this way. The time from capture to swallowing (the handling time) was measured in each encounter. Handling time varied with prey size and molting stage. Using an approach similar to that of Werner and Hall (1974) [Sect. 3.2.3(5)], Stein used the data to predict the prey size that would optimize the predation efficiency of the bass (pursuit plus handling time divided by energy gain).

The presence of a predator was found to influence the behavior of crayfish (Stein and Magnuson 1976). Various activity patterns were quantified for 3 days without fish. Bass were then introduced into some aquaria, and crayfish behavior was monitored for 3 more days. In the presence of the predator, active behavior patterns (such as walking, climbing, grooming, and feeding) were reduced, and the crayfish spent more time hiding in the substrate. Crayfish in tanks with bass also preferred pebble to sand because the former substrate offered greater opportunity for hiding; this preference was not seen when no fish were added. In all cases, behavioral effects were most noticeable among prey groups most susceptible to predation (juveniles and nonreproductive adults).

(3) Evaluation. The evaluation of fish-macroinvertebrate tests as hazard assessment tools is included with the evaluation of fish-fish systems in Sect. 3.2.5(3).

3.2.5 Fish-Fish

Predator-prey interactions among fish have been the subject of numerous laboratory investigations during the past 10 years. Most experiments have been designed to compare the vulnerability of two or more groups of prey. The groups may be different species (Coble 1973; Herting and Witt 1967; Mauck and Coble 1971) or members of the same species differing in size, color, form (Coble 1973; Mauck and Coble 1971), physiological condition (Coble 1970; Herting and Witt 1967; Vaughan 1979), or previous exposure to chemical or physical stress (Baker and Modde 1977; Coutant 1973; Coutant et al. 1974; Deacutis 1978; Goodyear 1972; Kania and O'Hara 1974; Sullivan et al. 1978; Sylvester 1972, 1973; Woltering et al. 1978; Wolters and Coutant 1976; Yocum and Edsall 1974). Examples of recent research and a discussion of methodological details are presented in this section.

(1) Examples of recent research. The focus of many predator-prey studies with fish has been the effects of toxicants or thermal stress on the susceptibility of prey to predation. Kania and O'Hara (1974) exposed groups of mosquito fish (Gambusia affinis) to 0.005 to 0.1 mg/L of mercury and offered each group, along with equal numbers of untreated mosquito fish, to largemouth bass (Micropterus salmoides). After 60 h, all the remaining mosquito fish were collected and counted. It was found that short exposure to low levels of mercury impaired the normal escape behavior of the prey, and predation was heavier on the treated group than on the controls. The effect was a function of mercury concentration and was seen as low as 0.01 mg/L, which is well below the lethal concentration for this fish.

Woltering et al. (1978) studied the effects of ammonia on the interaction between largemouth bass and mosquito fish. The approach differed from that of Kania and O'Hara (1974); predator and prey were both exposed to the toxicant continuously throughout the experiment. Ammonia concentrations above 0.34 mg/L caused physiological and behavioral changes in the predator, resulting in a lowered predation rate. The effect was greatest at high prey densities, where the predator was actively harassed by the prey. Like Kania and O'Hara (1974), Woltering et al. (1978) observed changes in the predator-prey interaction at toxicant concentrations below the lethal level.

The effects of acute and chronic exposure to cadmium on the vulnerability of fathead minnow (Pimephales promelas) to predation by largemouth bass were examined by Sullivan et al. (1978). Subtle behavioral changes in the prey increased their vulnerability at cadmium concentrations less than one-hundredth of the reported maximum allowable toxicant concentration (MATC) for this species. These changes are described in detail by Sullivan and Atchison (1978).

Increased predation on thermally stressed fish was reported in a series of papers by Coutant and co-workers (Coutant 1973; Coutant et al. 1974; Coutant et al. 1979; Wolters and Coutant 1976). In one study (Coutant 1973), juvenile rainbow trout (Salmo gairdneri) and chinook salmon (Oncorhynchus tshawytscha) were exposed to elevated temperatures for varying lengths of time and then placed in a tank with adult rainbow trout. When about 50% of the prey had been consumed, the survivors were removed and counted. The stressed fish exhibited disorientation, erratic swimming, unnatural posture, and reduced escape abilities; consequently, they suffered higher predation than unstressed prey. The effects were related to the exposure temperature and exposure time and were significant at 11% of the median lethal time or 2.5°C below the median lethal temperature. The experiments were intended to simulate the actual experience of juvenile fish near the thermal discharge of the Hanford, Washington, nuclear reactor.

In a subsequent study, Coutant et al. (1974) acclimated juvenile channel catfish (Ictalurus punctatus) and largemouth bass to several above-normal temperatures and then placed them with adult largemouth bass at 16°C. When the acclimation temperature was 7 to 9°C higher than the predation temperature, the prey were "benumbed" and rested on the bottom rather than seeking refuge. The predators recognized and preferentially selected the shocked fish. A much greater thermal shock is necessary to kill these fish. Wolters and Coutant (1976) observed similar effects with cold-shocked bluegill (Lepomis macrochirus). Other studies on thermal effects include those by Deacutis (1978) with killifish (Fundulus majalis) feeding on larvae of Atlantic silverside (Menidia menidia) and flounder (Paralichthys dentatus); by Sylvester (1972, 1973) with coho salmon (Oncorhynchus kisutch) feeding on sockeye salmon fry (O. nerka); and by Yocum and Edsall (1974) with yellow perch (Perca flavescens) feeding on fry of lake whitefish (Coregonus clupeaformis).

Goodyear (1972) demonstrated increased predation by largemouth bass on mosquito fish that had been exposed to gamma radiation. In this experiment, the prey were provided with refuge from the predator, and nonirradiated fish could survive for 20 days with only 5% losses. However, irradiated fish tended to wander out of the refuge, and 60% were consumed in 20 days. Goodyear proposed the method as a simple screening test for toxicants.

Several investigators (Coble 1970; Herting and Witt 1967; Vaughan 1979) have studied the influence of disease, parasitism, and viral infection on the predator-prey interaction. Herting and Witt (1967) presented bowfin (Amia calva) with pairs of prey species including golden shiner (Notegonus chrysoleucas), bluegill, green sunfish (Lepomis cyanellus), and largemouth bass. The preference of bowfin for one prey species over the other could be reversed if one of the prey species was diseased, parasitized, or suffered from handling stress. For example, normal bluegill were less vulnerable than green sunfish when both were offered together to the predator, but bluegill suffering from columaris disease were more vulnerable than green sunfish. A similar reversal was seen when largemouth bass parasitized by trematodes were offered together with healthy golden shiners. The authors concluded that the changes in relative vulnerability were due to sluggish behavior, which drew the attention of the predator (bowfin prefer slow-moving or stationary prey) and reduced agility and stamina of the prey. Vaughan (1979) as well as Coble (1970) observed no increased vulnerability in bluegill infected with lymphocystis virus or in fathead minnows infected with yellow grub (Clinostomum marginatum) respectively. Vaughan (1979) suggested that these negative results were due to the absence of noticeable behavioral changes in the infected prey.

(2) Methodological details. Most experiments on fish predator-prey interactions have been conducted in flow-through aquaria containing 100 to 750 L of water or in pools holding up to 3600 L of water. Deacutis (1978) studied predation by small killifish in 9-L tubs; at the other end of the size range, Mauck and Coble (1971) performed experiments in 0.04-ha ponds. Ginetz and Larkin (1975) constructed experimental troughs in a salmon spawning channel for studies of rainbow trout feeding on sockeye salmon fry. Most workers, however, have used conventional fish tanks.

In many cases, cover or refuge was provided for prey and/or predators. Cover has consisted of artificial vegetation (Coble 1973; Sullivan et al. 1978; Vaughan 1979), tree limbs (Mauck and Coble 1971), or bricks (Coble 1973). In Goodyear's (1972) studies of largemouth bass predation on mosquito fish, a shallow refuge area was provided for the prey, separated from the main portion of the aquarium by a coarse screen. The screen was necessary because some bass would pursue the prey into the shallow area, whereas others would not, creating variability in the experimental results. Shallow refuge areas were used by Kania and O'Hara (1974) and Woltering et al. (1978) in experiments with the same two species. Provision of refuge or cover for the prey increases their chances of survival and creates a more realistic environment for the predator-prey interaction. When no cover is present, the prey are usually consumed within minutes. Wolters and Coutant (1976) did not provide cover and reported difficulty in terminating some of their experiments before 50% of the prey were consumed since this sometimes occurred in less than 1 min. With cover, and especially with a refuge, experiments can be continued for several weeks if desired (Goodyear 1972).

Experiments have been conducted using fish from laboratory stocks as well as fish from the field. In either case, the fish must be preconditioned to the experimental situation. Acclimation to a particular temperature or light intensity can affect the performance of predator and prey (Coutant et al. 1974; Ginetz and Larkin 1976; Sylvester 1972; Wolters and Coutant 1976; Yocum and Edsall 1974). Learned behavior on the part of both animals also plays an important role in predation studies and can be a source of unexpected variability in the results. For instance, Baker and Modde (1977) reported that bluegills were timid in their first two encounters with blacktail shiners (Notropis venustus), but beginning with the third trial, they became more aggressive and actively searched for prey. Most investigators have trained the predators to feed under experimental conditions; Goodyear (1972) and Woltering et al. (1978) conditioned the prey to the predator as well.

In comparisons of predation on different groups of prey, the different groups may be offered to the predator simultaneously or in separate trials. When more than one prey type is present in one aquarium, differential marking is sometimes necessary to distinguish the groups. Many workers (e.g., Coutant 1973; Sullivan et al. 1978) used cold branding to identify treated and control prey. Kania and O'Hara (1974) used a radioisotope (^{197}Hg) to tag mosquito fish exposed to mercury; FitzGerald and Keenleyside (1978) suggested ^{131}I for the same purpose. Some marking techniques may affect the vulnerability of the prey. For example, Baker and Modde (1977) demonstrated that blacktail shiners marked with a particular stain were selected by largemouth bass and bluegill over unmarked shiners. Fin clipping is another marking technique that can affect the predator-prey interaction (Mauck and Coble 1971).

When alternative prey are presented to the predator simultaneously, the ratio of prey abundances can influence selection by the predator (Coutant 1973; Coutant et al. 1979). Results of an experiment may then depend on the proportions of prey added initially and on changes in those proportions during the test. To minimize this factor, experiments are often terminated before half of the prey are consumed (Coutant 1973; Coutant et al. 1974; Mauck and Coble 1971; Vaughan 1979; Wolters and Coutant 1976).

When different groups of prey are presented to the predator in separate trials, the problems of differential marking and prey proportions are avoided, but identical conditions must be carefully maintained from one trial to the next. The size, experience, and physiological condition of the animals are important factors in predation experiments. Predators are usually starved for 24 h or more before each experiment to achieve a uniform degree of hunger. Yocum and Edsall (1974) exposed the same predators to stressed and nonstressed prey alternately, with each group of predators serving as its own control. (A similar approach is often used in studies of fish predation on zooplankton--see Sect. 3.2.3).

In a few instances, predators and prey have been exposed to stress together in the same experimental chamber instead of exposing the prey separately and then adding them to the tank. The studies of Tagatz (1976) and Farr (1978) are discussed in Sect. 3.2.4(1), and those of Woltering et al. (1978) are described above. We found no reports of experiments in which only predators were exposed to a toxicant or other stress.

The outcome of a fish predator-prey experiment is usually determined by counting the surviving prey. When different prey groups are presented to predators in separate trials, analysis of variance is used to test for treatment effects (e.g., Ginetz and Larkin 1976; Sylvester 1973). When different prey groups are presented simultaneously, the results are often expressed as some type of selection index (e.g., Baker and Modde 1977; Coutant 1973; Coutant et al. 1974; Herting and Witt 1967; Mauck and Coble 1971; Wolters and Coutant 1976). Alternatively, a chi-square test may be used to compare the proportions of prey consumed with the proportions initially present (e.g., Coble 1973; Kania and O'Hara 1974). Sullivan et al. (1978) developed a special statistical technique for analyzing predation results.

A few investigators have measured the results of predator-prey experiments in ways other than counting survivors. Yocum and Edsall (1974) and Deacutis (1978) counted the number of attacks, captures, and escapes during experiments. This approach made it possible to differentiate effects on prey attractiveness (as indicated by frequency of attacks) from effects on escape abilities (as indicated by the ratio of captures or escapes to attacks). In both these studies, heat-stressed prey were attacked less frequently, but captured more successfully, than controls. Sylvester (1972) recorded the time of capture of each prey and expressed the results as the mean survival time of the prey. Yocum and Edsall (1974) found this approach unsatisfactory with yellow perch feeding on whitefish fry because individual predators differed greatly in the time taken to discover the prey. Woltering et al. (1978) measured the growth of predators during 10-day experiments; the results reflected the same trends as numbers of prey consumed.

(3) _Evaluation_. The studies of Tagatz (1976) and Farr (1977 1978) on predation by fish on grass shrimp are well-known examples of chemically induced alterations in prey behavior leading to increased susceptibility to predation. The predator's role in these

experimental systems is to detect the behavioral alterations. If a human observer were equally perceptive, the tests could be simplified to single-species behavioral bioassays. The same is true of most of the fish-fish studies discussed in this section. As stated above, the major justification for employing this type of predator-prey system in hazard assessment is its extreme sensitivity to chemical stress.

In most other respects, what has been said in Sect. 3.2.3(6) about fish-zooplankton interactions applies here as well. Fish-shrimp and fish-fish systems are somewhat more complex than fish-zooplankton systems, since a refuge or cover should be provided for the prey to permit ecologically significant behavioral effects to be revealed. Another difference between these experiments and those with zooplankton is that shrimp or fish prey may have equal or greater economic importance than the predator.

<u>There are no serious obstacles to the development and standardization of predator-prey test procedures with shrimp or fish as prey.</u> A predation experiment could be a convenient sequel to a single-species acute bioassay. For example, shrimp could be exposed to a range of chemical concentrations for determination of an acute LC_{50}. The animals from the sublethal treatments could then be presented to a predator to determine whether their survival abilities had been impaired. An integrated testing sequence such as this would provide a more ecologically meaningful indication of the potential hazards of a chemical than conventional bioassays alone, with no serious increase in cost.

3.2.6 Conclusions and Recommendations

All the predator-prey interactions discussed, except for protozoan predation, are of known ecological significance. Many have been shown to be highly sensitive to chemicals and other types of disturbance. Tests for chemical effects on the interaction between any two species are not likely to provide reliable information about interactions between other species pairs or to permit accurate predictions of effects that would occur in the context of a whole community or ecosystem. Therefore, the most suitable position for predator-prey tests in a chemical hazard assessment sequence is immediately after screening tests.

Laboratory systems with zooplankton predators and prey are probably the most efficient for chemical testing. Many zooplankton species are easily cultured, and large reproductive populations can be maintained in static aquaria. Predation tests can be conducted in small, static systems. Experiments can be completed in 8 h or less, and the surviving prey can be preserved to be enumerated later. Because zooplankton are nonvisual predators, lighting is not a critical factor, and experiments can be conducted in darkness. Learning, social interactions, and disturbances caused by observers are much less important in zooplankton-zooplankton systems than in fish systems. The most likely mechanisms for chemical effects on zooplankton predation are: (1) reduced swimming speed of predators or prey, (2) reduced capture success of predators, or (3) reduced escape success of prey. The sensitivity of these mechanisms to chemicals is unknown. Replicability of zooplankton-zooplankton systems is probably good. Species that might be suitable predators in chemical test systems include Mesocyclops edax and Cyclops spp., while Diaptomus spp., Bosmina longirostris, and Ceriodaphnia spp. would be appropriate prey.

Fish-zooplankton predation tests are somewhat more complicated than tests with zooplankton predators. Fish cultures require more space than zooplankton cultures, and continuous flow systems are necessary for most species. Likewise, predation studies involving fish generally require large volumes and/or continuous flow. Lighting conditions and background must be carefully controlled to ensure repeatable results with these visual predators. Effects of learning, social behavior, and unintentional disturbances are more likely to occur with fish than with zooplankton predators. All these factors imply that fish-zooplankton systems would be less amenable to chemical hazard assessment than zooplankton-zooplankton systems. However, experiments with fish might be faster than zooplankton predation tests since fish consume more prey in a given time than do zooplankton.

Possible mechanisms for chemical effects on fish-zooplankton interactions include: (1) impaired vision of the fish; (2) reduced swimming speed of predator or prey; and (3) reduced avoidance ability of prey. The sensitivity of fish-zooplankton systems to chemicals is unknown, but might be enhanced if zooplankton with well-developed escape abilities (such as Diaptomus spp.) were used as the prey. Replicability may be a problem with these systems because so many experimental variables can affect the results.

Because of the social and economic importance of many planktivorous fish, an attempt should be made to develop an efficient fish-zooplankton test system. The problems discussed above indicate that test procedures would have to be specified in considerable detail, but the problems are not insurmountable in developing a protocol. Common bioassay organisms such as rainbow trout, bluegill, and Daphnia could be readily applied to predator-prey experiments.

Predation experiments with fish as predators and macroinvertebrates or fish as prey have the same technical complications as fish-zooplankton experiments, but to a greater degree. Nevertheless, relatively simple fish-fish systems have been successfully used to test for effects of stress. The sensitivity of fish-shrimp and fish-fish systems to chemicals has been demonstrated; indeed, these are the only predator-prey systems for which we have information on chemical effects. The largemouth bass-mosquito fish systems of Goodyear (1972), Kania and O'Hara (1974), and Woltering et al. (1978) have proved quite amenable to effects testing, as have many other systems described in Sects. 3.2.4 and 3.2.5. The background of experience with chemical effects tests in such systems may offset the inherent difficulty of devising suitable test protocols. It is recommended, therefore, that a tentative protocol be developed for fish-fish (or fish-shrimp) experiments and that they be compared with zooplankton-zooplankton and fish-zooplankton systems before a final decision is reached on the best system for hazard assessment. <u>It is also recommended that research be conducted to devise sensitive, objective indicators of subtle behavioral effects, with the ultimate objective of replacing fish-fish and fish-shrimp tests with simple, single-species behavioral assays since alteration of prey behavior is the most likely mechanism of chemical effect on these interactions.</u>

To summarize the recommendations in this section, tests with fish as predators and either fish or shrimp as prey are well-known and could be standardized for chemical hazard assessment in the near future. Tests with zooplankton as predators or prey are potentially easier to use than fish predation tests, but further research must be conducted before zooplankton-zooplankton or fish-zooplankton systems can be adapted to chemical testing. Protozoa-protozoa predation tests are not recommended for development in this context.

3.3 Parasitism

It is widely recognized that the incidence of parasitism or disease in a population is determined partially by the physiological state of the host organism and that various environmental stressing agents can reduce the host's resistance to infection (Snieszko 1974; Wedemeyer 1970). Snieszko (1974) cited several instances of increases in parasitic infections in fish exposed to pesticides. Draggan (1977) reported indirect evidence of effects of chromium on the interaction between carp eggs and a fungal parasite. However, these observations were incidental to studies conducted for other purposes. Effects of drugs on parasitism and disease are, of course, the subject of clinical parasitology, which is outside the scope of this review.

The only example found of an experiment specifically designed to measure chemically induced susceptibility to parasitism was that of Couch and Courtney (1977). These authors examined penaeid shrimp from the Gulf of Mexico and found a high incidence of <u>Baculovirus</u> infection in the population. Infected shrimp were identified by microscopic examination of hepatopancreatic cell nuclei. A group of 925 shrimp was exposed to 0.7 µg/L Aroclor® (a polychlorinated biphenyl) for 35 days, and the incidence of parasitic infection in the population was compared with a control group held under similar conditions. Infected shrimp initially comprised 23.3% of the population. After 35 days, 45.7% of the control group were parasitized, compared with 75% of the shrimp exposed to PCB. Mortality was 13% in controls and 50% in treated shrimp. It was impossible to separate direct PCB toxicity from mortality resulting from increased parasitism without a parallel experiment using noninfected animals. The authors recognized the need for such an experimental design, but found it to be impossible due to an inability to raise shrimp xenobiotically and to detect latent viral infections in apparently healthy shrimp. Possible mechanisms for the observed effects of PCB on this host-parasite system were: (1) loss of resistance of shrimp to new viral infections; (2) enhancement of latent infections; (3) increased virulence of the virus; or (4) increased cannibalism on intoxicated individuals (cannibalism being one mechanism by which the virus is transmitted through the population). PCB was found to accumulate in the site of infection (the hepatopancreas), but not in tail muscle, which was uninfected.

The large numbers of animals involved in this study and the number of histopathological examinations required to determine the effect of one chemical at one concentration in one treatment group lead to questions about the practicality of this system for routine chemical hazard assessment. An earlier attempt to demonstrate the same effect using fewer individuals and shorter exposure times was inconclusive (Couch 1976). Moreover, the effect of PCB on the shrimp-<u>Baculovirus</u> system is probably not generalizable to any other host-parasite interaction. A chemical that failed to produce an effect in the shrimp-<u>Baculovirus</u> test would not necessarily be innocuous in other situations. We conclude that there are no host-parasite systems amenable to development as hazard assessment tests at this time. It is recommended that the parasitological literature be surveyed to evaluate the possiblity of developing a hazard assessment protocol.

3.4 Plant-Herbivore Interactions

The major plant communities in aquatic ecosystems are phytoplankton and macrophytes. Grazing on macrophytes has been studied very little by ecologists, and no relevant laboratory studies were found in our review of the literature. Grazing by zooplankton on phytoplankton is recognized as an important component of ecosystem energy flow and nutrient cycling and as a possible determinant of plankton community structure, but it too has received little attention. One reason for this is that methods for measuring plankton grazing rates, either in situ or in the laboratory, are still poorly developed. The sensitivity of zooplankton grazing to chemical stress is not known and should be investigated.

A phytoplankton-zooplankton hazard assessment test would be essentially a single-species bioassay, with zooplankton grazing rate as the measured response. Inert particles could be (and often are) substituted for algae in this type of test without changing the nature of the experiment significantly. The literature was not searched thoroughly for laboratory phytoplankton-zooplankton systems because our attention was directed towards areas with more promise for chemical hazard assessment.

It should be noted that grazing is one of the important processes in mixed flask culture model ecosystems [Sect. 3.6.3(1)]. It is, however, difficult to separate grazing from other processes occurring simultaneously in these systems.

3.5 Symbiosis

No published reports of chemical effects on symbiotic interactions among aquatic organisms were found. Because symbiosis represents a high degree of specialization on the part of the interacting species, chemical effects on one species pair would probably not be relevant to other pairs. With the possible exception of zooxanthellae in coral polyps, symbiosis is less important in aquatic ecosystems than any of the other interactions reviewed in this report. Symbiosis does not seem to be a logical subject for inclusion in a chemical hazard assessment program.

3.6 Ecosystem Properties

All organisms in nature live in ecosystems. The structural and functional properties of ecosystems determine the context in which organisms, populations, and communities develop, persist, and interact. Therefore, chemical effects on ecosystem properties have the potential to influence all the components of the ecosystem. In some situations, effects on ecosystem properties may be direct consequences of easily observed effects on dominant organisms, and knowledge of the responses of those organisms may be sufficient to infer hazards to ecosystems. In other instances, the mechanisms of ecosystem effects may be obscure. In either case, the ramifications of ecosystem-level effects on all components of an ecosystem can be unpredictable and far-reaching. This is the major justification for the development of methods to assess the hazards of chemicals to ecosystems.

This section reviews the properties of aquatic ecosystems and discusses the central issue of laboratory studies at the ecosystem level--the problem of predicting effects on natural ecosystems from responses measured in simplified laboratory systems. Finally, some general types of laboratory model ecosystems, or microcosms, that might be adaptable for chemical hazard assessment under TSCA are described.

3.6.1 Properties of Aquatic Ecosystems

An ecosystem is essentially an energy processing unit. Incoming solar energy is converted first to chemical energy and finally to heat. Because the energy processing capacity of an ecosystem depends on a steady supply of inorganic nutrients, the ecosystem expends a certain fraction of the energy it processes to ensure that nutrients are retained and recycled. Cycling of essential elements is accomplished through interactions among components of the ecosystem.

These interactions confer a degree of homeostatic control, which permits the maintenance of maximum persistent biomass in the face of environmental fluctuations (Whittaker and Woodwell 1972; Reichle et al. 1975). The existence of ecosystem homeostasis is implied by the persistence of complex natural systems through time. Elucidation of homeostatic mechanisms is a primary objective of ecosystem analysis.

Ecosystem function may be conceived in terms of superimposed flows of energy and matter. Conversion of solar energy in photosynthesis is accompanied by production of organic matter from inorganic elements. Chemical energy is released as heat by respiration, and the elements in organic matter are returned to inorganic form. In a mature ecosystem, the two portions of the matter-energy conversion are approximately in balance, at least over an annual cycle.

Thus, ecosystem metabolism consists of two basic processes, an anabolic or productive process and a catabolic or regenerative process. The productive process is mediated almost entirely by green plants; the rate of this process is termed gross primary productivity (GPP). The regenerative process is a function of both autotrophs and heterotrophs and represents the total energetic cost of operating the ecosystem. The difference between GPP and total ecosystem respiration (R_E) is the net ecosystem productivity (NEP), which represents storage of energy in biomass or detritus (Reichle et al. 1975). The ratio of GPP to R_E, usually referred to as P/R, is one index of ecosystem metabolism that has been measured in several aquatic ecosystems. Odum (1956) proposed the use of P/R for classifying ecosystems as autotrophic (P/R > 1) or heterotrophic (P/R < 1) and noted that either type of system tends to approach P/R = 1 over time. Odum (1969) listed P/R = 1 as an attribute of mature ecosystems, concluding that P/R could be used as an index of relative maturity. P/R ratios approximating 1 have been found in many laboratory microcosms (Beyers 1962, 1963; Copeland 1965; Gorden et al. 1969; Giddings and Eddlemon 1978; Harris et al. 1980) and natural systems (Riley 1956; Odum 1957; Odum and Hoskin 1958; Jordan and Likens 1975).

Microcosm studies consistently demonstrate that P/R departs from 1 when a system is disturbed. Microcosms grown at 23°C had a P/R of 1.09 at that temperature. When the temperature was lowered to 13°C, P/R rose to 1.27; and at 33°C, P/R was 0.81 (Beyers 1962). Microcosms dominated by turtle grass growing at 1500 foot candles (fc) had a P/R approximating 1. When the light was reduced to 230 fc, both P and R declined immediately, and P/R fell below 1. After 90 days, P and R had returned to their initial level; P/R was about 1; and the turtle grass community had been replaced by blue-green algae (Copeland 1965). Increased grazing pressure has the same effect as decreased light intensity: a decrease in both P and R, with P/R falling below 1 (McConnell 1962; Beyers 1963). In pond microcosms, P/R fell from 1.0 to 1.4 at steady state to 0 or below (i.e., negative net production) when arsenic was added and returned to 1.0 after 3 weeks (Giddings and Eddlemon 1978). Various toxic substances added to large experimental pools produced the same result (Whitworth and Lane 1969). Thus, P/R appears to be a reliable indicator of stress-induced changes in ecosystem metabolism.

Nutrient cycling is more difficult to measure than ecosystem metabolism. The easiest and most common approach to monitoring nutrient conditions in aquatic ecosystems is to measure the concentrations of dissolved inorganic nutrients. The extremely low concentrations of dissolved inorganic phosphorus and nitrogen in most lakes and ponds are evidence of the close coupling between rates of supply and rates of uptake by aquatic plants. Because of this coupling, changes in nutrient regimes may not be reflected in ambient nutrient concentrations (Schindler et al. 1971). Nutrient concentrations in sediment interstitial water may be more sensitive indicators of altered nutrient cycling than open-water nutrient concentrations (Harris et al. 1980). In a system with well-defined boundaries, the balance between nutrient inputs and outputs is a measure of the ability of the system to retain nutrients; retention of nutrients is a characteristic of mature, undisturbed ecosystems (Likens et al. 1977; Odum 1969).

Aquatic autotrophs, especially phytoplankton, respond rapidly to changes in nutrient regimes. The physiological state of autotrophs is very dependent on their nutrient status. The nutrient status of autotrophs can be assessed by measuring their response to nutrient enrichment, by determining nutrient concentrations in plant tissues, or by means of various physiological indicators such as alkaline phosphatase activity and enhancement of dark CO_2 fixation by ammonium.

Techniques exist for measurement of specific microbial processes contributing to the cycling of nutrients, including nitrogen fixation, nitrification, denitrification, sulfate reduction, and methanogenesis. Other components of the nutrient cycle, such as uptake by plants and regeneration from detritus, can be measured by isolating these processes from competing processes. However, determination of nutrient flux in whole ecosystems generally requires isotopic tracers such as ^{32}P and ^{15}N.

Very little is known about the sensitivity of nutrient cycling to toxic chemicals in aquatic ecosystems. It is possible that the structural and functional redundancy of most ecosystems would compensate for chemical effects on individual components of the nutrient cycle. Indeed, such stabilizing redundancy is one aspect of the homeostatic character of mature ecosystems. However, if a chemical were to disrupt nutrient cycling significantly, the effects on the ecosystem would be serious and unpredictable.

Techniques for measuring or predicting effects of chemicals on aquatic ecosystem properties are in an early developmental stage.

There is very little information by which to compare the sensitivity of ecosystem properties to chemicals with the sensitivity of conventional bioassay organisms. Neither do we know the degree to which responses of one ecosystem are likely to occur in other ecosystems. Research is needed on the whole gamut of potential ecosystem-level effects in a variety of ecosystems so that general answers to these questions may begin to emerge. Such research must be supported by conceptual advances in ecosystem analysis and by the development of practical techniques for measuring ecosystem properties. Thus, the search for tools for hazard assessment at the ecosystem level is inseparable from basic research into the ecology of whole ecosystems.

3.6.2 Realism and Generality

In discussing the applications of model ecosystems to chemical hazard evaluation, a distinction is often made between "generic" systems, which exhibit properties common to all ecosystems without mimicking any natural ecosystem in particular, and systems that simulate some specific ecosystem in greater or lesser detail. Such a distinction is necessary because two of the criteria for an ecosystem-level test protocol are not wholly compatible--namely, the requirements of realism and generality. Realistic simulation of any single ecosystem is achieved at the expense of generality; yet a test cannot provide information relevant to a range of ecosystem types without sacrificing some ability to represent a particular ecosystem in detail. These conflicting demands are frequently lumped together and termed "extrapolation," which refers to the general problem of using laboratory experiments to make inferences about natural phenomena. Such lumping of concepts is dangerous. The confusion arising from misunderstanding the dual nature of extrapolation has fueled much controversy about the utility and role of model ecosystems in hazard assessment.

Realistic simulation of some ecosystems is inherently more difficult than others. In terrestrial ecosystems, the size of the dominant vegetation may be the critical factor limiting the degree of simulation possible in the laboratory. In contrast, aquatic model ecosystems are constrained mainly by the dimensions of the dominant physical processes (mixing, turbulence, flow). The physical features of ponds, for example, are much easier to incorporate into laboratory systems than those of rivers, streams, or pelagic environments. Years of experience with one type of aquatic microcosm may lead investigators to make sweeping statements about the degree of realism that microcosms can achieve without appreciating that realism is a function of the ecosystem being modeled.

Likewise, some aspects of aquatic ecosystems are more readily reproduced in the laboratory than others. Realistic simulation of higher trophic levels is typically not possible in small laboratory systems. However, decomposer communities can be easily incorporated into model ecosystems. A major goal of research with any type of model ecosystem should be to identify those aspects of the system that most accurately represent the natural prototype.

It is important here to distinguish between structural and functional similarity. Exact duplication of the absolute abundances of all species is not necessary for reasonable simulation of the important processes occurring in an ecosystem. Unless a particular species has some economic, social, or aesthetic importance, its abundance may be of little concern to us. We are more concerned with the continued well-being of the system as a whole than with its structural details. Because of the functional redundancy of most ecosystems, some species can be entirely replaced by others without altering the overall productivity or persistence of the ecosystem. Conversely, research with gnotobiotic microcosms has shown that assemblages of the same species can be quite different in their functional characteristics. This is not to deny the value of good simulation of ecosystem structure in a laboratory system, but rather to emphasize that species abundance is not the only, or the best, measure of the success of simulation.

These thoughts lead quite naturally to a consideration of the other criterion for a hazard assessment tool--namely, generality. If a model ecosystem and a natural ecosystem may be functionally similar in spite of structural differences, then the same comparison might be made between natural ecosystems. That is, we may be able to distinguish certain universal ecosystem properties measurable in all systems and, by studying these properties and their response to toxic chemicals, make inferences that would be meaningful in any ecosystem. This concept is the basis for the abstract model ecosystems originated by Beyers (described by Gorden et al. 1969) and since adapted and modified by many theoretical and applied ecologists. Such model ecosystems, consisting of a few species of bacteria, algae, and invertebrates, have no natural counterparts; in a strict structural sense, they are totally unrealistic, and yet they exhibit features such as succession, metabolic balance, and homeostasis that are characteristic of all terrestrial and aquatic ecosystems. Most people who use these experimental systems consider them to be fully valid ecosystems, to be studied just as one studies lakes, streams, and other naturally occurring ecosystems. Abstract model ecosystems have often been suggested as ecosystem-level "white rats," implying that they might be used to deduce general ecosystem properties in the same way as laboratory rats have been used to investigate the principles of mammalian physiology.

Unfortunately, the universal ecosystem properties of which we are currently aware are of little recognized social or economic relevance in themselves. The causal connections between population-level phenomena and ecosystem properties have yet to be elucidated. Thus, a chemical effect observed in an abstract model ecosystem might indicate a potential for disruption of processes in natural ecosystems, but the nature of those disruptions cannot at present be predicted.

The problem of generalizing from model ecosystem results to different natural ecosystems will remain an obstacle in system-level hazard assessment until more comparative data are available for natural systems. There are a number of substances (e.g., certain trace elements and pesticides, and petroleum products) for which dose-response observations have been made in many natural ecosystems. Such data could be compiled to provide frequency distribution curves of ecosystem sensitivity against which the sensitivity of particular laboratory ecosystem tests could be compared. Construction of such data bases represents an empirical approach to "calibrating" laboratory systems for general predictions of safe exposure levels in nature.

As a chemical progresses through the hazard assessment testing sequence, the need for general indicators of potential effects diminishes, and the need for realism in the testing situation increases. At the initial screening level, information about the relative hazards of chemicals helps determine the need for more extensive testing. A general, or abstract, model ecosystem may be useful at this stage for ranking chemicals in order of potential effects on ecosystem processes. The rankings would be expected to be more consistent among different ecosystems, and hence more generalizable, than would qualitative or quantitative predictions of effects. Thus, any laboratory system exhibiting ecosystem properties could be used to identify those chemicals with the greatest potential for affecting ecosystems. The major criterion for such a laboratory system is its ability to generate rankings that are consistent with the actual hazard potential of the chemicals in nature, rather than its ability to simulate specific ecosystem effects. Test chemicals could be compared with selected standard reference chemicals to identify those with the greatest potential for environmental effects.

Once a chemical has been indicated to be hazardous and the types of ecosystems likely to be exposed are known (through the exposure assessment process), realistic simulation becomes the major objective of ecosystem-level tests. The realism of model ecosystems is sometimes evaluated in terms of how well they "track" their natural prototypes through time. The question might be raised, how well does _any_ ecosystem track another ecosystem? If a model ecosystem were perfected to the extent that it was identical in every measurable aspect to its natural prototype, it would be imperfect with respect to every other natural ecosystem. Since chemical hazard assessments under TSCA will usually be concerned with protecting more than a single ecosystem (although, especially in the later stages of the assessments, concern might be limited to one _type_ of ecosystem), perfect tracking does not seem to be a reasonable criterion for realistic simulation. Rather, the "validity" of a model ecosystem could be assessed by comparing its behavior with the _range_ of natural ecosystems. A laboratory ecosystem designed with realistic simulation as the major objective should be typical, but not necessarily identical to any particular example, of its ecosystem type.

A model ecosystem that satisfies this criterion becomes a reasonable substitute for a field experiment. When a chemical is tested in a realistic microcosm or in the field, the experiment results are scrutinized to determine which observed effects might be expected to occur in other ecosystems and which are situation-specific. Direct toxic effects on components of the test system are probably generalizable in that the same effects would occur in other situations where the same organisms receive the same exposure to the chemical. The difficulty arises in distinguishing direct toxic effects from indirect effects caused by interactions among ecosystem components. An intimate knowledge of the ecology of the test system is necessary if this distinction is to be made. Likewise, prediction of indirect effects in other ecosystems requires an understanding of the structure and function of these ecosystems as well. At present, our ability to predict indirect chemical effects in whole ecosystems is rudimentary (see Sect. 5). Results of a model ecosystem experiment are best viewed as examples of what could occur in a typical ecosystem. The predictive power of model ecosystems will depend on the growth of our basic understanding of ecosystem dynamics.

3.6.3 Potentially Useful Model Ecosystems

The number and diversity of aquatic model ecosystems is staggering. For the purposes of this review, six general categories have been selected for detailed discussion. Large, outdoor systems (e.g., Pilson et al. 1977) have been omitted as have the more complicated laboratory devices (e.g., Cooper and Copeland 1973), because construction of large numbers of replicate systems would be impractical. Other systems (e.g., Metcalf et al. 1971) have been omitted because, in the reviewer's opinion, they do not adequately represent ecosystem processes and are, therefore, unsuitable for testing chemicals for ecosystem-level effects. The six categories reviewed below range from nonrepresentational flask ecosystems to realistic simulations of natural ecosystems. Many of these systems have been used to test chemical effects, but none are so developed that a standardized test procedure has been specified. Few have been extensively compared with natural ecosystems. Therefore, "what has been done" is given less attention than "what can be done." No attempt has been made to document specific details of construction or operation of these systems; the reader is referred to the examples listed in the bibliography and to the general reviews of aquatic microcosm technique that have appeared in recent years (Warren and Davis 1971; Cooke 1977; Giddings 1980b; see also the papers contained in Giesy 1980).

(1) <u>Mixed flask cultures</u>. To many people, the word "microcosm" refers to a flask containing a mixed culture of bacteria, algae, and

microinvertebrates. In terms of sheer numbers of publications, mixed flask cultures are the most commonly used type of aquatic model ecosystem. Beyers was perhaps the first to use these systems for ecological research (Gorden et al. 1969). He inoculated an artificial growth medium with microorganisms from a sewage oxidation pond and maintained the cultures until a stable biotic composition was achieved. These cultures are still in existence, and the original species are still present. The organisms include several species of algae, <u>Paramecium</u>, a flagellate, rotifers, an ostracod, and 11 species of bacteria (Gorden et al. 1969). The strategy of inoculating artificial media with organisms collected from lakes, ponds, streams, aquaria, horse troughs (Ollason 1977), cemetery urns (Leffler 1977), and other sources appears to be consistently successful in producing simple, relatively stable model ecosystems (Bryfogle and McDiffett 1979; Cooper 1973; Kelly 1971; Kurihara 1978a,b; McConnell 1962, 1965; Neill 1972; Reed 1976; Thomas 1978; Waide et al. 1980). Gorden et al. (1969) demonstrated that these simple systems exhibit many of the properties common to all terrestrial and aquatic ecosystems (Odum 1969). They have also been used to study population- and community-level phenomena, and in a few instances, the effects of toxicants have been examined.

Because of their simplicity and small scale (usually less than 1 L), mixed flask cultures are relatively easy to mass produce for experiments with large numbers of replicates. The variablity among replicates can be minimized by cross-inoculating periodically during the first few weeks of growth. This ensures that random extinctions do not affect the composition of the community that eventually develops. Gorden (1967) noted the importance of including at least a few individuals of the larger species (particularly ostracods) in the inoculum of each culture since the presence or absence of these organisms has a disproportionate effect on the rest of the community. With these precautions, the coefficients of variation (CVs) of most measurements of ecosystem structure and function can be held below 50% (Kelly 1971; Leffler 1977). Even these values may be misleadingly high since oscillations occurring in some parameters may be identical, but out of phase among replicates, which results in high CVs at any single point in time. Waide et al. (1980) and Taub (personal communication) have attempted to overcome this problem by plotting microcosm behavior in a two-dimensional phase space with, for example, pH and dissolved oxygen levels as the two axes; identical, but out-of-phase, replicates will have identical trajectories in such a phase space.

Reproducing the same ecological characteristics from one experiment to the next is more difficult than producing good replicates within one experiment. Of course, natural sources of inocula will change between experiments. An alternative is the gnotobiotic approach (Taub 1969a,b,c; Nixon 1969), which establishes experimental communities by adding known numbers of organisms from stock monocultures. This method has the added advantage that initial population sizes may be manipulated by the experimenter. A major disadvantage is that pure stock cultures of all members of the community must be maintained; therefore, the cost in time and money of conducting an experiment is substantially increased. Another drawback of the gnotobiotic approach is that the organisms brought together in these artificial communities may not be representative of natural, co-adapted species assemblages. For this reason, gnotobiotic communities are probably not reliable for studies of ecosystem-level properties; most of Taub's research (1969a,b,c; Taub 1976; Taub and Crow 1980; Taub et al. 1980) focuses instead on population interactions.

Leffler's approach to the problem of achieving consistent results from one experiment to the next is to examine properties of mixed flask cultures that are insensitive to changes in community composition (Leffler, personal communication). Leffler is currently evaluating mixed flask cultures as screening tools for chemical hazard assessment. His strategy is to measure the effects of chemicals on a few easily measured integrative properties of the model ecosystems and to rank chemicals in order of the concentrations required to produce an observable effect. Leffler hypothesizes that these rankings will be consistent among mixed cultures with differing species composition even if the absolute values of the measured parameters are not consistent. As discussed in Sect. 3.6.2, the rankings, not the observed effects, constitute the output of this experimental design. The model ecosystems are used to identify chemicals capable of disrupting ecosystem processes, but do not specify which processes are disrupted or how these effects might be manifested in natural systems. Since many single-species bioassays have the same objective (ranking of chemicals by potential hazard), model ecosystems would be valuable primarily if they were more sensitive than conventional bioassay organisms or if they generated different rankings than those of conventional tests. If ecosystem-level screening tests merely echoed the results of simpler, more easily standardized bioassays, their use for screening chemicals would be questionable.

(2) _Periphyton communities_. Periphyton (also known as aufwuchs) is the community of organisms attached to or associated with benthic substrates or the submerged surfaces of macrophytes. The periphyton community includes bacteria, algae, and many kinds of invertebrates (Odum 1971). Periphyton are found in nearly all aquatic habitats. In stream ecosystems, periphyton are usually the major primary producers. They are invariably present in laboratory streams and can be a nuisance in pelagic model ecosystems (Harte et al. 1978). Although the periphyton community is only one part of an aquatic ecosystem, its functions include all the major ecosystem processes such as primary production, respiration, decomposition, and nutrient uptake, transformation, and regeneration (Rodgers et al. 1980). Periphyton communities have been used as indicators of ecosystem stress (Patrick 1973; Rodgers et al. 1980).

Periphyton communities are easily produced in laboratory systems. Typically, water from a natural stream, lake, or marine coastal ecosystem is circulated over glass slides, porcelain plates, or other artificial substrates, and organisms in the water colonize the substrates within a few days. Alternatively, an artificial medium may be used, with periphyton-covered rocks as an inoculum.

The ecology of laboratory periphyton communities has been thoroughly studied by McIntire (McIntire et al. 1964; Phinney and McIntire 1965; McIntire 1968a,b; McIntire 1973). In these systems, the species composition of the community became uniform over the substrate (gravel) within 1 month, and biomass was fairly constant after 2 to 3 months. McIntire noted that the plant communities "remained surprisingly constant" for at least 2 years, varying only in the relative abundance of species. He stated that "a well-developed periphyton community as a unit has a characteristic growth form and responds metabolically to external environmental factors [light, temperature, CO_2, dissolved oxygen, current] in a predictable way" (McIntire 1968a).

Laboratory systems for periphyton studies are usually designed in such a way that samples of the substrate can be removed for measurements of biomass, pigments, metabolism, or species abundance without disturbing the rest of the system (Bott et al. 1977; Gerhart et al. 1977; Kehde and Wilhm 1972; Kevern and Ball 1965; McIntire et al. 1964; Rodgers et al. 1980; Wulff 1971). Phinney and McIntire (1965) placed trays of substrate from the laboratory stream into chambers for measurement of photosynthesis and respiration at different temperatures and light intensities. Effects of toxicants could be studied in the same way. Replicate samples from a laboratory stream could be placed in chambers with test solutions, and effects on metabolism (Phinney and McIntire 1965; Rodgers et al. 1980) or rates of degradation of organic matter (Bott et al. 1977) could be measured over short periods of time. One stream system could provide enough replicate samples of the community for many toxicity tests, and if the community remains stable as McIntire et al. (1964) indicate that it should, experiments performed at different times would be comparable. Few other experimental systems offer the combination of stability, replicability, biotic complexity, and ease of handling found in laboratory periphyton communities.

Chronic effects of chemicals on laboratory periphyton communities have been studied by Gerhart et al. (1977) and by Rodgers et al. (1980). Whereas a single laboratory stream can supply material for many short-term tests, long-term experiments require that each stream be used for only one treatment regime. Obviously, the number of tests that can be performed by a single laboratory is severely limited. However, the stability of laboratory periphyton communities makes them ideal for chronic effects studies, providing a smooth baseline against which treatment effects can be measured. Rodgers et al. (1980) compared the variability and sensitivity of several structural and functional parameters, including dry weight, ATP, chlorophyll-a, CO_2 assimilation in the light and dark, and SO_4 assimilation in the light and dark. They found that functional measurements were much more consistent than structural measurements, and consequently, significant treatment effects were more readily detected with the functional parameters. Gerhart et al. (1977) also detected no effects on biomass or chlorophyll in their experiments, but they did observe minor (not statistically significant) changes in species abundance in communities exposed to coal leachate. They reported "excellent replicability of diatom communities" among their three control systems. No functional parameters were measured.

Results of laboratory periphyton studies, in the opinion of Kevern and Ball (1965), are consistent with ecological theory and with observations on natural systems. If light, temperature, and water flow are realistically reproduced, these laboratory systems are probably representative of natural periphyton communities. The major artificiality in laboratory systems may be the absence (in most studies) of grazers. Studies of grazer effects (Admiraal 1977; Kehde and Wilhm 1972; McIntire 1968a) have produced conflicting results, and further research in this area is warranted.

(3) <u>Sediment cores</u>. The sediment is the site of many important processes in aquatic ecosystems including decomposition of organic matter, nutrient regeneration, and degradation of contaminants. Exchanges between the sediment and the overlying water play a major role in nutrient cycles and in controlling chemical conditions in lakes and marine environments (Golterman 1976; Hutchinson 1975; Mortimer 1941, 1942; Pomeroy et al. 1965). Because processes occurring in the sediment and at the sediment-water interface are difficult to measure in situ, the technique of extracting sediment cores with overlying water for study in the laboratory has been widely used by ecologists. If cores are maintained at ambient temperatures, with aeration and mixing of the water to simulate natural conditions, ecological processes and effects of chemicals can be examined over extended periods of time. The methodological approach is essentially identical for studies in hypolimnetic, littoral, or coastal marine environments.

Sediment cores, unlike terrestrial soil cores (Sect. 4.2), have not been used extensively in research on chemical contaminants. The following discussion is based on work performed at EPA's Gulf Breeze Environmental Research Laboratory (Pritchard et al. 1979) and at the Utah Water Research Laboratory at Utah State University (Porcella et al. 1976). Much of the information presented here comes from personal communications with H. P. Pritchard (Gulf Breeze ERL) and Allen Medine (formerly of Utah State University, presently at the University of Connecticut). An outline for a chemical testing protocol using sediment cores was formulated by these two scientists at the Workshop on Methods for Measuring Effects of Chemicals on Aquatic Ecosystem Properties held in conjunction with this project (Giddings 1981).

The Gulf Breeze cores are extracted intact from an estuarine salt marsh. They are used primarily in short-term (up to 21 days) studies of microbial degradation of organic contaminants. Because of the relatively short duration of the experiments, semicontinuous replacement of the overlying water is not necessary. Like Medine's microcosms, the Gulf Breeze cores are sealed, and various chemical measurements can be made on the air leaving the systems. Although these microcosms are designed for degradation experiments, Pritchard believes that they could be used to study the effects of chemicals on microbial communities and possibly (if larger cores were used) on benthic invertebrates.

Medine and Porcella's systems consist of homogenized lake sediment, artificial medium, and a gas phase. The sediment is homogenized to promote uniformity among replicate systems. An artificial medium is used to facilitate mass balance calculations; 10% of the water volume is replaced each day. The systems are completely sealed so that gas production and consumption in the microcosms can be measured. Cores are illuminated to simulate shallow littoral habitats or darkened to simulate hypolimnetic regions. These cores can be used to measure the effects of chemicals on major biogeochemical cycles (C, N, S) including denitrification and N-fixation, microbial respiration, organic matter decomposition, primary production (in illuminated systems), and species diversity. Both Medine and Pritchard report good agreement among replicate cores.

A number of experimental factors have been found to influence the behavior of sediment cores. Medine emphasizes the importance of sediment and water characteristics on measured variables, especially nutrient exchange across the sediment-water interface. Pritchard notes that the microbial activity in his systems is affected by the dimensions of the core, the water:sediment ratio, and the sediment surface area. The Gulf Breeze researchers have also investigated the effects of homogenizing the sediment and observed that cores with homogenized sediments degrade some organic chemicals faster than intact cores, at least over 8 to 15 days. Medine's experiments run for several months, and it is conceivable that the stimulation of microbial activity caused by mixing the sediment disappears once the initial flush of nutrients is exhausted.

The sediment core technique could be applied at almost any level of a hazard assessment scheme. Simple static systems like the Gulf Breeze cores are amenable to short-term tests of chemical effects, whereas Medine's complex semicontinuous flow cores are suitable for long-term studies. The Gulf Breeze researchers have also experimented with continuous-flow, sediment-water systems for long-term degradation experiments. Intact cores with natural water should provide realistic sitespecific simulation for short experiments. Realistic simulation is probably not possible over long periods (Pritchard), but even homogenized cores with artificial medium can reproduce the general features of natural sediments (Medine). <u>Sediment cores definitely merit further development as hazard assessment tools</u>.

(4) <u>Pelagic microcosms</u>. The pelagic zones of lakes and coastal ecosystems present serious problems for microcosm simulation. The structure and function of pelagic ecosystems are strongly influenced by water movements, which carry planktonic organisms up and down in the water column (thereby exposing them to a range of nutrient and light regimes) and resupply the surface water with nutrients from the bottom water and the littoral zone (Nixon et al. 1980). Currents also transport plankton communities horizontally, bringing them into contact with other patches containing different organisms and different nutrient conditions (Margalef 1968). Enclosure of a pelagic system alters the vertical distribution of organisms and dissolved substances, cuts off nutrient inputs, and creates homogeneity in the place of patchiness. Primary production per unit volume of a phytoplankton community is usually low in pelagic microcosms; thus, fish are difficult to maintain without seriously altering community structure (Jassby et al. 1977b). Pelagic ecosystems are inherently variable and unpredictable, and pelagic microcosms are no less so (Giddings 1980).

Many aquatic ecosystems can be satisfactorily reproduced in the laboratory if natural physical conditions are simulated (Giddings 1980). Perez et al. (1977) attempted to duplicate the physical conditions of lower Narragensett Bay in 150-L pelagic microcosms. The microcosms were stirred with paddles to create turbulence equal to that of the bay, as measured by dissolution rates of hard sugar or gypsum. Microcosm water was replaced with bay water semicontinuously at a turnover rate approximately equal to that of the bay. The natural temperature regime was maintained by pumping bay water through a water bath around the microcosms. The natural photoperiod was reproduced. Experiments with light intensity are discussed later. A small benthic component was included in each microcosm, consisting of an intact sediment core in an opaque box through which microcosm water was circulated at a rate approximating that estimated for the bay. The ratio of sediment surface area to water volume was equal to the overall surface/volmume ratio of the bay. In short, an effort was made to establish conditions in the laboratory as close as possible to estimates or measurements from the natural ecosystem.

In their first experiment, Perez et al. (1977) found that, when the average light intensity in the microcosm water column was equal to the estimated average light intensity in the bay water column, an algal bloom occurred. Reasons for this bloom are still unknown (Perez, personal communication). Because grazers were more abundant in the microcosms than in the bay, the bloom probably did not result from reduced grazing. Release from nutrient limitation is a possibility; nitrogen concentrations in the bay water were quite high, but phosphorus (which was not measured) may have limited algal growth in the bay. Whatever the cause, Perez found that the bloom could be prevented by reducing the light intensity to 15% of that in the bay water column. Although imposing light limitation succeeded in holding algal growth in check, the fact that light levels were many times higher in the bay implies that the natural algal community was not light-limited. Consequently, subsequent experiments on the effects of turbulence, water turnover time, and sediment surface area are difficult to interpret. This research demonstrated the difficulty of simulating pelagic conditions in laboratory microcosms.

Because exchange rates of nutrients, organisms, and suspended material between the pelagic and benthic components were a major uncertainty in the original design, Perez is now developing a modification of the benthic-pelagic coupling in these microcosms. The modified systems will include a sediment core and a 1-m water column set up alongside the pelagic tank; turbulence near the sediment surface and exchanges with the pelagic portion will be under direct experimental control (Perez, personal communication). For chemical testing, Perez has constructed pelagic microcosms entirely of glass. The fate, transport, and effects of radio-labelled 2-ethyl-hexylphthalate were studied in a series of experiments lasting 30 to 90 days each. Perez reports good replicability in these experiments for measurements related to the fate and transport of the chemical, with more variability in measurements of phytoplankton, zooplankton, and bacteria (Perez, personal communication). He concludes that pelagic microcosms are useful for intensive studies of chemicals of particular interest, but are impractical for screening.

Researchers at Lawrence Berkeley Laboratory (LBL) have experimented with freshwater pelagic microcosms for several years (Dudzik et al. 1979; Jassby et al. 1977a,b; Harte et al. 1978, 1980). These microcosms are 50- or 700-L tanks containing natural water or artificial medium and a naturally derived lake plankton community. Turbulence is created by gentle aeration. There is no water replacement and no benthic component (the latter will be included in future experiments; J. Harte, personal communication).

A serious problem encountered in the early work with these microcosms was the growth of periphyton on the walls of the tanks. After several months of operation, the chemistry and biology of the systems were dominated by the periphyton, making realistic simulation of pelagic conditions impossible. Attempts at mechanical and biological control of side growth were ineffectual. The researchers concluded that the microcosms were most useful in the early stages of community development (before periphyton growth became significant), which were likened to the seasonal blooms observed in most temperate lakes (Dudzik et al. 1979; Harte et al. 1980; Jassby et al. 1977a,b). Eventually, a strategy of periodic transfer of the cultures to clean vessels proved successful in avoiding the periphyton problem (Harte et al. 1980). Perez (personal communication) eliminates wall growth in his pelagic marine microcosms by scraping the walls daily.

The LBL microcosms were used to test a technique for predicting the sensitivity of lakes to stress. The sensitivity prediction was based on the response of a sample of the pelagic community to organic enrichment. Microcosms with different initial nutrient levels were constructed and monitored for 2 months. The sensitivity of the microcosms was assessed by using the organic enrichment method, and the systems were then treated with ammonium, iron, or phenol and monitored for another 2 months. The predicted sensitivity of each type of system was compared with the actual response of the system to perturbation. The features measured in the microcosms included phytoplankton and zooplankton populations, nutrient concentrations, and (in some experiments) diurnal pH changes for estimation of primary productivity. The authors concluded that taxonomic enumeration was best able to characterize the response of pelagic microcosms to stress (Harte et al. 1978, 1980). Nutrient concentrations were insensitive to the chemical perturbations, possibly because of the disproportionate influence of periphyton on the water chemistry. Productivity estimates were sometimes difficult because the small pH changes could be detected only by measurements too precise for most instruments (Harte et al. 1978).

Microcosm research at LBL is progressing in three areas. First, tracking studies have been undertaken to compare pelagic microcosms with the natural lake ecosystems from which they were derived. It has been found that the phytoplankton community dynamics of the microcosms can be made to approximate those of the lake for up to 2 months if (1) the natural temperature regime is reproduced and (2) microcosm wall growth is controlled. A second area of research is the extension of Perez's benthic-pelagic coupling to freshwater systems. Finally, experiments on chemical effects are continuing, with the emphasis on interactions between chemicals and organic enrichment, and on the resulting alterations in decomposition rates and nutrient cycling (Harte, personal communication).

Considerable work remains before the applicability of pelagic microcosms to chemical hazard assessment can be determined. If detailed plankton counts are necessary for evaluating the response to chemicals, then these systems are not practical for testing large numbers of chemicals. The labor required for species enumeration is excessive, and special training in plankton identification is required. The replicability of plankton counts is generally poor (Harte et al. 1978). Reproducing species dynamics from one experiment to the next may be difficult. In addition, the true significance of population changes is not apparent, since major shifts in plankton communities can occur without altering community functions (Harte et al. 1980; O'Neill and Giddings 1979).

Attention must be given to measurements of <u>ecosystem properties</u> in pelagic microcosms. Production and respiration should be fairly easy to monitor in these systems by measuring diurnal fluctuations in dissolved oxygen. Various approaches to detecting chemical effects on nutrient cycling were described in Section 3.6.1. Further development of pelagic microcosms for chemical assessment is proceeding along these lines at LBL. Comparisons between pelagic microcosms and natural pelagic ecosystems should address these ecosystem-level properties instead of, or in addition to, the taxonomic structure of the plankton community. Strategies for improving the ability of microcosms to simulate natural pelagic ecosystems must be devised. <u>In their current state of development, pelagic microcosms are useful tools for basic research and some special applications, but they are not yet ready for standardization as TSCA hazard assessment protocols.</u>

(5) <u>Pond microcosms</u>. The development and characterization of pond microcosms has been the objective of a research program initiated at Oak Ridge National Laboratory (ORNL) in 1975. Very similar model ecosystems have been under study at EPA's Athens Environmental Research Laboratory (Brockway et al. 1979) and have been included in the chemical environmental assessment program of the Monsanto Company (Eggert et al. 1979; Gledhill and Saeger 1979). The evaluation presented in this section is based primarily on the results of the ORNL study (Harris et al. 1980).

Of all natural aquatic ecosystems, shallow ponds are the least distorted by encapsulation under laboratory conditions. Mature pond microcosms are ecologically quite similar to temperate ponds in midsummer. The dominant pond plants and animals (except fish, in most cases) thrive in pond microcosms. Microcosm periphyton and sediment communities contain the same taxonomic groups in roughly the same proportions as natural ponds. Water chemistry in microcosms is often similar to the parent ecosystem even after months in the laboratory. Most importantly, effects of chemical perturbations in ponds appear to be reproduced accurately in pond microcosms. One reason for this realism is that the physical conditions characteristic of ponds (shallow depth, lack of turbulence) are easily reproduced in aquaria. Another is that virtually all of the important ecological components and processes of whole pond ecosystems can be included in microcosms. This is not true for other aquatic ecosystem types, which must be broken down into subsystems (such as periphyton, sediment, or plankton) for study. Consequently, results of pond microcosm studies can be applied to natural systems with fewer assumptions and extrapolations than results derived from other experimental systems.

The pond microcosms developed at ORNL, Athens, and Monsanto are all derived by placing natural sediment, water, and samples of natural pond communities into aquaria and allowing the systems to evolve. The communities undergo a succession exhibiting many universal features of ecosystem development (Odum 1969) and culminating in a well-regulated system in which chemical and biological meaurements fluctuate within narrow limits. Although the exact course of succession may differ among replicate microcosms and between experiments, the mature communities are usually very similar. Coefficients of variation among mature replicates are below 20% for most measurements, particularly production, respiration, and the P/R ratio (Brockway et al. 1979; Giddings and Eddlemon 1979; and references cited therein). Pond microcosms can remain in this stable, reproducible condition for many months and are thus ideal for studies of chronic effects of chemicals on whole ecosystems.

Pond microcosms are extremely simple to construct and operate. The fact that three laboratories have independently established similar experimental protocols for microcosm experiments is evidence of this. The microcosms designed by these laboratories are ecologically very similar despite different source materials. Thus, we conclude that the technique could be used successfully in any laboratory, with the quality of results dependent mainly on accurate measurements and analyses rather than on system design.

The research groups at Athens and Monsanto have used pond microcosms primarily for studies of chemical transport and degradation. The ORNL program originally had similar objectives, but it was realized that the microcosms could also be used to measure ecosystem-level effects. Experiments have been conducted on the effects of arsenic (Giddings and Eddlemon 1978, 1979; Harris et al. 1980) and a coal-derived oil (Giddings 1979). A second, more comprehensive experiment with a synthetic oil began in August 1980 and will be followed by an experiment with the same material in outdoor ponds; this combination of studies should permit a thorough evaluation of the utility of pond microcosms for predicting effects in larger systems. <u>Based on results obtained so far, our tentative conclusion is that effects can be realistically simulated in the laboratory systems. The principal question that remains is not, "Do pond microcosms accurately represent ponds?", but rather, "To what extent are ponds representative of other aquatic ecosystems of interest?"</u>

Pond microcosms would not be convenient for screening large numbers of chemicals--experiments require too much time (about 2 months to reach maturity) and space. They could be extremely useful at intermediate and upper levels of a hazard assessment program. The hazard evaluation process at Monsanto incorporates pond microcosms for predictive and confirmative studies after initial screening with simpler systems (Gledhill and Saeger 1979).

(6) <u>Model streams</u>. To a much greater degree than other ecosystems discussed above, streams are open systems in which processes occurring at a given point influence conditions downstream. Energy and nutrient fluxes in streams may be more "spiral" than cyclic (Webster 1978). Therefore, the ecosystem really includes the entire length of the stream from headwater to mouth. For this reason streams are, in the opinion of Warren and Davis (1971), "among the most difficult freshwater systems to model." Critical parameters in the design of model streams include inflowing water quality (especially nutrient levels and organic content), bottom type, depth, current velocity, temperature, and light (Warren and Davis 1971).

Participants in the Workshop on Methods for Measuring Effects of Chemicals on Aquatic Ecosystem Properties (Giddings 1981) recognized three major classes of model streams: closed (completely recirculating) systems, partially recirculating systems, and open (once-through flow) systems. These system types generally fall along a gradient from small, completely recirculating laboratory devices to large-scale outdoor streams. The smaller, recirculating model streams are easier to construct and operate, are less expensive, and require less laboratory space than the larger systems. The methodology of smaller systems is also more easily transferred to other laboratories than larger systems. In the opinion of the workshop participants (Giddings 1981), statistical analysis of results is easiest with small model streams. The inherent variability of larger models means that more samples are needed to achieve a given level of confidence in the measurements and that temporal trends are more difficult to detect. Finally, responses to chemicals are more easily interpreted in small systems, where cause and effect are more easily distinguished than in complex systems. Because of these factors, simple laboratory recirculating streams come closest to satisfying the operational criteria for a TSCA hazard assessment tool.

However, the same systems that are most amenable for routine chemical hazard assessment may be the least generalizable to natural ecosystems. Small recirculating model streams lack the openness that is the distinctive feature of stream ecosystems; only larger, open systems are enough like natural streams to permit reliable predictions. Even with larger model streams, doubts about ecological realism were expressed by participants in the workshop (Giddings 1981). Because of the difficulty of reproducing the structure and function of stream ecosystems, model streams may be most useful for studies at the organism or population level. Warren and Davis (1971) mention many potential research applications, including studies of animal behavior, habitat selection, food selection, territoriality, predation, and competition. Studies of community structure, ecosystem metabolism, diversity, and stability are not recommended since factors controlling these properties may or may not be included in the model system (Giddings 1980).

Our conclusion is that model streams, while potentially useful in many areas of applied and basic ecological research, are not promising for chemical hazard assessment under TSCA. At best, they might be employed in advanced stages of testing when transport and fate have been fully characterized and probable ecological effects have been carefully defined. In such cases, the model ecosystems must be specifically designed to incorporate the processes and components relevant to the questions being asked.

3.6.4 Conclusions and Recommendations

The relevant characteristics of the model ecosystem types discussed above are summarized in Table 3.1. The second column

TABLE 3.1. CHARACTERISTICS OF MODEL ECOSYSTEMS

System type	Ability to replicate	Realism	Generality	Potential application
Mixed flask culture	High	Low	High?	Screening
Periphyton community	Med-high	Med-high	Medium?	Intermediate or advanced testing
Sediment core	Med-high	Medium	Medium?	Intermediate or advanced testing
Model ponds	Medium	High	Medium?	Intermediate or advanced testing
Pelagic microcosms	Low-med	Low-med	Medium?	Research
Model streams	Low	Low-med	Medium?	Research

heading in this table, "Ability to Replicate," refers to all aspects of constructing and using many replicate test units. Variability among replicates (largely a function of the response being measured) is one factor included here. "Realism" implies the ability of the model ecosystem to simulate a particular natural ecosystem, and "generality" was discussed in Sect. 3.6.2. Without a great deal more comparative data on aquatic ecosystem functions and responses to chemicals, generality is difficult to evaluate for any model ecosystem; the entries under this heading are highly subjective and likely to change as our knowledge improves.

The only model ecosystem potentially efficient enough for routinely testing large numbers of chemicals is the naturally derived mixed flask culture. If these systems are found to be more sensitive to chemicals than conventional assays, the ecosystem tests could replace certain less sensitive and less efficient single-species tests such as the algal growth test. If the model ecosystem tests rank chemicals differently from conventional tests (that is, if ecosystem-level hazards are not predictable from single-species bioassays), mixed flask cultures could be used in conjunction with the existing battery of tests. Either of these possibilities is contingent on the outcome of the ecosystem tests being relatively independent of the system's species composition since any particular taxonomic structure may be difficult to repeat exactly in successive experiments.

Sediment cores, periphyton communities, and model ponds are all potentially useful in intermediate or advanced stages of hazard assessment. Model ponds require more time and space than the other two systems and are, therefore, somewhat less efficient for routine testing. Sediment and periphyton systems also have the advantage that they can be applied to almost any aquatic ecosystem. Model ponds, on the other hand, are whole ecosystems, whereas the sediment and periphyton systems represent only parts of whole ecosystems. Model ponds are the most realistic type of model ecosystem. All three of these laboratory systems merit further development. Strategies need to be developed for making these systems as widely representative as possible.

Pelagic microcosms and model streams are still too unwieldy and unpredictable for use as TSCA testing tools. They are neither as efficient nor as realistic as model ponds, but they have been quite useful for basic ecological research and could be of value for special applications in chemical testing.

3.7 REFERENCES

Admiraal, W. 1977. Experiments with mixed populations of benthic estuarine diatoms in laboratory microecosystems. Bot. Mar. 20:479-485.

Akre, B. G., and D. M. Johnson. 1979. Switching and sigmoid functional response curves by damselfly naiads with alternative prey available. J. Anim. Ecol. 48:703-720.

Allan, D. 1973. Competition and the relative abundance of two cladocerans. Ecology 54:484-498.

Anderson, R. S. 1970. Predator-prey relationships and predation rates for crustacean zooplankters from some lakes in western Canada. Can. J. Zool. 48:1229-1240.

Baker, J. A., and T. Modde. 1977. Susceptibility to predation of blacktail shiners stained with bismarck brown Y. Trans. Am. Fish. Soc. 106:334-338.

*Bethel, W. M., and J. C. Holmes. 1977. Increased vulnerability of amphipods to predation owing to altered behavior induced by larval acanthocephalans. Can. J. Zool. 55:110-115.

Beyers, R. J. 1962. Relationship between temperature and the metabolism of experimental ecosystems. Science 136:980-982.

Beyers, R. J. 1963. The metabolism of twelve aquatic laboratory microecosystems. Ecol. Monogr. 33:281-306.

Bott, T. L., J. Preslan, J. Finlay, and R. Brunker. 1977. The use of flowing-water microcosms and ecosystem streams to study microbial degradation of leaf litter and nitrilotriacetic acid (NTA). IN Developments in Industrial Microbiology, Washington, D. C. 18:171-184.

Brandl, Z., and C. H. Fernando. 1974. Feeding of the copepod Acanthocyclops vernalis on the cladoceran Ceriodaphnia reticulata under laboratory conditions. Can. J. Zool. 52:99-105.

Brandl, Z., and C. H. Fernando. 1978. Prey selection by the cyclopoid copepods Mesocyclops edax and Cyclops vicinus. Verh. Int. Ver. Limnol. 20:2505-2510.

---

*Cited only in Appendix A.

Brockway, D. L., J. Hill, IV, J. R. Maudsley, and R. R. Lassiter. 1979. Development, replicability and modeling of naturally derived microcosms. Int. J. Environ. Stud. 13:149-158.

Brooks, J. L., and S. I. Dodson. 1965. Predation, body size, and composition of plankton. Science 150:28-35.

Bryfogle, B. M., and W. F. McDiffett. 1979. Algal succession in laboratory microcosms as affected by an herbicide stress. Am. Midl. Nat. 101:344-354.

Cairns, Jr., J. 1980. Estimating hazard. BioScience 30:101-107.

Coble, D. W. 1970. Vulnerability of fathead minnows infected with yellow grub to largemouth bass predation. J. Parasitol. 56:395-396.

Coble, D. W. 1973. Influence of appearance of prey and satiation of predator on food selection by northern pike (Esox lucius). J. Fish. Res. Board Can. 30:317-320.

Confer, J. L. 1971. Intrazooplankton predation by Mesocyclops edax at natural prey densities. Limnol. Oceanogr. 16:663-666.

Confer, J. L., and P. I. Blades. 1975a. Omnivorous zooplankton and planktivorous fish. Limnol. Oceanogr. 20:571-579.

Confer, J. L., and P. I. Blades. 1975b. Reaction distance to zooplankton by Lepomis gibbosus. Verh. Int. Ver. Limnol. 19:2493-2497.

Confer, J. L., and J. M. Cooley. 1977. Copepod instar survival and predation by zooplankton. J. Fish. Res. Board Can. 34:703-706.

Confer, J. L., G. L. Howick, M. H. Corzette, S. L. Kramer, S. Fitzgibbon, and R. Landesberg. 1978. Visual predation by planktivores. Oikos 31:27-37.

*Cooke, A. S. 1971. Selective predation by newts on frog tadpoles treated with DDT. Nature 229:275-276.

Cooke, G. D. 1977. Experimental aquatic laboratory ecosystems and communities. pp. 59-103. IN Cairns, Jr., J. (ed.), Aquatic Microbial Communities. New York, Garland Publishing.

---

*Cited only in Appendix A.

Cooper, D. C. 1973. Enhancement of net primary productivity by herbivore grazing in aquatic laboratory microcosms. Limnol. Oceanogr. 18:31-37.

Cooper, D. C., and B. J. Copeland. 1973. Responses of continuous-series estuarine microecosystems to point-source input variations. Ecol. Monogr. 43:213-236.

Copeland, B. J. 1965. Evidence for regulation of community metabolism in a marine ecosystem. Ecology 46:563-564.

Couch, J. A. 1976. Attempts to increase Baculovirus prevalence in shrimp by chemical exposure. Prog. Exp. Tumor Res. 20:304-314.

Couch, J. A., and L. Courtney. 1977. Interaction of chemical pollutants and virus in a crustacean: A novel bioassay system. Ann. N.Y. Acad. Sci. 298:497-504.

Coutant, C. C. 1973. Effect of thermal shock on vulnerability of juvenile salmonids to predation. J. Fish. Res. Board Can. 30:965-973.

Coutant, C. C., H. M. Ducharme, Jr., and J. R. Fisher. 1974. Effects of cold shock on vulnerability of juvenile channel catfish (Ictalurus punctatus) and largemouth bass (Micropterus salmoides) to predation. J. Fish. Res. Board Can. 31:351-354.

Coutant, C. C., R. B. McLean, and D. L. DeAngelis. 1979. Influences of physical and chemical alterations on predatorprey interactions. pp. 57-68. IN Clepper, H. (ed.), Predator-Prey Systems in Fisheries Management. Sport Fishing Inst., Washington, D.C.

*Crow, M. E., and F. B. Taub. 1979. Designing a microcosm bioassay to detect ecosystem level effects. Int. J. Environ. Stud. 13:141-147.

*Cushing, C. E., and F. L. Rose. 1970. Cycling of zinc-65 by Columbia River periphyton in a closed lotic microcosm. Limnol. Oceanogr. 15:762-767.

Deacutis, C. F. 1978. Effect of thermal shock on predator avoidance by larvae of two fish species. Trans. Am. Fish. Soc. 107:632-635.

Dodson, S. I. 1970. Complementary feeding niches sustained by size-selective predation. Limnol. Oceanogr. 15:131-137.

---

*Cited only in Appendix A.

Dodson, S. I. 1974a. Zooplankton competition and predation: An experimental test of the size-efficiency hypothesis. Ecology 55:605-613.

Dodson, S. I. 1974b. Adaptive change in plankton morphology in response to size-selective predation: A new hypothesis of cyclomorphosis. Limnol. Oceanogr. 19:721-729.

Draggan, S. 1977. Interactive effect of chromium compounds and a fungal parasite on carp eggs. Bull. Environ. Contam. Toxicol. 17:653-659.

Drenner, R. W., J. R. Strickler, and W. J. O'Brien. 1978. Capture probability: the role of zooplankter escape in the selective feeding of planktivorous fish. J. Fish. Res. Board Can. 35:1370-1373.

Dudzik, M., J. Harte, A. Jassby, E. Lapan, D. Levy, and J. Rees. 1979. Some considerations in the design of aquatic microcosms for plankton studies. Int. J. Environ. Stud. 13:125-130.

Eggers, D. M. 1977. The nature of prey selection by planktivorous fish. Ecology 58:46-59.

Eggert, C. R., R. G. Kaley, and W. E. Gledhill. 1979. Application of a laboratory freshwater lake model in the study of linear alkylbenzene sulfonate (LAS) biodegradation. pp. 451-461. IN Bourquin, A. W. and P. H. Pritchard (eds.), Microbial Degradation of Pollutants in Marine Environments. EPA-600/9-79-012.

*Eisler, R. 1973. Latent effects of Iranian crude oil and a chemical oil dispersant on Red Sea molluscs. Isr. J. Zool. 22:97-105.

Farr, J. A. 1977. Impairment of antipredator behavior in Palaemonetes pugio by exposure to sublethal doses of parathion. Trans. Am. Fish. Soc. 106:287-290.

Farr, J. A. 1978. The effect of methyl parathion on predator choice of two estuarine prey species. Trans. Am. Fish. Soc. 107:87-91.

*Ferens, M. C., and R. J. Beyers. 1972. Studies of a simple laboratory microecosystem: Effects of stress. Ecology 53:709-713.

Fielding, A. H., and G. Russell. 1976. The effect of copper on competition between marine algae. J. Ecol. 64:871-876.

---

*Cited only in Appendix A.

Fisher, J. W., C. B. Harrah, and W. O. Berry. 1980. Hydrazine: Acute toxicity to bluegills and sublethal effects on dorsal light response and aggression. Trans. Am. Fish. Soc. 109:304-309.

Fisher, N. S., E. J. Carpenter, C. C. Remsen, and C. F. Wurster. 1974. Effects of PCB on interspecific competition in natural and gnotobiotic phytoplankton communities in continuous and batch cultures. Microb. Ecol. 1:39-50.

FitzGerald, G. J., and M. H. A. Keenleyside. 1978. Technique for tagging small fish with I^{131} for evaluation of predator-prey relationships. J. Fish. Res. Board Can. 35:143-145.

*Fraleigh, P. C. 1971. Ecological succession in an aquatic microcosm and a thermal spring. Ph.D. dissertation, Univ. Ga.

*Frank, P. W. 1957. Coactions in laboratory populations of two species of Daphnia. Ecology 38:510-519.

Galbraith, Jr., M. G. 1967. Size-selective predation on Daphnia by rainbow trout and yellow perch. Trans. Am. Fish. Soc. 96:1-10.

Gause, G. F. 1934. The Struggle for Existence. Williams and Wilkins, Baltimore.

Gause, G. F., N. P. Smaragdova, and A. A. Witt. 1936. Further studies of interaction between predators and prey. J. Anim. Ecol. 5:118.

Gerhart, D. Z., S. M. Anderson, and J. Richter. 1977. Toxicity bioassays with periphyton communities: Design of experimental streams. Water Res. 11:567-570.

Gerritsen, J. 1978. Instar-specific swimming patterns and predation of planktonic copepods. Verh. Int. Ver. Limnol. 20:2531-2536.

Gerritsen, J., and J. R. Strickler. 1977. Encounter probabilities and community structure in zooplankton: A mathematical model. J. Fish. Res. Board Can. 34:73-82.

Giddings, J. M. 1979. Pollution studies in aquatic microcosms. Third Int. Symp. on Aquatic Pollutants, Oct. 15-17, 1979, Jekyll Island, Ga. (abstract).

Giddings, J. M. 1980. Types of aquatic microcosms and their research applications. IN Giesy, J. P. (ed.), Microcosms in Ecological Research (in press).

---

*Cited only in Appendix A.

Giddings, J. M. 1981. Methods for measuring effects of chemicals on aquatic ecosystem properties. IN Hammons, Anna S. (ed.), Ecotoxicological Test Systems: Proceedings of a Series of Workshops, ORNL-5709; EPA 560/6-81-004, Oak Ridge National Laboratory.

Giddings, J. M., and G. K. Eddlemon. 1978. Photosynthesis/respiration ratios in aquatic microcosms under arsenic stress. Water Air Soil Pollut. 9:207-212.

Giddings, J. M., and G. K. Eddlemon. 1979. Some ecological and experimental properties of complex aquatic microcosms. Int. J. Environ. Stud. 13:119-123.

Giesy, J. P. (ed.), 1980. Symposium on microcosms in ecological research. Augusta, Ga. November, 1978 (in press).

Ginetz, R. M., and P. A. Larkin. 1976. Factors affecting rainbow trout (Salmo gairdneri) predation on migrant fry of sockeye salmon (Oncorhynchus nerka). J. Fish. Res. Board Can. 33:19-24.

Gledhill, W. E., and V. W. Saeger. 1979. Microbial degradation in the environmental hazard evaluation process. pp. 434-442. IN Bourquin, A. W. and P. H. Pritchard (eds.), Microbial Degradation of Pollutants in Marine Environments. EPA-600/9-79-012.

Golterman, H. L. (ed.), 1976. Interactions between sediments and fresh waters. Proc. of an International Symposium held at Amsterdam, the Netherlands, September 6-10, 1976. Dr. W. Junk, D. V. Publishers, Wageningen, Netherlands.

Goodyear, C. P. 1972. A simple technique for detecting effects of toxicants or other stresses on a predator-prey interaction. Trans. Am. Fish. Soc. 101:367-370.

Gorden, R. W. 1967. Heterotrophic bacteria and succession in a simple laboratory aquatic microcosm. Ph.D. dissertation, Univ. Ga.

Gorden, R. W., R. J. Beyers, E. P. Odum, and R. G. Eagon. 1969. Studies of a simple laboratory microecosystem: Bacterial activities in a heterotrophic succession. Ecology 50:86-100.

*Goulden, C. E., and L. L. Hornig. 1980. Population oscillations and energy reserves in planktonic cladocera and their consequences to competition. Proc. Nat. Acad. Sci. (in press).

Green, J. 1967. The distribution and variation of Daphnia lumholzi (Crustacea: Cladocera) in relation to fish predation in Lake Albert, East Africa. J. Zool. 151:181-197.

---

*Cited only in Appendix A.

Hall, D. J., W. E. Cooper, and E. E. Werner. 1970. An experimental approach to the production dynamics and structure of freshwater animal communities. Limnol. Oceanogr. 15:839-928.

Hall, D. J., S. T. Threlkeld, C. W. Burns, and P. H. Crowley. 1976. The size-efficiency hypothesis and the size structure of zooplankton communities. Annu. Rev. Ecol. Syst. 7:177-208.

Hansen, S. R., and S. P. Hubbell. 1980. Single-nutrient microbial competition: Qualitative agreement between experimental and theoretically forecast outcomes. Science 207:1491-1493.

Harris, W. F., B. S. Ausmus, G. K. Eddlemon, S. J. Draggan, J. M. Giddings, D. R. Jackson, R. J. Luxmoore, E. G. O'Neill, R. V. O'Neill, M. Ross-Todd, and P. Van Voris. 1980. Microcosms as potential screening tools for evaluating transport and effects of toxic substances. EPA-600/3-80-042.

Harte, J., D. Levy, E. Lapan, A. Jassby, M. Dudzik, and J. Rees. 1978. Aquatic microcosms for assessment of effluent effects. Electrical Power Research Institute EA-936.

Harte, J., D. Levy, J. Rees, and E. Saegebarth. 1980. Making microcosms an effective assessment tool. IN Giesy, J. P. (ed.), Microcosms in Ecological Research, (in press).

Herting, G. E., and A. Witt, Jr. 1967. The role of physical fitness of forage fishes in relation to their vulnerability to predation by bowfin (Amia calva). Trans. Am. Fish. Soc. 96:427-430.

Hushon, J. M., R. J. Clerman, and B. O. Wagner. 1979. Tiered testing for chemical hazard assessment. Environ. Sci. Technol. 13:1202-1207.

Hutchinson, G. E. 1975. A Treatise on Limnology. Vol. 1., J. Wiley and Sons, New York.

Janssen, J. 1976. Selectivity of an artificial filter feeder and suction feeders on calanoid copepods. Am. Midl. Nat. 95:491-493.

Jassby, A., M. Dudzik, J. Rees, E. Lapan, D. Levy, and J. Harte. 1977a. Production cycles in aquatic microcosms. EPA-600/7-77-097.

Jassby, A., J. Rees, M. Dudzik, D. Levy, E. Lapan, and J. Harte. 1977b. Trophic structure modifications by planktivorous fish in aquatic microcosms. EPA-600/7-77-096.

Jordan, M., and G. E. Likens. 1975. An organic carbon budget for an oligotrophic lake in New Hampshire, U.S.A. Verh. Int. Ver. Limnol. 19:994-1003.

Kania, H. J., and J. O'Hara. 1974. Behavioral alterations in a simple predator-prey system due to sublethal exposure to mercury. Trans. Am. Fish. Soc. 103:134-136.

Kehde, P. M., and J. L. Wilhm. 1972. The effects of grazing by snails on community structure of periphyton in laboratory streams. Am. Midl. Nat. 87:8-24.

Kelly, R. A. 1971. The effects of fluctuating temperature on the metabolism of freshwater microcosms. Ph.D. dissertation, Univ. N. C.

Kerfoot, W. C. 1974. Egg-size cycle of a cladoceran. Ecology 55:1259-1270.

Kerfoot, W. C. 1975. The divergence of adjacent populations. Ecology 56:1298-1313.

Kerfoot, W. C. 1977a. Competition in cladoceran communities: The cost of evolving defenses against copepod predation. Ecology 58:303-313.

Kerfoot, W. C. 1977b. Implications of copepod predation. Limnol. Oceanogr. 22:316-325.

Kerfoot, W. C. 1978. Combat between predatory copepods and their prey: Cyclops, Epischura, and Bosmina. Limnol. Oceanogr. 23:1089-1102.

Kevern, N. R., and R. C. Ball. 1965. Primary productivity and energy relationships in artificial streams. Limnol. Oceanogr. 10:74-87.

Kindig, A. 1979. Investigations for streptomycin-induced algal competitive dominance reversals. Experimental Report ME25, FDA Contract No. 223-76-8348, Univ. of Wash.

*Klotz, R. L., J. R. Cain, and F. R. Trainor. 1976. Algal competition in an epilithic river flora. J. Phycol. 12:363-368.

Kurihara, Y. 1978a. Studies of succession in a microcosm. Sci. Rep. Tohoku Univ. Fourth Ser. (Biol.) 37:151-160.

Kurihara, Y. 1978b. Studies of the interaction in a microcosm. Sci. Rep. Tohoku Univ. Fourth Ser. (Biol.) 37:161-178.

*Landry, M. R. 1978. Predatory feeding behavior of a marine copepod, Labidocera trispinosa. Limnol. Oceanogr. 23:1103-1113.

---

*Cited only in Appendix A.

*Lange, W. 1974. Competitive exclusion among three planktonic blue-green algal species. J. Phycol. 10:411-414.

Leffler, J. W. 1977. A microcosm approach to an evaluation of the diversity-stability hypothesis. Ph.D. dissertation, Univ. of Ga.

Li, J. L., and H. W. Li. 1979. Species-specific factors affecting predator-prey interactions of the copepod Acanthocyclops vernalis with its natural prey. Limnol. Oceanogr. 24:613-626.

Likens, G. E., F. H. Bormann, R. S. Pierce, J. S. Eaton, and N. M. Johnson. 1977. Biogeochemistry of a Forested Ecosystem. Springer-Verlag, New York. 146 pp.

Luckinbill, L. S. 1973. Coexistence in laboratory populations of Paramecium aurelia and its predator Didinium nasutum. Ecology 54:1320-1327.

Luckinbill, L. S. 1974. The effects of space and enrichment on a predator-prey system. Ecology 55:1142-1147.

Lynch, M. 1979. Predation, competition, and zooplankton community structure: An experimental study. Limnol. Oceanogr. 24:253-272.

Margalef, R. 1968. Perspectives in Ecological Theory. Chicago, U. Chicago Press. 111 pp.

*Marshall, J. S. 1969. Competition between Daphnia pulex and D. magna as modified by radiation stress. Ecol. Soc. Am. Annu. Meet., Univ. of Vt., August 17-22, 1969.

Mauck, W. L. and D. W. Coble. 1971. Vulnerability of some fishes to northern pike (Esox lucius) predation. J. Fish. Res. Board Can. 28:957-969.

May, R. M. 1973. Stability and Complexity in Model Ecosystems. Princeton Univ. Press, Princeton, N. J.

McConnell, W. J. 1962. Productivity relations in carboy microcosms. Limnol. Oceanogr. 7:335-343.

McConnell, W. J. 1965. Relationship of herbivore growth to rate of gross photosynthesis in microcosms. Limnol. Oceanogr. 10:539-543.

---

*Cited only in Appendix A.

McIntire, C. D. 1968a. Physiological-ecological studies of benthic algae in laboratory streams. J. Water Pollut. Control Fed. 40:1940-1952.

McIntire, C.D. 1968b. Structural characteristics of benthic algal communities in laboratory streams. Ecology 49:520-537.

McIntire, C. D. 1973. Periphyton dynamics in laboratory streams: A simulation model and its implications. Ecol. Monogr. 43:399-420.

McIntire, C.D., R. L. Garrison, H. K. Phinney, and C. E. Warren. 1964. Primary production in laboratory streams. Limnol. Oceanogr. 9:92-102.

McQueen, D. J. 1969. Reduction of zooplankton standing stocks by predacious Cyclops bicuspidatus thomasi in Marion Lake, British Columbia. J. Fish. Res. Board Can. 26:1605-1618.

*Medine, A. J., D. B. Porcella, and V. D. Adams. 1980. Heavy metal and nutrient effects on sediment oxygen demand in three-phase aquatic microcosms. IN J. P. Giesy (ed.), Microcosms in Ecological Research (in press).

Metcalf, R. L., G. K. Sangha, and I. P. Kapoor. 1971. Model ecosystem for the evaluation of pesticide biodegradability and ecological magnification. Environ. Sci. Technol. 5:709-713.

*Mickelson, M. J., H. Maske, and R. C. Dugdale. 1979. Nutrient-determined dominance in multispecies chemostat cultures of diatoms. Limnol. Oceanogr. 24:298-315.

Mortimer, C. H. 1941. The exchange of dissolved substances between mud and water in lakes. J. Ecol. 29:280-329.

Mortimer. C. H. 1942. The exchange of dissolved substances between mud and water in lakes. J. Ecol. 30:147-201.

Mosser, J. L., N. S. Fisher, and C. F. Wurster. 1972. Polychlorinated biphenyls and DDT alter species composition in mixed cultures of algae. Science 176:533-535.

*Muller, W. A., and J. J. Lee. 1977. Biological interactions and the realized niche of Euplotes vannus from the salt marsh aufwuchs. J. Protozool. 24:523-527.

Mullin, M. M. 1979. Differential predation by the carnivorous marine copepod, Tortanus discaudatus. Limnol. Oceanogr. 24:774-777.

---

*Cited only in Appendix A.

Neill, W. E. 1972. Effects of size-selective predation on community structure in laboratory aquatic microcosms. Ph.D. dissertation, Univ. of Texas.

*Neill, W. E. 1975. Experimental studies of microcrustacean competition, community composition, and efficiency of resource utilization. Ecology 56:809-826.

Nixon, S. W. 1969. A synthetic microcosm. Limnol. Oceanogr. 14:142-145.

Nixon, S. W., B. A. Buckley, D. Alonso, and M. E. Q. Pilson. 1980. Turbulent mixing in aquatic microcosms. IN Giesy, J. P. (ed.), Microcosms in Ecological Research. (in press).

O'Brien, J. W. 1979. The predator-prey interaction of planktivorous fish and zooplankton. Amer. Sci. 67:572-581.

O'Brien, W. J., D. Kettle, and H. Riessen. 1979. Helmets and invisible armor: Structures reducing predation from tactile and visual planktivores. Ecology 60:287-294.

O'Brien, W. J., and D. Schmidt. 1979. Arctic Bosmina morphology and copepod predation. Limnol. Oceanogr. 24:564-568.

O'Brien, W. J., N. A. Slade, and G. L. Vinyard. 1976. Apparent size as the determinant of prey selection by bluegill sunfish (Lepomis macrochirus). Ecology 57:1304-1310.

O'Brien, W. J., and G. L. Vinyard. 1978. Polymorphism and predation: The effect of invertebrate predation on the distribution of two varieties of Daphnia carinata in South India ponds. Limnol. Oceanogr. 23:452-460.

Odum, E. P. 1969. The strategy of ecosystem development. Science 164:262-270.

Odum, E. P. 1971. Fundamentals of Ecology, 3rd ed. Saunders, W. B., Philadelphia, 574 pp.

Odum, H. T. 1956. Primary production in flowing waters. Limnol. Oceanogr. 1:102-117.

Odum, H. T. 1957. Trophic structure and productivity of Silver Spring, Florida. Ecol. Monogr. 27:55-112.

---

*Cited only in Appendix A.

Odum, H. T., and C. M. Hoskin. 1958. Comparative studies on the metabolism of marine waters. Publ. Inst. Mar. Sci., Univ. of Tex. 5:16-46.

Ollason, J. G. 1977. Freshwater microcosms in fluctuating environments. Oikos 28:262-269.

O'Neill, R. V., and J. M. Giddings. 1979. Population interactions and ecosystem function: Phytoplankton competition and community production. pp. 103-123. IN Innis, G. S. and R. V. O'Neill (eds.), Systems Analysis of Ecosystems. International Co-operative Publishing House, Fairland, Md.

Patrick, R. 1973. Use of algae, especially diatoms, in the assessment of water quality. pp. 76-95. IN Cairns, Jr., J. and K. L. Dickson (eds.), Biological Methods for the Assessment of Water Quality. ASTM Special Technical Publication 528, American Society for Testing and Materials, Philadelphia.

Perez, K. T., G. M. Morrison, N. F. Lackie, C. A. Oviatt, S. W. Nixon, B. A. Buckley, and J. F. Heltshe. 1977. The importance of physical and biotic scaling to the experimental simulation of a coastal marine ecosystem. Helgol. Wiss. Meeresunters. 30:144-162.

Phinney, H. K., and C. D. McIntire. 1965. Effect of temperature on metabolism of periphyton communities developed in laboratory streams. Limnol. Oceanogr. 10:341-344.

Pilson, M. E. Q., G. A. Vargo, P. Gearing, and J. N. Gearing. 1977. The marine ecosystems research laboratory: A facility for the investigation of effects and fates of pollutants. IN Proceedings of the 2nd National Conference, Interagency Energy/Environment R&D Program, Washington, D. C., June 6-7, 1977.

Pomeroy, L. R., E. E. Smith, and C. M. Grant. 1965. The exchange of phosphate between estuarine water and sediment. Limnol. Oceanogr. 10:167-172.

Porcella, D. B., V. D. Adams, and P. A. Cowan. 1976. Sediment-water microcosms for assessment of nutrient interactions in aquatic ecosystems. pp. 293-322. IN Middlebrooks, E., D. H. Falkenborg, and T. E. Maloney (eds.), Biostimulation and Nutrient Assessment. Ann Arbor: Ann Arbor Science.

Pritchard, P. H., A. W. Bourquin, H. L. Frederickson, and T. Maziarz. 1979. System design factors affecting environmental fate studies in microcosms. pp. 251-272. IN Bourquin, A. W. and P. H. Pritchard (eds.), Microbial Degradation of Pollutants in Marine Environments. EPA-600/9-79-012.

Reed, C. C. 1976. Species diversity in aquatic microecosystems. Ph.D. dissertation, Univ. of N. Colo.

Reichle, D. E., R. V. O'Neill, and W. F. Harris. 1975. Principles of energy and material exchange in ecosystems. pp. 27-43. IN: Van Dobben, W. H. and R. H. Lowe-McConnell (eds.), Unifying Concepts in Ecology. W. Junk, the Hague.

Riley, G. A. 1956. Factors controlling phytoplankton populations on Georges Bank. J. Mar. Res. 6:54-73.

Robertson, A., C. W. Gehrs, B. D. Hardin, and G. W. Hunt. 1974. Culturing and ecology of Diaptomus clavipes and Cyclops vernalis. EPA-660/3-74-006.

Rodgers, J. H., Jr., J. R. Clark, K. L. Dickson, and J. Cairns, Jr. 1980. Nontaxonomic analyses of structure and function of aufwuchs communities in lotic microcosms. IN Giesy, J. P. (ed.), Microcosms in Ecological Research (in press).

Russell, G., and A. H. Fielding. 1974. The competitive properties of marine algae in culture. J. Ecol. 62:689-698.

Salt, G. W. 1967. Predation in an experimental protozoan population (Woodruffia-Paramecium). Ecol. Monogr. 37:113-144.

Salt, G. W. 1968. The feeding of Amoeba proteus on Paramecium aurelia. J. Protozool. 15:275-280.

Salt, G. W. 1969. A measure of culture-induced changes in a laboratory population of protozoa. Ecology 50:135-137.

Salt, G. W. 1974. Predator and prey densities as controls of the rate of capture by the predator Didinium nasutum. Ecology 55:434-439.

Salt, G. W. 1979. Density, starvation, and swimming rate in Didinium populations. Am. Nat. 113:135-143.

Schindler, D. W., F. A. J. Armstrong, S. K. Holmgren, and G. J. Brunskill. 1971. Eutrophication of Lake 227, Experimental Lakes Area, Northwestern Ontario, by addition of phosphate and nitrate. J. Fish. Res. Board Can. 28:1763-1782.

Snieszko, S. F. 1974. The effects of environmental stress on outbreaks of infectious diseases of fishes. J. Fish. Biol. 6:197-208.

Sprules, W. G. 1972. Effects of size-selective predation and food competition on high altitude zooplankton communities. Ecology 53:375-386.

Stein, R. A. 1977. Selective predation, optimal foraging, and the predator-prey interaction between fish and crayfish. Ecology 58:1237-1253.

Stein, R. A., and J. J. Magnuson. 1976. Behavioral response of crayfish to a fish predator. Ecology 57:751-761.

Strickler, J. R. 1977. Observation of swimming performances of planktonic copepods. Limnol. Oceanogr. 22:165-170.

Sugiura, K., S. Sato, M. Goto, and Y. Kurihara. 1976a. Effects of beta-BHC on aquatic microcosm. Chemosphere 1:39-44.

Sugiura, K., S. Sato, M. Goto, Y. Kurihara. 1976b. Toxicity assessment using an aquatic microcosm. Chemosphere 2:113-118.

Sullivan, J. F., and G. J. Atchison. 1978. Predator-prey behavior of fathead minnows, *Pimephales promelas*, and largemouth bass, *Micropterus salmoides*, in a model ecosystem. J. Fish. Biol. 13:249-253.

Sullivan, J. F., G. J. Atchison, D. J. Kolar, and A. W. McIntosh. 1978. Changes in the predator-prey behavior of fathead minnows (*Pimephales promelas*) and largemouth bass (*Micropterus salmoides*) caused by cadmium. J. Fish. Res. Board Can. 35:446-451.

Sylvester, J. R. 1972. Effect of thermal stress on predator avoidance in sockeye salmon. J. Fish. Res. Board Can. 29:601-603.

Sylvester, J. R. 1973. Effect of light on vulnerability of heat-stressed sockeye salmon to predation by coho salmon. Trans. Am. Fish. Soc. 102:139-142.

Tagatz, M. E. 1976. Effect of mirex on predator-prey interaction in an experimental estuarine ecosystem. Trans. Am. Fish. Soc. 105:546-549.

Taub, F. B. 1969a. A biological model of a freshwater community: A gnotobiotic ecosystem. Limnol. Oceanogr. 14:136-142.

Taub, F. B. 1969b. A continuous gnotobiotic (species defined) ecosystem. pp. 101-120. IN Cairns, Jr., J. (ed.), The Structure and Function of Fresh-Water Microbial Communities. Research Monograph 3, Virginia Polytechnic Institute and State University, Blacksburg, Va.

Taub, F. B. 1969c. Gnotobiotic models of freshwater communities. Verh. Int. Ver. Limnol. 17:485-496.

Taub, F. B. 1976. Demonstration of pollution effects in aquatic microcosms. Int. J. Environ. Stud. 10:23-33.

Taub, F. B., and M. E. Crow. 1980. Synthesizing aquatic microcosms. IN Giesy, J. P. (ed.), Microcosms in Ecological Research (in press).

Taub, F. B., M. E. Crow, and H. J. Hartmann. 1980. Responses of aquatic microcosms to acute mortality. IN Giesy, J. P. (ed.), Microcosms in Ecological Research (in press).

Thomas, C. L. 1978. A microcosm study of the interactions of nutrients and cadmium in aquatic systems. M.S. Thesis, Univ. of Ga.

Thompson, D. J. 1978. Towards a realistic predator-prey model: life history of the damselfly, Ischnura elegans. J. Anim. Ecol. 47:757-767.

*Tilman, D. 1977. Resource competition between planktonic algae: An experimental and theoretical approach. Ecology 58:338-348.

*Titman, D. 1976. Ecological competition between algae: Experimental confirmation of resource-based competition theory. Science 192:463-465.

U. S. Environmental Protection Agency. 1979. Toxic substances control. Discussion of premanufacture testing policy and technical issues: Request for comment. Fed. Reg. 44:16240-16292.

Van den Ende, P. 1973. Predator-prey interactions in continuous culture. Science 54:562-564.

Vaughan, G. E. 1979. Comparative vulnerability of bluegills with and without lymphocystis disease to predation by largemouth bass. Prog. Fish Cult. 41:163-164.

Veilleux, B. G. 1979. An analysis of the predatory interaction between Paramecium and Didinium. J. Anim. Ecol. 48:787-803.

Vinyard, G. L., and W. J. O'Brien. 1975. Dorsal light response as an index of prey preference in bluegill (Lepomis macrochirus). J. Fish. Res. Board Can. 32:1860-1863.

Vinyard, G. L., and W. J. O'Brien. 1976. Effects of light and turbidity on the reactive distance of bluegill (Lepomis macrochirus). J. Fish. Res. Board Can. 33:2845-2849.

---

*Cited only in Appendix A.

Waide, J. B., J. E. Schindler, M. C. Waldron, J. J. Hains, S. P. Schreiner, M. L. Freedman, S. L. Benz, D. R. Pettigrew, L. A. Schissel, and P. J. Clarke. 1980. A microcosm approach to the study of biogeochemical systems: 2. Responses of aquatic laboratory microcosms to physical, chemical and biological perturbations. IN Giesy, J. P. (ed.), Microcosms in Ecological Research (in press).

*Ward, D. V., B. L. Howes, and D. F. Ludwig. 1976. Interactive effects of predation pressure and insecticide (temefos) toxicity on populations of the marsh fiddler crab Uca pugnax. Mar. Biol. 35:119-126.

Ware, D. M. 1972. Predation by rainbow trout (Salmo gairdneri): The influence of hunger, prey density, and prey size. J. Fish. Res. Board Can. 29:1193-1201.

Ware, D. M. 1973. Risk of epibenthic prey to predation by rainbow trout (Salmo gairdneri). J. Fish. Res. Board Can. 30:787-797.

Warren, C. E., and G. E. Davis. 1971. Laboratory stream research: Objectives, possibilities, and constraints. Annu. Rev. Ecol. Syst. 2:111-144.

Warshaw, S. J. 1972. Effects of alewives (Alosa pseudoharengus) on the zooplankton of Lake Wononskopomuc, Conn. Limnol. Oceanogr. 17:816-825.

Webster, J. R. 1978. Analysis of potassium and calcium dynamics in stream ecosystems on three southern Appalachian watersheds of contrasting vegetation. Ph.D. dissertation, Univ. Ga.

Wedemeyer, G. 1970. The role of stress in the disease resistance of fishes. pp. 30-35. IN Snieszko, S. F. (ed.), A Symposium on Diseases of Fishes and Shellfishes. Am. Fish. Soc., Washington, D.C.

Wells, L. 1970. Effects of alewife predation on zooplankton populations in Lake Michigan. Limnol. Oceanogr. 15:556-565.

Werner, E. E. 1974. The fish size, prey size, handling time relation in several sunfishes and some implications. J. Fish. Res. Board Can. 31:1531-1536.

Werner, E. E., and D. J. Hall. 1974. Optimal foraging and size selection of prey by the bluegill sunfish (Lepomis macrochirus). Ecology 55:1042-1052.

---

*Cited only in Appendix A.

Whittaker, R. H., and G. M. Woodwell. 1972. Evolution of natural communities. pp. 137-159. IN Wiens, J. A. (ed.), Ecosystem Structure and Function. Oregon State University Press, Corvallis, Oregon.

Whitworth, W. R., and T. H. Lane. 1969. Effects of toxicants on community metabolism in pools. Limnol. Oceanogr. 14:53-58.

Woltering, D. M., J. L. Hedtke, and L. J. Weber. 1978. Predator-prey interactions of fishes under the influence of ammonia. Trans. Am. Fish. Soc. 107:500-504.

Wolters, W. R., and C. C. Coutant. 1976. The effect of cold shock on the vulnerability of young bluegill to predation. pp. 162-164. IN Esch, G. W. and R. W. McFarlane (eds.), Thermal Ecology II. CONF-750425.

Wulff, B. L. 1971. Structure and productivity of marine benthic diatom communities in a laboratory model ecosystem. Ph.D, dissertation, Ore. State U.

Yocum, T. G., and T. A. Edsall. 1974. Effects of acclimation temperature and heat shock on vulnerability of fry of lake whitefish (Coregonus clupeaformis) to predation. J. Fish. Res. Board Can. 31:1503-1506.

Zaret, T. M. 1972. Predators, invisible prey, and the nature of polymorphism in the cladocera (Class Crustacea). Limnol. Oceanogr. 17:171-184.

Zaret, T. M. 1975. Strategies for existence of zooplankton prey in homogeneous environments. Verh. Int. Ver. Limnol. 19:1484-1489.

Zaret, T. M., and W. C. Kerfoot. 1975. Fish predation on Bosmina longirostris: Body-size selection versus visibility selection. Ecology 56:232-237.

LABORATORY TESTS FOR CHEMICAL EFFECTS ON
TERRESTRIAL POPULATION INTERACTIONS
AND ECOSYSTEM PROPERTIES

G. W. Suter, II
Environmental Sciences Division
Oak Ridge National Laboratory

SECTION 4

LABORATORY TESTS FOR CHEMICAL EFFECTS ON TERRESTRIAL POPULATION INTERACTIONS AND ECOSYSTEM PROPERTIES

The potential multispecies laboratory test systems discussed in this section were selected on the basis of a literature review and workshops on population interactions and ecosystem properties (Suter 1980a, b). Highest priority was given to systems that had been used for testing effects of chemicals. Somewhat lower priority was given to systems that were well studied and documented, but that were designed for such uses as pure research or studies of chemical transport. Lowest priority was given to systems that had (1) been little studied or (2) had not been studied at all as complete laboratory systems, but that had been suggested by one of the workshop panels.

Potential test systems are identified and evaluated in the text of this section and in Appendix B. The criteria used for test evaluation include (1) the state of development of a system, (2) sensitivity of the system, (3) ability of the system to simulate responses in the real world, (4) the ecological and economic importance of the organisms and processes included, (5) cost, (6) technical difficulty, (7) the availability of system components, (8) the range of responses displayed by the system, and (9) the time to response.

Multispecies test systems should be included in a chemical hazard assessment scheme because of (1) the effects of ecological systems on the activity of test chemicals, (2) the effects of the system context on the responses of the individual components, and (3) the effects of chemicals on holistic properties of systems.

Ecological systems may affect the activity of a test chemical by chemically or physically transforming it, by concentrating or diluting it, or by changing its availability. The soil microflora may degrade or detoxify a chemical or may even increase toxicity through partial oxidation. The soil itself may affect the availability and toxic properties of a chemical by sorption and abiotic oxidation and reduction. Higher organisms may take up chemicals and partially or completely metabolize them, sequester them in relatively inactive tissues such as the cuticle, or pass them to exploiters in a concentrated form.

The response of an individual organism or population to a chemical may be modified by its interactions with other system components. For example, chemicals may affect the ability to avoid predation, find prey, compete, or subsist on toxic or marginally nourishing hosts. Because interactions between organisms often result in stress or increased energy expenditure, traditional response parameters may be more sensitive to chemicals in multispecies systems. Because interactions of organisms or populations require behavioral and physiological responses which are not displayed in isolation, the range of measurable responses to a chemical is greater in multispecies than in single species systems. Therefore, the responses of the individual components in a multispecies test system may be both more realistic and more sensitive than if that component were tested alone.

Holistic properties, those which are characteristic of an entire hierarchical level of organization, can measurably respond to test chemicals. These include collective properties which are summarizations of the properties of system components and emergent properties which are not summarizations of the properties of components (Salt 1979). Collective properties such as diversity, foodweb connectivity, and community production and respiration provide indices of the state of the system. In many cases, the responses of these collective properties have greater practical importance than the responses of the individual component organisms or populations (e.g., soil respiration is more important than the respiration of any individual microbial population). Collective properties can be no more sensitive than the most sensitive component, but they can be considerably less sensitive. Functional or numerical replacement of sensitive species by insensitive analog species can result in the masking of toxic effects when collective properties are measured (O'Neill and Giddings 1979). This structural and functional redundancy is, however, a property of natural systems and does not invalidate the use of collective properties as indicators of the effects of chemical on communities.

Emergent properties are often attributed to communities and ecosystems on the basis of loosely supported teleological arguments or loose definitions of emergence. Emergent properties are probably uncommon in communities and ecosystems because selection has relatively little opportunity to act on these higher organizational levels (Salt 1979). The replacement rate of communities is very low relative to those of populations within a community and individuals within a population so that selective pressure is less intense at higher organizational levels. In addition, community-level selective pressure must act in the face of gene flow to the constituent populations from other communities. Recent successes in predicting the properties of communities with models based on the properties of populations (O'Neill and Giddings 1979; Shugart and West 1980) suggest that emergent properties need not be invoked at the community and ecosystem level.* Therefore, the only emergent properties which

---

*A less restrictive definition of emergent properties is used in systems theory. The components of such systems (e.g., transitors or plant populations) are treated as having properties which are independent of the system into which they are assembled. The system merely reduces the range of behavior of the components. The emergent

appear to be testable in multispecies systems are those associated with interactions of pairs of coevolved species such as the formation of nodules by legumes and rhizobia and of lichen thalli by algae and fungi.

4.1 Population Interactions

This section is organized according to competition, predation, and the other conventional classes of population interactions. This organization is not meant to imply that tests can be developed to represent these interactions in the same sense that rats serve to represent mammal species of varying sensitivity. The class Mammalia is composed of organisms that share a large number of physiological processes, but the class of interactions called competition, for example, has no mechanistic commonality. Exploitation competition consists of division of a limiting resource (Park 1954), which can occur by a contest or scramble (Nicholson 1954). Interference competition (Park 1954) consists of the many other mechanisms by which one organism reduces another organism's use of a limiting resource including allelopathy, interspecific territoriality, predation, and physical contact. The large number of distinct mechanisms of interaction, which are called competition because they share a common outcome, are unlikely to respond in a qualitatively similar manner to chemical substances. Similar arguments can be made concerning predation, symbiosis, herbivory, and parasitism.

This problem is not serious for tests that are used only for screening chemicals and not for predicting specific effects. Screening tests only need to be sensitive to a wide range of chemicals and to produce a representative relative ranking of toxicity. The outcome of many population interactions is highly sensitive to normal ecological variables, and it seems likely that they would also be more sensitive to chemicals than a single-species bioassay. This supposition has rarely been tested, however, and is not always supported by the evidence (e.g., Kochhar et al. 1980). This use of population interaction tests would, like the use of second stressor in bioassays, simply be a method of increasing or broadening sensitivity

---

properties of systems theory (e.g., signal amplification or community biomass) are simply a result of the topology of the system (Caswell et al. 1972). If this general model is as correct for ecosystems as for electrical circuits, ecosystems have no emergent properties in Salt's (1979) sense. Predictions of effects of toxicants on ecosystem properties are made on the basis of individual responses of individual organisms which are assumed to be independent of the system context (e.g., West et al. 1980). Emergent properties according to systems theory require better models rather than better tests (see Sect. 5).

over that of a standard, single-species test. Development of multispecies test systems simply for their sensitivity is not recommended.

Predictive tests (those that actually predict responses in the field) are necessary to establish the significance of responses observed in screening tests. For this purpose, tests must be representative of classes of interactions that are economically or ecologically important and yet are so narrowly defined as to encompass a generally uniform set of response mechanisms. Examples of these tests might include predation by hymenopteran parasitoids and herbivory by homopterans.

Another general problem concerns the definition of a population interaction test system. Because the results of population interactions are defined in terms of changes in population size and composition, the test systems must allow completion of multiple life cycles by each component species. This requirement might be circumvented in many instances by developing predictive indicators of response. One strategy is to use experimental designs and mathematical models that permit the prediction of outcome from data on a single generation, such as those developed for competition by DeWit (Sect. 4.1.1). Another strategy is to isolate components of the interaction that are both sensitive to toxicants and important to the outcome of the interaction, such as (possibly) predator searching efficiency or photosynthesis rates of competing plants. Finally, stress symptoms such as reduced larval size in competing _Drosophila_ may provide early indicators of the ultimate outcome of the system.

Test systems developed using these strategies would only be indicative of effects on population interactions and not truly predictive because they inevitably ignore some components of the interaction. Tests of predator searching, for example, typically treat the prey as passive fodder. All test systems that do not include numerous generations exclude the possibility of evolutionary responses. It will be important to determine the magnitude of error induced by simplifying the interactions relative to errors induced by extrapolating between different groups of interacting species and by extrapolating from the laboratory to the field.

4.1.1 Competition

"Competition occurs when a number of animals [or plants] (of the same or different species) utilize common resources the supply of which is short; or if the resources are not in short supply, competition occurs when animals [or plants] seeking that resource nevertheless harm one or the other in the process" (Birch 1957). As indicated in Sect. 4.1, this widely quoted definition of competition includes a broad variety of mechanisms of interaction, more than one of which is often involved in a particular two-species interaction. Operationally, competition is said to occur when the fitness of one population is reduced by the presence of another population that uses a common resource.

Different approaches to the analysis of competition have developed. Because Park's Triboleum competition system [Sect. 4.1.1 (2)] invariably results in extinction of one species, the response of this system is expressed in terms of time to extinction and is modeled by a stochastic version of the Lotka-Voltera competition equations (Leslie 1958). Results from competition systems that are stable (i.e., do not lead to extinction) or that cannot be carried to termination because of the long generation times of the organisms involved have results expressed as changes in relative frequency. These are analyzed in terms of DeWit's (1960) ratio diagrams (Fig. 4.1). Data are fit to the model:

$$\log (O_1/O_2) = \log \alpha + \beta \log (I_1/I_2),$$

where O_1/O_2 is the ratio of the output frequencies of the two species, and I_1/I_2 is the ratio of the input frequencies. The intercept ($\log \alpha$) provides a measure of the fitness differential when the input ratio equals 1, whereas β measures the change in relative fitness with varying input frequency. A line with a slope of 1 [Fig. 4.1 (line a)] indicates that fitness is independent of the relative frequency, and one species will become extinct. A line with a slope <1 [Fig. 4.1 (line b)] indicates that the less frequent species is favored, and a stable equilibrium frequency exists at the intersection of the fitted line with the diagonal. A slope >1 [Fig. 4.1 (line c)] indicates that the more frequent species is favored, and the equilibrium is unstable. Maximum likelihood methods provide a more efficient analysis of this model than the traditional least squares regression (Adams and Duncan 1979). The experimental design used with this analysis is the replacement series. The total input density is kept constant, and the ratio of the two species is varied (e.g., 0:5, 1:4, 2:3, 3:2, 4:1, 5:0).

(1) _Microbial competition_. Microbial competition has received considerable attention. However, nearly all such work has been performed using liquid culture (Alexander 1971; Fredrickson 1977; Meers 1973) because the use of soil greatly inhibits the extraction, identification, and enumeration of microorganisms. Studies that realistically address competition in the soil (e.g., Rennie and Schmidt 1977) require elaborate techniques such as the fluorescent antibody technique. Because of this problem, tests for effects on microbial competition should be limited to liquid cultures that simulate aquatic systems. Further, interest in soil microorganisms primarily concerns the processes that they perform rather than the species performing them. Microbial processes are discussed in Sect. 4.2.

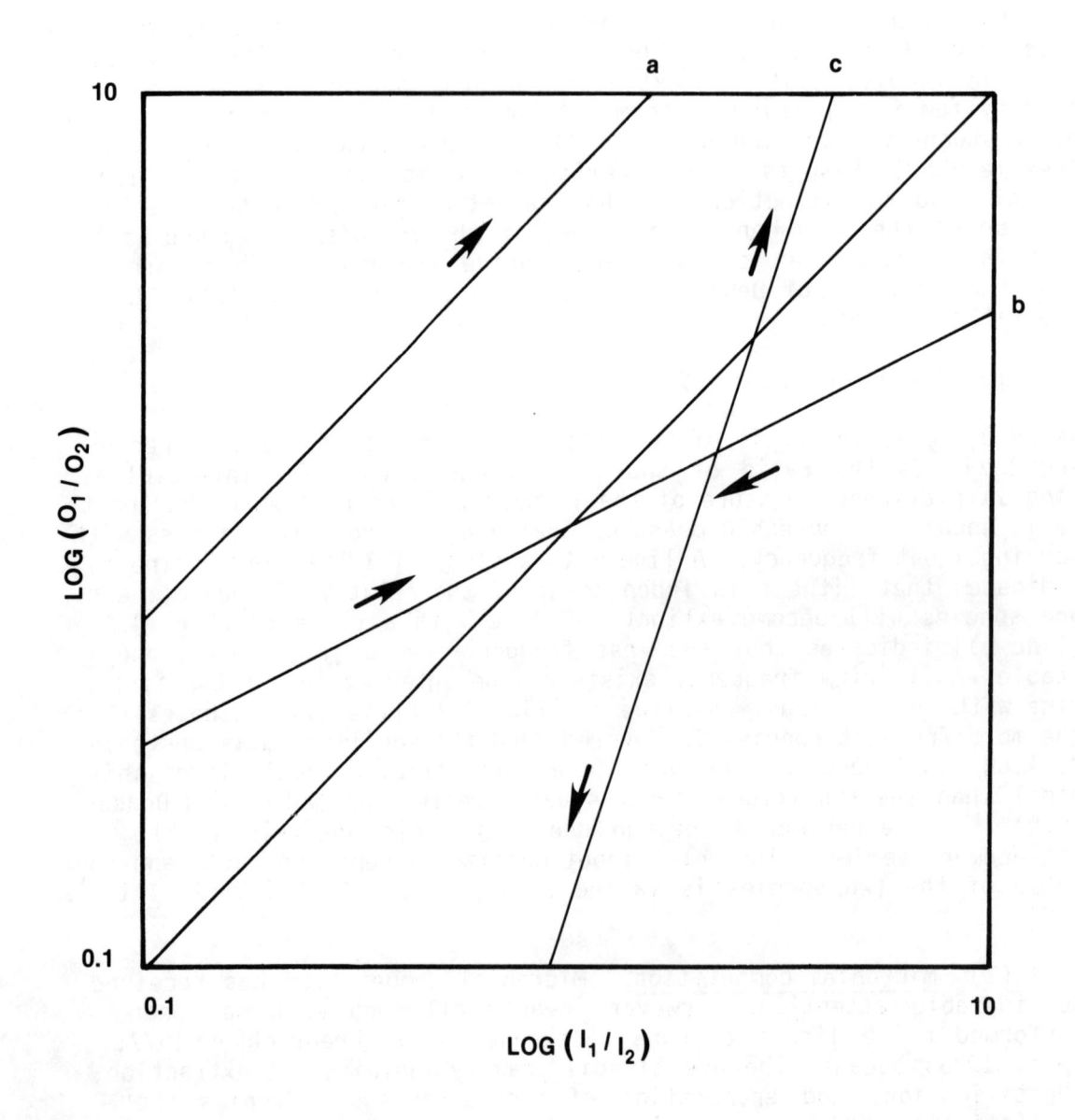

FIGURE 4.1. RATIO DIAGRAM: I_1/I_2 = THE RATIO OF THE INPUT FREQUENCIES OF SPECIES 1 AND 2 AND O_1/O_2 = THE RATIO OF OUTPUT FREQUENCIES.

(2) Plant competition. Because autotrophic plants lack the diverse resource base and behavioral repertoire of heterotrophic organisms, plant competition is both intense and mechanistically limited. Plants engage in exploitation competition for space (light), water, and mineral nutrients. Interference competition between plants primarily involves allelochemicals released as leachates from living or dead tissues or as root exudates. The hypothesis that plant competition is a relatively uniform process is supported by White and Harper's (1970) determination that a wide variety of combinations of plant species in the field and laboratory give a good fit to the equation of Yoda et al. (1973) for the relationship of weight (w) to density (p) in self-thinning communities: $w = cp^{-3/2}$, where c is a constant.

Socially important plant competitors include weeds and crops, more and less commercially desirable species of trees, and components of mixed-species crop and pasture systems. Some pairs of plant species such as mixed barley and oat crops (DeWit 1960) engage in pure exploitation competition [Fig. 4.1 (line a)]. Apparent stable equilibria due to rare species advantage include species of Avena (Jain 1969) and Papaver (Harper and McNaughton 1962). Interference competition could be demonstrated using any allelopathic plant (Rice 1974 and 1979). Allelopathy could result in an advantage to the more common species [Fig. 4.1 (line c)].

Competition between pasture grasses and legumes is a relatively well-studied system that is also commercially important. Clover-grass mixtures are frequently used in seeded pastures to maximize yield and nutritional quality of the pasture. Bennett and Runeckles (1977) found that 0.09 ppm ozone changed the crimson clover-annual ryegrass competitive balance from favoring clover to favoring ryegrass. Kochhar et al. (1980) found that ladino clover growth was reduced by fescue competition and by 0.03 ppm ozone, but the combination of ozone and fescue produced no greater growth decrement than either factor produced alone. However, leachate from ozone-exposed fescue, but not control fescue, inhibited clover nodulation. While the differences in the results of these two studies may be attributable in part to differences in experimental design and techniques, they suggest that generalization may be difficult even between closely related systems. A tentative protocol for a clover-grass competition test is presented in Suter (1981a).

Alternative candidates for plant competition exist in profusion. Competitors could be chosen to represent taxonomic groups (i.e., monocot-dicot) life forms (i.e., tree-herb or annual-perennial) or community types (i.e., tilled agriculture or old field). Which of these organizational schemes would provide the strongest basis for predictive generalization is not clear.

Plant competition tests should be designed as replacement series with at least three ratios (each species alone and an equal mix).

Plants would ideally be grown to maturity because of differences in responses to chemicals in different phenological stages and the importance of effects on production of propagules. Nevertheless, shorter tests have some applicability because vegetative biomass of immature plants is the parameter of interest in many managed systems. Competitive outcomes measured by harvesting vegetation can be analyzed in terms of relative yield (r = the yield of a species in the mixture/monoculture yield), total relative yield (RYT = $r_1 + r_2$), and the crowding coefficient ($k_{1'2} = r_1/r_2$).

(3) <u>Arthropod competition</u>. The arthropod competition systems discussed below represent over 90% of the laboratory studies of terrestrial arthropod competition. They are all saprophytic systems. Competitive interactions between herbivores have received relatively little attention. Any herbivorous arthropod that is a significant competitor of a pest species is likely to be a pest itself. Although damage may be somewhat reduced by interference competition between pests, there are no positive outcomes from such competition, and therefore it has little appeal to management-oriented entomologists. Competition between predators, and particularly among parasitoids, has important effects on the success of biocontrol. Therefore, these interactions have been somewhat better studied. Arthropod herbivore, predator, and parasitoid competition are discussed in Sects. 4.1.2 and 4.1.3(2).

(a) <u>Drosophila</u>. The members of the genus <u>Drosophila</u> are among the most studied organisms in biology. Hundreds of papers have been published on competition among more than a dozen species of <u>Drosophila</u> over a period of 45 years (beginning with L'Heritier and Teissier 1937). Because this work has been dominated by population geneticists, emphasis has been placed on the evolution of fitness under competition. The response of <u>Drosophila</u> competition to chemicals has not been studied.

Depending on the pair of <u>Drosophila</u> species and physical conditions chosen, a particular species may become extinct. This species may be indeterminant (Barker and Podger 1970; Miller 1964), or both species may coexist indefinitely even though they occupy the same niche by the criterion of the Lotka-Voltera competition equations (Ayala 1970, 1971). Coexistence can be explained by an increase in fitness with decreasing frequency [Fig. 4.1 (line a)] or by evolved shifts in competitive advantage. Complete shifts in dominance have been observed in competition between <u>D. melanogaster</u> and <u>D. simulans</u> (Moore 1952) and between <u>D. serrata</u> and both <u>D. pseudoobscura</u> and <u>D. melanogaster</u> (Ayala 1966), supporting the evolutionary model. Relatively stable frequency ratios that support the DeWit model of frequency dependence have been obtained using the following pairs: <u>D. pseudoobscura</u> and <u>D. willistoni</u> (Ayala 1971); <u>D. pseudoobscura</u> and <u>D. serrata</u>; and <u>D. nebulosa</u> and <u>D. serrata</u> (Ayala 1969). These stable frequencies are achieved with varying input frequencies.

Drosophila experiments have traditionally been conducted in 250-mL or smaller bottles or vials with a yeast-containing medium covering the bottom. Various alternative container designs that offer some advantages in manipulation have been used, but none of them are widely accepted. Media, vials, anesthetizing equipment, and some Drosophila species and a large variety of mutant types are commercially available. The use of flies with conspicuous genetic markers makes sorting relatively easy.

Although the number of adult flies of each species is the standard parameter in Drosophila competition experiments, a variety of other parameters, including stage-specific viability, length of stages, weight of adults, wing length, and the ratios of numbers, weights, and development times of males and females, have been used. All these parameters have been shown to respond to the effects of competition, but their response to chemicals is unknown.

The utility of Drosophila competition as a screening test is suggested not only by the sensitivity of the outcome to temperature, light, and other physical parameters, but also by its response to radiation. Moth and Barker (1977) found that viability of flies was significantly reduced by 35 µCi of ^{32}P in 30 mL of medium. Blaylock and Shugart (1972) found that treatments of 250 and 500 rads, but not 1000 rads, increased the fitness of inbred D. simulans in competition with inbred D. melanogaster. They concluded from this and previous studies that low levels of radiation in a largely homozygous population results in heterosis, but at high levels the effects of deleterious genes predominate. Because Drosophila species have been shown to coexist in the field in fruit, oak fluxes, and fungi (Atkinson 1979; Budnik and Brncic 1974), this laboratory system represents a natural phenomenon. The outcome of competition among Drosophila or other saprophagic flies is not, however, of such importance that a predictive test system is desirable.

A Drosophila competition test might be simply based on changes in relative frequency after one generation at one frequency. This test would only require a few small vials, and by using D. melanogaster and D. simulans (the best-studied species pair), it could be completed in 2 weeks. The sensitivity of the test could probably be increased by using three input frequencies so that the parameters of the DeWit competition model could be estimated. While Drosophila competition may play an important role in the development of a theory of ecotoxicology, it does not appear to be sufficiently representative of important interactions in the field to warrant its use as a test protocol.

(b) Other flies. Although the great preponderance of literature on competition between flies is concerned with Drosophila, significant work has been done on other species. These include species of blowfly (Ullyett 1950), housefly and blowfly (Pimentel, Feinberg et al. 1965), and varieties of housefly (Boggild and Keiding

1958; Sokal and Sullivan 1963). In addition to being less well studied than Drosophila, these species require more space and therefore would be more expensive to maintain. Therefore, they are not recommended.

(c) Tribolium. Competition between flour beetles of the genus Tribolium has been studied at least as much as Drosophila competition. More than 100 papers have been published on Tribolium competition since Park's (1948) seminal monograph. These studies have been concerned with the ways in which competition leads to extinction of one or the other member of the pair T. confusum (cf) and T. castaneum (cs). The characteristic of this system that has attracted the most attention is the indeterminacy of outcome. At certain initial frequencies of specified populations and at specified temperatures and humidity, the surviving species cannot be predicted. This indeterminacy indicates a fine competitive balance. Therefore, Tribolium competition, like Drosophila competition, may be highly sensitive to a wide range of chemicals.

The Tribolium system is easily initiated by placing the desired proportions of the two species in shell vials containing 8 g of whole wheat flour with 5% yeast. All life stages are removed by sieving at monthly intervals and placing in fresh medium. A tentative testing protocol proposed for this system calls for operating the system under conditions that produce an indeterminant outcome (Suter 1980a). The primary response criterion proposed is determinacy of outcome. That is, an effect has been demonstrated if one species becomes extinct in all chemically treated replicates. Time to extinction would be a secondary response criterion. The difficulty with this proposal is that the indeterminate systems require about 2 years for completion. This large time requirement results from the longevity of the adult beetles [323 days for cf and 213 for cs (Mertz 1972)] and their relatively long generation time (30 days). If, as was conjectured in the proposed protocol, the determinacy of the outcome could be predicted with 90% accuracy after 150 days, the system is still not as rapid as other screening tests. A single generation test for Tribolium competition would require a month, and there is no basis for predicting outcome from the results of a single generation as there is for Drosophila.

Because these species exist almost entirely as pests of stored grain products, the laboratory system is the "natural" system. The outcome of competition in these "natural" systems is, however, immaterial to the grain products owner. The particular combination of exploitation competition with predation and cannibalism that characterizes this system is unlikely to respond in a manner that is predictive of interaction in any important group of organisms.

(d) Other grain insects. Park was preceded in the study of competition among grain insects by Crombie (1945, 1946), who studied the beetles T. confusum, Rhizopertha dominica, and Oryzaephilus surinamensis and the moth Sitotroga cerealella. These studies, like those of Park, were initiated to investigate problems in population biology. Crombie's systems were supplanted by Park's because of the greater theoretical appeal of competition between sibling species. More recently, LeCato (1975a, 1975b, and 1978) reexamined systems of taxonomically diverse graminivorous insects with the idea of reducing grain losses by encouraging predation. If this idea ever proves useful (the research has been at least temporarily discontinued), the effects of fumigants and residues of pesticides or other chemicals in the grain would be critical.

(e) Soil arthropods. Detritivorous soil and litter arthropods show a remarkable combination of high species diversity and low feeding specificity (Anderson 1962). This "enigma" gives the problem of soil arthropod competition theoretical importance. These organisms can be maintained as competitors on a totally artificial system of plaster of Paris and charcoal (Culver 1974; Longstaff 1976) or in soil-litter microcosms (Anderson 1978). The former system is too artificial to represent effects of chemicals in the field and is too poorly understood and developed to be appealing as a screening test. On the other hand, microarthropods in soil and litter are relatively difficult to extract quantitatively and census. These organisms are important primarily because of their collaborative role in decomposition and nutrient cycling. Tests for these processes are discussed in Sect. 4.2.

(4) Other animals. No competition tests are recommended for competition among nonarthropod animals. Nematodes approach the arthropods in ecological importance, but they are difficult to identify and are therefore poor candidates for a population test. Vertebrates are obviously important, but testing for effects on competition between populations of even the smallest species (as opposed to simple behavioral interactions) would require an excessively large area and long time period.

4.1.2 Herbivore-Plant

This section considers herbivorous insects feeding on flowering plants. These two groups dominate the earth's biota, accounting for more than 60% of procaryotic species (Gilbert 1979). Insects account for the great preponderance of herbivory, rivaled only by ungulates in semiarid grasslands. Ungulate herbivory, for obvious reasons, is not considered for laboratory test systems.

While herbivores may act as predators (by killing individual plants) or as overtly mutualistic symbionts, most herbivores are functionally analogous to parasites, consuming the tissues or fluids of the host plant without directly killing it (Gilbert 1979). It has been hypothesized that consumption of plant parts by herbivores generally increases the overall fitness of the host plants (Owen and Wiegert 1976); the success of programs to control exotic weeds by importing herbivorous insects from the weed's area of origin suggests that such cryptomutualism is not the rule. Certainly, intensive agricultural and sylvicultural practices tend to uncouple such mutualistic relationships, resulting in highly "virulent" herbivores. Nevertheless, the fact that herbivorous insects can modify the allocation of plant resources in ways that are not always detrimental (Harris 1973) suggests that net plant production must be measured by tissue type and age to understand herbivore effects.

Herbivores that feed on vegetation can be divided into chewing and sucking types. Sucking insects have several advantages as test organisms: (1) they are typically small, and many of them can be crowded on a single plant; (2) many of them are either immobile or relatively inactive except during dispersal phases; (3) they are highly sensitive to changes in plant physiology as reflected in sap chemistry; (4) many of them produce several generations per year; and (5) most economically important species have several known predators that may be added to the system (Sect. 4.1.3). While these insects may be highly sensitive to chemicals that are taken up by the plant (witness the efficiency of systemic pesticides), they would be insensitive to chemicals deposited on the leaf surface. For such chemicals, an external chewing insect test system would be required.

Because of the relatively long life cycles of flowering plants, herbivore-plant population interaction tests would probably be limited to growing the plant through seed set. Even with this reduction in scope, there are no apparent existing laboratory systems for this interaction (effects of herbivory over one full life cycle of the plant). Population ecologists have avoided the problems of maintaining live plants by using insects that can be raised on inert media (e.g., Drosophila and Tribolium). Agricultural and ecosystem entomologists typically raise insects on stems or individual leaves of plants when determining consumption rates or pesticide response. Whole-plant cages (Adams and Van Emden 1972) are seldom used, in part because of effects of the cage on light, humidity, and other environmental conditions. Large (>0.5 m^2) cages that contain several potted plants probably provide better conditions, but if each plant is to be treated as a replicate, nonflying insects must be used, and mobile forms such as apterous aphids must be constrained by barriers (Adams and Van Emden 1972). Because the great majority of studies of plant-herbivore interactions are conducted in the field, there is little experience with these laboratory systems. <u>Test systems would need to be largely developed from scratch, but there do not appear to be major technical problems.</u>

The life cycles of many herbivorous insects are sufficiently long and complex that most insects and the plants could not practically be raised through multiple life cycles in routine tests. Indicator tests that only include the activities of certain life stages might be developed for those population interactions. These tests must be chosen to include stages in development that are likely to be sensitive to a variety of chemicals (ecdysis may be an example) and those stages that are sensitive to the resistance mechanisms of the host plants. Antibiotic plant defensive mechanisms act at various stages in the life cycle of the insect to inhibit growth, reduce survival, disrupt development, or reduce reproduction (Waiss et al. 1977). Test chemicals may reduce or enhance host plant resistance.

This section emphasizes herbivores using domestic plants because (1) these species are well known, (2) the plants are easily cultivated, (3) many of the insects can be obtained from culture (Dickerson et al. 1980) and maintained on defined artificial diets, and (4) their social relevance is obvious. Highly coevolved herbivore-plant species pairs from natural communities may, however, prove to be more sensitive and more representative of the majority of the earth's biota. This possibility should be considered during development of advanced test systems.

(1) <u>Sucking Insect-Plant</u>. While some hemipterans are important herbivores, the majority of sucking herbivorous insects are homopterans. As previously mentioned, these insects have several advantages as test organisms. The herbivore-plant species pairs discussed in this section were selected primarily on the basis of a recent workshop held at ORNL (Suter 1981a).

(a) <u>Aphid-alfalfa</u>. The spotted alfalfa aphid (<u>Therioaphis trifolli</u>) is an important pest of alfalfa in California and other western states. <u>It is a good candidate for a test system to represent this class of interactions because it involves an economically important host plant that can be easily and rapidly grown.</u> The system could be readily extended to include predators [Sect. 4.1.3(2)], and it might be possible to create an aphid competition test by adding the pea aphid (<u>Acyrthosiphon pisum</u>), which is also a pest of alfalfa in California. While no suitable experimental or testing system has been demonstrated for these species, it should be relatively easy to adapt the techniques of mass rearing aphids on potted alfalfa seedlings (Finney et al. 1960) to testing by using whole-plant cages.

(b) <u>Aphid-grain</u>. Individual, whole-plant cages were used by Windle and Franz (1979) in a study of the effects of greenbugs (<u>Schizaphis graminum</u>) on competition between barley varieties. Greenbugs, a chronic pest of small grains, caused a reversal in competitive dominance as measured by the crowding coefficient [Sect. 4.1.1(2)] in aphid-resistant and susceptible varieties. Effects of aphids on plant production were demonstrated within 2 weeks, but the effect changed from positive to negative between weeks 2 and 6.

(c) <u>Whitefly-plant</u>. The greenhouse whitefly (<u>Trialeurodes vaporariorum</u>) is an important pest of greenhouse crops with over 200 host plants. The relevance of this system to greenhouse culture is both its chief advantage and its chief disadvantage. The test and real world conditions are identical, but whiteflies are insignificant in the United States outside of greenhouses and citrus groves. The greenhouse whitefly can be raised on potted beans, cotton, tomatoes, or any of its many other host plants. It has a generation time of 21 days at 20°C, which includes a crawler stage of the first instar, scale-like second and third instars, a "pupa" and winged adult. Although whole greenhouses have been used as experimental units in whitefly control studies, a test system would use whole-plant cages (Nechols and Tauber 1977).

(d) Scale-plant. Scale insects (Coccoidea) present considerable advantages for determining life table data because of their sessile nature and the record of mortality provided by the shells. The brown soft scale (Coccus hesperidum) uses citrus and other tropical and subtropical trees and a large variety of greenhouse plants. Its development may be completed in 26 days at 27°C, and the primarily parthenogenic females may produce over 200 progeny (Saakyan-Baranova 1964). This scale is easily maintained in the laboratory on Coleus or Begonia.

(2) Chewing insect-plant. Chewing herbivores, primarily Coleoptera, Lepidoptera, and Orthoptera, are ecologically and economically important and represent a distinct mode of plant-insect-chemical interaction. Most of them are difficult to maintain in the laboratory over multiple generations because the adults are relatively large and highly mobile and have different requirements from the larvae. Because many of them are also voracious, they would require relatively large plants to moderate herbivory to a level at which plant responses could be measured.

No clearly preferable insect-plant species pair for this test system exists. A recent workshop recommended that tests for chewing herbivore-plant interactions should utilize the corn earworm (cotton bollworm, tomato fruit worm, Heliothis zea) and possibly the corn rootworm, japanese beetle, Cactoblastis, gypsy moth, and a grasshopper because they are well studied, economically important, and have documented exploiters (Suter 1981a). The corn earworm could be easily cultured because it is hearty and euryphagous, but it is fairly large and is probably insensitive to pesticides and other chemicals. Some other species such as the gypsy moth and Cactoblastis are relatively unsuitable because they use slowly growing hosts. The alfalfa caterpillar (Colias eurytheme) and green cloverworm (Plathypena scabra) are somewhat smaller important species which consume alfalfa, an easily and rapidly grown herb.

The fact that the young and the adults share the same habitat gives grasshoppers and other orthoptera an advantage over lepidoptera. Some beetles, such as the Mexican bean beetle (Epilachna varivestis), share this advantage even though they are homometabolous and small.

The physical test system for this relationship in most cases must be some sort of whole-plant cage. Dyer and Bokhari (1976) maintained individual grasshoppers (Melanoplus sanguinipes) for 18 days in single plant cages containing hydroponic blue grama grass (Bouteloua gracilis). Larger cages containing several plants will be required for true studies of population interactions. Soil-dwelling herbivores such as the corn rootworm can be maintained in pots or even in plastic pouches (Ortman and Branson 1976). Nonflying insects may be isolated by placing a sticky trap around each plant (Robinson et al. 1978). This technique provides a measure of emigration which could indicate a change in herbivore preference.

4.1.3 Predator-Prey

Predation is often defined functionally as all forms of exploitation that regularly result in death of the exploited species. That definition is used here except for herbivory because herbivory is predominately nonlethal. The definition includes parasitoids and microbial "parasites" such as Bdellovibrio, but not pathogens and true parasites, which typically do not kill or consume a large fraction of an individual host.

Predator effectiveness is the product of the predation rate and the population growth rate of the herbivore and behavioral response to predation. Predation rates are the product of changes in predator density (numerical responses) and the predation rate per individual (functional responses) (Solomon 1949). Most laboratory studies of terrestrial predation are concerned with the components of the functional response, searching rate, capture rate, handling time, and satiation. Numerical responses are relatively neglected because of the difficulty of maintaining predators and prey together in the laboratory for multiple generations. Prey species are typically presented to the predator under circumstances that do not permit an appropriate behavioral response by the prey; they very seldom reproduce in the experimental system, and they may even be replaced by artificial prey (e.g., Holling 1966; Gardner 1966).

(1) Microbe-microbe. While most studies of microbes that kill and consume other microbes are concerned with protozoan predators, the predatory habit is also practiced by a variety of bacteria and fungi. Microbial predation may be considered beneficial if the prey is a plant pathogen (e.g., Habte and Alexander 1975) or detrimental if it is a beneficial species such as Rhizobium (e.g., Danso et al. 1975).

Because of the relative difficulty of quantitatively extracting and enumerating microbes in soil, it is recommended that any tests involving enumeration of microbial predators and prey be conducted in aquatic systems. Predation on plant pathogens can be evaluated in terms of the presence of plant pathology. The best example of this type of system is the control of Rhizoctonia solani through destruction of its sclerotia by Tricoderma harzisnum. A test protocol for this system using damping-off of radishes as the measured response has been tentatively proposed (Suter 1981a). Respiration and transformation of mineral nutrients by prey organisms have also been used as indicators of the effects of microbial predators (e.g., Telegdy-Kovats 1932). These responses are discussed as ecosystem processes [Sect. 4.2.5 (4)].

(2) *Arthropod-predators*. Traditionally defined predators kill their prey before consuming them or kill them by consuming them rather rapidly. Parasitoids differ in that they kill their host (prey) by consuming them over a relatively long time. It has been argued on theoretical grounds that parasitoids are better adapted than most other predators to control the populations of herbivorous insects (Doutt and DeBach 1964). This argument is borne out by the predominance of parasitoids in successful insect biocontrol programs. Therefore, parasitoids are emphasized in this section.

The relatively high sensitivity of arthropod predators to pesticides suggests that they may provide sensitive toxicological tests. Pesticide applications commonly eliminate arthropod predators, often resulting in the creation of secondary pests and the resurgence of primary pests to greater abundance than before treatment. The effectiveness of a predator as a biocontrol agent can be verified in the field by applying pesticides at concentrations that eliminate the predator without damaging the prey populations (DeBach and Huffaker 1971). The effectiveness of predation may be even more sensitive than predator mortality.

Laboratory studies of predators as potential biocontrol agents generally are not concerned with the population biology of the predator and prey species. Population interactions are studied in the field. Laboratory studies of the relative toxicity of pesticides to predators and prey generally measure mortality rather than effects on the predation process. Therefore, laboratory test systems for arthropod predator-prey population interactions cannot readily be adapted from existing experimental systems for biocontrol agents. As a rule, ecological experiments use easily manipulated, interesting, or unusual species (Sects. (a), (e), and (f) below) rather than important species.

Searching capacity has been found to be the most important indicator of the ability of predators in biocontrol programs to maintain pest populations below an economic threshold (Huffaker et al. 1971). Therefore, some basis for using predation rate as an indicator of predator-prey population interactions exists. Nevertheless, tests that only use predation rate or its components should be supported by studies of true population interactions.

(a) *Parasitoid-gall midge*. The California endemic midge *Rhopalomyia californica* (Cecidomyiidae) that forms galls on *Baccharis pilularis* is attacked by 12 species of hymenopteran parasitoids.

Force (1970, 1974) has performed field and laboratory investigations of this "community" to elucidate the means by which this diversity of parasitoids is maintained and its effect on the midge. The community experiments are performed in 48- by 38- by 40-cm screened cages with 40 Bacharis seedlings in small pots. The cages are kept in a greenhouse. The midge and the six parasitoid species used in these experiments are not available from culture, but they are readily obtained by collecting galls and are easily maintained in the laboratory. The life cycles of three parasitoids investigated are 27, 38, and 46 days.

Six species of parasitoids can be maintained together in a cage for at least 100 days. The outcome is determined by details of the biology of the parasitoids, including restraint from and success in superparasitism, multiparasitism, and hyperparasitism. This system is particularly well developed for studying population interactions between parasitoid competitors and between parasitoids and their host. It does not represent an economically important species association, and none of the biological constituents are commercially available. The physical system of large, whole-plant cages could serve as a model for test systems using other species.

(b) Parasitoid-whitefly. Since the 1920s the parasitoid Encarsia formosa has been used as a biocontrol agent for the greenhouse whitefly (Helgesen and Tauber 1974). At 18°C the fecundity of the whitefly is 10 times as great as that of Encarsia although the rate of development is equal; at 26°C the fecundity is equal, and the rate of development of the parasitoid is twice that of the whitefly (Hussey and Bravenboer 1971). Encarsia attacks the scale larvae of the whitefly, and parasitized scales are blackened and therefore readily recognized. Encarsia completes its life cycle in 2 to 4 weeks. This species pair is well studied; its dynamics in the greenhouse are relatively predictable (Burnett 1967), and the parasitoid is commercially available.

(c) Parasitoid-aphid. Three parasitoids of the spotted alfalfa aphid, Praon exsoletum (P. palitans), Trioxys complanatus (T. utilis), and Aphelinus asychis (A. semiflavus), have been the subjects of intensive laboratory study. Force and Messenger's (1964a and b, 1965) system of alfalfa stem "bouquets" in 3.5- by 15-cm glass tubes was designed to study the effects of physical conditions on the life history parameters of the parasitoids and on larval parasitoid competition. This system permits examination of parasitoid development and hunting efficiency of the adults although searching is minimized by the small chambers. A larger system with whole plants would permit examination of true population interactions and would permit studies of searching. Chemicals might affect the outcome of competition resulting from multiple parasitism, or they might diminish the ability of A. asychis to discriminate parasitized hosts.

(d) *Predator-aphid.* The best-studied predators of aphids are coccinellid (ladybird) beetles. Populations of the spotted alfalfa aphid are reduced by native coccinellid predators of the genera *Hyspodamia* and *Coccinella*. These predators have been the subject of considerable field investigation (Hagen, van den Bosch, and Dahlsten 1971) and would contribute to the completeness of a test system based on alfalfa and the spotted alfalfa aphid.

Laboratory studies of predation by coccinellids on aphids have been conducted using *C. septempunctata* on *Acyrithasiphon pisum* and *Aphis fabae* (Murdoch and Marks 1973) and *Adalia bipunctata* on *Drepanosiphon platanoides* (Dixon 1970), but these studies do not include full life cycles. Several species of coccinellids are commercially available.

Other aphid predators that could be used in a test system include green lacewings (*Chrysopa*), syrphid flies (*Syrphus*, *Metasyrphus*, etc.), and damsel bugs (*Nabis*). These predators are not as well studied or as readily available as coccinellids.

(e) *Parasitoid-grain moth.* Species of Lepidoptera from five families infest stored grains, pulses, nuts, and their products (Benson 1973). They are attacked by parasitoids from five families of Hymenoptera and one species of Diptera. Because of the economic importance of grain insects and their ease of manipulation in the laboratory, they have been the subjects of many laboratory studies.

Parasitoid-grain moth experimental systems consist of sets of replicate chambers, ranging in size from 0.005 to 13.8 m^3. Several containers of grain or other substrate are placed in the chambers with moths and parasitoids. The life cycles of a typical moth *Ephesta (Anagasta) kuhniella* and parasitoid *Exidechthis canescens* are 41 to 106 days and 21 to 33 days, respectively, at 27°C. The system could be elaborated by incorporating multiple prey and parasitoid species or the oophagous mite *Blattisocius*.

Because the parasitoids discover prey by probing the substrate with the ovipositers, searching efficiency is the key factor in the parasitoid population even in small (0.61-m^3) chambers (Benson 1973). By providing refuges for the moth larvae, the system can be made to persist for 2 years or more in 0.13-m^3 chambers (Flanders and Badgley 1963). Thus, the system lends itself to tests of both predation rate and true population interactions. This system has considerable advantages because of extensive previous laboratory study and ease of manipulation resulting from the use of grain rather than whole plants to support the herbivore. The chief disadvantage of the system is that it is only directly relevant to grain storage. While the mechanisms of parasitoid-host interaction may be sufficiently uniform to permit generalization from this system, chemically treated grain would not be directly analogous to any important mode of ecosystem contamination.

(f) <u>Parasitoid-bean weevil</u>. Another set of important and rather extensive laboratory studies of predation are those conducted by Syunro Utida on the parasitoids of the azuki bean weevil (<u>Callosobruchus chinensis</u>) (summarized in Utida 1957). Bean weevils were raised on azuki beans in petri dishes and exposed to the braconid parasitoid <u>Heterospilus prosopidis</u>, alone or in competition with the chalcid parasitoid, <u>Neocatolaccus namezophagus</u>. To study population fluctuations, Utida counted the populations at 7- to 10-day intervals and ran the experiments for several months. Generation time for the bean weevils is three weeks. <u>As a potential test system, this experimental system shares the advantages and disadvantages of the parasitoid grain moth system already described</u>. While the azuki bean weevil is not readily available in the United States, a similar system has recently been developed utilizing another bean weevil (<u>Zabrotes subfasciatus</u>) with the parasitoids <u>H</u>. <u>prosopidis</u> and <u>Anisopteromalus calandrae</u> (Kistler 1980).

(g) <u>Parasitoid-fly</u>. This system was developed by David Pimentel to investigate the mechanisms of predator-prey coexistence. The system consists of an array of 1, 16, or 30 plastic boxes connected by plastic tubes (Pimentel et al. 1963). The boxes contain vials of medium on which houseflies (<u>Musca domestica</u>), blowflies (<u>Phaenicia sericata</u>), bluebottle flies (<u>Phormia regina</u>), or greenbottle flies (<u>Phaenicia sericata</u>) are raised. These serve as prey for the hymenopteran parasitoid <u>Nasonia vitripennis</u>. The predation rate of another fly pupa parasitoid (<u>Muscidifurax raptor</u>) has been studied relative to <u>N</u>. <u>vitripennis</u> (DeBach and Smith 1941) and could be used as a competitor in this system. The housefly, blowfly, and <u>Nasonia</u> have life cycles of 13, 14, and 14 days respectively. These three species are commercially available.

This system is similar to the parasitoid-grain moth system because its population ecology is relatively well known, and it is based on a medium that is convenient, but not directly relevant to field conditions. Searching efficiency of the parasitoid is not an important factor in the system as constituted so it is not useful for tests on predation rate. This system emphasizes the coevolution of fecundity of the parasitoid and resistance of the fly. It would be difficult, however, to demonstrate that coevolution was reduced by a chemical.

Such a system could be developed using <u>Drosophila</u> and the parasitoid <u>Pseudeucoila bochei</u>. Use of these species should allow some miniaturization of the system. In addition, there has been far more experience with <u>Drosophila</u> than with houseflies or blowflies.

(h) <u>Ground-dwelling beetle-prey</u>. Staphylinid and carabid beetles are common predators of ground-dwelling arthropods and molluscs. While these beetles have been shown in the field to be important predators of a variety of insect pests, few laboratory studies have been performed on them.

Harris and Oliver (1979) examined predation by the staphylinid *Philonthus creunatus* on the eggs and larvae of the hornfly *Haematobia irritans*. Hornfly eggs were placed on manure pats, which were placed on either a soil-vermiculite mixture or a section of sod. Beetles were added in varying densities, and the emerging flies were counted. While this system appears to realistically simulate the field situation, it was sustained for less than a full generation of either the predator or prey. Because the beetles primarily consume the egg stage of the fly, behavior of the prey is not an important component of the system, and chemical exposure of the prey should begin before the predation test.

Small carabids such as *Notiophilus* can consume collembola in simple arenas (Eijsackers 1978). Because collembola can be raised on plaster, charcoal, and yeast, a test of predation behavior could be easily developed. A population test would require soil for the immature carabids, which would considerably complicate enumeration of both prey and predator.

Because neither of these systems for predator-prey interactions using ground-dwelling beetles appears promising, development is not recommended. It should be possible to introduce these predators into Pimentel's fly system [Sects. 4.1.1(3) and 4.1.3(2)] to test the generality of the responses observed.

(i) *Spider-prey*. Although spiders are major predators in many natural ecosystems, interest in their role as predators has been limited because they have not been shown to control outbreaks of insect pests. Laboratory studies of spider predation have been concerned with spider behavior; those that study the functional response to prey density most closely approximate a population interaction test (Haynes and Sisojevic 1966; Gardner 1966; Hardman and Turnbull 1974). *Drosophila*, which were used as prey in these studies, are easily obtained and cultured, but spiders are not commercially available, and techniques for rearing spiders are only now being developed.

(j) *Mite-mite*. Unlike insect predators and prey, herbivorous and predatory mites have been well studied as interacting populations in realistic laboratory conditions (Table 4.1). This is probably due, in large part, to Huffaker and Kennett's (1956) demonstration that the dynamics of mite predatory-prey interactions in strawberry fields are adequately simulated by laboratory studies. Most of these experimental systems consist of mites on arrays of potted plants in a greenhouse or environmental chamber, with water or grease barriers used to isolate treatments or individual plants within treatments. Although the mites are counted in sample leaves or plants, the outcome is typically described in terms of control (the herbivore population reaches levels that damage the plant). The control of a herbivore by a predator depends not only on the pair of species used but also on physical conditions, the characteristics of the host plant, and the input ratio of the predator and prey. Systems

TABLE 4.1. LABORATORY STUDIES OF MITE-MITE PREDATION

Study	Predator	Prey	Host
Huffaker and Kennett 1956	Typhlodromus cucumeris T. reticulatus	Tarsonemus pallidus	Strawberry
Huffaker 1958, Huffaker et al. 1963	Typhlodromus occidentalis	Eotetranychus sexmaxulatus	Oranges
Collyer 1958	Typhlodromus tiliae	Panonychus ulmi	Prunus sp.
Chant 1961	Phytoseiulus persimilis	Tetranychus telarius	Red kidney bean
Herbert 1962	Typhlodromus pyri	Bryobia arboria	Apple
Van de Vrie 1962	Typhlodromus tiliae T. tiliarum	Panonychus ulmi	Apple
Collyer 1964	Typhlodromus pyri T. finlandicus	Aculus fockeui Panonychus ulmi	Bullace
Hussey et al. 1965	Phytoseiglus riegeli	Tetranychus urticae	Cucumber
McMurtry and Scriven 1968	Amblyseius hibisci	Oligonychus punicae	Avocado
Burnett 1970	Amblyseius fallacis	Tetranychus urticae	Alfalfa

that are near the balance point between control and escape of the prey might be highly sensitive to chemical perturbations. The test might be scored on the basis of the presence or absence of large numbers of mites. For most of the systems listed in Table 4.1, this outcome would be reached in less than a month.

Huffaker's system of predator and prey mites on oranges (Huffaker et al. 1963) had considerable heuristic value in the development of ecology. This system is, however, much more difficult to relate to the real world than a system on plants, and its elaborate array of 252 partially covered oranges was difficult to establish and maintain.

(3) <u>Vertebrate predators</u>. Holling's (1959) laboratory studies of the functional response of deer mice (<u>Peromyscus maniculatus</u>) hunting pine sawfly (<u>Neodiprion sertifler</u>) cocoons were important to the development of the theory of predation. Similar studies of predatory behavior in enclosed arenas have since been conducted using a variety of other vertebrates (e.g., Craig 1978). <u>This type of system is not a good candidate for protocol development because relatively large arenas are required (3 by 1.2 by 1.8 m in Holling's case), population responses are not included, and behavioral effects of chemicals on vertebrates are already being tested in relation to human health effects</u>.

4.1.4 Host-Parasite

The experimental determination of effects of chemicals on host-parasite interaction has been treated as a rather complex, single-species problem. In one view, the parasite is considered as a second stress that, like thermal shock, modifies the intensity of the host's response to the chemical. Alternatively, chemicals are treated as potential drugs that may rid the host of the parasite. In neither case are the host and parasite treated as a system of interacting populations. This situation partly reflects a general lack of interest by experimental ecologists in parasitism relative to other types of population interactions as a result of the apparent absence of an experimentally tractable conceptual scale. The appropriate scale for laboratory population experiments lies somewhere between the microscale of medical physiology, described above, and the macroscale at which epidemiologists model or monitor the spread of infection and the evolution of virulence and resistance.

<u>Even if a laboratory host-parasite population system were found or developed, it would not necessarily be a good test system</u>. Because host-parasite relations are highly intimate and coevolved, their dynamics are dominated by peculiarities of structure and physiology that are not readily generalized.

For these reasons, host-parasite population interactions are not considered further in this document. Parasites of insects and plants that might be developed as traditional tests for effects on virulence are discussed in the report of a recent ORNL workshop (Suter 1981a).

4.1.5 Symbiosis

Symbiotic relationships are defined as those which benefit at least one of the partner species without harming either; these include Odum's (1971) commensalism, mutualism, and protocooperation. Because of the great diversity of ways in which one species may benefit another, the mechanisms of symbiosis are probably less uniform than those of most other classes of population interactions. They range from very intimate obligate relationships such as the termite-intestinal flagellate relationship to the rather loose commensal relationships such as phoresy.

This section deals primarily with the symbiotic relationships between higher plants and mycorrhizal and nitrogen-fixing microorganisms. Because these relationships are ubiquitous and important to primary production, they have the broadest relevance and greatest ecological and social importance of any symbiotic relationship. Lichens are considerably less important, but are obvious candidates for a testing protocol because of their use in air pollution monitoring.

(1) __Lichens__. Although many of the algal and fungal symbionts that form lichens are capable of independent existence, the symbiotic unit is functionally and reproductively distinct from its constituents. The existence of an independent taxonomic nomenclature for lichens reflects the proto-organismal character of lichens. Because lichen tests are performed by collecting whole lichens rather than by bringing together the constituent symbionts (a difficult and seldom successful procedure), lichen tests are procedurally identical to single-species tests. Therefore, it can be argued that lichens do not constitute a multispecies test system.

Lichens are highly sensitive to gaseous air pollutants, particularly SO_2 (Ferry et al. 1973). They may also be sensitive to organic vapors and aerosols. Lichen tests are performed by exposing a piece of thallus that has been activated by wetting to the chemical vapor or aerosol. Potential response parameters include respiration, photosynthesis growth, pigmentation, potassium loss, and death.

(2) __Rhizobium-legume__. Although nitrogen fixation is carried out by a variety of free-living microbes and microbes living symbiotically with higher plants (Alexander 1971), the __Rhizobium__-legume symbiosis is the predominate source of fixed nitrogen in terrestrial ecosystems. Because of the agricultural importance of legumes, numerous tests have been conducted to determine the effects of agricultural chemicals on __Rhizobium__-legume symbiosis. Because the sensitivity of in vitro __rhizobia__ is poorly correlated with sensitivity of the whole plant-microbe system (Lin et al. 1972, Fisher 1976, and Fisher et al.

1978), only whole-system tests should be considered. Rhizobia-inoculated seeds or sprouts can be grown on agar slants or in soil or artificial media (vermiculite, sand, etc.). The growth medium can significantly influence response to a chemical. Because simple media such as vermiculite may decrease rather than increase the sensitivity of the test without reducing variability (Smith et al. 1978), soil should be used as the growth medium for the sake of realism.

The ultimate socially relevant response of this system is productivity of the legume partner. Parameters that may be measured include weight of plant parts, number and weight of propagules, frequency of flowering, stem elongation, and damage symptoms. Nitrogen content of plant parts provides an integrative measure of nitrogen fixation and is also an indicator of forage quality. Direct indicators of the symbiotic relationship include the number, position, size, and color of nodules; leghaemoglobin content; and nitrogen fixation rate of the whole system or of excised roots or nodules. None of these parameters are clearly more sensitive to toxicants than the others (Table 4.2), and most are easily determined. The N fixation rate and plant N content determinations require some analytic sophistication, but at least one of these parameters should be determined as an indication of the effectiveness of the nodules.

The few time-course studies shown in Table 5.2 indicate that sensitivity of the system generally diminishes with time. This may be simply explained by degradation of the test chemical and adaptation of the symbionts, or it may be the result of reduction in sensitivity of the symbiont pair with age. Letchworth and Blum (1977) found that sensitivity of clover top weight and number of nodules to ozone decreased with the age at which the plants were exposed. Nodulation of the first root (crown nodules) is more variable than nodulation of lateral roots (Tu 1977) and thus may be more sensitive to toxicants. <u>Therefore, a short-term test using legume seedlings may be sensitive and may indicate the potential for interference problems with establishment and reproduction of legumes</u>. A more realistic test for pasture legumes and natural legumes would be provided by the fescue-clover competition system discussed in Sect. 4.1.1(2), but this system is less well developed.

(3) <u>Mycorrhizae</u>. Most flowering plants form mycorrhizal associations with fungi. The primary benefit ascribed to mycorrhizae is enhanced uptake of phosphorus. Mycorrhizae may also enhance uptake of other nutrients and water and protect the plant from root diseases. While the mycorrhizal association is generally beneficial to the higher symbiont, under certain environmental conditions, mycorrhizae may be neutral or even parasitic. Chemicals may not only deprive plants of the benefits of mycorrhizal symbiosis, but may modify the symbiotic nature of the association.

The benefits of this association can be measured directly in terms of the quantity and quality of plant production. The

TABLE 4.2. RELATIVE FREQUENCY OF SIGNIFICANT RESPONSES BY PARAMETERS OF THE RHIZOBIUM-LEGUME SYMBIOSIS TO TOXIC CHEMICALS

Study	Legume weight Top	Legume weight Roots	Legume weight Total	Damage	Seed production	Flowering	Stem elongation	N content of the legume	Total nodules	Nodule size	Leghaemoglobin content	% infection	N fixation
Pareek and Gaur 1970	$0/6^a$ (28)^b				0/6 (28)			$2/6^+$ (28) $3/6^-$	$1/6^+$ (28) $2/6^-$		$3/6^+$ (28) $3/6^-$		
DDT	$4/6^-$ (49)				$1/6^+$ (49) $3/6^-$			$5/6^-$ (49)	$2/6^+$ (49) $4/6^-$		$3/6^+$ (49) $3/6^-$		
Selim et al. 1970 Dieldrin and Lindane	$2/4^-$ (60)	$2/4^-$ (60)	$2/4^-$ (60)			$4/4^-$ (60)	$1/4^-$ (60)	$2/4^-$ (60)	$4/4^-$ (60)	$2/4^-$ (60)			
Carlyle and Thorpe 1947 2-4, D (Na and NH$_3$ salts)				$15/24^+$ (134)					$23/24^-$ (34)				
Letchworth and Blum 1977: O$_3$	$2/2^-$ (7-28)	$2/2^-$ (7-28)						$2/2^-$ (7-28)	$2/2^-$ (7-28)			0/2 (7-28)	
Grossbard 1970: 4 herbicides			$1/6^+$	0/6				$1/6^+$				$2/6^-$	
Tu 1978 3 insecticides and 4 combinations	$4/7^-$ (21) 0/7 (56)	$5/7^-$ (21) 0/7 (56)							$4/7^-$ (21) 0/7 (56)				$6/7^-$ (21) 0/7 (56)

TABLE 4.2 (continued)

Study	Legume weight Top	Legume weight Roots	Legume weight Total	Damage	Seed production	Flowering	Stem elongation	N content of the legume	Total nodules	Nodule size	Leghaemoglobin content	% infection	N fixation
Fisher et al. 1978 8 surfactant fungicides	12/15$^-$ (56) 3/15$^-$ (84)												8/15$^-$ (56) 4/15$^-$ (84)
Maning, Feder and Papia 1972: O_3	1/1$^-$ (20) 1/1 (60)	1/1$^-$ (20) 1/1 (60)			1/1$^-$ (20) 1/1 (60)		1/1$^-$ (20) 1/1 (60)		1/1$^-$ (20) 1/1 (60)	1/1$^-$ (20) 1/1 (60)			
Fisher 1976: 8 fungicides			0/16 (77)					0/16 (77)			0/14 (77)		1/14$^+$ 2/14$^-$ (77)
Smith et al. 1978 7 pesticides				26/112$^+$ (21)								61/112$^-$ (21)	
Kulkarni et al. 1974 4 insecticides				0/4 (56)		0/4 (56)		0/4 (56)	4/4$^-$ (56)	0/4 (56)	0/4 (56)		

^{a}The fraction indicates the number of significant responses out of the total number of combinations of toxicants and soils. The sign (+ or -) indicates that the parameter increased or decreased.

^{b}Numbers in parentheses indicate the number of days after addition of the chemicals that responses were measured.

mycorrhizal association itself can be examined according to the extent of infection. Ectomycorrhizal infection can be readily evaluated in terms of the amount of root covered with a mycelial mantle. Endomycorrhizae do not significantly modify the appearance of infected roots and therefore must be evaluated microscopically. Preparation techniques have been developed by Ambler and Young (1977) and Kormanik et al. (1980). These techniques are used to measure percent infection and the frequency of arbuscules and vesicles. These measures of infection are likely to respond more rapidly than plant production to a chemical that affects the association and may be more sensitive than plant production. The large clamydospores of endomycorrhizae are readily removed by wet sieving, but clamydospore production is less sensitive than root infection to pesticides (Menge et al. 1979). Of 39 combinations of crops and pesticides, 24 resulted in reduced endomycorrhizal infection (Menge et al. 1979).

It may also be possible to develop a test system based on the ability of mycorrhizae to suppress root diseases. Mycorrhizae may inhibit pathogens (1) by producing antibiotics, (2) by stimulating the root to produce antibiotics, (3) by modifying root exudates, or (4) by forming a physical barrier to infection (Marx 1969). A root disease that produced a rapid visible response and that was suppressed by mycorrhizae would form an easily scored and possibly sensitive test system.

Because of the taxonomic, functional, and structural differences between endomycorrhizae and ectomycorrhizae, test systems should be developed for both types of associations. The difference in sensitivity between the two types is unknown, but endomycorrhizae recover more slowly because they do not form airborne spores. Tentative protocols for *Pisolithus tinctorius* and loblolly pine (ectomycorrhizae) and *Glomus* spp. and a grass (endomycorrhizae) have been proposed by participants in a recent workshop at ORNL (Suter 1981a). These protocols call for rather long test runs (105 and 84 days), but it may be possible to distinguish effects of chemicals on infection rates more rapidly. Any test system that includes a plant can serve as a test for the mycorrhizal association if suitable inoculum is included. Any phytotoxicity test that uses nonmycorrhizal plants is likely to give results that are irrelevant to field conditions.

4.1.6 Community Composition

The properties that are unique to the community level of organization include species composition, succession, food web structure, species turnover rate, and diversity. Multicellular plants and macroinvertebrate and vertebrate animals are too large and long-lived to display these properties in the laboratory. Microbes and microinvertebrates, as previously mentioned, are difficult to extract quantitatively, identify, and enumerate. Because the soil community's composition is not sufficiently important relative to its function to justify a difficult and expensive test, no tests for terrestrial community properties are recommended.

4.1.7 Summary

While terrestrial ecosystem-level responses to chemicals have received some attention (Sect. 4.2), population interactions have been neglected. The only interactions that have received significant toxicological attention and therefore could be adopted in the near term as TSCA test standards are the legume-rhizobia and mycorrhizal fungus-plant associations. Development is needed to arrive at acceptable protocols for these symbiotic associations because there has been no consistency in the techniques used to date. The test systems suggested in a recent ORNL workshop (Suter 1981a) would be a good starting point. In addition, the opinions expressed at that workshop and in Sect. 4.1.5 concerning appropriate response parameters must be confirmed by systematic testing with reference chemicals. The economic and ecological importance of these plant-microbe associations makes development of these tests highly desirable.

Drosophila and Tribolium competition, Pimentel's fly and wasp systems, and the parasitoid-grain moth system constitute a second class of potential test systems. These are highly developed experimental systems, which could be readily implemented but for which there is no toxicological experience. These systems may be quite sensitive, but their ability to generate relevant predictions is questionable. Because these systems are relatively well understood and fairly easily operated, they might be examined concurrently with the developing test protocols to better understand the way in which chemicals affect general classes of population interactions.

Finally, there is a group of potential test systems that is neither well studied toxicologically nor well developed as experimental systems, but that appears worthy of long-term development. This category includes general interactions: plant competition, herbivory, and predation. The best candidate for a plant competition test is clover-grass because of its economic importance, its seminatural character, and the work done on its response to ozone. No strong bases for selecting a particular species of host plant and a sucking or chewing insect for herbivory tests exist. For the reasons listed in Sect. 4.1.2, small homoptera appear to be good subjects for a population interaction test. Hymenopteran parasitoids are the best candidates for the predators in a predator-prey test because they are small, important as biocontrol agents, and well studied. While the parasitoid-grain moth and fly systems are relatively well studied and easily maintained, a system involving parasitoids of homoptera raised on whole plants should be much more representative of natural and agronomic systems. A similarly realistic test for conventional predators would include a coccinellid or neuropteran predator and a homopteran prey raised on whole plants. Mite predator-prey systems are relatively well developed, compact, and rapid. They would be

<u>ideal test systems if they can be shown to be representative of insects as well as mites</u>.

The potential for combining categories of tests is obvious. One can easily imagine, for example, a test system involving competition between clover and grass that is inoculated with <u>Rhizobium</u> and mycorrhizae and that supports competing herbivores and predators. Such a system would have considerable appeal as a highly inclusive and realistic screening test, but simpler systems would be necessary to explain the cause of the observed responses.

The use of any of these tests for broad predictions of ecological effects will depend on a considerable increase in our knowledge of the nature of ecological processes. Some bases for that knowledge will result from the process of test development.

4.2 Ecosystem Properties

The two basic processes which are characteristic of ecosystems are the cycling of nutrient elements and the capture and transfer of energy. While chemical contaminants may modify the physical and chemical components of these processes by affecting soil pH or by chelating metal ions, TSCA chemicals are unlikely to occur in the environment at concentrations sufficient to have significant direct effects on soil chemistry unless large spills occur. Effects on the terrestrial biota are likely to be far more significant.

This section discusses the parameters measured in tests for effects on nutrient dynamics, primary production, and saprophytic metabolism in terrestrial ecosystems. Nonsaprophytic secondary production is not considered because it is much less readily measured as a whole ecosystem characteristic than as a component of specific population interactions (Sect. 4.1). Problems of selecting the size and components of test systems are also discussed. Examples of synthetic and excised test systems are briefly described in terms of their relative applicability to toxicological testing.

4.2.1 Parameters

(1) <u>Primary productivity</u>. The ecological importance and social relevance of certain ecosystem processes are evident. For example, the ecologist's primary production is the forester's and agriculturalist's yield. This parameter might be a sufficient test criterion in itself, except that response to chemicals may be very slow because of the mediation by effects on soil chemistry, reproductive success, herbivore and pathogen activity, or other factors. <u>Hazard evaluation procedures involving any system that contains plants should include primary production, measured in terms of dry mass yield because of its importance and ease of determination.</u> Transient effects on primary production from which the plant recovers can be detected by CO_2 uptake or O_2 release, but if these effects are

not reflected in yield, their importance is questionable. Other, easily measured plant characteristics that may aid in the interpretation of test results include (a) symptoms of damage such as chlorosis and necrosis, (b) phenological parameters such as time to flowering, and (c) physiological parameters such as the nutrient status of the leaves.

(2) <u>Nutrient cycling</u>. Processes that influence soil fertility (nutrient cycling processes), such as transformations and movement of nutrient elements and degradation of organic materials, also have obvious social relevance. Nutrient transformations include fixation, mineralization, and oxidation-reduction reactions. The most important transformations in terms of biological production are those that involve the macronutrients. Of these, the best candidates for toxicological testing are nitrogen and sulfur, the macronutrients whose dynamics are dominated by biological processes. (Carbon dynamics are considered in terms of photosynthesis and respiration.) Nitrogen is the most important, but not all steps in the N cycle are important in all systems. Nitrogen fixation makes an insignificant contribution in most agricultural systems because of fertilization (fixation by legumes is an exception) and in mature natural systems because of the dominance of internal cycling. Nitrogen is often important in natural pastures and immature natural ecosystems, and nitrogen mineralization (ammonification) is important in natural systems. Nitrification is considered undesirable in many agricultural systems because of nitrate leaching and is a minor process in many natural systems because of rapid immobilization of ammonia. Biological nitrogen immobilization is important in nearly all systems, but it is difficult to measure directly; indirect indicators include plant N content and available N concentrations. Denitrification is limited under aerobic conditions, and inhibition of this process would generally not be considered detrimental.

Loss of nutrient elements by leaching can be important to ecosystem maintenance and productivity if sufficiently large and sustained. It has also been hypothesized to be a rapid and highly sensitive indicator of ecosystem stress (O'Neill et al. 1977). The terrestrial portion of a recent microcosm research program at ORNL was based on this premise (Harris 1980). The synthesis of this effort concluded that Ca and NO_3 leaching would be sufficient parameters for use in a toxicology screening test (Ross-Todd et al. 1980). Ca concentrations in leachate had the least variance and the greatest sensitivity of the nutrients considered [Mg, Ca, dissolved organic carbon (DOC), K, NO_3, P, and NH_4] followed by Mg, which was highly correlated with Ca. NO_3 loss was much more variable than Ca and Mg, but was highly sensitive.

The mechanisms of nutrient loss in these test systems, particularly Ca loss, are not understood. The large importance of cation exchange processes and carbonate chemistry relative to biological processes in most soils raises important questions of interpretation. When Jackson et al. (1979) used Na_2SO_4 as a nontoxic control salt for Na_3AsO_4, Ca leaching was higher in the controls than in the experimentals. Van Voris et al. (1978) added ^{45}Ca to the surface of a Cd-contaminated grassland core. They concluded that "the Ca isotope was totally retained in the top 2.5 cm of the soil indicating that the Ca loss was not due to cation exchange since the ion exchange sites were not saturated." The results can be realistically explained by isotopic dilution, the process of displacement of native Ca on exchange sites by ^{45}Ca; the experiment, therefore, did not eliminate exchange processes as a major factor in Ca loss. The coincidental occurrence of increased Ca loss and decreased CO_2 efflux cited by Van Voris et al. (1978) is suggestive, but it does not establish a biological cause for Ca loss.

Nutrient export becomes even more difficult to interpret when organic chemicals are tested. Metabolism of an organic chemical leads to immobilization of nutrients, masking any leakage of nutrients from stressed biota. This process might explain why hexachlorobenzene caused greater Ca loss at lower concentrations in a soil core study by Ausmus et al. (1979). Gile et al. (1979) examined the effects of four organic agricultural chemicals on nutrient loss. Leaching of most nutrients was unaffected or reduced by the chemicals, again suggesting that immobilization was stimulated. Because most TSCA test substances will be organic, this could be a serious disadvantage to using nutrient export tests to predict effects.

Other problems with nutrient leaching studies concern interpretation of results in terms of effects in the field. Leaching of nutrients from a 5- to 15-cm-deep soil core does not mean that the nutrients will appear in surface or ground water or that they are lost to the biotic community. In many, if not most cases, nutrients leached from the A horizon are retained in lower soil horizons. In this case the nutrient is not lost, but rather has been mobilized and transferred to another relatively immobile pool. This movement would be advantageous to deeper-rooted plant species. A second problem is the inability to adequately interpret the seriousness of the observed response. In soil microcosms, a toxicant-elevated nutrient loss rate typically returns to control levels within 3 weeks, even though toxicant and nutrient concentrations in the soil have not appreciably declined. A parameter that is that resilient will only be useful if it is indicative of longer-term ecosystem responses.

Another approach to determining the effect of chemicals on nutrient dynamics is to measure nutrient availability by extraction. Such extractions are conventionally performed by shaking a soil slurry formed with dried, screened soil and a chemical extractant. Jackson and Hall (1978) leached soil cores with extractant solutions, thereby deriving estimates of available Ca, NH_3, NO_3, and PO_4 that were lower than those obtained from slurries, but that were more sensitive to the effects of heavy metals. Like nutrient leaching, nutrient availability would respond to effects on mineralization and immobilization. It has the advantage over nutrient leaching of explicitly taking into account ion exchange processes, but its response is less often significant, and the direction of response is less regular (Ausmus et al. 1979; Jackson et al. 1979; and Jackson et al. 1978).

(3) <u>Community metabolism</u>. The most common measure of soil metabolism is CO_2 efflux. Chemicals that are toxic and persistent and to which the biota cannot adapt will simply depress CO_2 efflux. Chemicals that serve as substrates or supply mineral nutrients would elevate CO_2 efflux. Chemicals that are toxic but leave no residues such as fumigants, that are readily degraded, or to which the biota adapts cause a short depression in CO_2 efflux, followed by a rebound to very high levels and a slower return to predisturbance levels. This pattern also occurs in response to drying or physical disturbance of the soil, in which case the cycle typically requires 5 to 14 days. It is one of the major determinants of the equilibration period required for soil test systems. Elevated CO_2 efflux during the rebound period is generally attributed to the degradation of microbes killed by the disturbance.

If CO_2 efflux is measured continuously by infrared gas analysis, cycles in the system's carbon balance can be monitored. The number of distinguishable cyclic frequencies was used by Van Voris et al. (1978) as an indicator of the functional complexity of microcosms. This index, however, was used to predict response to a toxicant rather than as an indicator of response. The functional significance of these cycles is unknown.

Carbonaceous substrates are frequently added to the soil to examine effects of chemicals on a specific degradation process or to ease the CO_2 determination by increasing the efflux rate. In the absence of evidence that degradation of a specific substrate is particularly sensitive to toxic chemicals, it is probably best to maximize realism by using no amendment or by using only whole plant material. In this way, the range of microbes involved in the test is maximized. If, as Domsch (1970) has hypothesized, autochthonous organisms and those that degrade resistant substances are most sensitive to toxic effects, degradation of native soil organic matter may be a sensitive process. If carbonaceous amendments are used, the time until peak respiration may be more sensitive than total respiration (Domsch 1970; Spalding 1978).

Other methods of determining soil community metabolism include O_2 uptake, heat production, and ATP concentration. Methods of measuring O_2 consumption (a) are less precise and therefore less sensitive than CO_2 efflux (Lighthart et al. 1977), (b) do not represent microbial respiration as completely as CO_2 (Stotzky 1965), and (c) therefore would only be useful if the respiratory quotient (RQ) was of interest. Klein (1977) found that RQ was a sensitive indicator of seasonal changes in the microbial community, but it was not affected by any of the 14 salts of heavy metals that significantly reduced CO_2 efflux (Lighthart et al. 1977).

ATP assays are difficult and expensive to perform, are not amenable to time course analysis because of their destructive nature, and do not seem to offer any particular advantages over other indices of soil metabolism.

The sensitivity of soil metabolism to toxic chemicals is questionable. The only good body of evidence for disruption of decomposition by pollutants is that for heavy metals (Coughtrey et al. 1979; Harris 1980; Jackson and Watson 1977; Lighthart et al. 1977; Ruhling and Tyler 1973; Spalding 1978; Tyler 1976). This effect is generally attributed to metal toxicity. However, it has been attributed to total salt concentration by Lighthart et al. (1977) because sodium salts were as effective as heavy metal salts of equivalent ionic strength. Spalding (1978) concluded that the effect of heavy metals on soil respiration primarily resulted from the formation of resistant metal-organic complexes rather than from direct toxicity. These mechanisms would not contribute to the effects of organic compounds on decomposition. The effect of most organic compounds would be to increase metabolism by serving as a microbial substrate.

Enzyme activity determinations are used to indicate the potential of soils to perform certain chemical transformations. Results of enzyme assays reflect changes in the character of ecosystems less directly than the parameters previously discussed. Therefore, enzyme assays could only be recommended if they were known to be particularly sensitive to chemicals or particularly rapid and inexpensive. Because available evidence indicates that neither of these cases is true, enzyme assays are not recommended.

Transformation of chemical contaminants is also an ecosystem function. While this process typically results in detoxification, partial oxidation of chemicals can result in increased toxicity. One chemical may also decrease the rate of degradation of a second chemical, leading to undesired toxic effects and contamination of food or enhancing the effectiveness of agricultural chemicals that degrade too rapidly (Kaufman 1977). Effects of one pesticide on the degradation of another have been demonstrated by Kaufman et al. (1970, 1971, 1977). In addition to pesticides, the soil biota degrades toxic chemicals from the air, chemical spills, and buried or land-farmed wastes. The soil biota is also responsible for scavenging inorganic gaseous pollutants from the atmosphere. The extent and potential importance of interference with this process by chemicals is unknown.

(4) <u>Summary</u>. Table 4.3 summarizes the results of several studies that have examined the effects of toxic substances on more than one ecosystem process. Fungal and bacterial counts are included because they are frequently determined in studies of ecosystem processes. Few of these studies consider primary production, but the

results of one study suggest that it is more sensitive to organic chemicals than microbial processes and populations (Eno and Everett 1977) and should be determined in any system containing plants. CO_2 efflux is a rapid and sensitive indicator of biotic response, but it may increase or decrease depending on time since the perturbation, the degradability and persistence of the test chemical, the nutrient status of the system, and other factors. It should be measured over time to clarify the nature of the response. Mineralization of nitrogen and other nutrients is an important process that is relatively sensitive to metal salts (Liang and Tabatabi 1977) and moderately rapid. Nitrification and nitrogen fixation appear to be somewhat less sensitive and are as likely to increase as to decrease. The few results from ATP assays do not appear promising, particularly in light of the relatively high expense and difficulty of this assay. Enzyme assays, in addition to being difficult to interpret, appear to be relatively insensitive to perturbations. Nutrient leaching is sensitive to metal salts and is quite rapid in some cases, but to date the results with organic compounds are not promising. Nutrient availability appears to be less sensitive, consistent, and rapid than nutrient leaching.

There is good evidence that heavy metals disrupt ecosystem processes at concentrations that do not acutely affect most individual organisms. However, the studies cited herein and reviews of insecticide and herbicide effects on terrestrial ecosystems (Brown 1978; Greaves et al. 1976; Cullimore 1971) indicate that soil microbes and the ecosystem processes that they conduct are typically less sensitive to organic chemicals than individual organisms and populations. Because most TSCA-regulated chemicals are organic, they are more likely to behave like organic agrochemicals than metals. Nevertheless, effects on ecosystem processes are sufficiently important that a simple system to measure CO_2 efflux and N mineralization in soil should be included in any testing scheme. Other parameters such as nutrient leaching are potentially useful but require further development.

4.2.2 Test Components

While component ecosystem processes such as ammonification can be conducted by a single bacterial clone in a liquid minimum medium, the realism of responses measured in that system are highly questionable. Most microbial ecologists would agree that minimal realism requires a mixed microbial culture in soil. Some would argue further that because the presence of litter, plant roots, and soil invertebrates significantly modify the absolute and relative rates of soil processes, they must also be included in a test system for any basic ecosystem process. The importance of these components in determining responses to chemicals has not been investigated. CO_2 efflux has been measured in a wide variety of test systems, but its response shows no trends with increasing system complexity (Table 4.3). Nutrient leaching in response to metals is not clearly affected by the presence

TABLE 4.3. RELATIVE FREQUENCY OF SIGNIFICANT RESPONSES BY ECOSYSTEM PROCESS PARAMETERS TO TOXIC CHEMICALS IN LABORATORY SYSTEMS

System (toxicant)	Primary pro- duction	Nutrient leaching	Nutrient avail- ability	Nitrogen fixation	Ammoni- fication	Nitri- fication	CO_2 efflux amended	CO_2 efflux Not amended	O_2 uptake	ATP	Enzyme assays	Bacteria counts	Fungal counts
SOIL													
Atlas, et al. 1978 (3 herbicides and 2 fungicides)				0/2[a] (84)[b]		0/6 (84)	1/8- (84)	0/6 (84)			2/4- (84)	0/6 (84)	1/5- (84)
Bartha et al. (29 pesticides)						3/29+ 22/29- (6-18)	7/17+ (30)[d]	2/17- (30)[d]					
Eno and Everett 1958 (10 pesticides)	8/10- (17)					3/10+ 3/10- (30)		4/10+ (30)				0/10 (30)	1/10+ (30)
Kudeyarow and Jenkinson 1976 (CS_2 and $CHCl_3$)					4/4+ (10)	4/4+ (10)		4/4+ (10)	4/4+ (10)				
Liang and Tabatabi 1977 (21 metal salts)					64/84- (20)	20/84- (20)							
Tu 1978 (32 pesticides)				7/32- 9/32+ 1/32± (2-6)								4/32- 7/32+ (2-6)	9/32- 5/32+ 3/32± (2-6)
Tu 1970 (4 pesticides)					7/8+ (7)	6/8- (2)			8/8+ [1]			1/8- [56] 1/8+ [28] 6/8± [7-56]	4/8- [7-56] 2/8+ [14-28] 1/8± [7-14]
Tu 1980 (7 pesticides)						0/14 (14) 4/14+ (28)			13/14+ [1]		11/24+ (2) 12/24- (7) 16/24+ (14)	13/14- (7) 7/14- (14) 4/14+ (28)	12/14- (7) 6/14+ (14)
LITTER													
Spalding 1979 (7 metal salts)								6/7- (3-28)			5/63- 9/63+ (1-28)		
SOIL-LITTER													
Lighthart et al. 1977 (20 metal salts)								12/20- 1/20+ (20)	6/20- (20)				

129

TABLE 4.3. (continued)

System (toxicant)	Primary production	Nutrient leaching	Nutrient availability	Nitrogen fixation	Ammonification	Nitrification	CO$_2$ efflux Amended	CO$_2$ efflux Not amended	O$_2$ uptake	ATP	Enzyme assays	Bacteria counts	Fungal counts
SOIL CORE													
Ausmus et al. 1979 (hexachlorobenzene)		1/1+ [1][c]	0/1 (21)					1/1− (21)					
Gile et al. 1979 (Methyl parathion, dieldrin, 2, 4, 5-T and hexachlorobenzene)		2/20+ 5/20− (56)						0/1 (49)					
Jackson et al. 1977 (As)		2/4+ (?)								0/2 (?)	0/8 (?)		
GRASSLAND CORE													
Jackson et al. 1979 (As)	0/1 (107)	5/6+ 1/6− [1−107]	3/5+ (107)							0/1 (107)		1/1+ (107)	1/1+ (107)
Van Voris et al. 1978 (CdCl$_2$)		1/1+ [1]						1/1− (14)		1/1− (62)		1/1+ (62)	1/1+ (62)
TREECOSM													
Jackson et al. 1978; Ausmus 1978 (Pb smelter dust)		4/5+ (611)	4/5− (611)					1/1+ [130]		1/1+ (611)		1/1+ (611)	1/1− (611)

[a]The fraction indicates the number of significant responses out of the total number of combinations of toxicants and soils. The sign indicates the direction of response; ± indicates that the direction changed over time.
[b]Numbers in parentheses indicate the number of days after addition of the toxicant that responses were measured.
[c]Numbers in brackets indicate the number of days in a time series of measurements when a significant response was first measured after addition of the toxicant.
[d]Total response for period indicated.

of plants although the treecosm responses may have been slowed by the trees and litter (Jackson et al. 1978). Extraneous components (those which do not qualitatively affect system response) would increase the cost of a test, would complicate interpretation of results, and might interfere with measurements. No ecosystem components have been shown to be extraneous in this sense.

Soil structure also can be considered a system component. Ausmus and O'Neill (1978) found that intact soil cores and homogenized soil columns did not differ in CO_2 efflux, but the homogenized soil lost significantly more DOC in leachate with a larger percent variation. In another study (Jackson et al. 1979; Jackson and Levine 1979) arsenic transport and nutrient concentrations in leachate before As treatment did not differ in 30-cm-diameter intact and homogenized soil columns; extractable Ca and PO_4 levels showed inconsistent differences. Leaching of DOC was higher in the intact columns (contradicting the result described above), and ATP concentration and fungal biomass were significantly reduced in the intact columns, but not in the homogenized columns. Although homogenized soil would seem intuitively to be less variable than intact cores, there were no consistent differences in variability in these studies. Therefore, the choice between intact and homogenized soil structures may be made on the basis of convenience. Small cores are most easily obtained by extraction, but larger systems such as the treecosm would probably be more easily assembled.

4.2.3 Soil Type

The problem of selecting a soil type for use in tests of terrestrial ecosystem processes is essentially the same as the problem of choosing species for tests of species interactions. The choice is critical to the outcome of the test because the responsiveness of ecosystem processes to chemicals is highly dependent on soil type.

One possible solution to the problem is to simply prescribe limits on soil texture, organic carbon content, and pH. This is the simplest solution and is probably the only one that is currently feasible, but unidentified discrepancies in results would still occur, and the range of field situations to which the test could apply would be limited. A second possible solution is to designate a standard soil or a series of standard soils that are representative of major regional soil types. This solution would produce relatively consistent results, but would require that EPA or some other agency be responsible for distributing certified standard soil. Another approach is to allow testing laboratories to select their test soil, but to require the use of standard reference chemicals as positive controls. This solution is based on the assumption that relative sensitivity of soils to different chemicals is nearly constant, at least within broad categories of chemicals and soils. This assumption will need to be tested before reference chemicals are proposed.

In some cases, the production, distribution, and use of a chemical may be so delimited as to allow identification of a small number of soils which could be affected by the chemical. In these cases, testing of the potentially affected soils would increase test validity at the cost of not producing standard results.

4.2.4 Size

The size of a test system is determined by (1) the components and processes that must be included, (2) the amount of material necessary for measurement of the response parameters, and (3) the necessity of reducing variance by increasing the volume of material. If plants or macroinvertebrates are included in the system, their requirements are likely to determine the minimum size. Laboratory systems are not large enough to support vertebrate animals without unrealistically severe disruption of the system (Gile and Gillett 1979; Metcalf et al. 1979). The volume of soil or litter in purely microbial systems is usually determined by the volumes required for chemical analysis or measurement of gas uptake or efflux.

Studies that consider the effect of size on system response are rare. Ross-Todd et al. (1980) analyzed the results of two experiments that considered the effect of size (10 x 10 cm vs 30 x 15 cm and 15 x 25 cm vs 30 x 25 cm) on response of grassland cores to As. The larger cores produced generally higher concentrations of nutrients in leachate, but the relative variability of this parameter was inconsistent. Leachate concentration showed a clearer treatment effect (was more sensitive) in the larger cores. CO_2 efflux was less variable in the larger cores. These results suggest that fewer large systems would be required to show a statistically significant treatment effect, but this advantage must be balanced against the higher cost of preparing and maintaining larger systems.

4.2.5 Synthetic Systems

This section discusses synthetic systems, those that are assembled or constructed from ecosystem components. The basic components are soil, plants, animals, and nonliving organic matter. The applicability of these systems to tilled fields where strong structural relationships of soil, litter, and plants do not develop is obvious. Natural ecosystems are probably less well simulated by these test systems than by excised, intact systems, but the differences in response have not been demonstrated in work to date.

Only one or a few key references are cited for each test system in this and the following section. A more complete set of references is provided in the bibliography (Appendix D).

(1) <u>Soil systems</u>. Most studies of terrestrial ecosystem processes are performed by microbiologists using natural microflora in soil. The soil may be dried, sieved, ground, formed into a slurry, or

amended with substrate materials. Slurries, like liquid cultures and agar plates, do not realistically represent the soil. Grinding is unnecessarily destructive, and sieving should be kept to a minimum to retain crumb structure. Drying is also unnecessary and reduces the diversity of the microflora. Soil amendments increase the rate and magnitude of microbial activities, making measurement easier, but they may qualitatively modify the effects of a test chemical if they are not representative of common substrates in the field. Glucose greatly decreases the sensitivity of microbial respiration to pesticides (Bartha 1967).

Soil systems (test systems consisting of soil and microbiota) can be used to test effects on any of the ecosystem processes previously discussed except those that require plants (primary production and plant uptake of nutrients). Decades of work by agronomic microbiologists indicate that nutrient dynamics and the effectiveness of soil fumigants in agricultural systems are adequately represented by soil systems. Untilled, natural systems may not be adequately represented by these systems because of the importance of litter-root-soil structure relationships.

Schemes for testing the effects of chemicals on soil processes have been suggested by Johnen and Drew (1977), Atlas et al. (1978), the U.S. EPA (1979), and the participants in a recent workshop held by ORNL (Suter 1981b). None of these schemes have been subject to validation, standardization, or interlaboratory transfer, but the test proposed at the ORNL workshop appears to best fit the requirements of TSCA.

(2) _Litter_. This system is identical to the soil system except that litter, rather than soil, is the medium (Spalding 1979). Litter responses to chemicals have received much less attention because forests have less economic importance than field crops and have received less intentional input of chemicals. Litter alone does not represent forest ecosystems as well as litter and soil and offers no significant advantage in cost or rapidity of response. Therefore, it does not appear to be a good candidate for protocol development.

(3) _Soil-litter_. This system is essentially a combination of the previous two, a layer of sifted litter on top of a layer of homogenized and sieved soil. In the form developed by Bond et al. (1976), the system is enclosed in an apparatus that permits continuous and simultaneous measurement of CO_2 efflux, O_2 uptake, and heat output. It is designed to make possible complete and accurate measurement of the integrated responses of the forest floor microbial community to toxicants. This system would be suitable for development as a test protocol if it was simplified by only measuring respiration as CO_2 efflux. Coefficients of variation for CO_2 efflux from this system are low (<10%) and comparable to those for intact forest soil cores (Ausmus and O'Neill 1978).

(4) _Gnotobiotic soil_. Rather than using a natural, undefined community of microflora and fauna in soil test systems, a defined community can be assembled in sterilized soil (Coleman et al. 1977). These gnotobiotic systems are useful research tools and are likely to be sensitive because they lack functional redundancy. However, they are expensive and difficult to maintain and are unlikely to respond as realistically to test chemicals as natural soil communities. <u>For these reasons, gnotobiotic systems are not good candidates for test protocols.</u>

(5) _Soil-plant_. These systems are designed to reveal the effect or fate of agricultural chemicals applied to field crops.

(a) _Pot_. This is essentially a test for effects of pesticides on crop plants using a pot of field soil in which effects on the microbial community and microbial processes are determined (Eno and Everett 1958). The use of large pots makes it possible to grow the plants to maturity and examine effects on reproduction and yield. <u>The simplicity of this system and the large mass of experience with growing potted plants in greenhouses makes this an appealing test system for effects of chemicals on agricultural systems.</u>

(b) _Lichtenstein_. This system consists of corn seedlings grown in layers of contaminated and uncontaminated homogenized soil contained in an 86- by 154-mm-high plastic cylinder, resting in a leachate collector (Lichtenstein et al. 1977). The only validation provided for this system is comparison of the results for a pesticide (N-2596) with an independent field study. In that study, far shorter persistence was found in the soil of field plots planted to rye than was found in the Lichtenstein system (Lichtenstein et al. 1977). This system is also essentially a pot test, except that the pots are not large enough to grow the plants to maturity.

(c) _Agroecosystem chamber_. This system consists of crop plants (cotton or tomatoes at five plants/chamber) grown on a 15-cm layer of sieved soil in a 115 cm high x 150 cm x 50 cm closed glass box with controlled air flow (Nash et al. 1977). The system is designed to provide a complete description of pesticide fate by permitting the measurement of volatilization and residues in soil, plants, and leachate. No attempts to field validate this system have been reported. The chief advantage of this system for effects studies is that the air flow system would permit measurement of whole system respiration.

(d) _Summary_. As effects tests, these systems are essentially plants in different-sized pots, one of which has a cover to control air flow. This type of system could be adapted to measure nutrient leaching in agricultural ecosystems, and microbial processes can be measured if the potting medium is not artificial. With the deliberate addition of a pathogen, herbivore, or another plant, a more realistic ecosystem process test and a test for population interactions are presumably obtained. The primary technical problem concerns the size of pot that is necessary to support the processes of interest.

(6) <u>Soil, litter, plant, and animal</u>. These systems represent attempts to assemble true microcosms--laboratory systems that contain all the major components and processes of a selected terrestrial ecosystem.

(a) <u>Odum</u>. This system consists of natural soil and litter and small plants of five different taxa in a 16.2-cm-diameter plastic desiccator (Odum and Lugo 1970). An air flow of 2.5 L/min was maintained through ports in the lid, and CO_2 content was measured with an infrared gas analyzer. Because the soil and litter were not subjected to harsh treatments and the flora consisted of whole transplants, a representative invertebrate fauna was included.

The purpose of this system was to supplement a field study of radiation effects on a tropical forest. The system permitted greater resolution in metabolic measurements than did the unconfined ecosystem. Neither respiration nor photosynthesis was found to be affected in these systems by 25,000 r of gamma radiation. The lack of effects on respiration was not surprising because respiration is dominated by the microflora, which are resistant to radiation. The absence of effects on photosynthesis was somewhat unexpected because damage to plants outside the microcosms was observed at that radiation level, but the photosynthetic enzyme system is resistant to radiation at levels that cause morphological damage to plants. The baseline respiration rate was two orders of magnitude lower in the microcosms than in the field.

(b) <u>Witkamp</u>. These systems were designed as research tools to study the dynamics of fallout isotopes (^{137}Cs) and mineral nutrients under various physical and biological conditions (Witkamp 1976). They consist of a glass or plastic cylinder 7 to 13 cm in diameter by 10 to 13 cm deep, with a leachate port to which various combinations of soil, litter, soil fauna, and seedling trees may be added. They have not been used for chemical testing, but have the advantage that their nutrient dynamics have been modeled and are relatively well understood. <u>The approach of using major system elements as components in a factorial design would be useful for determining mechanisms of toxic response</u>. Transfer rates are generally higher in these systems than in the field, but the mechanisms and pathways are qualitatively similar (Witkamp 1976).

(c) <u>Metcalf</u>. The original version of this system consisted of sloping soil in an aquarium with a crop and terrestrial fauna on the high end and water and aquatic flora and fauna on the low end (Metcalf et al. 1971). More recently, this system has been supplanted by a more efficient design. It consists of either 400 g of vermiculite or 3000 g of soil planted with corn (Metcalf et al. 1979).

After 10 days, saltmarsh caterpillars, slugs, earthworms, and pillbugs are added. On day 15 a vole is added, and on day 20 the system is terminated. The primary purpose of this system is to analyze the fate of pesticides in agricultural systems. Effects are determined incidentally by measuring plant growth and noting deaths of animals.

The only validation provided for this system is a general comparison of pesticide fate in the system and the field. Results agree "very closely" (Metcalf et al. 1979). If this system were adapted for use in effects testing, the vole should be deleted. The voles greatly disrupt the systems by burrowing and typically consume the entire flora and fauna of the system. This situation is obviously not typical of the role of voles in ecosystems, and the diet provided is probably no more realistic than commercially prepared food for laboratory mice. The use of screw-topped jars provides a cheap and easily closed system for gas analysis.

(d) <u>Terrestrial microcosm chamber (TMC)</u>. The TMC is essentially an enlargement and elaboration of the Metcalf system. It consists of a 1 x 0.75 x 0.6 m glass box with ports for airflow, water addition as rain or a "spring," and a leachate port (Gile and Gillett 1979). It contains 20 cm of synthetic soil, alfalfa, rye grass, two species of nematodes, earthworms, enchaetraeid worms, two species of pillbugs, mealworms, crickets, snails, and a pregnant vole. Like the Metcalf system, it is used primarily to study the fate of pesticides and secondarily to determine effects.

The TMC results with Dieldrin were validated by comparison with published field and laboratory studies. While many results are comparable, others are not. The concentration of residues in the vole are more than an order of magnitude higher than would be expected from field studies. The problems of including a mammal in a microcosm are reduced but not eliminated in this larger system.

The advantages of this larger, elaborate system over the Metcalf system have largely to do with studies of fate. If the vole is deleted, the Metcalf system has no significant relative disadvantages as a test system and is considerably cheaper and easier to operate.

4.2.6 Excised Systems

Systems that are excised, intact from the field, are discussed in this section. These systems were developed out of the belief that the structural relationships of soil, litter, and plants are critical to ecosystem dynamics.

(1) <u>Soil core</u>. A 5-cm-diameter by 5- or 10-cm-deep soil core is encased in a heat-shrunk polyvinylchloride (PVC) sleeve and supported on a leachate collector. Aboveground vegetation may be removed or left in place. The system was designed to serve as a general-purpose

test system for determining the fate and effects of toxic materials. This is the only one of the six systems discussed at the 1977 Workshop on Terrestrial Microcosms for which a testing protocol was proposed (Gillett and Witt 1979; see also Harris 1980). No attempt has been made to field validate this specific system, but the nutrient leaching results have been related to the general body of evidence on nutrient loss summarized by O'Neill et al. (1977). This system, which was developed at ORNL, has been used at the Corvallis Environmental Research Laboratory to test pesticides and herbicides (Gile et al.). The Corvallis study did not obtain the same regular increase in nutrient leaching that was obtained at ORNL even though one common chemical (hexachlorobenzene) was used; it is not clear whether the disparity is due to differences in the soils used or other factors.

(2) Grassland core. This system consists of intact cores that are sufficiently large (15- to 30-cm diameter by 10 to 25 cm) to support a representative portion of a grassland community. The 15-cm diameter cores of Van Voris et al. (1978) supported averages of 14 individual plants of 6.3 species. The version of this system recommended by Harris (1980) is supported on a Plexiglass disk with central port and encased in a heat-shrunk PVC sleeve. This system was designed to test the fate and effects of chemicals in grassland communities. Jackson et al. (1979) attempted to validate this system in the field. While nutrient leaching and soil ATP levels in the cores were affected by As, no response was measured in the field. Because the cores were kept in the field and because untreated cores and plots were comparable, this result implies that enclosure increases the sensitivity of these parameters.

(3) Sod. This system consists of a 16-cm diameter by 7-cm deep section of sod contained in a closed 4-L Nalgene jar (Campbell 1973). Ports are provided in the lid for periodic measurement of CO_2 production by infrared gas analysis. This system was designed to display the response of grassland ecosystems to stress. It is similar to the grassland core, but has no provision for monitoring nutrient loss. It offers no particular advantage as a test system.

(4) Treecosm. This system consists of an intact 45- x 45- x 25-cm block of forest soil containing an approximately 2-m-tall red maple sapling and associated ground flora (Jackson et al. 1978). The primary purpose of this system was to investigate the ability of microcosms to simulate a specific field perturbation and elucidate the mechanisms of the observed field response.

Comparison of treecosm results with studies by Jackson and Watson (1977) of the effects of smelter emissions on Crooked Creek watershed partially validate the system. While the pattern of uptake of metals from the smelter dust was similar to that at Crooked Creek, differences in transfer rates were sufficient to prevent development of a predictive transport model of Crooked Creek watershed from the treecosm results (Luxmore and Begovich 1979). This disparity was attributed to the physical conditions of the greenhouse in which the treecosms were kept. While the treecosms were treated to simulate areas at Crooked Creek receiving high metal deposition rates, the small increase in macronutrient pools observed in treecosm litter better simulated areas that received intermediate levels of deposition. Low macronutrient levels were observed in tree tissues at Crooked Creek, but not in the treecosm. The increased leaching of macronutrients from treated treecosms suggests a mechanism for the decreased macronutrient levels in the soil at Crooked Creek. The elevated soil respiration rates and ATP concentrations observed in treated treecosms contrast sharply with the reduced respiration and elevated litter biomass observed at Crooked Creek. Reduced fungal lengths in treated treecosms correspond to the reduction in amino sugar concentrations observed at Crooked Creek.

The disparities between treecosm and field results may be attributed to the greenhouse environment or to differences in soil and biota between Crooked Creek, Missouri, and Oak Ridge, Tennessee, the source of the treecosms. It seems likely, however, that many of the disparities are attributable to the 20-month period of the treecosm experiment, which is relatively short in terms of forest dynamics. The high levels of internal nutrient cycling in trees buffer them against changes in soil chemistry. This characteristic also delays any soil responses that depend on changes in characteristics of the litter fall or root dynamics.

Because trees and their mycorrhizal symbionts dominate the dynamics of forest ecosystems, the treecosm is the minimum system that displays all the major forest ecosystem processes. Assembling such a large system from soil, litter, and a nursery tree would probably be easier than excising a large block of soil, but might increase the equilibration period and reduce realism. The size of the system could be reduced by using a seedling rather than a sapling tree, but the effects of this change are unknown. It would be highly desirable to establish that inexpensive and rapidly responding parameters such as nutrient leaching from soil cores are not only indicative of system stress, but are predictive of changes in forest production or other socially valued parameters. <u>In the absence of such an ideal test, the treecosm should be developed as a confirmatory test for forest ecosystem responses to stress.</u>

(5) <u>Outcrops</u>. This system consists of excised sections of small isolated communities that have developed in depressions on rock outcrops (McCormick and Platt 1962). The excised sections are arranged in a concrete trough, which is sloped to provide drainage. The major appeal of this system is that an entire, clearly defined, simple community is recreated. <u>However, this community type is not sufficiently common to support harvesting for TSCA testing or to be considered an important community type. In addition, the peculiar hydrology of these systems makes them unrepresentative of most terrestrial</u>

ecosystems. These considerations preclude the development of this system as a testing protocol.

4.2.7 Summary

There has been no consistent line of laboratory system (microcosm) development oriented toward ecosystem processes that would lead to a clearly useful test system for ecosystem processes. Most terrestrial microcosms have been developed to suit the needs of a specific research program rather than as generally applicable testing tools. In addition, most microcosm research has been concerned with the transport and fate of chemicals rather than with their effects. Therefore, only a simple ecosystem-level test system can be recommended for immediate use.

This system would consist of soil with and without a realistic organic amendment. Parameters measured would include CO_2 efflux, nitrogen mineralization, and nitrification. A system of this type (see Suter 1981b, for a proposed protocol) would be reasonably rapid and inexpensive while providing a realistic test of ecologically important and relatively well-understood processes of terrestrial ecosystems. Because of the considerable experience of microbial ecologists with this type of system, development would consist primarily of determining whether soil characteristics can be defined to give comparable results among different laboratories. This exercise should include the development of positive controls.

Considerably more development will be required before more complex microcosms can be used as test systems. Basic questions about microcosm design, optimum size, and the importance of components such as litter, plants, and animals remain unresolved. It is still not clear that microcosms display important responses to chemicals that are not apparent in or predictable from simpler plant, animal, and microbe toxicity tests. Parameters such as nutrient leaching rates and the frequency distribution of community CO_2 exchange must be better understood in terms of their mechanisms and responses to chemicals before they can be used in standardized predictive test systems.

Development of microcosms as test systems must proceed by an orderly consideration of component interactions. Physical and biological components (including the microflora) should be treated as elements in a factorial design. A few well-studied pesticides or other chemicals should be used as surrogates for TSCA-regulated chemicals to maximize the bases for validation and comparison with standard test systems. Such a program would provide a firm basis for support of test protocol.

4.3 REFERENCES

Adams, J. B., and H. F. Van Emden. 1972. The biological properties of aphids and their host plant relationships. pp. 47-104. IN H. F. Van Emden (ed.), Aphid Technology, Academic Press, New York.

Adams, W. T. and G. T. Duncan. 1979. A maximum likelihood statistical method for analyzing frequency-dependent fitness experiments. Behav. Genet. 9:7-21.

Alexander, M. 1971. Microbial Ecology. John Wiley and Sons, Inc., New York. 511 pp.

Ambler, J. R., and J. L. Young. 1977. Techniques for determining root length infected by vesicular-arbuscular mycorrhizae. Soil Sci. Soc. Am. J. 41:551-555.

Anderson, J. M. 1962. The enigma of soil animal species diversity. pp. 51-58. IN Murphy, P. W. (ed.), Progress in Soil Zoology. Butterworths, London.

Anderson, J. M. 1978. Competition between two unrelated species of soil cryptostigmata (Acari) in experimental microcosms. J. Anim. Ecol. 47:787-803.

Atkinson, W. D. 1979. A field investigation of larval competition in domestic Drosophila. J. Anim. Ecol. 48:91-102.

Atlas, R. M., D. Pramer, and R. Bartha. 1978. Assessment of pesticide effects on non-target soil microorganisms. Soil Biol. Biochem. 10:231-239.

Ausmus, B. S., S. Kimbrough, D. R. Jackson, and S. Lindberg. 1979. The behavior of hexachlorobenzene in pine forest microcosms: Transport and effects on soil processes. Environ. Pollut. 13:103-111.

Ausmus, B. S., and E. G. O'Neill. 1978. Comparison of carbon dynamics of three microcosm substrates. Soil Biol. Biochem. 10:425-429.

Ayala, F. J. 1966. Reversal of dominance in competing species of _Drosophila_. Am. Nat. 100(910):81-83.

Ayala, F. J. 1969. Experimental invalidation of the principle of competitive exclusion. Nature 224:1076-1079.

Ayala, F. J. 1970. Competition, coexistence, and evolution. pp. 121-158. IN Hecht, M. K. and W. C. Steere (eds.), Essays in Evolution and Genetics in Honor of Theodosius Dobzhansky. Appleton-Century-Crofts, New York.

Ayala, F. J. 1971. Competition between species: Frequency dependence. Science 171:820-824.

Barker, J. S. F., and R. N. Podger. 1970. Interspecific competition between Drosophila melanogaster and Drosophila simulans: Effects of larval density on viability, developmental period and adult body weight. Ecology 51:170-189.

Bennett, J. P., and V. C. Runeckles. 1977. Effects of low levels of ozone on plant competition. J. Appl. Ecol. 14:877-880.

Benson, J. F. 1973. The biology of Lepidoptera infesting stored products, with special reference to population dynamics. Biol. Rev. 48:1-26.

Birch. L. C. 1957. The meanings of competition. Am. Nat. 91:5-18.

Blaylock, B. G., and H. H. Shugart, Jr. 1972. The effect of radiation-induced mutations on the fitness of Drosophila populations. Genetics 72:469-474.

Boggild, O., and J. Keiding. 1958. Competition in house fly larvae. Oikos 9(1):1-25.

Bond, H., B. Lighthart, R. Shimabuku, and L. Russell. 1976. Some effects of cadmium on coniferous forest soil and litter microcosms. Soil Sci. 121(5):278-287.

Brown, A. W. A. 1978. Ecology of Pesticides. John Wiley and Sons, Inc., New York. 525 pp.

Budnik, M., and D. Brncic. 1974. Preadult competition between Drosophila pavani and Drosophila melanogaster, Drosophila simulans, and Drosophila willistoni. Ecology 55:657-661.

Burnett, T. 1967. Aspects of the interaction between a chalcid parasite and its aleurodid host. Can. J. Zool. 45:539-578.

Burnett, T. 1970. Effect of temperature on a greenhouse acarine predator-prey population. Can. J. Zool. 48:555-562.

Campbell, S. D. 1973. The effect of cobalt-60 gamma-rays on terrestrial microcosm metabolism. Ph.D. Dissertation. Univ. of Mich., Ann Arbor, Mich. 144 pp.

Carlyle, R. E., and J. D. Thorpe. 1947. Some effects of ammonium and sodium 2,4-dichlorophenoxyacetates on legumes and the *Rhizobium* bacteria. J. Am. Soc. of Agron. 39:929-936.

Caswell, H., H. E. Koenig, J. A. Resh, and Q. E. Ross. 1972. An introduction to systems science for ecologists. pp. 4-78. IN Patten, B. C. (ed.) Systems Analysis and Simulation in Ecology, Volume II. Academic Press, New York.

Chant, D. A. 1961. An experiment in biological control of *Tetranychus telarius* (L.) (Acarina: Tetranychidae) in a greenhouse using the predacious mite *Phytoseiulus persimilis* Athias-Henriol (Phytoseiidae). Can. Entomol. 93:437-443.

Coleman, D. C., C. V. Cole, R. V. Anderson, M. Blaha, M. K. Campion, M. Clarholm, E. T. Elliott, H. W. Hunt, B. Shaefer, and J. Sinclair. 1977. An analysis of rhizosphere-saprophage interactions in terrestrial ecosystems. Ecol. Bull. (Stockholm) 25:299-309.

Collyer, E. 1958. Some insectary experiments with predacious mites to determine their effect on the development of *Metatetranychus ulmi* (Koch) populations. Entomol. Exp. Appl. 1:138-146.

Collyer, E. 1964. The effect of an alternative food supply on the relationship between two *Typhlodromus* species and *Panonychus ulmi* (Koch) (Acarina). Entomol. Exp. Appl. 7:120-124.

Coughtrey, P. J., C. H. Jones, M. H. Martin, and S. W. Shales. 1979. Litter accumulation in woodlands contaminated by Pb, Zn, Cd and Cu. Oecologia (Berlin) 39:51-60.

Craig, R. B. 1978. An analysis of the predatory behavior of the loggerhead shrike. Auk 95:221-234.

Crombie, A. C. 1945. On competition between different species of graminivorous insects. Proc., R. Soc. London, Series B-Biological Sciences. 132:362-395.

Crombie, A. C. 1946. Further experiments on insect competition. Proc., R. Soc. London, Series B-Biological Sciences. 133:76-109.

Cullimore, D. R. 1971. Interaction between herbicides and soil micro-organisms. Residue Reviews 35:65-80.

Culver, D. 1974. Competition between Collembola in a patchy environment. Rev. Ecol. Biol. Sol. 11(4):533-540.

Danso, S. K. A., S. O. Keya, and M. Alexander. 1975. Protoza and the decline of *Rhizobium* populations added to soil. Can. J. Microbiol. 21:884-895.

DeBach, P., and C. B. Huffaker. 1971. Experimental techniques for evaluation of the effectiveness of natural enemies. pp. 113-140. IN Huffaker, C. B. (ed.), Biological Control. Plenum Press, New York.

DeBach, P., and H. S. Smith. 1941. The effect of host density on the rate of reproduction of entomophagous parasites. J. Econ. Entomol. 34:741-745.

De Telegdy-Kovats, L. 1932. The growth and respiration of bacteria in sand cultures in the presence and absence of protozoa. Ann. Appl. Biol. 19:65-86.

DeWitt, C. T. 1960. On competition. Versl. Landbouwkd. Onderz. 66.8:1-82.

Dickerson, W. A., et. al. 1980. Arthropod species in culture. Entomol. Soc. of Am. Hyattsville, MD. 93 pp.

Dixon, A. F. G. 1970. Factors limiting the effectiveness of the coccinellid beetle, Adalia bipunctata (L.), as a predator of the sycamore aphid, Drepanosiphon platanoides (Schr.). J. Anim. Ecol. 39:739-751.

Domsch, K. H. 1970. Effects of fungicides on microbial populations in soil. pp. 42-46. IN Pesticides in the Soil: Ecology, Degradation and Movement Int. Symp. on Pesticides in the Soil. Mich. State Univ., East Lansing, Mich.

Doutt, R. L., and P. DeBach. 1964. Some biological control concepts and questions. Chap. 5. IN DeBach, P. (ed.), Biological Control of Insect Pests and Weeds. Reinhold Publ. Co., N.Y. 844 pp.

Dyer, M. I., and U. G. Bokhari. 1976. Plant-animal interactions; studies of the effects of grasshopper grazing on the blue grama grass. Ecology 59:762-772.

Eijsackers, H. 1978. Side effects of the herbicide 2,4,5-T affecting the carabid Notiophilus biguttatus Fabr., a predator of springtails. Z. Angew. Entomol. 86:113-128.

Eno, C. F., and P. H. Everett. 1977. Effects of soil applications of ten chlorinated hydrocarbon insecticides on soil microorganisms and the growth of stringless black valentine beans. J. Environ. Qual. 6(1):235-238.

Ferry, B. W., M. S. Baddeleym and D. L. Hawksworth. 1973. Air Pollution and Lichens. The Athlone Press of the Univ. of London. 389 pp.

Finney, G. L., B. Puttler, and L. Dawson. 1960. Rearing of three spotted alfalfa aphid hymenopterous parasites for mass release. J. Econ. Entomol. 53(4):655-659.

Fisher, D. J. 1976. Effects of some fungicides on Rhizobium trifolii and its symbiotic relationship with white clover. Pestic. Sci. 7:10-18.

Fisher, D. J., A. L. Hayes, and C. A. Jones. 1978. Effects of some surfactant fungicides on Rhizobium trifolii and its symbiotic relationship with white clover. Ann. of Appl. Biol. 90(1):73-84.

Flanders, S. E., and M. E. Badgley. 1963. Prey-predator interactions in self-balanced laboratory populations. Hilgardia. 35(8):145-183.

Force, D. C. 1970. Competition among four hymenopterous parasites of an endemic insect host. Ann. Entomol. Soc. of Am. 63:1675-1688.

Force, D. C. 1974. Ecology of insect host-parasitoid communities. Science 184:624-632.

Force, D. C., and P. S. Messenger. 1964a. Duration of development, generation time, and longevity of three hymenopterous parasites of Therioaphis maculata, reared at various constant temperatures. Ann. of the Entomol. Soc. of Am. 57(4):405-413.

Force, D. C., and P. S. Messenger. 1964b. Fecundity, reproductive rates and innate capacity for increase of three parasites of Therioaphis maculata (Buckton). Ecology 45:706-715.

Force, D. C., and P. S. Messenger. 1965. Laboratory studies of competition among three parasites of the spotted aphis Thirioaphis maculata (Buckton). Ecology 46:853-859.

Fredrickson, A. G. 1977. Behavior of mixed cultures of microorganisms. Annu. Rev. Microbiol. 31:63-87.

Gardner, B. T. 1966. Hunger and characteristics of the prey in the hunting behavior of salticid spiders. J. Comp. Physiol. Psychol. 62(3):475-478.

Gilbert, L. E. 1979. Development of theory in the analysis of insect-plant interactions. pp. 117-154. IN Horn, D. J., G. R. Stairs, and R. D. Mitchell (eds.), Analysis of Ecological Systems. Ohio State Univ. Press, Columbus, Ohio.

Gile, J. D., J. C. Collins, and J. W. Gillett. 1979. The soil core microcosm - A potential screening tool. EPA-600/3-79-089, U.S. Environmental Protection Agency, Corvallis, Oregon. 41 pp.

Gile, J. D., and J. W. Gillett. 1979. Fate of ^{14}C-dieldrin in a simulated terrestrial ecosystem. Arch. Environ. Contam. Toxicol. 8:107-124.

Gillett, J. W., and J. M. Witt (eds.). 1979. Terrestrial Microcosms. IN Proc., Workshop on Terrestrial Microcosms, Symposium on Terrestrial Microcosms and Environmental Chemistry. NSF/RA 790034, National Science Foundation, Washington, D.C. 35 pp.

Greaves, M. P., H. A. Davies, J. A. P. Marsh, and G. I. Wingfield. 1976. Herbicides and soil microorganisms. Crit. Rev. Microbiol. 5(1):1-38.

Grossbrad, E. 1970. Effect of herbicides on the symbiotic relationship between Rhizobium trifolii and white clover. pp. 47-59. IN Symposium on White Clover Research, Queens Univ. Belfast, 1969.

Habte, M., and M. Alexander. 1975. Protozoa as agents responsible for the decline of Xanthomonas campestris in soil. Appl. Microbiol. 29(2):159-164.

Hagen, K. S., R. van den Bosh, and D. L. Dahlsten. 1971. The importance of naturally-occurring biological control in the Western United States. pp. 253-293. IN Huffaker, C. B. (ed.), Biological Control, Plenum Press, New York.

Hardman, J. M., and A. L. Turnbull. 1974. The interaction of spatial heterogeneity, predator competition and the functional response to prey density in a laboratory system of wolf spiders (Araneae: Lycosidae) and fruit flies (Diptera: Drosophilidae). J. Anim. Ecol. 43:155-171.

Harper, J. L., and I. H. McNaughton. 1962. The comparative biology of closely related species living in the same area. VII. Interference between individuals in pure and mixed populations of Papaver species. New Phytol. 61:175-188.

Harris, P. 1973. Insects in the population dynamics of plants. pp. 201-209. IN Van Emden, H. F. (ed.), Symp. R. Entomol. Soc. London: Number Six. Insect/Plant Relationships. Blackwell Scientific Publications, Oxford.

Harris, R. L., and L. M. Oliver. 1979. Predation of Philonthus flavolimbatus on the horn fly. Environ. Entomol. 8:259-260.

Harris, W. F. (ed.). 1980. Microcosms as potential screening tools for evaluating transport and effects of toxic substances: Final report. ORNL/EPA-Y. Oak Ridge National Laboratory, Oak Ridge, Tennessee. 382 pp.

Haynes, D. L., and P. Sisojevic. 1966. Predatory behavior of *Philodromus rufus* Walckenaer (Araneae: Thomisidae). Can. Entomol. 98(2):113-133.

Helgesen, R. G., and M. J. Tauber. 1974. Biological control of greenhouse whitefly, *Trialeurodes vaporariorum* (Aleyrodidae: Homoptera), on short-term crops by manipulating biotic and abiotic factors. Can. Entomol. 106:1175-1188.

Herbert, H. J. 1962. Influence of *Typhlodromus* (T.) Pyri scheuten on the development of *Bryobia arborea* m. & a. populations in the greenhouse. Can. Entomol. 94:870-873.

Holling, C. S. 1966. The functional response of invertebrate predators to prey density. Mem. Entomol. Soc. Can. 48:1-88.

Huffaker, C. B. 1958. Experimental studies on predation: Dispersion factors and predator-prey oscillations. Hilgardia 27(14):343-383.

Huffaker, C. B., and C. E. Kennett. 1956. Experimental studies on predation: predation and cyclamen-mite populations on strawberries in California. Hilgardia. 26(4):191-222.

Huffaker, C. B., P. S. Messenger, and P. DeBach. 1971. The natural enemy component in natural control and the theory of biological control. pp. 16-67. IN Huffaker, C. B. (ed.), Biological Control. Plenum Press, New York.

Huffaker, C. B., K. P. Shea, and S. G. Herman. 1963. Experimental studies on predation: Complex dispersion and levels of food in an acarine predator-prey interaction. Hilgardia. 34(9):305-330.

Hussey, N. W. and L. Brovenboer. 1971. Control of pests in greenhouse culture by the introduction of natural enemies. IN: Huffaker, C. B. (ed.), Biological Control. Plenum Press, New York. pp. 195-216.

Hussey, N. W., and W. J. Parr. 1965. Observations on the control of *Tetranychus urticae* Koch on cucumbers by the predatory mite *Phytoseiulus riegeli* Dosse. Entomol. Exp. Appl. 8:271-281.

Jackson, D. R., B. S. Ausmus, and M. Levine. 1979. Effects of arsenic on nutrient dynamics of grassland microcosms and field plots. Water, Air, Soil Pollut. 11:13-21.

Jackson, D. R., and J. M. Hall. 1978. Extraction of nutrients from intact soil cores to assess the impact of chemical toxicants on soil. Pedobiologica 18:272-278.

Jackson, D. R., and M. Levine. 1979. Transport of arsenic in grassland microcosms and field plots. Water, Air, Soil Pollut. 11:3-12.

Jackson, D. R., J. J. Selvidge, and B. S. Ausmus. 1978. Behavior of heavy metals in forest microcosms. 1. Transport and distribution among components. Water, Air, Soil Pollut. 10:3-11.

Jackson, D. R., C. D. Washburne, and B. S. Ausmus. 1977. Loss of Ca and NO_3-N (calcium, nitrate-nitrogen) from terrestrial microcosms as an indicator for assessing contaminants of soil pollution. Water, Air, Soil Pollut. 8(3):279-284.

Jackson, D. R., and A. P. Watson. 1977. Disruption of nutrient pools and transport of heavy metals in a forested watershed near a lead smelter. J. Environ. Qual. 6:331-338.

Jain, S. K. 1969. Comparative ecogenetics of two *Avena* species occurring in central California. Evol. Biol. 3:73-117.

Johnen, B. G., and E. A. Drew. 1977. Ecological effects of pesticides on soil microorganisms. Soil Sci. 123(5):319-324.

Kaufman, D. D. 1970. Pesticide metabolism. pp. 73-86. IN Pesticides in the Soil: Ecology, Degradation, and Movement. International Symposium on Pesticides in the Soil. Mich. State Univ., East Lansing, Mich.

Kaufman, D. D. 1977. Biodegradation and persistence of several acetamide, acylanilide, azide, carbamate, and organophosphate pesticide combinations. Soil Biol. Biochem. 9(1):49-57.

Kaufman, D. D., J. Blake, and D. E. Miller. 1971. Methylcarbamates affect acylanilide herbicide residues in soil. J. Agric. Food Chem. 19:204-206.

Kaufman, D. D., P. C. Kearney, D. W. Von Endt, and D. E. Miller. 1970. Methylcarbamate inhibition of phenylcarbamate metabolism in soil. J. Agric. Food Chem. 18:513-519.

Kistler, R. A. 1980. The functional response as a determinant of stability in an experimental mini-ecosystem. Bull. Ecol. Soc. Am. 61:146.

Klein, D. A. 1977. Seasonal carbon flow and decomposer parameter relationships in a semiarid grassland soil. Ecology 58(1):184-190.

Kochhar, M., U. Blum, and R. A. Reinert. 1980. Effects of O_3 and (or) fescue on ladino clover: Interactions. Can. J. Bot. 58(2):241-249.

Kormanik, P. P., W. C. Bryan, and R. C. Schultz. 1980. Procedures and equipment for staining large numbers of plant root samples for endomycorrhizal assay. Can. J. Microbiol. (in press).

Kudeyarov, V. N., and D. S. Jenkinson. 1975. The effects of biocidal treatments on metabolism in soil - VI. Fumigation with carbon disulphide. Soil Biol. Biochem. 8:375-378.

Kulkarni, J. H., J. S. Sardeshpande, and D. J. Bagyaraj. 1974. Effect of four soil-applied insecticides on symbiosis of Rhizobium with Arachis hypogaea Linn. Plant Soil 40(1):169-172.

LeCato, G. L. 1975a. Interactions among four species of stored-product insects in corn: A multifactorial study. Ann. Entomol. Soc. Am. 66(4):677-679.

LeCato, G. L. 1975b. Predation by red flour beetle on sawtoothed grain beetle. Environ. Entomol. 4(1):504-506.

LeCato, G. L. 1978. Functional response of red flour beetles to density of cigarette beetles and the role of predation in population regulation. Environ. Entomol. 7(1):77-80.

Leslie, P. H. 1958. A stochastic model for studying the properties of certain biological systems by numerical methods. Biometrika 45:16-31.

Letchworth, M. B., and U. Blum. 1977. Effects of acute ozone exposure on growth, nodulation and nitrogen content of ladino clover. Environ. Pollut. 14:303-312.

L'Heritier, P., and G. Teissier. 1937. Elimination des forms mutants dans les populations des drosophiles. Cas des Drosophiles Bar. C. R. Soc. Biol. (Paris) 124:880-882.

Liang, C. N., and M. A. Tabatabai. 1977. Effects of trace elements on nitrogen mineralization in soils. Environ. Pollut. 12:141-147.

Lichtenstein, E. P., K. R. Schulz, and T. T. Liang. 1977. Fate of fresh and aged soil residues of the insecticide (14C)-N-2596 in a soil-corn-water ecosystem. J. Econ. Entomol. 70:169-175.

Lighthart, B., H. Bond, and M. Ricard. 1977. Trace element research using coniferous forest soil/litter microcosms. EPA-600/3-77-091. U.S. Environmental Protection Agency, Corvallis, Ore. 51 pp.

Lin, S., B. R. Funke, and J. T. Schulz. 1972. Effects of some organophosphate and carbamate insecticides on nitrification and legume growth. Plant Soil 37:489-496.

Longstaff, B. C. 1976. The dynamics of collembolan populations: Competitive relationships in an experimental system. Can. J. Zool. 54(6):948-962.

Luxmore, R. J. and C. L. Begovich. 1979. Simulated heavy metal fluxes in tree microcosms and a deciduous forest-A review. ISEM J. 1:48-60.

McCormick, J. F., and R. B. Platt. 1962. Effects of ionizing radiation on a natural plant community. Radiat. Bot. 2:161-188.

McMurtry, J. A., and G. T. Scriven. 1968. Studies on predator-prey interactions between Amblyseius hibisci and Oligonychus punicae: Effects of host-plant conditioning and limited quantities of an alternate food. Ann. Entomol. Soc. Am. 61:393-397.

Manning, W. J., W. A. Feder, and P. M. Papia. 1972. Influence of long-term low levels of ozone and benomyl on growth and nodulation of pinto bean plants. Phytopathology 62(5):497.

Marx, D. H. 1969. Antagonism of mycorrhizal fungi to root pathogenic fungi and soil bacteria. Phytopathology 59:153-163.

Meers, J. L. 1973. Growth of bacteria in mixed cultures. Microbiol. Ecol. 136-181.

Menge, J. A., E. L. V. Johnson, and V. Minassian. 1979. Effect of heat treatment and three pesticides upon the growth and reproduction of the mycorrhizal fungus Glomus fasciculatus. New Phytol. 82(2):473-480.

Mertz, D. M. 1972. The Tribolium model and the mathematics of population growth. Annu. Rev. Ecol. Syst. 3:51-78.

Metcalf, R. L., L. K. Cole, S. G. Wood, D. J. Mandel, and M. L. Milbrath. 1979. Design and evaluation of a terrestrial model ecosystem for evaluation of substitute pesticide chemicals. EPA-600/3-79-004/1-79. Final Report R-80-3249. Corvallis Environ. Res. Lab., U.S. Environmental Protection Agency, Corvallis, Ore. 20 pp.

Metcalf, R. L., G. K. Sangha, and I. P. Kapoor. 1971. Model ecosystem for the evaluation of pesticide biodegradability and magnification. Environ. Sci. Tech. 5(8):709-713.

Miller, R. S. 1964. Interspecies competition in laboratory populations of Drosophila melanogaster and Drosophila simulans. Am. Nat. 98(901):221-238.

Moore. J. A. 1952. Competition between Drosophila melanogaster and Drosophila simulans. II. The improvement of competitive ability through selection. Genetics 38:813-817.

Moth, J. J., and J. S. F. Barker. 1977. Interspecific competition between *Drosophila melanogaster* and *Drosophila simulans*: Effects of adult density on adult viability. Genetica 47(3):203-218.

Murdoch, W. W., and J. R. Marks. 1973. Predation by coccinellid beetles: Experiments on switching. Ecology 54:160-167.

Nash, R. G., M. L. Beall, Jr., and W. G. Harris. 1977. Toxaphene and 1,1,1-trichloro-2,2-bis(p-chlorophenyl) ethane (DDT) losses from cotton in an agroecosystem chamber. J. Agric. Food Chem. 25(2):336-341.

Nechols, J. R., and M. J. Tauber. 1977. Age-specific interaction between the greenhouse whitefly and *Encarsia formosa*: Influence of host on the parasite's oviposition and development. Environ. Entomol. 6:143-149.

Nicholson, A. J. 1954. An outline of the dynamics of animal populations. Aust. J. Zool. 2:9-65.

Odum, E. P. 1971. Fundamentals of Ecology. W. B. Saunders Company, Philadelphia. 574 pp.

Odum, H. T., and A. Lugo. 1970. Metabolism of forest-floor microcosms. pp. 135-156. IN Odum, H. T. (ed.), Tropical Rain Forest. U.S. Atomic Energy Commission, Washington, D.C.

O'Neill, R. V., B. S. Ausmus, D. R. Jackson, R. I. Van Hook, P. Van Voris, C. Washburne, and A. P. Watson. 1977. Monitoring terrestrial ecosystems by analysis of nutrient export. Water, Air, Soil Pollut. 8:271-277.

O'Neill, R. V., and J. M. Giddings. 1979. Population interactions and ecosystem function. pp. 103-123. IN: Innis, G. S. and R. V. O'Neill (eds.), Systems Analysis of Ecosystems. International Cooperative Publishing House, Fairland, Md.

Ortman, E. E., and T. F. Branson. 1976. Growth pouches for studies of host plant resistance to larvae of corn rootworms. J. Econ. Entomol. 69:380-382.

Owen, D. F., and R. G. Wiegert. 1976. Do consumers maximize plant fitness? Oikos 27(3):488-492.

Pareek, R. P., and A. C. Gaur. 1970. Effect of dichloro diphenyl trichloro-ethane (DDT) on Symbiosis of *Rhizobium sp.* with *Phaseolus aureus* (green gram). Plant Soil 33:297-304.

Park, T. 1948. Experimental studies of interspecies competition. 1. Competition between populations of lour beetles, *Tribolium confusum* Duval and *Tribolium castaneum* Herbst. Ecol. Monogr. 18:265-308.

Park, T. 1954. Experimental studies of interspecies competition. 11. Temperature, humidity and competition in two species of *Tribolium*. Physiol. Zool. 27:177-238.

Pimentel, D., E. H. Feinberg, P. W. Wood, and J. T. Hayes. 1965. Selection, spatial distribution, and the coexistence of competing fly species. Am. Nat. 99(905):97-109.

Pimentel, D., W. P. Nagel, and J. L. Madden. 1963. Space-time structure of the environment and the survival of parasite-host systems. Am. Nat. 97:141-167.

Rennie, R. J., and E. L. Schmidt. 1977. Autecological and kinetic analysis of competition between strains of *Nitrobacter* in soils. Ecol. Bull. (Stockholm) 25:431-441.

Rice, E. L. 1979. Allelopathy--an update. Bot. Rev. 45:15-109.

Robinson, J. F., J. A. Klun, and T. A. Brindley. 1978. European corn borer: A nonpreference mechanism of leaf feeding resistance and its relationship to 1,4-benzoxazin-3-one concentration in dent corn tissue. J. Econ. Entomol. 71:461-465.

Ross-Todd, M., E. G. O'Neill, and R. V. O'Neill. 1980. Synthesis of terrestrial microcosm results. pp. 242-264. IN Harris, W. F. (ed.), Microcosms as Potential Screening Tools for Evaluating Transport and Effects of Toxic Substances: Final Report. ORNL/EPA-600/7-79, Oak Ridge National Laboratory, Oak Ridge, Tenn.

Ruhling, A., and G. Tyler. 1973. Heavy metals pollution and decomposition of spruce needle litter. Oikos 24:402-416.

Saakyan-Baranova, A. A. 1964. On the biology of the soft scale *Coccus hesperidum* L. (Homoptera, Coccoidea). Entomol. Rev. 1:135-147.

Salt, G. W. 1979. A comment on the use of the term emergent properties. Am. Nat. 113:145-148.

Selim, K. G., S. A. Z. Mahmoud, and M. T. El-Mokadem. 1970. Effect of dieldrin and lindane on the growth and nodulation of *Vicia faba*. Plant Soil 33:325-329.

Shugart, H. H., and D. C. West. 1980. Forest succession models. BioScience 30:308-313.

Smith, C. R., B. R. Funke, and J. T. Schulz. 1978. Effects of insecticides on acetylene reduction by alfalfa, red clover and sweetclover. Soil Biol. Biochem. 10(6):463-466.

Sokal, R. R., and R. L. Sullivan. 1963. Competition between mutant and wild-type house-fly strains at varying densities. Ecology 44(2):314-322.

Solomon, H. N. 1949. The natural control of animal populations. J. Anim. Ecol. 18:1-37.

Spalding, B. P. 1978. The effect of biocidal treatments on respiration and enzymatic activities of douglas-fir needle litter. Soil Biol. Biochem. 10:537-543.

Spalding, B. P. 1979. Effects of divalent metal chlorides on respiration and extractable enzymatic activities of douglas-fir needle litter. J. Environ. Qual. 8:105-109.

Stotzky, G. 1965. Microbial respiration. pp. 1550-1572. IN: Black, C. A. (ed.), Methods of Soil Analysis, Part 2, Chemical and Microbial Properties. American Society of Agronomy, Inc., Madison, Wis.

Suter, G. W. 1981a. Methods for measuring effects of chemicals on terrestrial population interaction. IN Hammons, Anna S. (ed.), Ecotoxicological Test Systems: Proceedings of a Series of Workshops, ORNL-5709; EPA 560/6-81-004, Oak Ridge National Laboratory.

Suter, G. W. 1981b. Methods for measuring effects of chemicals on terrestrial ecosystem properties. IN Hammons, Anna S. (ed.), Ecotoxicological Test Systems: Proceedings of a Series of Workshops, ORNL-5709; EPA 560/6-81-004, Oak Ridge National Laboratory.

Telegdy-Kovats, L. He. 1932. The growth and respiration of bacteria in sand cultures in the presence and absence of protozoa. Ann. Appl. Biol. 19:5-86.

Tu, C. M. 1977. Effects of pesticide seed treatments on Rhizobium japonicum and its symbiotic relationship with soybean. Bull. Environ. Contam. Toxicol. 18(2):190-199.

Tu, C. M. 1978. Effect of pesticides on acetylene reduction and microorganisms in a sandy loam. Soil Biol. Biochem. 10:451-456.

Tyler, G. 1976. Heavy metal pollution, phosphatase activity, and mineralization of organic phosphorus in forest soils. Soil Biol. Biochem. 8:327-332.

Ullyett, G. C. 1950. Competition for food and allied phenomena in sheep-blowfly populations. Philos. Trans. R. Soc. London, Ser. B. 234:77-174.

U.S. Environmental Protection Agency. 1979. Toxic substances control act premanufacture testing of new chemical substances (OTS-050003; FRL-1069-1) Fed. Regist. 44(53):16240-16292.

Van De Vrie, M. 1962. The influence of spray chemicals on predatory and phytophagous mites on apple trees in laboratory and field trials in the Netherlands. Entomophaga 3(3)243-250.

Van Voris, P., R. V. O'Neill, H. J. Shugart, and W. R. Emanual. 1978. Functional complexity and ecosystem stability: An experimental approach. ORNL/TM-6199. Oak Ridge National Laboratory, Oak Ridge, Tenn. 120 pp.

Waiss, A. C., Jr., B. G. Chan, and C. A. Elliger. 1977. Host plant resistance to insects. pp. 115-128. IN Hedin, P. A. (ed.), ACS Symposium Series 62. American Chemical Soc., Washington, D. C.

West, D. C., S. B. McLaughlin, and H. H. Shugart. 1980. Simulated forest response to chronic air polluation stress. J. Environ. Qual. 9:43-49.

White, J., and J. L. Harper. 1970. Correlated changes in plant size and number in plant populations. J. Ecol. 58:467-485.

Windle, P. N., and E. H. Franz. 1979. The effects of insect parasitism on plant competition: Greenbugs and barley. Ecology 60(3):521-529.

Witkamp, M. 1976. Microcosm experiments on element transfer. Int. J. Environ. Stud. 10(1):59-63.

Yoda, K., T. Kira, H. Ogawa, and H. Hozumi. 1963. Self-thinning in overcrowded pure stands under cultivated and natural conditions. J. Biol. Osaka City Univ. 14:107-129.

MATHEMATICAL MODELS USEFUL IN CHEMICAL HAZARD ASSESSMENT

L. W. Barnthouse
Environmental Sciences Division
Oak Ridge National Laboratory

SECTION 5

MATHEMATICAL MODELS USEFUL IN CHEMICAL HAZARD ASSESSMENT

Mathematical models and laboratory test systems are similar in that both can be viewed, for the purpose of hazard assessment, as analogues of natural ecosystems. However, they are not interchangeable. Whereas laboratory systems are composed of real organisms, mathematical models consist solely of mathematical representations of organisms. Thus, models are more tenuously connected to reality than are laboratory systems. Many alternative models (in principle, an infinite number) of any real ecosystem are possible. Moreover, similar, and equally plausible, models of the same ecosystem can yield radically different predictions about the response of the system to chemical stress. The all-important subject of model validation has in the past received too little attention and is the single greatest limitation on the use of mathematical models in hazard assessment. According to Shugart and O'Neill (1979), model validation is the most important problem remaining in the field of ecological modeling. The limitless variety of models and modeling methods confers advantages as well as disadvantages. In comparison to laboratory test systems, mathematical models are extraordinarily versatile. The number and identity of components included in a model, the detail with which each component is modeled, and the method used to analyze the model can be tailored to the specific needs of each hazard assessment.

This section focuses on general types of models rather than on specific models. There are two reasons for this emphasis. First, the number of types of models is far smaller than the number of individual models. The various types of models differ in applicability and practicality to a greater extent than do different models within the same type. Moreover, describing the characteristics, advantages, and disadvantages of types of models provides insights that can facilitate the design and evaluation of future models. Second, different types of models are required for different purposes. Many ways exist in which models can be used to evaluate hazards, from initial screening of classes of substances for potential effects to site-specific evaluations of specific substances. Selecting the best models for any given assessment involves both technical and nontechnical decisions that can only be made by persons involved in that assessment.

Relatively little work has been done on developing and applying mathematical models to predict effects of toxic substances on multi-population systems and ecosystems. Many existing ecosystem simulation models and environmental fate models could be modified for toxic effects prediction. In addition to relatively complex simulation models, broad classes of simpler, more generalized models and modeling methodologies appear to be potentially useful in toxic effects assessment. Many of these models are not useful for site-specific assessments, and their predictions are primarily qualitative rather than quantitative. However, where applicable (e.g., in preliminary screening), they can be much more rapidly and inexpensively applied than can detailed simulation models.

In addition to the types of models available, evaluation criteria are discussed in this section. These criteria are important because they are needed (1) for judging the usefulness of models proposed for chemical effects assessment, (2) for designing future models, and (3) for deciding how specific models can best be utilized. These criteria relate not only to the properties of the models, but also to the match between the capabilities of the models and the objectives of hazard evaluation schemes. Much of the information discussed in this section is the result of a workshop, Mathematical Models Useful in Toxicity Assessment, sponsored by ORNL and EPA (Barnthouse 1981).

5.1 Available Models and Modeling Methodologies

During the workshop on mathematical models, three general categories of potentially useful models were discussed:

1. Ecosystem simulation models.

2. Generalized multipopulation models.

3. Alternative methodologies.

This section contains brief descriptions of the types of models and methodologies included in each category and of the advantages and disadvantages of each type for predicting the effects of chemical substances.

5.1.1 Ecosystem Simulation Models

Of the various kinds of models that can be used to predict effects of chemical substances on multipopulation complexes and ecosystems, ecosystem simulation models are the best known and the only kind to have had significant practical applications to date. They incorporate far more detailed representations of abiotic and biotic processes than do the other models discussed here. The major advantage of this detail is that the physical and chemical processes that govern the fate of chemical substances in the environment and the biological processes that govern the effects of these substances on organisms can be more realistically modeled. However, the complexity necessitated by this detail makes these models comparatively difficult and expensive to use. They frequently require extensive modification to be implemented on a computing system other than the one for which they were designed. These models are difficult for persons other than the original developers to use, unless extensive documentation (which is rare) is available. Perhaps more important, large amounts of relatively costly data are required to calibrate ecosystem simulation models. Reference data sets that can be used to calibrate models and to verify predictions made by models will be required before ecosystem simulation models can be profitably used in risk assessments.

(1) <u>Terrestrial simulation models</u>. Local, regional, and even global-scale models have been developed to predict the transport and fate of anthropogenic materials in terrestrial ecosystems. The best developed of these are the local-scale cycling models that are used to predict doses to man resulting from radioisotope releases (Hoffman et al. 1977). Regional-scale models of DDT cycling and bioaccumulation have been used in legal proceedings related to DDT regulation (Harrison et al. 1970). Global-scale models are now being developed to assess and predict changes in atmospheric CO_2 levels due to fossil fuel combustion (Emanuel et al. 1980). The local and regional models can be used to predict the transport and bioaccumulation of chemical substances, provided that sufficient information on the relevant chemical properties of the substances is available. A major disadvantage of all these models is that they assume that the modeled substance behaves like a tracer and has no effects on the modeled system. All would require substantial modification and validation to predict effects.

Nonlinear ecosystem simulation models such as the biome models developed under the auspices of the International Biological Program (IBP) (e.g., Innis 1972) can, at least in principle, be used to predict chemical effects. The most important limitation to their use is that unusually large quantities of data are required to calibrate them. Even when calibrated, independent data sets (not usually available) are required for validation, i.e., to show that they can accurately predict the effects of stress on ecosystems.

Forest succession models (e.g., Shugart and West 1977) are now being used to simulate the effects of SO_x and forest management practices on the structure and productivity of forests. These models require minor modifications to predict effects of chemical substances, and the predictions made (changes in timber yield) are socially relevant. Data requirements are less severe than for IBP-type models, but only soil compartments and vegetation are modeled. Although effects on animals of forest successional changes caused by chemical substances may be indirectly inferred from model predictions, they cannot be predicted directly.

Other succession models have been used to evaluate environmental impacts on naturally occurring forests. Botkin (1973, 1977) considered the effects of CO_2 enrichment on plant growth and subsequent effects on forest dynamics. McLaughlin et al. (1978) and West et al. (1980) conducted model experiments on chronic air pollution stress expressed as a change in growth rates of pollution-sensitive trees.

A review of forest succession models by Shugart and West (1980) concluded that forest succession models can provide a necessary adjunct to laboratory-based assessments of environmental effects and that models will become increasingly important tools for prediction if human activities alter environmental conditions on a global scale.

(2) <u>Aquatic Simulation Models</u>. Many models have been developed to simulate the transport and fate of materials in aquatic ecosystems (e.g., Smith et al. 1977; Mogenson and Jorgensen 1979; Fagerstrom and Asell 1973). Some of these were constructed specifically to predict the transport and fate of chemical substances such as pesticides, PCBs, and heavy metals. Like the corresponding terrestrial fate models, they cannot be used to predict the effects of chemical substances on ecosystems. They must be modified or coupled to a model that can predict effects.

Nonlinear ecosystem simulation models exist for most types of aquatic ecosystems (e.g., Park et al. 1975; Scavia et al. 1976; Steele and Frost 1977; Kremer and Nixon 1978). Many of these models are detailed enough so that effects of chemical substances on organismal physiology can be extrapolated to population and ecosystem effects. The lower trophic levels (phytoplankton and zooplankton) are generally modeled in the greatest detail, and success at validating model predictions has been greatest at these levels.

A few models are now being developed that incorporate both sufficient physical and chemical detail to predict the fate of substances and enough biological detail to predict effects (e.g., Falco and Mulkey 1976). None of these models has been applied to date.

5.1.2 Generalized Multipopulation Models

Ecosystem simulation models are intended to be realistic representations of particular ecosystem types. Modifying them to model a different ecosystem can be time-consuming and expensive. Alternatively, it is also possible to construct simple, highly generalized multipopulation models that can be rapidly and inexpensively tailored to fit any system of interacting populations, aquatic or terrestrial. Using this modeling strategy, no attempt is made to model every component of an ecosystem; only those processes believed to be critically important are modeled. Transport phenomena are not incorporated in these models. Thus, they can be used to predict the effects of chemical substances on systems, but not the fate of those substances. These models are not thought to be appropriate for detailed chemical- and site-specific hazard assessments. They can be used in the early stages of an assessment to rapidly explore the possible effects of toxic substances. Results of these preliminary studies can aid in determining whether a more detailed modeling effort is warranted.

These models can be classified into four groups. In order of increasing complexity, these are:

1. Functionally simple, not environmentally coupled (e.g., DeAngelis et al. 1975; Canale 1970; Levin 1974; Hassell and Comins 1976).

2. Functionally simple, environmentally coupled (e.g., Emanuel and Mulholland 1975).

3. Functionally complex, not environmentally coupled (e.g., Hsu et al. 1977; Travis et al. 1980).

4. Functionally complex, environmentally coupled (e.g., Craig et al. 1979; Eggers 1975; Anderson and Ursin 1977).

Within each category, models can be either spatially homogeneous or spatially complex and either age-dependent or not. Although many of the cited examples were developed with particular systems of populations in mind, the principles used can be applied to any system.

5.1.3 Alternative methodologies

In additon to ecosystem simulation models and generalized multipopulation models, several less familiar modeling methods appear to be potentially useful in hazard assessment. Two of these, loop analysis and time-averaging, are methods of analyzing the qualitative behavior of systems of coupled differential equations. They could be applied to many of the generalized multipopulation models discussed in the previous section. A third method, input-output analysis, is a method of econometric analysis that has been modified for use in ecology. In addition to these newly developed methods, the well-developed (but infrequently applied) theory of population genetics may be useful in predicting the evolutionary responses of populations exposed to chemical substances.

(1) Loop analysis. Loop analysis (Levins 1974; Lane and Levins 1977) can be used to analyze partially specified systems of equations (i.e., systems in which the patterns of interaction among the component variables are known, but parameter values and functional forms are not). The definitions of the variables are entirely arbitrary (e.g., they can be populations, aggregated groups of populations, life-stages, or even physiological rates). Loop analysis has been used in theoretical studies of eutrophication (Lane and Levins 1977), but has not been used to predict effects of chemical substances. It can be used to predict the response of a multipopulation system to an applied stress, to identify critical parameters that should be measured, and to identify system properties that enhance or reduce impacts.

(2) <u>Time-averaging</u>. Time-averaging (Levins 1979) was designed to be complementary to loop analysis. In loop analysis, the system being modeled is assumed to be at, or at least close to, equilibrium. If the natural system being modeled is in reality far from equilibrium, conclusions drawn from loop analysis may not be valid. In contrast, time-averaging assumes that the system is fluctuating and is not at equilibrium.

Like loop analysis, time-averaging can be applied to any system of interacting populations or aggregates of populations. However, instead of focusing on average population (or aggregate population) sizes as in loop analysis, time-averaging focuses on the variances and covariances of the population sizes. In theory, measurements of these variances and covariances, and changes in variances and covariances in response to inputs of chemical substances, may be used to distinguish populations that are directly affected by a chemical substance from those that are indirectly affected. This application of time-averaging may be especially useful in interpreting the results of microcosm experiments.

(3) <u>Input-output analysis</u>. Input-output analysis is an econometric method that has been adapted for use in ecology (Hannon 1973; Finn 1976; Lettenmaier and Richey 1978). It has been used to compare material cycling patterns in different ecosystems. The analysis can be applied either to whole ecosystems or to subsystems within ecosystems. It has been hypothesized that structure and cycling indices derived by using input-output analysis may be useful as indicators of environmental stress. In theory, input-output analysis can be used to predict changes in material flow patterns in response to stress, but further development and testing are required before it is known whether this is feasible in practice.

(4) <u>Population genetics models</u>. Population biologists have used a variety of models to study the evolution of populations and systems of interacting populations in response to changes in their environments (e.g., Kimura and Ohta 1971). All of these models relate rates of changes in gene or phenotype frequencies to selective pressure, heritability, and genetic variance within populations. They can be used to predict adaptive responses of species to toxic substances and to predict the effects of those responses on population size, location, behavior, and interactions with other species.

Although population genetics models have not been used to predict the effects of chemical substances on populations, they are potentially valuable for this purpose because populations in nature frequently evolve in response to exposure to chemical substances. Pesticide tolerance in insects and antibiotic resistance in pathogens are notorious examples. Practical applications would require experimental work to measure the genetic variances in tolerance within and between populations for species of interest and to estimate selection intensities in the field.

5.2 Criteria for Evaluating and Selecting Models

No existing models have been demonstrated to be useful for predicting the effects of toxic substances on ecosystems. Moreover, no single model or model type can fulfill all regulatory needs. For this reason, one task at the workshop on Mathematical Models Useful in Toxicity Assessment was development of criteria that could be used to evaluate the usefulness of existing models, modified versions of existing models, and new models. These criteria include not only the properties of the models themselves, but also the match between the capabilities (and deficiencies) of the models and the objectives of a hazard assessment scheme. The criteria selected are defined as follows:

1. **The degree of modification required for handling toxic material inputs.** Can toxic material inputs be modeled directly? Are the physical and chemical processes that govern the transport and fate of toxic materials included in the model? Are the biological processes directly affected by toxic materials included in the model?

2. **Data requirements.** Is the amount of data required for parameterizing the model consistent with the available resources (i.e., time and money)?

3. **Generality.** Can the model be used for only one geographic region or ecosystem type, or can it be easily applied to others?

4. **Ease of validation.** Has the model been validated against baseline data? Are the output variables (i.e., those that must be measured to test the model's predictions) easily measurable? Do modifications required for handling toxic materials invalidate the model? Can the model be tested with microcosm systems and with field data?

5. **Social relevance.** Is the model output relevant to regulatory needs?

6. **Relevance to monitoring.** Does the model suggest an environmental monitoring protocol? For example, does it suggest indicator variables that are easily measurable and that could be used as early warnings of environmental effects.

7. **Spatial/temporal scales.** Do the spatial and temporal scales of the model match the basic impact scale?

8. **Ease of use.** Is the model documentation comprehensible, consistent, and complete? Is the computer code readily available? How much modification is required to implement the code on a different computer system?

9. __Acceptance by the scientific community, especially the ecological community__. Is the model based on biological ideas and mathematical procedures accepted by most of the ecological community?

Figure 5.1 presents a scheme that could be used to identify specific models for use in such evaluations. The scheme uses aquatic ecosystem simulation models as examples, but it could apply equally to any type of model. It is exceedingly important to note that the choice of the best model(s) for any given hazard assessment involves a number of decisions that require active participation by the Office of Toxic Substances. These decisions include formulating the specific legal or social questions that the model will be expected to answer and specifying whether the purpose of the assessment is the screening of many substances for potential effects or the detailed evaluation of particular substances in connection with regulatory actions.

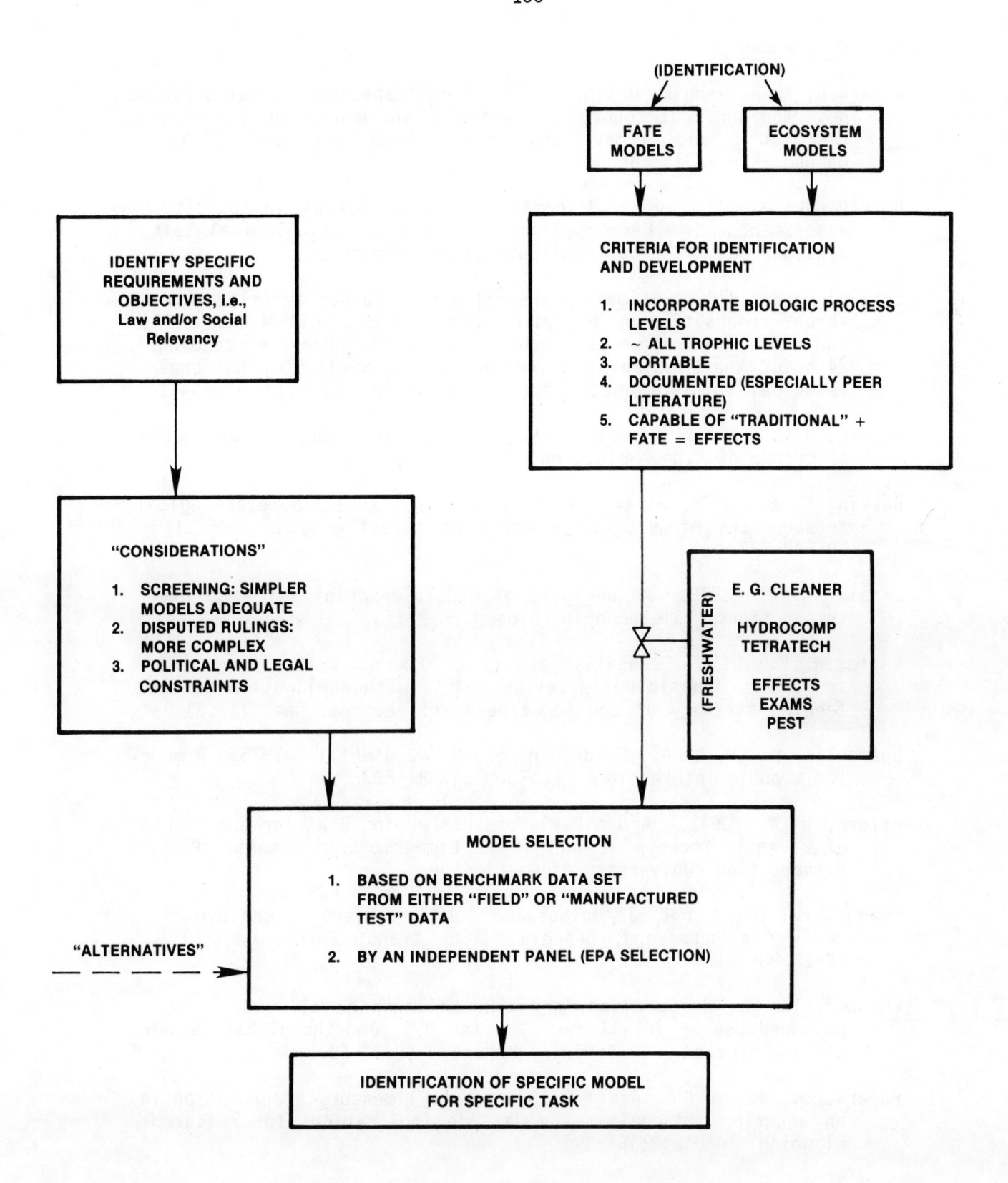

```
                                    (IDENTIFICATION)
                                   ↙            ↘
                            ┌──────────┐    ┌──────────┐
                            │  FATE    │    │ ECOSYSTEM│
                            │  MODELS  │    │  MODELS  │
                            └────┬─────┘    └────┬─────┘
                                 └────┬──────────┘
                                      ↓
┌──────────────────────┐    ┌────────────────────────────────┐
│ IDENTIFY SPECIFIC    │    │ CRITERIA FOR IDENTIFICATION    │
│ REQUIREMENTS AND     │    │ AND DEVELOPMENT                │
│ OBJECTIVES, i.e.,    │    │                                │
│ Law and/or Social    │    │ 1. INCORPORATE BIOLOGIC PROCESS│
│ Relevancy            │    │    LEVELS                      │
└──────────┬───────────┘    │ 2. ~ ALL TROPHIC LEVELS        │
           │                │ 3. PORTABLE                    │
           │                │ 4. DOCUMENTED (ESPECIALLY PEER │
           │                │    LITERATURE)                 │
           │                │ 5. CAPABLE OF "TRADITIONAL" +  │
           │                │    FATE = EFFECTS              │
           │                └────────────────┬───────────────┘
           ↓                                 │
┌──────────────────────┐                     │        ┌──────────────┐
│ "CONSIDERATIONS"     │                     │        │ E. G. CLEANER│
│                      │                     │        │              │
│ 1. SCREENING: SIMPLER│              (FRESHWATER)    │  HYDROCOMP   │
│    MODELS ADEQUATE   │                     ⋈────────│  TETRATECH   │
│ 2. DISPUTED RULINGS: │                     │        │              │
│    MORE COMPLEX      │                     │        │   EFFECTS    │
│ 3. POLITICAL AND LEGAL                     │        │   EXAMS      │
│    CONSTRAINTS       │                     │        │   PEST       │
└──────────┬───────────┘                     │        └──────────────┘
           │                                 │
           ↓                                 ↓
          ┌──────────────────────────────────────────┐
          │ MODEL SELECTION                          │
          │                                          │
          │ 1. BASED ON BENCHMARK DATA SET           │
"ALTERNATIVES"          FROM EITHER "FIELD" OR "MANUFACTURED
       ----→│    TEST" DATA                         │
          │                                          │
          │ 2. BY AN INDEPENDENT PANEL (EPA SELECTION)│
          └────────────────────┬─────────────────────┘
                               ↓
                   ┌─────────────────────────────┐
                   │ IDENTIFICATION OF SPECIFIC MODEL │
                   │ FOR SPECIFIC TASK           │
                   └─────────────────────────────┘
```

FIGURE 5.1 SCHEME FOR SELECTING APPROPRIATE MODELS FOR USE IN HAZARD ASSESSMENTS.

5.3 References

Andersen, K. P., and E. Ursin. 1977. A multispecies extension to the beverton and holt theory of fishing, with accounts of phosphorus circulation and primary production. Medd. fra Dan. Fisk. Havunders. 7:313-345.

Barnthouse, L. W. 1981. Mathematical models useful in toxicity assessment. IN Hammons, Anna S. (ed.) Ecotoxicological Test Systems; Oak Ridge National Laboratory, (in press).

Botkin, D. B. 1973. Estimating the effects of carbon fertilization on forest composition by ecosystem simulation: IN G. M. Woodwell, and E. V. Pecan (eds.). Carbon and the Biosphere. Proceedings 24th Brookhaven Symposium in Biology. CONF-720510, National Technical Information Service, Springfield, Va. pp. 328-344.

Botkin, D. B. 1977. Forests, lakes, and the anthropogenic production of carbon dioxide. BioScience 27:325-331.

Botkin, D. B., J. F. Janak, and J. R. Wallis. 1972. Some ecological consequences of a computer model of forest growth. J. Ecol. 60:849-872.

Canale, R. P. 1970. An analysis of models describing predaor-prey interactions. Biotechnol. Bioeng. 12:353.

Craig, R. B., D. L. DeAngelis, and K. R. Dixon. 1979. Long- and short-term dynamic optimization models with application to the feeding strategy of the loggerhead shrike. Am. Nat. 113:31-51.

DeAngelis, D. L., R. A. Goldstein, and R. V. O'Neill. 1975. A model for trophic interaction. Ecology 56:881-892

Effers, D. M. 1975. A Synthesis of the Feeding Behavior and Growth of Juvenile Sockeye Salmon in the Limnetic Environment. Ph.D. dissertation, University of Washington.

Emanuel, W. R., and R. J. Mulholland. 1975. Energy based dynamic model for Lago Pond, Georgia. IEEE trans. Autom. Control. AC-20:98-101.

Emanuel, W. R., J. S. Olson, and G.G. Killough et al. 1980. The expanded use of fossil fuels by the U.S. and the global carbon dioxide problem. J. Environ. Manage. 10:37-49.

Fagerstrom, T., and B. Asell. 1973. Methyl mercury accumulation in an aquatic food chain. A model and implications for research planning. Ambio 2:164-171.

Falco, J. W., and L. A. Mulkey. 1976. Modeling the effect of pesticide loading on riverine ecosystems. IN Ott, W. R., (ed.), Environmental Modeling and Simulation. EPA-600/ 9-76-016/.

Finn, J. T. 1976. Measures of ecosystem structure and function derived from analysis of flows. J. Theor. Biol. 56:363-380.

Hannon, B. 1973. The structure of ecosystems. J. Theor. Biol. 41:535-646.

Harrison, H. L., et al. 1970. Systems studies of DDT transport. Science 170:503-508.

Hassell, M. P., and H. N. Comins. 1976. Discrete time models for two-species competition. Theor. Popul. Bio. 9:202-221.

Hoffman, F. O., C. W. Miller, D. L. Shaeffer, and C. T. Garten, Jr. 1977. Computer codes for the assessment of radionuclides released to the environment. Nuclear Safety 18:343-354.

Hsu, Hubbel, and Waltman. 1977. A mathematical theory of single nutrient competition in continuous cultures of microorganisms. SIAM J. of Appl. Math. 32:366-383.

Innis, G. S. 1972. Simulation models of grassland and grazing lands. Prep. No. 35, Grassland Biome, Natural Resource Ecology Laboratory, Colorado State University, Fort Collins.

Kimura, M., and T. Ohta. 1971. Theoretical aspects of population genetics. Monog. Popu. Biol. 4. Princeton University Press, Princeton, N. J.

Kremer, J. N., and S. W. Nixon. 1978. A Coastal Marine Ecosystem-Simulation and Analysis. Springer-Verlag.

Lane, P. A., and R. Levins. 1977. The dynamics of aquatic ecosystems 2. The effects of nutrient enrichment on model plankton communities. Limnol. Oceanogr. 22(3):454-471.

Lettenmaier, D. P., and J. E. Richey. 1978. Ecosystem modeling: A structural approach. J. Environ. Eng. Dive., Proc. Am. Soc. Civ. Eng. 104:1015-1021.

Levin, S. A. 1974. Dispersion and population interaction. Am. Nat. 108:207-228.

Levins, R. 1974. The qualitative analysis of partially specified systems. Ann. N.Y. Acad. Sci. 231:123-138.

Levins, R. 1979. Coexistence in a variable environment. Am. Nat. 114:765-783.

McLaughlin, S. B., D. C. West, H. H. Shugart, and D. S. Shriner. 1978. Air pollution effects on forest growth and succession: applications of a mathematical model. IN H. B. H. Cooper, (ed), Proceedings, 71st Meeting of the Air Pollution Control Association. Document No. 78-24.5 APCA., Houston, TX.

Mogenson, B. and S. E. Jorgensen. 1979. Modelling the distribution of chromium in a Danish firth. IN S. E. Jorgensen, (ed), Proc. 1st International Conference on the State of the Art in Ecological Modelling. Copenhangen 1978.

Park, R., et al. 1975. A generalized model for simulating lake ecosystems. Contribution No. 152, Eastern Deciduous Forest Biome, U. S. International Biological Program. Simulation Councils, Inc.

Scavia, D. B., J. Eadie, and A. Robertson. 1976. An Ecological Model for Lake Ontario. Model formulation, calibration, and preliminary evaluation. NOAA Technical Report ERL 371-GLERL 12.

Shugart, H. H., and R. V. O'Neill (eds.). 1979. Systems Ecology. Benchmark Papers in Ecology 9. Dowden, Hutchinson, Ross, Inc. Stroudsburg, Pa.

Shugart, H. H., and D. C. West. 1977. Development of an appalachian deciduous forest succession model and its application to assessment of the impact of the chestnut blight. J. Environ. Managem. 5:161-179.

Shugart, H. H., and D. C. West. 1980. Forest succession models. BioScience. 30:308-313.

Smith, J. H., et al. 1977. Environmental pathways of selected chemicals in freshwater systems, Part I. EPA 600/7-77-113.

Steele, J. H., and B. W. Frost. 1977. The structure of Plankton communities. Philos. Trans. R. Soc., London, Ser. B. 280:485-534.

Travis, C. C., W. M. Post, and D. L. DeAngelis. 1980. Analysis of compensatory Leslie matrix models for competing species. Theor. Pop. Biol. (in press).

West, D. C., S. B. McLaughlin, and H. H. Shugart. 1980. Simulated forest response to chronic air pollution stress. J. Environ. Qual. 9:43-49.

APPENDIX A*

SUMMARY TABLE OF
AQUATIC TEST SYSTEMS

---

*Complete references can be found in Section 3.7.

APPENDIX A
SUMMARY TABLE OF AQUATIC TEST SYSTEMS

Author(s)	System components	Measured responses	Duration of expt.	Expt'l. variables	Validation
A. COMPETITION					
Fielding and Russell 1976	Algae (_Ectocarpus siliculosis_, _Ulothrix flacca_, _Erythrotrichia carnea_) in batch culture	Final yield (biomass)	35 days	Cu	
Fisher et al. 1974	Algae (_Dunaliella tertiolecta_, _Thalassiosira pseudonana_) in batch and continuous culture	Population density	7 to 16 days	PCB	
Frank 1957	_Daphnia magna_, _D. pulicaria_	Population density, size classes, sex ratios, # of ephippia, # of shed parthenogenic eggs	60 days	Food source	
Goulden and Horning 1980	_Daphnia galeata mendotae_, _Bosmina longirostris_	Population density, age classes, mortality	64 to 108 days		
Hansen and Hubbell 1980	Bacteria (_Escherichia coli_, _Pseudomonas aeruginosa_) in continuous culture	Population density	60 to 120 h	Nutrient concentration, dilution rate	
Kindig 1979	Algae (_Scenedesmus_ sp., _Anabaena_ sp., _Chlorella_ sp., _Ankistrodesmus_ sp., _Selenastrum_ sp.) in batch cultures	Population density, optical density	32 to 58 days	Streptomycin	
Klotz et al. 1976	Algae (_Chlorella_ sp., _Achnanthes deflexa_) in semicontinuous culture	Population density	7 days	Sewage treatment plant effluent	
Lange 1974	Algae (_Microcystis aeruginosa_, _Nostoc muscorum_, _Phormidium foveolarum_) in batch culture	Population density, pH, COD	31 days		
Marshall 1969	_Daphnia magna_, _D. pulex_	Population density, # gravid females, # males, # shed ephippia, # eggs in brood chambers	100 weeks	Gamma radiation	
Mickelson et al. 1979	Algae (_Thalassiosira gravida_, _Skeletonema costatum_, _Chaetoceros septentrionalis_) in continuous culture	Population density	10 days	Dilution rate	
Mosser et al. 1972	Algae (_Thalassiosira pseudonana_, _Dunaliella tertiolecta_) in batch cultures	Population density, biomass	4 days	PCB, DDT	

Author(s)	System components	Measured responses	Duration of expt.	Expt'l. variables	Validation
Muller and Lee 1977	Ciliate (Euplotes vannus), nematode (Chromadorina germanica), foramaniferan (Allogromia laticollaris)	Population density	42 days	Food density	
Russell and Fielding 1974	See Fielding and Russell 1976	Final yield (biomass)	35 days	Light, temperature, salinity	
Tilman 1977, Titman 1976	Algae (Asterionella formosa, Cyclotella meneghiniana) in semi-continuous culture	Population density	42 days	Nutrient concentration, dilution rate	

B. PREDATION

Author(s)	System components	Measured responses	Duration of expt.	Expt'l. variables	Validation
Akre and Johnson 1979	Zooplankton (Anomalagrion hastatum, Daphnia magna, Simocephalus vetulus)	Prey survival	12 h	Prey density, prey species, predator hunger	
Baker and Modde 1977	Largemouth bass, bluegill, blacktail shiner	Prey survival	15 min	Stain	
Bethel and Holmes 1977	Amphipods, ducks, muskrats	Prey survival	5 to 15 min (ducks), 24 h (muskrats)	Parasitism	
Brandl and Fernando 1974	Zooplankton (Acanthocyclops vernalis, Ceriodaphnia reticulata)	Prey survival	5 days	Predator diet, prey size	
Brandl and Fernando 1978	Zooplankton (Cyclops vernalis, Mesocyclops edax, natural communities)	Prey survival	24 h	Predator density	
Confer 1971	Zooplankton (Mesocyclops edax, Diaptomus floridanus)	Prey survival	2 to 5 days	Prey size, prey density	
Confer and Blades 1975a,b	Bluegill, Daphnia magna, D. pulex, natural copepods	Reactive distance, capture success	Seconds	Prey size, light	
Confer et al. 1978	Lake trout, brook trout, Daphnia magna, D. pulex	Reactive distance	Seconds	Prey size, prey pigmentation, predator hunger, light, aquarium shape	
Cooke 1971	Newt, frog tadpole, gravel	# Attacks, # captures	1 to 5 min	DDT	
Coutant 1973	Rainbow trout, chinook salmon	Prey survival	3 to 10 min	Heat shock	
Coutant et al. 1974	Largemouth bass, channel catfish	Prey survival	30 min	Cold shock	
Deacutis 1978	Killifish, Atlantic silverside, flounder	# Attacks, # captures, # escapes	30 min	Heat shock	

Author(s)	System components	Measured responses	Duration of expt.	Expt'l. variables	Validation
Drenner et al. 1978	Gizzard shad, natural zooplankton community	Prey survival	1 to 13½ h		
Eisler 1973	Gastropod drill, mussel	Prey survival, # attacks, predator egg production	28 to 32 days	Crude oil, oil dispersant	
Farr 1977	Killifish, grass shrimp, sand	Prey survival, capture time	3 h	Methyl parathion, ethyl parathion	
Farr 1978	Killifish, grass shrimp, sheepshead minnow, sand	Prey survival	5 days	Methyl parathion	
Goodyear 1972	Largemouth bass, mosquito fish, refuge	Prey survival	20 days	Gamma radiation	
Gerritsen 1978	Zooplankton (Cyclops scutifer, Chaoborus sp.)	Prey survival	4 h	Prey size	
Herting and Witt 1967	Bowfin, various prey (fish)	Prey survival	24 h	Disease, parasitism, handling stress	
Kania and O'Hara 1974	Largemouth bass, mosquito fish, refuge	Prey survival	60 h	Hg	
Kerfoot 1977a, b	Zooplankton (Cyclops bicuspidatus, C. vernalis, Bosmina longirostris) -or-	# Encounters, # attacks, # injuries, # ingestions	5 h	Prey instar	
	Epischura nevadensis, Bosmina longirostris, Daphnia ambigua, Ceriodaphnia sp.)	Prey survival	3 days	Prey species, prey size	
Landry 1978	Zooplankton (Labidocera trispinosa, Acartia clausi, A. tonsa, Paracalanus parvis, Calanus pacificus	Prey survival	24 h	Prey species, prey size, prey density, jar size, anesthesia	
Li and Li 1979	Zooplankton (Acanthocyclops vernalis, rotifers, cladocerans, copepods)	Prey survival	24 h	Prey species, prey size	
Luckinbill 1973	Protozoa (Didinium nasutum, Paramecium aurelia)	Population density	6 to 33 days	Bacterial food, methyl cellulose	
Luckinbill 1974	Protozoa (Didinium nasutum, Paramecium aurelia)	Population density, population extinction	3 to 80 h	Culture volume	
Mullin 1979	Zooplankton (Tortanus discaudatus, Acartia clausi)	Prey survival	6 to 8 h	Prey instar, jar size	
O'Brien et al. 1976	Bluegill, Daphnia magna	Prey selection	Seconds	Prey size	

Author(s)	System components	Measured responses	Duration of expt.	Expt'l. variables	Validation
Salt 1967	Protozoa (*Woodruffia metabolica*, *Paramecium aurelia*)	Population density, generation time, searching rate, capture rate	~100 h		
Salt 1968	Protozoa (*Amoeba proteus*, *Paramecium aurelia*)	Population density, generation time, feeding rate	~300 h		
Salt 1974	Protozoa (*Didinium nasutum*, *Paramecium aurelia*)	Population density, generation time, feeding rate	6 to 72 h	Prey and predator densities	
Stein 1977	Smallmouth bass, crayfish, gravel	Prey survival, handling time	10 h to 7 days	Prey sex, moulting stage, substrate type	
Stein and Magnuson 1976	Smallmouth bass, crayfish, gravel	Prey behavior	3 days	Presence of predator	
Sullivan et al. 1978	Largemouth bass, fathead minnow, gravel, artifical plants	Prey survival	3 to 7 days	Cd	
Sylvester 1972	Coho salmon, sockeye salmon	Mean survival time	5 to 10 min	Heat shock	
Sylvester 1973	Coho salmon, sockeye salmon	Prey survival	15 min	Heat shock	
Tagatz 1976	Pinfish, grass shrimp, seagrass, sand	Prey survival	1 to 3 days	Mirex	
Thompson 1978	Damselfly nymph, *Daphnia magna*	Attack coefficient, handling time, prey survival	24 h	Prey density, temperature	
Van den Ende 1973	Bacteria (*Klebsiella aerogenes*), protozoa (*Tetrahymena pyriformis*) in continuous culture	Population density	1100 h		
Vaughan 1979	Largemouth bass, bluegill, refuge	Prey survival	Not specified	Viral infection	
Veilleux 1979	Protozoa (*Didinium nasutum*, *Paramecium aurelia*)	Population density, fission rate, feeding rate	Not specified		
Vinyard and O'Brien 1976	Bluegill, *Daphnia magna*	Prey selection	Seconds	Prey size	
Ward et al. 1976	Marsh fiddler crab in salt marsh plots	Population density	6 weeks	Insecticide	
Ware 1972	Rainbow trout, amphipods (*Crangonyx richmondensis*, *Hyalella azteca*), litter substrates	Prey survival, # attacks, # captures, handling time, reactive distance	50 min	Prey density, substrate type, predator hunger	
Werner 1974	Bluegill, green sunfish, *Daphnia magna*	Handling time	Minutes	Prey size, predator hunger	
Werner and Hall 1974	Bluegill, *Daphnia magna*	Prey survival, reactive distance	0.5 to 5 min	Prey size, prey density	

Author(s)	System components	Measured responses	Duration of expt.	Expt'l. variables	Validation
Woltering et al. 1978	Largemouth bass, mosquito fish, refuge	Prey survival, predator growth	10 days	NH_3	
Wolters and Coutant 1976	Largemouth bass, bluegill	Prey survival	1 to 30 min	Cold shock	
Yocum and Edsall 1974	Yellow perch, lake whitefish	# Attacks, # captures	30 min	Heat shock	
Zaret 1972	Fish (<u>Melaniris chagresi</u>), zooplankton (<u>Ceriodaphnia cornutum</u>)	Prey survival	1 h	Prey morphology	

C. PARASITISM

Couch and Courtney 1977	Shrimp, virus	% Infection, mortality	35 days	PCB	

D. MIXED FLASK CULTURES

Bryfogle and McDiffett 1979	Flask, water, pond inoculum	P, R, chlorophyll, biomass, populations	48 days	Herbicide	
Cooper 1973	Water, sterile pond sediment, pond water with zooplankton removed	P, R	40 days	Herbivorous fish	
Ferens and Beyers 1972	See Gorden 1967	P, R, chlorophyll, biomass	40 days	Gamma radiation	
Fraleigh 1971	See Gorden 1967	P, R, chlorophyll, biomass, total P	80 days	Phosphorus enrichment	
Gorden 1967	Artificial medium, inoculum from Beyers' original culture (algae, bacteria, <u>Paramecium</u>, rotifers, flagellate, ostracod)	P, R, populations, POM, DOM, thiamin, glyoxylate uptake	75 days	None	
Kelly 1971	Artificial medium, inoculum from lakes, ponds, streams	P, R, chlorophyll, carotenoids, biomass, alkalinity, CO_2, DOM, DIM, TOM, TIM, populations	59 weeks	Temperature	
Kurihara 1978a,b (see also Sugiura et al. 1976a,b)	Artificial medium, pond inoculum	P, R, biomass, populations	140 days	B-BHC, Cu	
Leffler 1977	Artificial medium; inoculum from aquaria, Beyers' cultures, ponds	P, R, populations, Element Distribution Index	18 weeks	Temperature	
McConnell 1962	Tap water, pond inoculum	P, R, organic matter	222 days	Nutrients	
McConnell 1965	Tap water, pond inoculum; <u>Tilapia</u> added later	P, R, fish biomass	1½ months	Herbivorous fish	
Neill 1972, 1975	Well water, algae, crustacea	P, populations, crustacean gut contents, microhabitat, survivorship, fecundity	>1 year	<u>Gambusia</u> predation	

Author(s)	System components	Measured responses	Duration of expt.	Expt'l. variables	Validation
Ollason 1977	Artificial medium, inoculum from horse trough	Populations	60 days	Light levels	
Reed 1976	Water, pond inoculum, various substrates	Populations	20 weeks	Nutrient enrichment	
Thomas 1978	Water, inoculum from various sources	Pigments, POM		Cd, nitrogen	
Waide et al. 1978	Artificial medium, pond inoculum	DO, pH, temp., conductivity, turbidity, fluorescence, total P, SRP, algal populations	70 days	Turbulence, light regime, pH, _Daphnia_ grazing	
Taub (1969a,b,c; 1976; Taub and Crow 1980; Taub, Crow, and Hartman 1980; Crow and Taub 1979)	Bacteria, algae, _Daphnia_, protozoa, rotifers, ostracod, artificial medium, sediment	Population density, pigments, optical density, biomass, productivity	1 to 2 months	Algicide, insecticides, organic enrichment, Hg, Cd, PCB	
E. PERIPHYTON COMMUNITIES					
Admiraal 1977	Recirculating sea water, natural periphyton on natural sediment	Chlorophyll, populations	4 to 23 weeks	Source of sediment, nutrient enrichment	
Bott et al. 1977	Recirculating stream water, periphyton colonizers, various substrates	Carbon flux; litter decomposition; NTA decomposition		Cu	Compared w/natural stream
Cushing and Rose 1970	Recirculating river water, periphyton colonizers, glass tube substrate	^{65}Zn uptake		None	
Gerhart et al. 1977	Partially recirculating lake water, model stream, periphyton colonizers, porcelain substrates	Chlorophyll, populations, biomass	25 days	Coal leachate	
Kedhe and Wilhem 1972	Recirculating stream water, periphyton colonizers, snails, microscope slide substrates	Biomass, chlorophyll, populations	92 days	Grazing	
Kevern and Ball 1965	Recirculating artificial medium, periphyton inoculum on rock substrates	Water chemistry, P, R	>1 month	Temp., light, EDTA	
McIntire et al. 1964	Partially recirculating stream water in wooden troughs, gravel, periphyton colonizers	P, R, biomass, chlorophyll, populations	2 years	None	
McIntire 1968a,b	As above, plus snails	"		Light, temp.	
Phinney and McIntire 1965	"	"		Temp.	

Author(s)	System components	Measured responses	Duration of expt.	Expt'l. variables	Validation
F. OTHER MODEL ECOSYSTEMS					
Medine et al. 1980; Porcella et al. 1976	Homogenized sediment, artificial medium, air, and sediment biota	Nutrient dynamics, ecosystem metabolism	80 to 120 days	Heavy metals	
Pritchard et al. 1979	Intact sediment core, natural water, sediment biota	(Biodegradation and contaminant transport)	8 to 21 days	Organic contaminants	
Dudzik et al. 1979; Harte et al. 1978, 1980; Jassby et al. 1977a,b	Artificial medium, natural lake plankton	Population dynamics, nutrient concentrations	6 weeks to several months	Phenol, NH_4, Fe	
Harris et al. 1980	Natural sediment, pond water, macrophyte community, and associated biota	Ecosystem metabolism, nutrient dynamics, water chemistry, taxonomic groups	2 to 12 months	Arsenic, coal-derived oil	
Brockway et al. 1979	Sand, natural sediment, river water, detritus	Ecosystem metabolism, nutrients, water chemistry	Undetermined		
Eggert et al. 1979	Natural sediment, pond water, pond biota	(Biodegradation and contaminant transport)	2 to 4 months	Organic contaminants	

APPENDIX B*

SUMMARY TABLE OF
TERRESTRIAL TEST SYSTEMS

---

*Complete references can be found in Section 4.3.

APPENDIX B
SUMMARY TABLE OF TERRESTRIAL TEST SYSTEMS[a]

Test system	Components	Measured responses	Response time (days)	Cost	Perturbations tested	Validation
4.1 Population interactions						
4.1.1 Competition						
(1) Microbes Rennie and Schmidt 1977	Natural populations of two *Nitrobacter* species in NO_2-enriched soils in screwcap tubes.	Number of bacteria, oxidation rate.	14 (exp)[b]	Moderate		
(2) Plants Bennett and Runeckles 1977	Seeds of grass and clover are seeded as monocultures and a mixture in 15.6-cm pots of a fertilized soil mix and thinned to 12 plants per pot.	Leaf area, weight of parts, number of tillers.	42 (exp)	Low	Ozone	In progress
(3) Arthropods						
(a) Drosophila Ayala 1969	Adult flies added to 0.47-L bottles with culture medium (simplest and most common system).	Number of adults, adult weight, ratios of weight and numbers by sex, wing length, viability, length of life stages, and time to extinction.	18 to 23 (generation)	Low	Radiation	
(b) Other flies Housefly-blowfly Pimentel et al. 1965	Houseflies and blowflies in 9.5x13.3x19-cm boxes with vials of larval medium, either singly or in sets of 4 or 16 boxes connected by plastic tubing.	Numbers of adults and time to extinction.	>14 (generation)	Moderate (1 cell), high (16 cell)		
Blowfly-blowfly Ullyett 1950	Newly hatched larvae of 2 blowfly species are placed on 140 g of beef in a 45x45x10-cm box.	Larva and puparium weight and length, fecundity, sex ratio, mortality, number at each life stage.		Moderate		
(c) Tribolium Park 1957	Adult beetles added to 8 g of flour and yeast in a shell vial in an incubator.	Number of adults and larvae and time to extinction.	480-1000 (extinction) 30 (generation)	Moderate		

Test system	Components	Measured responses	Response time (days)	Cost	Perturbations tested	Validation
(d) Other grain insects Crombie 1945	Adult insects or eggs are added to 10 g of cracked wheat in jars in an incubator.	Number of adults, fecundity, longevity, length, and weight.	~ 365 (exp)	Low		
(e) Soil arthropods Longstaff 1976	Collembola are maintained in a 15.7-cm² x 3-cm dish with a floor of moist plaster of Paris, charcoal, and yeast.	Number of individuals by size class.	84 to >168 (exp)	Low		
Anderson 1978	Microarthropods are removed by drying from intact 9x9x10-cm litter-soil columns in plastic containers and replaced with the competing species.	Number of individuals by soil horizon and microhabitat.	14 (exp)	Moderate		Numbers and distribution were compared to the field.

4.1.2 Herbivory

(1) Sucking insects

(a) Aphid-alfalfa	No system developed.					
(b) Aphid-grain Windle and Franz 1979	2 Cultivars of barley planted together and singly, 69 seeds/25.5-cm pot with 100 aphids/pot contained by cellulose nitrate collars.	Number of barley leaves and fillers, height, and dry weight. Number of aphids and damage.	14 to 42 (exp)	Moderate		
(c) Whitefly-plant	See 4.1.3(2)(b)					
(d) Scale-plant	No system developed.					
(2) Chewing insects Grasshopper-grass Dyer and Bokhari 1976	Blue gramma grass grown in a flask of nutrient solution with a grasshopper contained on the plant top by a screen cage.	Changes in solution pH, plant growth; grasshopper intake rate, digestive efficiency, growth, and amount of litter cut.	18 (exp)	Moderate		
Corn-rootworm-corn Ortman and Branson 1976	Newly hatched rootworms are added to plastic pouches of soil containing corn seedlings.	Growth rate and % survival of rootworms.	10 (exp)	Low		

Test system	Components	Measured responses	Response time (days)	Cost	Perturbations tested	Validation
4.1.3 Predation						
(1) Microbes Habte and Alexander 1975	10^{10} Xanthomonas cells were added to 10 g of sterile and non-sterile soil in 150 mL dilution bottles.	Counts of bacteria and predators.	3 (exp)	Moderate		
(2) Arthropods						
(a) Parasitoid-gall midge Force 1970	40 Baccharis seedlings in small pots are placed in groups of 10 at weekly intervals into 48x38x40-cm screen cages. Eight adult midges are added with each group of plants, and 1 to 4 species of wasps are added at appropriate times.	Life table statistics for the wasps; frequency of parasitism and multiparasitism.	60 to 200 (exp)	High		
(b) Parasitoid-whitefly Nechols and Tauber 1977	Tobacco plants were held in 1-m^3 screen cages. Individual adult whiteflies were allowed to oviposite within single-leaf cages, and newly emerged parasitoids were added at different intervals for 8 to 12 h.	Parasitization rate; parasitoid and whitefly development and mortality.		Moderate		
McClanahan 1970	Eight potted cucumbers in an isolated 3.2x5.2-m section of greenhouse were exposed to 690 adult whiteflies, and 15 days later, 210 adult parasitoids. Pesticide was sprayed at intervals.	Numbers of parasitized and unparasitized whiteflies over time and numbers of adult whiteflies and parasitoids at termination.	75 (exp)	Moderate	Oxthioquinox	

Test system	Components	Measured responses	Response time (days)	Cost	Perturbations tested	Validation
(c) Parasitoid-aphid Force and Messenger 1964, 1965	Aphids were raised on alfalfa stems in vials of water within 3.5x15-cm glass tubes held vertically in an environmental chamber. Host and parasitoid densities and number of parasitoid species were varied.	Parasitoid survival, development rate, fecundity, and percent parasitization and super parasitization of the host.	1 (hunting) 9 to 38 (development)	Moderate		
(d) Predator-aphid Murdock and Marks 1973	Single ladybird larvae were placed on potted bean plants with different ratios of two aphid species. Plants were isolated by "Fluon"-coated plastic collars.	Prey selection, predator, and prey behavior.	0.36 (hunting)	Moderate		
(e) Parasitoid-grain moth Benson 1974	Moths and wasps were raised in 90x90x75-cm cages with 81 cardboard trays containing 50 g of wheat-feed each. Nine trays were replaced each week.	Numbers of wasps and moths by developmental stage.	35 (moth life cycle) 59 (exp)	Moderate		
(f) Parasitoid-bean weevil Utida 1957	Bean weevils were raised on beans in petri dishes and exposed to one or two species of parasitoids.	Number of weevils and wasps.	21 (weevil life cycle) 1050 (exp)	Moderate		
(g) Parasitoid-fly Pimentel et al. 1963	Single 9.5x13.3x19-cm plastic boxes or arrays of 16 or 30 boxes connected by 0.64-cm plastic tubes containing vials of fly medium, parasitoid wasps, and houseflies or blowflies.	Numbers of flies and wasps	42 to 132 (extinction of single cell system) 133 to 224 (16 cell system) 574 (30 cell system)	Moderate		

Test system	Components	Measured responses	Response time (days)	Cost	Perturbations tested	Validation
(h) Ground-dwelling beetles Harris and Oliver 1979	Staphylinid beetles preyed on horn fly eggs and larvae on manure pats placed on a soil-vermiculite mixture on a 32x28x5-cm piece of sod covered with mesh.	Number of emerging flies.	14 (fly development)	Moderate		
(i) Spiders Hardman and Turnbill 1974	7.5-cm³ boxes or arrays of eight 7.6x7.6x 5.6-cm trays with "Fluon"-coated sides connected by 25x24-cm arched plastic bridges. Predators and prey were subadult lycosid spiders and vestigial-winged Drosophila.	Number of flies killed.	6 (hunting)	Moderate		
(j) Mites Huffaker 1956	Two groups of 36 field-infected potted strawberries were arranged on greenhouse benches. One group was sprayed with parathione to eliminate the predator.	Numbers of predators and prey.	<9 to 365 (predator effect seen, length of experiment)	Moderate		
Huffaker et al. 1963	Mite herbivores and predators were placed on a random subset of 252 partially covered oranges, which rested in glass coasters on 3 wire mesh shelves, which were connected by wooden dowels.	Numbers of predators and prey.	490 (maximum length of experiment)	Moderate		
4.1.4 Parasitism	No systems discussed.					
4.1.5 Symbiosis						
(1) Lichens	No systems discussed.					
(2) Rhizobium-Legume Pareek and Gaur 1970	Inoculated seeds sown in pots of seived soil that had been sprayed with pesticide.	Plant and seed weight and N content, number of nodules, and leghaemoglobin content.	28 to 91 (nodule formation-plant maturation)	Moderate	>40 pesticides and ozone	Some field studies have been done, but not to validate laboratory studies.

Test system	Components	Measured responses	Response time (days)	Cost	Perturbations tested	Validation
(3) Mycorrhizae Wilde and Persidsky 1956	Seedlings in pots of soil inoculated with mycorrhizal fungi in a greenhouse.	Plant weight, number of fungal propagules, % of root length infected.	240 (exp)	Moderate	Numerous pesticides	

4.2 Ecosystems

4.2.5 Synthetic systems

Test system	Components	Measured responses	Response time (days)	Cost	Perturbations tested	Validation
(1) Soil Atlas et al. 1978	Sieved soil in a flask, bottle, or other container.	Microbe numbers, respiration, nutrient dynamics, enzyme assays, ATP assays.	1 to >100 (exp)	Low	Many chemicals	Informal; decades of experience indicate general validity.
(2) Litter Spalding 1979	Sorted litter in a container.	Respiration and enzyme assays.	1 to 28 (time to response)	Low	7 heavy metals	None; related generally to field studies.
(3) Litter and soil Bond et. al. 1976	Sieved soil (150 g) and seived litter (15 g) in a beaker or lined can in a gas and temperature control system.	Respiration, heat output, microbe numbers.	20 (exp)	High	20 metal salts, O_3, and SO_2	None; related generally to field studies.
(4) Gnotobiotic soil Coleman et. al. 1977	_Pseudomonas_ sp. _Acanthamoeba_ sp., and _Mesoplogaster_ sp. in 20 g of dried, sifted, and sterilized soil in a 50-mL Erlenmeyer flask.	CO_2 efflux, N and P mineralization and immobilization and numbers of bacteria, protozoa, and nematodes.	14 (exp)	High		
(5) Plant and soil (a) Pot Eno and Everett 1958	7.6-L pots of field soil with 10 bean plants.	Plant germination, plant production, microbe numbers, respiration, and nitrification.	17 (exp)	Moderate	10 insecticides	
(b) Lichtenstein et al. 1977	Layers of toxicant-contaminated and uncontaminated homogenized soil with corn plants, in a 86-mm-diameter, 1-L plastic cylinder mounted on a leachate collecter.	Toxicant fate, (soil, plant, and leachate); plant biomass; plant symptoms.	22 (exp)	Low	Phorate, Stauffer N-2596, Eptam, and Phorate	Compared to field trial for N-2596.

Test system	Components	Measured responses	Response time (days)	Cost	Perturbations tested	Validation
(c) Agroecosystem chamber Nash et al. 1977	Crop plants grown on 15 cm of seived soil in a 115-cm-high x 150 cm x 50 cm closed glass box.	Toxicant fate (air, soil, leachate and plant).	35 (exp)	Moderate	Toxaphene, DDT, Silvex, Zineb, Maneb	
(6) Soil, litter, plant and animal						
(a) Odum - Odum and Lugo 1970	Natural soil, litter, a flowering plant, fern, moss, lichen, and algae in a 16.2-cm-diameter plastic desiccator.	CO_2 exchange.		Moderate	Radiation	Compared to the radiated forest from which the components were derived.
(b) Witkamp Witkamp and Frank 1970	Round containers 7 to 13-cm-diameter by 10 to 13-cm with a leachate port, soil or sand, litter, millipedes, snails, and seedlings.	Mineral nutrient dynamics, CO_2 efflux, and litter weight.	98 (exp)	Moderate		
(c) Metcalf Metcalf et al. 1979	Corn seedlings grown in vermiculite or soil with earthworms, isopods, slugs, saltmarsh caterpillars, and a vole in a 19-L wide-mouth jar. Ports in the lid and base permit air and leachate sampling.	Pesticide fate, plant growth, and faunal numbers.	20 (exp)	Moderate	15 pesticides	Pesticide fate is comparable to that reported from the field.
(d) Terrestrial microcosm chamber Gile and Gillett 1979	A 1x0.75x0.6-m glass box with 20 cm of synthetic soil, alfalfa, ryegrass, nematodes, earthworms, enchytraeid worms, isopods, mealworms, crickets, snails, and a pregnant vole. Ports allow air and leachate sampling.	Pesticide fate, faunal numbers, and vole behavior.	67 (exp)	High	Dieldrin	Compared to published field and laboratory studies of dieldrin.

Test system	Components	Measured responses	Response time (days)	Cost	Perturbations tested	Validation
4.2.6 Excised systems						
(1) Soil core Jackson et al. 1977	5-cm-diameter x 5- or 10-cm intact soil core encased in heat-shrunk plastic and supported on a leachate collector.	Nutrient loss, respiration, toxicant loss, and degradation. Microbe biomass, soil enzymes.	30 to 59 (exp)	Low	As, dieldrin, methyl parathion, 2, 4, 5-T, and hexachlorobenzene.	None.
(2) Grassland core Jackson and Levine 1978; Van Voris et al. 1978	15 to 30-cm-diameter x 10 to 25-cm grassland cores encased in plastic and supported on a leachate collecter.	Toxicant loss and uptake, nutrient loss, soil ATP, CO_2 flux, plant biomass, soil arthropod, nematode, bacteria, and fungi.	100 to 175	Moderate	As, Cd	
(3) Sod Campbell 1973	16-cm diameter x 7-cm-deep sod in a nalgene jar.	Respiration, photosynthesis, plant symptoms, species abundance.	<1 (time to response of respiration and photosynthesis) 45 (plant damage symptoms)	Moderate	Radiation	None
(4) Treecosm Jackson et al. 1978	An intact block of forest soil 45x45x25-cm with one ~2-m sapling and associated ground flora sealed with epoxy in wood boxes.	Transport, nutrient loss, respiration, ATP, microbe density, primary production.	300 (exp)		Pb smelter dust	Yes; results are qualitatively but not quantitatively confirmed by field studies and modeling.
(5) Outcrop McCormick and Platt 1962	Excised 90x90-cm segments of granite outcrop communities arranged in a 1x6.5-m concrete trough.	Plant growth; plant reproduction, plant species density, soil erosion.	365 (exp)	High	Radiation	In terms of natural properties, but not response to toxicants.

[a]The study cited is representative of the system type described. Measured responses and perturbations are listed for all known experiments of each type, not just the study cited.

[b]Notes in parentheses indicate how response time was determined; (exp) indicates that the length of the experiment, which may be arbitrary, was used.

APPENDIX C

ALPHABETICAL BIBLIOGRAPHY
AQUATIC AND TERRESTRIAL TEST SYSTEMS

BIBLIOGRAPHY

Abbott, W. 1966. Microcosm studies on estuarine waters. I. The replicability of microcosms. J. Water Pollut. Control Fed. 38:256-270.

Abbott, W. 1967. Microcosm studies on estuarine waters. II. The effects of single doses of nitrate and phosphate. J. Water Pollut. Control Fed. 39:113-122.

Abbott, W. 1969. High levels of nitrate and phosphate in carboy microcosm studies. J. Water Pollut. Control Fed. 14:1748-1751.

Adams, J. B., and H. F. Van Emden. 1972. The biological properties of aphids and their host plant relationships. pp. 47-104. IN Van Emden, H. F. (ed.), Aphid Technology. Academic Press, New York.

Adams, W. T., and G. T. Duncan. 1979. A maximum likelihood statistical method for analyzing frequency-dependent fitness experiments. Behavior Genetics 9:7-21.

Admiraal, W. 1977. Experiments with mixed populations of benthic estuarine diatoms in laboratory microecosystems. Bot. Mar. 20:479-485.

Akre, B. G., and D. M. Johnson. 1979. Switching and sigmoid functional response curves by damselfly naiads with alternative prey available. J. Anim. Ecology 48:703-720.

Alexander, M. 1971. Microbial Ecology. John Wiley and Sons, Inc., New York. 511 pp.

Allan, D. 1973. Competition and the relative abundance of two cladocerans. Ecology 54:484-498.

Allen, S. D., and T. D. Brock. 1968. The adaptation of heterotrophic microcosms to different temperatures. Ecology 49:343-346.

Ambler, J. R., and J. L. Young. 1977. Techniques for determining root length infected by vesicular-arbuscular mycorrhizae. Soil Sci. Soc. Am. J. 41:551-555.

Anderson, J. M. 1962. The enigma of soil animal species diversity. pp. 51-58. IN Murphy, P. W. (ed.), Progress in Soil Zoology. ButterworthsLondon.

Anderson, J. M. 1978. Competition between two unrelated species of soil Cryptostigmata (Acari) in experimental microcosms. J. Anim. Ecol. 47:787-803.

Anderson, R. S. 1970. Predator-prey relationships and predation rates for crustacean zooplankters from some lakes in western Canada. Can. J. Zool. 48:1229-1240.

Anderson, R. V., E. T. Elliott, J. F. McClellan, D. C. Coleman, C. V. Cole, and H. W. Hunt. 1978. Trophic interactions in soils as they affect energy and nutrient dynamics. III. Biotic interactions of bacteria, amoebae, and nematodes. Microbio. Ecol. 4:361-371.

Anderson, R. V., D. C. Coleman, C. V. Cole, E. T. Elliott, and J. F. McClellan. 1979. The use of soil microcosms in evaluating bacteriophogic nematode response to other organisms and effects on nutrient cycling. Int. J. Environ. Stud. 13:175-182.

Andison, H. 1940. The soft scale (Coccus hesperidum) infesting holly on Vancouver Island. Proc. Entomol. Soc. B.C. 36:3-5.

Armitage, B. J. 1980. Effects of temperature on periphyton biomass and community composition in the Browns Ferry experimental channels. IN Giesy, J. P. (ed.), Microcosms in Ecological Research (in press).

Atkinson, W. D. 1979. A field investigation of larval competition in domestic Drosophila. J. Anim. Ecol. 48:91-102.

Atlas, R. M., D. Pramer, and R. Bartha. 1978. Assessment of pesticide effects on non-target soil microorganisms. Soil Biol. Biochem. 10: 231-239.

Atz, J. W. 1949. The balanced aquarium myth. The Aquarist 14:159-160.

Ausmus, B. S., G. J. Dodson, and D. R. Jackson. 1978. Behavior of heavy metals in forest microcosms. III. Effects on litter-soil carbon metabolism. Water Air Soil Pollut. 10:19-26.

Ausmus, B. S., S. Kimbrough, D. R. Jackson, and S. Lindberg. 1979. The behavior of hexachlorobenzene in pine forest microcosms: Transport and effects on soil processes. Environ. Pollut. 13:103-111.

Ausmus, B. S., and E. G. O'Neill. 1978. Comparison of carbon dynamics of three microcosm substrates. Soil Biol. Biochem. 10:425-429.

Ayala, F. J. 1966. Reversal of dominance in competing species of Drosophila. The Am. Nat. 100(910):81-83.

Ayala, F. J. 1967. Improvement in competitive ability of two species of Drosophila. Genetics 56:542-543.

Ayala, F. J. 1969. Evolution of fitness. IV. Genetic evolution of interspecific competitive ability in Drosophila. Genetics 61: 737-747.

Ayala, F. J. 1969. Experimental invalidation of the principle of competitive exclusion. Nature 224:1076-1079.

Ayala, F. J. 1970. Competition, coexistence, and evolution. pp. 121-158. IN Hecht, M. K., and W. C. Steere (eds. Essays in Evolution and Genetics in Honor of Theodosius Dobzh. Appleton-Century-Crofts, New York.

Ayala, F. J. 1971. Competition between species: Frequency dependence. Science 171:820-824.

Ayala, F. J. 1972. Competition between species. Am. Sci. 60:348-357.

Ayala, F. J., M. E. Gilpin, and J. G. Ehrenfeld. 1973. Competition between species: Theoretical models and experimental tests. Theor. Popul. Biol. 4:331-356.

Backman, P. A., and E. M. Clark. 1977. Effect of carbofuran and other pesticides on vesicular-arbuscular mycorrhizae in peanuts. Nematropica 7:13-18.

Baker, J. A., and T. Modde. 1977. Susceptibility to predation of blacktail shiners stained with Bismarck Brown Y. Trans. Am. Fish. Soc. 106:334-338.

Bakker, K., H. J. P. Eijsackers, J. C. van Lenteren, and E. Meelis. 1972. Some models describing the distribution of eggs of the parasite Pseudeucoila (Hym., Cynip.) over its hosts, larvae of Drosophila melanogaster. Oecologia 10:29-57.

Bams, R. A. 1967. Differences in performance of naturally and artificially propagated sockeye salmon migrant fry, as measured with swimming and predation tests. J. Fish. Res. Board Can. 24:1117-1153.

Barker, J. S. F. 1971. Ecological differences and competitive interaction between Drosophila melanogaster and Drosophila simulans in small laboratory populations. Oecologia 8:139-156.

Barker, J. S. F., and R. N. Podger. 1970. Interspecific competition between Drosophila melanogaster and Drosophila simulans: Effects of larval density on viability, developmental period and adult body weight. Ecology 51:170-189.

Bartha, R., and D. Pramer. 1965. Features of a flask and method of measuring the persistence and biological effects of pesticides in soil. Soil Sci. 100:68-70.

Bartha, R., R. P. Lanzilotta, and D. Pramer. 1967. Stability and effects of some pesticides in soil. Appl. Microbiol. 15:67-75.

Batchelder, A. R. 1975. Eutrophication of microponds. J. Environ. Qual. 4:520-526.

Bazzaz, F. A., and J. L. Harper. 1976. Relationship between plant weight and numbers in mixed populations of Sinapsis abla (L.) Rabenh. and Lepidium sativum. J. Appl. Ecol. 13:211-216.

Beall, M. L., Jr., R. G. Nash, and P. C. Kearney. 1976. Agroecosystem--a laboratory model ecosystem to simulate field conditions for monitoring pesticides. pp. 790-793. Proc., EPA Conf. on Environ. Modeling anSimulation, Cincinnati, Oh., April 19-22.

Bennett, J. P., and V. C. Runeckles. 1977. Effects of low levels of ozone on plant competition. J. Appl. Ecol. 14:877-880.

Benson, J. F. 1960. Population dynamics of Bracon hebetor Say (Hymenoptera: Braconidae) and Ephestia cautella (Walker) (Lepidoptera: Phycitidae) in a laboratory ecosystem. J. Anim. Ecol. 43:71-86.

Benson, J. F. 1973. The biology of Lepidoptera infesting stored products, with special reference to population dynamics. Biol. Rev. 48:1-26.

Bethel, W. M., and J. C. Holmes. 1977. Increased vulnerability of amphipods to predation owing to altered behavior induced by larval acanthocephalans. Can. J. Zool. 55:110-115.

Beyers, R. J. 1962. Relationship between temperature and the metabolism of experimental ecosystems. Science 136:980-982.

Beyers, R. J. 1962. Some metabolic aspects of balanced aquatic microcosms. Am. Zool. 2:391.

Beyers, R. J. 1963. A characteristic diurnal metabolic pattern in balanced microcosms. Publ. Inst. Mar. Sci., Univ. Texas 9:19-27.

Beyers, R. J. 1963. The metabolism of twelve aquatic laboratory microecosystems. Ecol. Monogr. 33:281-306.

Beyers, R. J. 1964. The microcosm approach to ecosystem biology. Amer. Biol. Teach. 26:491-498.

Beyers, R. J. 1965. The pattern of photosynthesis and respiration in laboratory microecosystems. IN Goldman, C. R. (ed.), Primary Productivity in Aquatic Environments. Mem. Ist. Ital. Idrobiol. 18:61-74.

Beyers, R. J., P. C. Fraleigh, B. Braybog, and H. Morrissett. 1968. The effects of gamma radiation on simplified microecosystems. Sav. River Ecol. Lab. Ann. Report, pp. 176-182.

Birch, L. C. 1957. The meanings of competition. Am. Nat. 91:5-18.

Bird, G. W., J. R. Rich, and S. U. Glover. 1974. Increased endomycorrhizae of cotton roots in soil treated with nematocides. Phytopathol 64:48-51.

Bisson, P. A. 1978. Diet food selection by two sizes of rainbow trout (Salmo gairdneri) in an experimental stream. J. Fish. Res. Board Can. 35:971-975.

Blaylock, B. G. 1969. Effects of ionizing radiation on interspecific competition. pp. 61-67. IN Nelson, D. J., and F. C. Evans (eds.), Symposium on Radioecology. CONF-670503. U.S. Atomic Energy Commission, Washington, D.C.

Blaylock, B. G., and H. H. Shugart, Jr. 1972. The effect of radiation-induced mutations on the fitness of Drosophila populations. Genetics 72:469-474.

Boggild, O., and J. Keiding. 1958. Competition in house fly larvae. Oikos 9(1):1-25.

Bond, H., B. Lighthart, R. Shimabuku, and L. Russell. 1976. Some effects of cadmium on coniferous forest soil and litter microcosms. Soil Sci. 121(5):278-287.

Bond, H., B. Lighthart, and R. Volk. 1979. The use of soil/litter microcosms with and without added pollutants to study certain components of the decomposer community. pp. 111-123. IN Witt, J. M., and J. W. Gillett (eds.), Terrestrial Microcosms and Environmental Chemistry. NSF/RA 79-0026. National Science Foundation, Washington, D.C.

Bott, T. L., J. Preslan, J. Finlay, and R. Brunker. 1977. The use of flowing-water microcosms and ecosystem streams to study microbial degradation of leaf litter and nitrilotriacetic acid (NTA). IN Developments in Industrial Microbiology. Washington, D.C. 18:171-184.

Bott, T. L., K. Rogenmuser, and P. Thorne. 1978. Effects of No. 2 fuel oil, Nigerian crude oil, and used crankcase oil on benthic algal communities. J. Environ. Sci. Health, Part A 10:751-779.

Bourquin, A. W. 1977. Effects of malathion on microorganisms of an artificial salt-marsh environment. J. Environ. Qual. 6:373-378.

Bourquin, A. W., R. L. Garnas, P. H. Pritchard, F. G. Wilkes, C. R. Cripe, and N. I. Rubinstein. 1979. Interdependent microcosms for the assessment of pollutants in the marine environment. Int. J. Environ. Stud. 13:131-140.

Bourquin, A., L. Kiefer, and S. Cassidy. 1974. Microbial response to malathion treatments in salt marsh microcosms. Abstr. Annu. Meet. Am. Soc. Microbiol.

Bourquin, A. W., P. H. Pritchard, R. Vanolinda, and J. Samela. 1979. Fate of dimilin in estuarine microcosms. Abstr. Annu. Meeting Am. Soc. Microbiol.

Boyce, N. P., and S. B. Yamada. 1977. Effects of a parasite, *Eubothrium salvelini* (Cestoda: Pseudophyllidea), on the resistance of juvenile sockeye salmon, *Oncorhynchus nerka*, to zinc. J. Fish. Res. Board Can. 34:706-709.

Brandl, Z., and C. H. Fernando. 1974. Feeding of the copepod *Acanthocyclops vernalis* on the cladoceran *Ceriodaphnia reticulata* under laboratory conditions. Can. J. Zool. 52:99-105.

Brandl, Z., and C. H. Fernando. 1978. Prey selection by the cyclopoid copepods *Mesocyclops edax* and *Cyclops vicinus*. Verh. Int. Ver. Limnol. 20:2505-2510.

Branson, T. F. 1971. Resistance of the grass tribe Maydeae to larvae of the western corn rootworm. Ann. Entomol. Soc. Am. 64:861-863.

Brockway, D. L., J. Hill IV, J. R. Maudsley, and R. R. Lassiter. 1979. Development, replicability and modeling of naturally derived microcosms. Int. J. Environ. Studies 13:149-158.

Brooks, J. L., and S. I. Dodson. 1965. Predation, body size and composition of plankton. Science 150:28-35.

Brown, A. W. A. 1978. Ecology of pesticides. John Wiley and Sons, Inc., New York. 525 pp.

Bruning, K., R. Lingeman, and J. Ringelberg. 1978. Properties of an aquatic microecosystem. Part 3. Development of the decomposer subsystem and the phosphorus output stability. Verh. Int. Ver. Limnol. 20:1231-1235.

Bryfogle, B. M., and W. F. McDiffett. 1979. Algal succession in laboratory microcosms as affected by an herbicide stress. Am. Midl. Nat. 101:344-354.

Budnik, M., and D. Brncic. 1974. Preadult competition between *Drosophila pavani* and *Drosophila melanogaster*, *Drosophila simulans*, and *Drosophila willistoni*. Ecology 55:657-661.

Burnett, T. 1949. The effect of temperature on an insect host-parasite population. Ecology 30:113-134.

Burnett, T. 1960. Effects of initial densities and periods of infestation on the growth-forms of a host and parasite population. Can. J. Zool. 38:1063-1077.

Burnett, T. 1967. Aspects of the interaction between a chalcid parasite and its aleurodid host. Can. J. Zool. 45:539-578.

Burnett, T. 1970. Effect of simulated natural temperatures on an acarine predator-prey population. Physiol. Zool. 43:155-165.

Burnett, T. 1970. Effect of temperature on a greenhouse acarine predator-prey population. Can. J. Zool. 48:555-562.

Busch, D. 1978. Successional Changes Associated with Benthic Assemblages in Experimental Streams. Ph.D. dissertation, Oregon State University.

Butler, J. L. 1964. Interaction of Effects by Environmental Factors on Primary Productivity in Ponds and Microecosystems. Ph.D. dissertation, Oklahoma State University.

Cairns, J., Jr. 1979. Hazard evaluation with microcosms. Int. J. Environ. Stud. 13:95-99.

Cairns, J., K. L. Dickson, J. P. Slocomb, S. P. Almeida, and J. K. Eu. 1976. Automated pollution monitoring with microcosms. Int. J. Environ. Studies 10:43-49.

Campbell, S. D. 1973. The Effect of Cobalt-60 Gamma-Rays on Terrestrial Microcosm Metabolism. Ph.D. Dissertation. University of Michigan, Ann Arbor, Mich. 144 pp.

Capinera, J. L., and P. Barbosa. 1977. Influence of natural diet and larval density on gypsy moth, Lymantria dispar (Lepidoptera: Orgyiidae) egg mass characteristics. Can. Entomol. 109:1313-1318.

Carlyle, R. E., and J. D. Thorpe. 1947. Some effects of ammonium and sodium 2,4-Dichlorophenoxyacetates on legumes and the Rhizobium bacteria. J. of the Am. Soc. of Agronomy :929-936.

Carney, J. L., H. E. Garrett, and H. G. Hedrick. 1978. Influence of air pollutant gases on oxygen uptake of pine roots with selected mycorrhizae. Phytophathol. 68:1160-1163.

Chabora, P. C., and D. Pimentel. 1970. Patterns of evolution in parasite-host systems. Ann. Entomol. Soc. Am. 63:479-486.

Chant, D. A. 1961. An experiment in biological control of *Tetranychus telarius* (L.) (Acarina: Tetranychidae) in a greenhouse using the predacious mite *Phytoseiulus persimilis* Athias-Henriol (Phytoseiidae). Can. Entomol. 93:437-443.

Chiu, C., and C. A. Kouskolekas. 1978. Laboratory rearing of tea scale. Ann. Entomol. Soc. Am. 71:850-851.

Christiansen, K. 1967. Competition between Collembolan species in culture jars. Rev. Ecol. Biol. Sol. 4:439-462.

Coats, J. R., R. L. Metcalf, and I. P. Kapoor. 1974. Metabolism of the methoxychlor isotere, dianisylneopentane, in mouse, insects, and a model ecosystem. Pest. Biochem. Physiol. 4:201-211.

Coats, J. R., R. L. Metcalf, P. Y. Lu, D. D. Brown, J. F. Williams, and L. G. Hansen. 1976. Model ecosystem evaluation of the environmental impacts of the veterinary drugs phenothiazine, sulfamethazine, clopidiol, and diethylstilbestrol. Environ. Health Perspect. 18: 167-179.

Coble, D. W. 1970. Vulnerability of fathead minnows infected with yellow grub to largemouth bass predation. J. Parasitol. 56:395-396.

Coble, D. W. 1973. Influence of appearance of prey and satiation of predator on food selection by northern pike (*Esox lucius*). J. Fish. Res. Board Can. 30:317-320.

Cole, C. V., E. T. Elliott, H. W. Hunt, and D. C. Coleman. 1978. Trophic interactions in soils as they affect energy and nutrient dynamics. V. Phosphorus transformations. Microbiol. Ecol. 4:381-387.

Cole, L. K., and R. L. Metcalf. 1979. Predictive environmental toxicology of pesticides in the air, soil, water and biota of terrestrial model ecosystems. pp. 57-73. IN Witt, J. M., and J. W. Gillett (eds.), Terrestrial Microcosms and Environmental Chemistry. NSF/RA79-0026. National Science Foundation, Washington, D.C.

Cole, L. K., R. L. Metcalf, and J. R. Sanborn. 1976. Environmental fate of insecticides in terrestrial model ecosystems. Int. J. Environ. Stud. 10:7-14.

Cole, L. K., J. R. Sanborn, and R. L. Metcalf. 1976. Inhibition of corn growth by aldrin and the insecticides fate in the soil, air, crop and wildlife of a terrestrial model ecosystem. Environ. Entomol. 5: 583-589.

Coleman, D. C., C. V. Cole, R. V. Anderson, M. Blaha, M. K. Campion, M. Clarholm, E. T. Elliott, H. W. Hunt, B. Shaefer, and J. Sinclair. 1977. An analysis of rhizosphere-saprophage interactions in terrestrial ecosystems. Ecol. Bull. (Stockholm) 25:299-309.

Coleman, D. C., C. V. Cole, H. W. Hunt, and D. A. Klein. 1978. Trophic interactions in soils as they affect energy and nutrient dynamics. I. Introduction. Microbiol. Ecol. 4:345-349.

Coleman, D. C., R. V. Anderson, C. V. Cole, E. T. Elliott, L. Woods, and M. K. Campion. 1978. Trophic interactions in soils as they affect energy and nutrient dynamics. IV. Flows of metabolic and biomass carbon. Microbiol. Ecol. 4:373-380.

Collyer, E. 1958. Some insectary experiments with predacious mites to determine their effect on the development of Metatetranychus ulmi (Koch) populations. Ent. Exp. Appl. 1:138-146.

Collyer, E. 1964. The effect of an alternative food supply on the relationship between two Typhlodromus species and Panonychus ulmi (Koch) (Acarina). Entomol. Exp. Appl. 7:120-124.

Confer, J. L. 1971. Intrazooplankton predation by Mesocyclops edax at natural prey densities. Limnol. Oceanogr. 16:663-666.

Confer, J. L. 1972. Interrelations among plankton, attached algae, and the phosphorus cycle in open artificial systems. Ecol. Monogr. 42: 1-23.

Confer, J. L., and P. I. Blades. 1975. Omnivorous zooplankton and planktivorous fish. Limnol. Oceanogr. 20:571-579.

Confer, J. L., and P. I. Blades. 1975. Reaction distance to zooplankton by Lepomis gibbosus. Verh. Int. Vere. Limnol. 19:2493-2497.

Confer, J. L., and J. M. Cooley. 1977. Copepod instar survival and predation by zooplankton. J. Fish. Res. Board Can. 34:703-706.

Confer, J. L., G. L. Howick, M. H. Corzette, S. L. Kramer, S. Fitzgibbon, and R. Landesberg. 1978. Visual predation by planktivores. Oikos 31:27-37.

Cooke, A. S. 1971. Selective predation by newts on frog tadpoles treated with DDT. Nature 229:275-276.

Cooke, G. D. 1967. The pattern of autotrophic succession in laboratory microcosms. Bioscience 17:717-721.

Cooke, G. D. 1977. Experimental aquatic laboratory ecosystems and communities. pp. 59-103. IN Cairns, J., Jr. (ed.). Aquatic Microbial Communities. Garland Publishing, New York.

Cook, W. L., D. Fiedler, and A. W. Bourquin. 1980. Succession of microfungi in estuarine microcosms perturbed by carbaryl, methyl parathion and pentachlorophenol. Bot. Mar. 23:129-131.

Cooper, D. C. 1973. Enhancement of net primary productivity by herbivore grazing in aquatic laboratory microcosms. Limnol. Oceanogr. 18: 31-37.

Cooper, D. C., and B. J. Copeland. 1973. Responses of continuous-series estuarine microecosystems to point-source input variations. Ecol. Monogr. 43:213-236.

Copeland, B. J. 1965. Evidence for regulation of community metabolism in a marine ecosystem. Ecology 46:563-564.

Cornell, H., and D. Pinentel. 1978. Switching in the parasitoid _Nasonia vitripennis_ and its effects on host competition. Ecology 59:297-308.

Couch, J. A. 1976. Attempts to increase _Baculovirus_ prevalence in shrimp by chemical exposure. Prog. Exp. Tumor Res. 20:304-314.

Couch, J. A., and L. Courtney. 1977. Interaction of chemical pollutants and virus in a crustacean: A novel bioassay system. Annals N.Y. Acad. Sci. 298:497-504.

Coughtrey, P. J., C. H. Jones, M. H. Martin, and S. W. Shales. 1979. Litter accumulation in woodlands contaminated by Pb, Zn, Cd and Cu. Oecologia (Berlin) 39:51-60.

Coutant, C. C. 1973. Effect of thermal shock on vulnerability of juvenile salmonids to predation. J. Fish. Res. Board Can.30:965-973.

Coutant, C. C., D. K. Cox, and K. W. Moored, Jr. 1976. Further studies of cold shock effects on susceptibility of young channel catfish to predation. pp. 154-158. IN Esch, G. W., and R. W. McFarlane (eds.), Thermal Ecology. II. ERDA Technical Information Center, Oak Ridge, TN, CONF-750425.

Coutant, C. C., H. M. Ducharme, Jr., and J. R. Fisher. 1974. Effects of cold shock on vulnerability of juvenile channel catfish (_Ictalurus punctatus_) and largemouth bass (_Micropterus salmonids_) to predation. J. Fish. Res. Board Can. 31:351-354.

Coutant, C. C., R. B. McLean, and D. L. DeAngelis. 1979. Influences of physical and chemical alterations on predator-prey interactions. pp. 57-68. IN Clepper, H. (ed.), Predator-Prey Systems in Fisheries Management. Sport Fishing Inst., Washington, D.C.

Craig, R. B. 1978. An analysis of the predatory behavior of the loggerhead shrike. Auk. 95:221-234.

Crombie, A. C. 1945. On competition between different species of graminivorous insects. Proc. R. Soc. London, Series B--Biol. Sci. 132:362-395.

Crombie, A. C. 1946. Further experiments on insect competition. Proc. R. Soc. London, Series B--Biol. Sci. 133:76-109.

Cross, F. A., J. N. Willis, and J. P. Baptist. 1971. Distribution of radioactive and stable zinc in an experimental marine ecosystem. J. Fish. Res. Board Can. 28:1783-1788.

Crouthamel, D. A. 1977. A Microcosm Approach to the Effects of Fish Predation on Aquatic Community Structure and Function. Ph.D. dissertation, University of Georgia. 95 pp.

Crow, M. E., and F. B. Taub. 1979. Designing a microcosm bioassay to detect ecosystem level effects. Int. J. Environ. Stud. 13:141-147.

Cullimore, D. R. 1971. Interaction between herbicides and soil microorganisms. Residue Rev. 35:65-80.

Culver, D. 1974. Competition between Collembola in a patchy environment. Rev. Ecol. Biol. Sol. 11(4):533-540.

Cushing, C. D., and F. L. Rose. 1970. Cycling of zinc-65 by Columbia River periphyton in a closed lotic microcosm. Limnol. Oceanogr. 15:762-767.

Cushing, C. E., J. M. Thomas, and L. L. Eberhardt. 1974. Modelling mineral cycling by periphyton in a simulated stream system. Battelle Pacific Northwest Laboratories, CONF-740826-4. 10 pp.

Danso, S. K. A., S. O. Keya, and M. Alexander. 1975. Protoza and the decline of _Rhizobium_ populations added to soil. Can. J. Microbiol. 21:884-895.

Davis, G. E. 1963. Trophic Relations of Simplified Animal Communities in Laboratory Streams. Ph.D. dissertation, Oregon State University.

Davis, W. P., B. S. Hester, R. L. Yoakum, and R. G. Dorney. 1977. Marine ecosystem testing units: Design for assessment of benthic organism responses to low-level pollutants. Helgol. Wiss. Meeresunters. 30: 673-681.

Dawson, P. S. 1969. A conflict between Darwinian fitness and population fitness in *Tribolium* "competition" experiments. Genetics 62:413-419.

Dawson, P. S., and I. M. Lerner. 1962. Genetic variation and indeterminism in interspecific competition. Am. Natur. 96:379-380.

Deacutis, C. F. 1978. Effect of thermal shock on predator avoidance by larvae of two fish species. Trans. Am. Fish. Soc. 107:632-635.

De Bach, P. 1966. The competitive displacement and coexistence principles. Annu. Rev. Entomol. 11:183-212.

De Bach, P., and C. B. Huffaker. 1971. Experimental techniques for evaluation of the effectiveness of natural enemies. pp. 113-140. IN Huffaker, C. B. (ed.), Biological Control. Plenum Press, New York.

De Bach, P., and H. S. Smith. 1941. The effect of host density on the rate of reproduction of entomophagous parasites. J. Econ. Entomol. 34:741-745.

De Benedictis, P. A. 1977. The meaning and measurement of frequency-dependent competition. Ecology 58:158-166.

De Telegdy-Kovats, L. 1932. The growth and respiration of bacteria in sand cultures in the presence and absence of protozoa. Ann. Appl. Biol. 19:65-86.

De Witt, C. T. 1960. On competition. Versl. Landbouwkd. Onderz. 66.8:1-82.

De Witt, C. T. 1971. On the modeling of competitive phenomena. pp. 269-281. IN Den Boer, P. S., and G. R. Gradwell (eds.), Proceedings of the Advanced Study Institute on Dynamics of Numbers in Populations. Centre for Agricultural Publishing and Documentation, Wageningen.

De Witt, C. T., P. G. Tow and G. C. Ennik. 1966. Competition between legumes and grasses. Agricultural Research Report 687. Centre for Agricultural Publications and Documentation, Wageningen. 30 pp.

Dickerson, W. A., et al. 1980. Arthropod species in culture. Entomol. Soc. of Am. Hyattsville, Md. 93 pp.

Dickson, R. C., E. L. Laird, Jr., and G. R. Pesho. 1955. The spotted alfalfa aphid (yellow clover aphid on alfalfa). Hilgardia 24:93-118.

Di Salvo, L. H. 1971. Regenerative functions and microbial ecology of coral reefs: Labelled bacteria in a coral reef microcosm. J. Exp. Mar. Biol. Ecol. 7:123-136.

Dixon, A. F. G. 1970. Factors limiting the effectiveness of the coccinellid beetle, Adalia bipunctata (L.), as a predator of the sycamore aphid, Drepanosiphon platanoides (Schr.). J. Anim. Ecol. 39:739-751.

Dodson, S. I. 1970. Complementary feeding niches sustained by size-selective predation. Limnol. Oceanogr. 15:131-137.

Dodson, S. I. 1974. Adaptive change in plankton morphology in response to size-selective predation: A new hypothesis of cyclomorphosis. Limnol. Oceanogr. 19:721-729.

Dodson, S. I. 1974. Zooplankton competition and predation: An experimental test of the size-efficiency hypothesis. Ecology 55:605-613.

Domsch, K. H. 1970. Effects of fungicides on microbial populations in soil. pp. 42-46. IN Pesticides in the Soil: Ecology, Degradation, and Movement. Int. Symp. on Pesticides in the Soil. Michigan State University, East Lansing.

Domsch, K. H., and W. Paul. 1974. Simulation and experimental analysis of the influence of herbicides on soil nitrification. Arch. Microbiol. 97:283-301.

Doutt, R. L., and P. De Bach. 1964. Some biological control concepts and questions. Chap. 5. IN De Bach, P. (ed.), Biological Control of Insect s and Weeds. Reinhold Publ. Co., N.Y. 844 pp.

Draggan, S. 1977. Interactive effect of chromium compounds and a fungal parasite on carp eggs. Bull. Environ. Contam. Toxicol. 17:653-659.

Draggan, S. 1979. Effects of substrate type and arsenic dosage level on arsenic behavior in grassland microcosms. Part I: Preliminary results on ^{74}As transport. pp. 102-110. IN Witt, J. M., and J. W. Gillett (eds.), Terrestrial Microcosms and Environmental Chemistry. NSF/RA 79-0026. National Science Foundation, Washington, D.C.

Drenner, R. W., J. R. Strickler, and W. J. O'Brien. 1978. Capture probability: The role of zooplankter escape in the selective feeding of planktivorous fish. J. Fish. Res. Board Can. 35:1370-1373.

Dudzik, M., J. Harte, A. Jassby, E. Lapan, D. Levy, and J. Rees. 1979. Some considerations in the design of aquatic microcosms for plankton studies. Int. J. Environ. Stud. 13:125-130.

Duke, T. W., J. Willis, T. Price, and K. Fischler. 1969. Influence of environmental factors on the concentration of zinc-65 by an experimental community. pp. 355-362. Proc., 2nd Nat. Sympos. Radioecol., Ann Arbor, Mich., 1967.

Dyer, M. I., and U. G. Bokhari. 1976. Plant-animal interactions: Studies of the effects of grasshopper grazing on blue grama grass. Ecology 59:762-772.

Eggers, D. M. 1977. The nature of prey selection by planktivorous fish. Ecology 58:46-59.

Eggert, C. R., R. G. Kaley, and W. E. Gledhill. 1979. Application of a laboratory freshwater lake model in the study of linear alkylbenzene sulfonate (LAS) biodegradation. pp. 451-451. IN Bourquin, A. W., and P. H. Pritchard (eds.), Microbial Degradation of Pollutants in Marine Environments. EPA-600/9-79-012.

Eijsackers, H. 1978. Side effects of the herbicide 2,4,5-T affecting the carabid notiophilus biguttatus fabr., a predator of springtails. Z. Angew. Entomol. 86:113-128.

Eisler, R. 1973. Latent effects of Iranian crude oil and a chemical oil dispersant on Red Sea molluscs. Is. J. Zool. 22:97-105.

Elliott, E. T., C. V. Cole, D. C. Coleman, R. V. Anderson, H. W. Hunt, and J. F. McClellan. 1979. Amoebal growth in soil microcosms: A model system of C,N, and P trophic dynamics. Int. J. Environ. Stud. 13:169-174.

Elmgren, R., G. A. Vargo, J. F. Grassle, J. P. Grassle, D. R. Heinle, G. Langlois, and S. L. Vargo. 1980. Trophic interactions in experimental marine ecosystems perturbed by oil. IN Giesy, J. P. (ed.), Microcosms in Ecological Research (in press).

Eno, C. F., and P. H. Everett. 1977. Effects of soil applications of 10 chlorinated hydrocarbon insecticides on soil microorganisms and the growth of stringless black valentine beans. J. Environ. Qual. 6(1):235-238.

Evans, E. C., and R. S. Henderson. 1977. Elutriator/Microcosm System Pilot Model and Test. EPA-600/3-77-093.

Evans, E. C., III. 1977. Microcosm responses to environmental perturbants. Helgol. Wiss. Meeresunters. 30:178-191.

Everest, J. W. 1979. Predicting phosphorus movement and pesticide action in salt marshes with microecosystems. Office of Water Research and Technology W79-07006, OWRT-A-045-ALA(1). 90 pp.

Everest, J. W., and D. E. Davis. 1979. Phosphorus movement using salt marsh microecosystems. J. Environ. Qual. 8:465-468.

Farr, J. A. 1977. Impairment of antipredator behavior in Palaemonetes pugio by exposure to sublethal doses of parathion. Trans. Am. Fish. Soc. 106:287-290.

Farr, J. A. 1978. The effect of methyl parathion on predator choice of two estuarine prey species. Trans. Am. Fish. Soc. 107:87-91.

Ferens, M. C. 1971. The Effects of Gamma Radiation on a Laboratory Microecosystem. M.S. Thesis, University of Georgia.

Ferens, M. C., and R. J. Beyers. 1972. Studies of a simple laboratory microecosystem: Effects of stress. Ecology 53:709-713.

Ferry, B. W., M. S. Baddeleym, and D. L. Hawksworth. 1973. Air Pollution and Lichens. The Athlone Press of the University of London. 389 pp.

Fielding, A. H., and G. Russell. 1976. The effect of copper on competition between marine algae. J. Ecol. 64:871-876.

Finney, G. L., B. Puttler, and L. Dawson. 1960. Rearing of three spotted alfalfa aphid hymenopterous parasites for mass release. J. Econ. Entomol. 53(4):655-659.

Fisher, D. J. 1976. Effects of some fungicides on Rhizobium trifolii and its symbiotic relationship with white clover. Pest. Sci. 7:10-18.

Fisher, D. J., A. L. Hayes, and C. A. Jones. 1978. Effects of some surfactant fungicides on Rhizobium trifolii and its symbiotic relationship with white clover. Ann. of Appl. Biol. 90(1):73-84.

Fisher, N. S., E. J. Carpenter, C. C. Remsen, and C. F. Wurster. 1974. Effects of PCB on interspecific competition in natural and gnotobiotic phytoplankton communities in continuous and batch cultures. Microbial Ecol. 1:39-50.

FitzGerald, G. J., and M. H. A. Keenleyside. 1978. Technique for tagging small fish with I^{131} for evaluation of predator-prey relationships. J. Fish. Res. Board Can. 35:143-145.

Fitmarice, P. 1979. Selective predation on cladocera by brown trout Salmo trutta. J. Fish. Biol. 15:521-526.

Flanders, S. E. 1968. Mechanisms of population homeostasis in Anagasta ecosystems. Hilgardia 39:367-404.

Flanders, S. E., and M. E. Badgley. 1963. Prey-predator interactions in self-balanced laboratory populations. Hilgardia 35(8):145-183.

Force, D. C. 1970. Competition among four hymenopterous parasites of an endemic insect host. Ann. Entomol. Soc. of Am. 63:1675-1688.

Force, D. C. 1974. Ecology of insect host-parasitoid communities. Science 184:624-632.

Force, D. C., and P. S. Messenger. 1964. Duration of development, generation time, and longevity of three hymenopterous parasites of Therioaphis maculata, reared at various constant temperatures. Ann. of the Entomol. Soc. of Am. 57(4):405-413.

Force, D. C., and P. S. Messenger. 1964. Fecundity, reproductive rates and innate capacity for increase of three parasites of Therioaphis maculata (Buckton). Ecology 45:706-715.

Force, D. C., and P. S. Messenger. 1965. Laboratory studies of competition among three parasites of the spotted aphid Thirioaphis maculata (Buckton). Ecology 46:853-859.

Fraleigh, P. C. 1971. Ecological Succession in an Aquatic Microcosm and a Thermal Spring. Ph.D. dissertation, University of Georgia.

Fraleigh, P. C., and P. C. Dibert. 1980. Inorganic carbon limitation during ecological succession in aquatic microcosms. IN Giesy, J. P. (ed.), Microcosms in Ecological Research (in press).

Frank, P. W. 1957. Coactions in laboratory populations of two species of Daphnia. Ecology 38:510-519.

Fredrickson, A. G. 1977. Behavior of mixed cultures of microorganisms. Ann. Rev. Microbiol. 31:63-87.

Fredrickson, H. L., A. W. Bourquin, and P. H. Pritchard. 1979. A comparative study of the fate of pentachlorophenol, methyl parathion, and carbaryl in estuarine microcosms. Abstr. Annu. Meeting Am. Soc. Microbiol. 1979.

Furnass, T. I. 1979. Laboratory experiments on prey selection by perch fry (Perca fluviatilis). Freshwater Biol. 9:33-44.

Futuyma, D. J. 1970. Variation in genetic response to interspecific competition in laboratory populations of Drosophila. Am. Nat. 104:239-252.

Galbraith, M. G., Jr. 1967. Size-selective predation on Daphnia by rainbow trout and yellow perch. Trans. Am. Fish. Soc. 96:1-10.

Gallepp, G. W. 1979. Chironomid influence on phosphorus release in sediment-water microcosms. Ecology 60:547-556.

Gardner, B. T. 1966. Hunger and characteristics of the prey in the hunting behavior of salticid spiders. J. Comp. Physiol. Psychol. 62(3):475-478.

Gause, G. F. 1934. The Struggle for Existence. Williams and Wilkins, Baltimore.

Gause, G. F., N. P. Smaragdova, and A. A. Witt. 1936. Further studies of interaction between predators and prey. J. Anim. Ecol. 5:1-18.

Gerhart, D. Z., S. M. Anderson, and J. Richter. 1977. Toxicity bioassays with periphyton communities: Design of experimental streams. Water Res. 11:567-570.

Gerritsen, J. 1978. Instar-specific swimming patterns and predation of planktonic copepods. Verh. Int. Ver. Limnol. 20:2531-2536.

Gerritsen, J., and J. R. Strickler. 1977. Encounter probabilities and community structure in zooplankton: A mathematical model. J. Fish. Res. Board Can. 34:73-82.

Ghiorse, W. C., and M. Alexander. 1977. Effect of nitrogen dioxide on nitrate oxidation and nitrate-oxidizing populations in soil. Soil Biol. Biochem. 9:353-355.

Giddings, J. M. 1979. Pollution studies in aquatic microcosms. Third Int. Symp. on Aquatic Pollutants, Oct. 15-17, 1979, Jekyll Island, Ga. (abstract).

Giddings, J. M. 1980. Types of aquatic microcosms and their research applications. IN Giesy, J. P. (ed.), Microcosms in Ecological Research (in press).

Giddings, J. M. 1981. Methods for measuring effects of chemicals on aquatic ecosystem properties. IN Hammons, Anna S. (ed.), Ecotoxicological Test Systems: Proceedings of a Series of Workshops, ORNL-5709; EPA 560/6-81-004, Oak Ridge National Laboratory.

Giddings, J. M., and G. K. Eddlemon. 1977. The effects of microcosm size and substrate type on aquatic microcosm behavior and arsenic transport. Arch. Environ. Contam. Toxicol. 6:491-505.

Giddings, J. M., and G. K. Eddlemon. 1978. Photosynthesis/respiration ratios in aquatic microcosms under arsenic stress. Water, Air, and Soil Pollut. 9:207-212.

Giddings, J. M., and G. K. Eddlemon. 1979. Some ecological and experimental properties of complex aquatic microcosms. Int. J. Environ. Stud. 13:119-123.

Giddings, J. M., B. T. Walton, G. K. Eddlemon, and K. G. Olson. 1979. Transport and fate of anthracene in aquatic microcosms. pp. 312-320. IN Bourquin, A. W., and P. H. Pritchard (eds.), Microbial Degradation of Pollutants in Marine Environments. Environmental Protection Agency, EPA-600/9-79-012.

Giesy, J. P., Jr. 1978. Cadmium inhibition of leaf decomposition in an aquatic microcosm. Chemosphere 7:467-475.

Giesy, J. P. (ed.). 1980. Symposium on Microcosms in Ecological Research, Augusta, Ga., November, 1978 (in press).

Gilbert, J. J., and C. E. Williamson. 1978. Predator-prey behavior and its effect on rotifer survival in associations of Mesocyclops edax, Asplanchna girodi, Polyarthra vulgaris, and Keratella cochleuris. Oecologia 37:13-22.

Gilbert, L. E. 1979. Development of theory in the analysis of insect-plant interactions. pp. 117-154. IN Horn, D. J., G. R. Stairs, and R. D. Mitchell (eds.), Analysis of Ecological Systems. State U. Press, Columbus, Ohio.

Gile, J. D., J. C. Collins, and J. W. Gillett. 1979. The soil core microcosm--a potential screening tool. EPA-600/3-79-089. U.S. Environmental Protection Agency, Corvallis, Oregon. 41 pp.

Gile, J. D., and J. W. Gillett. 1979. Fate of ^{14}C-dieldrin in a simulated terrestrial ecosystem. Arch. Environ. Contam. Toxicol. 8:107-124.

Gile, J. D., and J. W. Gillett. 1979. Fate of selected fungicides in a terrestrial laboratory ecosystem. J. Agric. Food Chem. 27:1159-1164.

Gile, J. D., and J. W. Gillett. 1979. Terrestrial microcosm chamber evaluations of substitute chemicals. pp. 75-85. IN Witt, J. M., and J. W. Gillett (eds.), Terrestrial Microcosms and Environmental Chemistry. NSF/RA 79-0026. National Science Foundation, Washington, D.C.

Gillett, J. W., and J. D. Gile. 1976. Pesticide fate in terrestrial laboratory ecosystems. Int. J. Environ. Stud. 10:15-22.

Gillett, J. W., and J. M. Witt (eds.). 1979. Terrestrial microcosms. Proccedings of the Workshop on Terrestrial Microcosms, Symposium on Terrestrial Microcosms and Environmental Chemistry. NSF/RA 79-0034. National Science Foundation, Washington, D.C. 35 pp.

Gilpin, M. E., and F. J. Ayala. 1976. Schoener's model and Drosophila competition. Theor. Popul. Biol. 9:12-14.

Ginetz, R. M., and P. A. Larkin. 1975. Factors affecting rainbow trout (Salmo gairdneri) predation on migrant fry of sockeye salmon (Oncorhynchus nerka). J. Fish. Res. Board Can. 33:19-24.

Gledhill, W. E., and V. W. Saeger. 1979. Microbial degradation in the environmental hazard evaluation process. pp. 434-442. IN Bourquin, A. W., and P. H. Pritchard (eds.), Microbial Degradation of Pollutants in Marine Environments. EPA-600/9-79-012.

Golterman, H. L. (ed.). 1976. Interactions between sediments and fresh waters. Dr. W. Junk, D. V. (Publishers), Wageningen, Netherlands. Proc., of an international symposium held at Amsterdam, the Netherlands, September 6-10, 1976.

Goodyear, C. P. 1972. A simple technique for detecting effects of toxicants or other stresses on a predator-prey interaction. Trans. Am. Fish. Soc. 101:367-370.

Goodyear, C. P., C. E. Boyd, and R. J. Beyers. 1972. Relationships between primary productivity and mosquitofish (Gambusia affinis) production in large microcosms. Limnol. Oceanogr. 17:445-450.

Gorden, R. W. 1967. Heterotrophic Bacteria and Succession in a Simple Laboratory Aquatic Microcosm. Ph.D. dissertation, University of Georgia.

Gorden, R. W., R. J. Beyers, E. P. Odum, and R. G. Eagon. 1969. Studies of a simple laboratory microecosystem: Bacterial activities in a heterotrophic succession. Ecology 50:86-100.

Gorden, R. W., R. J. Beyers, E. P. Odum, and R. G. Eagon. 1969. Studies bacteria of playa lakes and microcosms. Southwest. Nat. 15:419-428.

Goulden, C. E., and L. L. Hornig. 1980. Population oscillations and energy reserves in planktonic cladocera and their consequences to competition. Proc. Nat. Acad. Sci. (in press).

Graham, H. M. 1959. Effect of temperature and humidity on the biology of *Therioaphis maculata* (Buckton). Univ. Calif., Berkeley, Publ. Entomol. 16:47-80.

Greaves, M. P., H. A. Davies, J. A. P. Marsh, and G. I. Wingfield. 1976. Herbicides and soil microorganisms. Crit. Rev. in Microbiol. 5(1): 1-38.

Green, J. 1967. The distribution and variation of *Daphnia lumholzi* (Crustacea: Cladocera) in relation to fish predation in Lake Albert, East Africa. J. Zool. 151:181-197.

Gross, C. F., and R. R. Robinson. 1968. Competition between ladino clover seedlings and established orchardgrass in nutrient solution cultures. Agron. J. 60:512-514.

Grossbrad, E. 1970. Effect of herbicides on the symbiotic relationship between *Rhizobium trifolii* and white clover. pp. 47-59. IN Symposium on White Clover Research, Queens Univ. of Belfast, 1969.

Guthrie, R. K., E. M. Davis, D. S. Cherry, and H. E. Murray. 1979. Biomagnification of heavy metals by organisms in a marine microcosm. Bull. Environ. Contam. Toxicol. 21:53-61.

Guttay, A. J. R. 1976. Impact of deicing salts upon the endomycorrhizae of roadside sugar maples. Soil Sci. Soc. Am. J. 40:952-954.

Habte, M., and M. Alexander. 1975. Protozoa as agents responsible for the decline of *Xanthomonas campestris* in soil. Appl. Microbiol. 29(2):159-164.

Habte, M., and M. Alexander. 1977. Further evidence for the regulation of bacterial populations in soil by protozoa. Arch. Microbiol. 113:181-183.

Habte, M., and M. Alexander. 1978. Mechanisms of persistence of low numbers of bacteria preyed upon by protozoa. Soil Biol. Biochem. 10:1-6.

Habte, M., and M. Alexander. 1978. Protozoan density and the coexistence of protozoan predators and bacterial prey. Ecology 59:140-146.

Hagan, K. S., R. van den Bosh, and D. L. Dahlsten. 1971. The importance of naturally-occurring biological control in the western United States. pp. 253-293. IN Huffaker, C. B. (ed.), Biological Control. Plenum Press, New York.

Hagstrom, A. 1977. The fate of oil in a model ecosystem. Ambio 6:229-231.

Hall, D. J., W. E. Cooper, and E. E. Werner. 1970. An experimental approach to the production dynamics and structure of freshwater animal communities. Limnol. Oceanogr. 15:839-928.

Hall, D. J., S. T. Threlkeld, C. W. Burns, and P. H. Crowley. 1976. zooplankton communities. Annu. Rev. Ecol. Syst. 7:177-208.

Halliday, J., and J. S. Pate. 1976. The acetylene reduction assay as a means of studying nitrogen fixation in white clover under sward and laboratory conditions. J. Br. Grassl. Soc. 31:29-35.

Hansen, S. R., and S. P. Hubbell. 1980. Single-nutrient microbial competition: Qualitative agreement between experimental and theoretically forecast outcomes. Science 207:1491-1493.

Hardman, J. M., and A. L. Turnbull. 1974. The interaction of spatial heterogeneity, predator competition and the functional response to prey density in a laboratory system of wolf spiders (Araneae: Lycosidae) and fruit flies (Diptera: Drosophilidae). J. Anim. Ecol. 43:155-171.

Harpaz, I. 1955. Bionomics of Therioaphis maculata (Buckton) in Israel. J. Econ. Entomol. 48:668-671.

Harper, J. L. 1961. Approaches to the study of plant competition. pp. 1-39. IN Mechanisms in Biological Competition, Symposia of the Society for Experimental Biology. XV. Academic Press, Inc., New York.

Harper, J. L. 1977. Population Biology of Plants. Academic Press, New York.

Harper, J. L., and I. H. McNaughton. 1962. The comparative biology of closely related species living in the same area. VII. Interference between individuals in pure and mixed populations of Papaver species. The New Phytol. 61:175-188.

Harris, P. 1973. Insects in the population dynamics of plants. IN Van Emden, H. F. (ed.),Symp. of the R. Entomol. Soc. of London: Number Six. Insect/Plant Relationships. Blackwell Scientific Publications, Oxford.

Harris, R. L., and L. M. Oliver. 1979. Predation of Philonthus flavolimbatus on the horn fly. Environ. Entomol. 8:259-260.

Harris, W. F., B. S. Ausmus, G. K. Eddlemon, S. J. Draggan, J. M. Giddings, D. R. Jackson, R. J. Luxmoore, E. G. O'Neill, R. V. O'Neill, M. Ross-Todd, and P. Van Voris. 1980. Microcosms as potential screening tools for evaluating transport and effects of toxic substances. EPA-600/3-80-042; ORNL/EPA-600/7-79.

Harte, J., D. Levy, E. Lapan, A. Jassby, M. Dudzik, and J. Rees. 1978. Aquatic microcosms for assessment of effluent effects. Electrical Power Research Institute EA-936.

Harte, J., D. Levy, J. Rees, and E. Saegebarth. 1980. Making microcosms an effective assessment tool. IN Giesy, J. P. (ed.), Microcosms in Ecological Research (in press).

Hassell, M. P. 1971. Parasite behavior as a factor contributing to the stability of insect host-parasite interactions. pp. 366-378. IN Den Boer, P. J., and G. R. Gradwell (eds), Proceedings of the Advanced Study Institute on Dynamics of Numbers in Populations. Center for Agricultural Publishing and Documentation, Wageningen.

Hassell, M. P., and C. B. Huffaker. 1969. Regulatory processes and population cyclicity in laboratory populations of Anagasta kuhniella (Zeller) (Lepidoptera: Phycitidae). III. The development of population models. Res. Popul. Ecol. 11:186-210.

Hatfield, C. T., and J. M. Anderson. 1972. Effects of two insecticides on the vulnerability of Atlantic salmon (Salmo salar) parr to brook trout (Salvelinus fontinalis) predation. J. Fish. Res. Board Can. 29:27-29.

Hawksworth, D. L., and F. Rose. 1976. Lichens as pollution monitors. Edward Arnold, London. 60 pp.

Haynes, D. L., and P. Sisojevic. 1966. Predatory behavior of Philodromus rufus Walckenaer (Araneae: Thomisidae). Can. Entomol. 98(2):113-133.

Heath, R. T. 1979. Holistic study of an aquatic microcosm: Theoretical and practical implications. Int. J. Environ. Stud. 13:87-93.

Heath, R. T. 1980. Are microcosms useful for ecosystem analysis? IN Giesy, J. P. (ed.), Microcosms in Ecological Research (in press).

Heinle, D. R., D. A. Flemer, R. T. Huff, S. T. Sulkin, and R. E. Ulanowicz. 1979. Effects of perturbations on estuarine microcosms. pp. 119-142. IN Dame, R. F. (ed.), Marsh-Estuarine Systems Simulation. U. of South Carolina Press, Columbus, S.C.

Helgesen, R. G., and M. J. Tauber. 1974. Biological control of greenhouse whitefly, Trialeurodes vaporariorum (Aleyrodidae: Homoptera), on short-term crops by manipulating biotic and abiotic factors. Can. Entomol. 106:1175-1188.

Helgesen, R. G., and M. J. Tauber. 1974. Pirimicarb, an aphicide nontoxic to three entomophagous arthropods. Environ. Entomol. 3:99-101.

Henderson, R. S., S. V. Smith, and E. C. Evans. 1976. Flow-through microcosms for simulation of marine ecosystems: development and intercomparison of open coast and bay facilities. Naval Undersea Center, San Diego, California. NUC-TP-519. 76 pp.

Hendrick, P. W. 1972. Factors responsible for a change in interspecific competitive ability in Drosophila. Evolution 26:513-522.

Henis, Y., A. Ghaffar, and R. Baker. 1978. Integrated control of Rhizoctonia solani damping-off of radish: Effect of successive plantings, PCNB, and Trichoderma harzianum on pathogen and disease. Phytopathology 68:900-907.

Herting, G. E., and A. Witt, Jr. 1967. The role of physical fitness of forage fishes in relation to their vulnerability to predation by bowfin (Amia calva). Trans. Am. Fish. Soc. 96:427-430.

Herbert, H. J. 1962. Influence of Typhlodromus (T.) Pyri Scheuten on the development of Bryobia arborea M. & A. populations in the greenhouse. Can. Entomol. 94:870-873.

Herzberg, M. A., D. A. Klein, and D. C. Coleman. 1978. Trophic interactions in soils as they affect energy and nutrient dynamics. II. Physiological responses of selected rhizosphere bacteria. Microb. Ecol. 4:351-359.

Hill, J., IV, and D. B. Porcella. 1974. Component description of sediment water microcosms. Utah State University Center for Water Resources W74-12868, OWRR-B-080-Utah, PRWG 121-122.

Hill, J., IV, H. P. Kollig, D. F. Paris, N. L. Wolfe, and R. G. Zepp. 1976. Dynamic behavior of vinyl chloride in aquatic ecosystem. Environmental Protection Agency, EPA-600/3-76-001.

Hirwe, A. S., R. L. Metcalf, P. Y. Lu, and L. C. Chio. 1975. Comparative metabolism of 1,1-bis-(p-chlorophenyl)-2,2-nitropropane (Prolan) in mouse, insects, and in a model ecosystem.

Hoffman, J. H., and V. C. Moran. 1977. Pre-release studies on *Tucumania tapiacola* Dyar (Lepidoptera: Pyridae), a potential biocontrol agent for jointed cactus. J. Entomol. Soc. South Afr. 40:205-209.

Hoffman, R. W., and A. J. Horne. 1980. On-site flume studies for assessment of effluent impacts on stream aufwuchs communities. IN Giesy, J. P. (ed.), Microcosms in Ecological Research (in press).

Holling, C. S. 1959. The components of predation as revealed by a study of small-mammal predation of the European pine sawfly. Can. Entomol. 91:293-320.

Holling, C. S. 1966. The functional response of invertebrate predators to prey density. Mem. Entomol. Soc. Can. 48:1-88.

Hough, J. A., and D. Pimentel. 1978. Influence of haste foliage on development, survival and fecundity of the gypsy moth. Environ.

Howarth, R. W., and S. G. Fisher. 1976. Carbon, nitrogen and phosphorous dynamics during leaf decay in nutrient enriched stream microecosystems. Freshwater Biol. 6:221-228.

Huckabee, J. W., and B. G. Blaylock. 1976. Microcosm studies on the transfer of mercury, cadmium, and selenium from terrestrial to aquatic ecosystems. Proc., Univ. Mo. Annu. Conf. Trace Subst. Environ. Health 8:219-228.

Hueck, H. J., and D. M. M. Adema. 1968. Toxicological investigations in an artifical ecosystem. A progress report on copper toxicity towards algae and *Daphnia*. Helgol. Wiss. Meeresunters. 17:188-199.

Huffaker, C. B. 1958. Experimental studies on predation: Dispersion factors and predator-prey oscillations. Hilgardia 27(14):343-383.

Huffaker, C. B. 1971. The phenomenon of predation and its roles in nature. pp. 327-343. IN Den Boer, P. J., and G. R. Cradwell (eds.), Dynamics of Populations, Proc. of the Advanced Study Institute on Dynamics of Numbers in Populations. Centre for Agricultural Publishing and Documentation, Wageningen.

Huffaker, C. B., and C. E. Kennett. 1956. Experimental studies on predation: Predation and cyclamen-mite populations on strawberries in California. Hilgardia 26(4):191-222.

Huffaker, C. B., C. E. Kennett, B. Matsumoto, and E. G. White. 1973. Some parameters in the role of enemies in the natural control of insect abundance. pp. 59-75. IN Southwood, T. R. E. (ed.), Insect Abundance. Blackwell Scientific Publications, Oxford.

Huffaker, C. B., P. S. Messenger, and P. De Bach. 1971. The natural enemy component in natural control and the theory of biological control. pp. 16-67. IN Huffaker, C. B. (ed.), Biological Control. Plenum Press, New York.

Huffaker, C. B., K. P. Shea, and S. G. Herman. 1963. Experimental studies on predation: Complex dispersion and levels of food in an acarine predator-prey interaction. Hilgardia 34(9):305-330.

Hura, M., E. C. Evans III, and F. G. Wood. 1976. Coastal water protection the Navy way. Environ. Sci. Technol. 10:1098-1103.

Hurlbert, S. H., J. Zedler, and D. Fairbanks. 1972. Ecosystem alteration by mosquitofish (Gambusia affinis) predation. Science 175:639-641.

Hussey, N. W., and L. Brovenboer. 1971. Control of pests in greenhouse culture by the introduction of natural enemies. pp. 195-216. IN Huffaker, C. B. (ed.), Biological Control. Plenum Press, New York.

Hussey, N. W., and W. J. Parr. 1965. Observations on the control of Tetranychus urticae Koch on cucumbers by the predatory mite Phytoseiulus riegeli Dosse. Entomol. Exp. and Appl. 8:271-281.

Hutchinson, G. E. 1975. A treatise on limnology. Vol. 1. J. Wiley and Sons, New York.

Isensee, A. R. 1976. Variability of aquatic model ecosystem derived data. Int. J. Environ. Stud. 10:35-41.

Isensee, A. R., and G. E. Jones. 1975. Distribution of 2,3,7,8-tetrachloro-dibenzene-p-dioxin (TCDD) in aquatic model ecosystems. Environ. Sci. Technol. 9:668-672.

Isensee, A. R., P. C. Kearney, E. A. Woolson, G. E. Jones, and V. P. Williams. 1973. Distribution of alkyl arsenicals in model ecosystems. Environ. Sci. Technol. 7:841-845.

Iyer, J. G., and S. A. Wilde. 1965. Effect of vapam biocide on the growth of red pine seedlings. J. For. 63:703-704.

Jackman, R. H., and M. C. H. Mouat. 1972. Competition between grass and clover for phosphate I. N. Z. J. Agric. Res. 15:653-666.

Jackson, D. R., B. S. Ausmus, and M. Levine. 1979. Effects of arsenic on nutrient dynamics of grassland microcosms and field plots. Water, Air, and Soil Pollut. 11:13-21.

Jackson, D. R., and J. M. Hall. 1978. Extraction of nutrients from intact soil cores to assess the impact of chemical toxicants on soil. Pedobiologica 18:272-278.

Jackson, D. R., and M. Levine. 1979. Transport of arsenic in grassland microcosms and field plots. Water, Air, and Soil Poll. 11:3-12.

Jackson, D. R., J. J. Selvidge, and B. S. Ausmus. 1978. Behavior of heavy metals in forest microcosms. 1. Transport and distribution among components. Water, Air, and Soil Pollut. 10:3-11.

Jackson, D. R., W. J. Selvidge, and B. S. Ausmus. 1978. Behavior of heavy metals in forest microcosms. II. Effects on nutrient cycling processes. Water Air Soil Pollut. 10:13-18.

Jackson, D. R., C. D. Washburne, and B. S. Ausmus. 1977. Loss of Ca and NO_3-N (calcium, nitrate-nitrogen) from terrestrial microcosms as an indicator for assessing contaminants of soil pollution. Water, Air, and Soil Pollut. 8(3):279-284.

Jackson, D. R., and A. P. Watson. 1977. Disruption of nutrient pools and transport of heavy metals in a forested watershed near a lead smelter. J. Environ. Qual. 6:331-338.

Jacobs, J. 1978. Coexistence of similar zooplankton species by differential adaptation to reproduction and escape in an environment with fluctuating food and enemy densities. Part 3. Laboratory experiments. Oecologia 35:35-54.

Jacobs, J. 1978. Influence of prey size, light intensity, and alternative prey on the selectivity of plankton feeding fish. Verh. Int. Ver. Limnol. 20:2461-2466.

Jain, S. K. 1969. Comparative ecogenetics of two Avena species occurring in central California. Evol. Biol. 3:73-117.

Jamieson, G. S., and G. G. E. Scudder. 1979. Predation in Gerris (Hemiptera): Reactive distances and locomotion rates. Oecologia 44:13-20.

Janssen, J. 1976. Feeding modes and prey size selection in the alewife (Alosa pseudoharengus). J. Fish. Res. Board Can. 33:1972-1975.

Janssen, J. 1976. Selectivity of an artificial filter feeder and suction feeders on calanoid copepods. Am. Midl. Nat. 95:491-493.

Jassby, A., M. Dudzik, J. Rees, E. Lapan, D. Levy, and J. Harte. 1977. Production cycles in aquatic microcosms. EPA-600/7-77-097.

Jassby, A., J. Rees, M. Dudzik, D. Levy, E. Lapan, and J. Harte. 1977. Trophic structure modifications by planktivorous fish in aquatic microcosms. EPA-600/7-77-096.

Jenkinson, D. S., and D. S. Powlson. 1976. The effects of biocidal treatments on metabolism in soil I. Fumigation with chloroform. Soil Biol. Biochem. 8:167-177.

Johnen, B. G., and E. A. Drew. 1977. Ecological effects of pesticides on soil microorganisms. Soil Sci. 123(5):319-324.

Johnson, D. L. 1978. Biological mediation of chemical speciation. Part 1. Microcosm studies of the diurnal pattern of copper species in sea water. Chemosphere 7:641-644.

Jordan, M., and G. E. Likens. 1975. An organic carbon budget for an oligotrophic lake in New Hampshire, U.S.A. Verh. Int. Ver. Limnol. 19:994-1003.

Kanazawa, J., A. R. Isensee, and P. C. Kearney. 1975. Distribution of carbaryl and 3,5-xylyl methylcarbamate in an aquatic model ecosystem. J. Agric. Food Chem. 23:760-763.

Kania, H. J., and R. J. Beyers. 1970. Feedback control of light input to a microecosystem by the system. Sav. River Ecol. Lab. Annu. Report, pp. 146-148.

Kania, H. J., and R. J. Beyers. 1974. NTA and mercury in artificial stream systems. Environmental Protection Agency, EPA-660/3-73-025.

Kania, H. J., R. L. Knight, and R. J. Beyers. 1976. Fate and biological effects of mercury introduced into artificial streams. Environmental Protection Agency, EPA-600/3-76-060.

Kania, H. J., and J. O'Hara. 1974. Behavioral alterations in a simple predator-prey system due to sublethal exposure to mercury. Trans. Am. Fish. Soc. 103:134-136.

Kapoor, I. P., R. L. Metcalf, A. S. Hirwe, P. Y. Lu, J. R. Coats, and R. F. Nystrom. 1972. Comparative metabolism of DDT, methoxychlor, and ethoxychlor in mouse, insects, and in a model ecosystem. J. Agr. Food Chem. 20:1-6.

Kapoor, I. P., R. L. Metcalf, R. F. Nystrom, and G. K. Sangha. 1970. Comparative metabolism of methoxychlor and DDT in mouse, insects, and in a model ecosystem. J. Agr. Food Chem. 18:1145-1152.

Kaufman, D. D. 1970. Pesticide metabolism. Pesticides in the soil: Ecology, degradation, and movement. IN International Symposium on Pesticides in the Soil. MSU, E. L., Mich.

Kaufman, D. D. 1977. Biodegradation and persistence of several acetamide, acylanilide, azide, carbamate, and organophosphate pesticide combinations. Soil Biol. Biochem. 9(1):49-57.

Kaufman, D. D., J. Blake, and D. E. Miller. 1971. Methylcarbamates affect acylanilide herbicide residues in soil. J. Agric. Food Chem. 19:204-206.

Kaufman, D. D., P. C. Kearney, D. W. Von Endt, and D. E. Miller. 1970. Methylcarbamate inhibition of phenylcarbamate metabolism in soil. J. Agric. Food Chem. 18:513-519.

Kawabata, Z., and Y. Kurihara. 1978. Computer simulation study of the relationships between the total system and subsystems in the early stages of succession of the aquatic microcosm. Sci. Rep. Tohoku Univ., Ser. 4 (Biol.) 37:179-204.

Kawabata, Z., and Y. Kurihara. 1978. Computer simulation study on the nature of the steady-state of the aquatic microcosm. Sci. Rep. Tohoku Univ. Ser. 4 (Biol.) 37:205-218.

Kawabata, Z., and Y. Kurihara. 1978. Effects of the consumer on the biomass and spatial heterogeneity in the aquatic microcosm. Sci. Rep. Tohoku Univ. Ser. 4 (Biol.) 37:219-234.

Kehde, P. M., and J. L. Wilhm. 1972. The effects of grazing by snails on community structure of periphyton in laboratory streams. Am. Midl. Nat. 87:8-24.

Kelly, R. A. 1971. The Effects of Fluctuating Temperature on the Metabolism of Freshwater Microcosms. Ph.D. dissertation, University of North Carolina.

Kerfoot, W. C. 1974. Egg-size cycle of a cladoceran. Ecology 55:1259-1270.

Kerfoot, W. C. 1975. The divergence of adjacent populations. Ecology 56:1298-1313.

Kerfoot, W. C. 1977. Competition in cladoceran communities: The cost of evolving defenses against copepod predation. Ecology 58:303-313.

Kerfoot, W. C. 1977. Implications of copepod predation. Limnol. Oceanogr. 22:316-325.

Kerfoot, W. C. 1978. Combat between predatory copepods and their prey: Cyclops, Epischura, and Bosmina. Limnol. Oceanogr. 23:1080-1102.

Kersting, K. 1975. The use of microsystems for the evaluation of the effects of toxicants. Hydrobiol. Bull. 9:102-108.

Kettle, D., and W. J. O'Brien. 1978. Vulnerability of arctic zooplankton species to predation by small lake trout (Salvelinus namaycush). J. Fish. Res. Board Can. 35:1495-1500.

Kevern, N. R. 1963. Primary Productivity and Energy Relationships in Artificial Streams. Ph.D. dissertation, Michigan State University.

Kevern, N. R., and R. C. Ball. 1965. Primary productivity and energy relationships in artificial streams. Limnol. Oceanogr. 10:74-87.

Kindig, A. 1979. Investigations for streptomycin-induced algal competitive dominance reversals. Experimental Report ME25, FDA Contract No. 223-76-8348, University of Washington.

King, C. E., and P. S. Dawson. 1972. Population biology and the Tribolium model. Evol. Biol. 5:133-277.

Kitchens, W. M. 1979. Development of a salt marsh microecosystem. Int. J. Environ. Stud. 13:109-118.

Kitchens, W. M., and B. J. Copeland. 1980. Succession in laboratory microecosystems subjected to thermal and nutrient addition. IN Giesy, J. P. (ed.), Microcosms in Ecological Research (in press).

Kitchens, W. M., R. T. Edwards, and W. V. Johnson. 1979. Development of a living salt marsh ecosystem model: A microecosystem approach. IN Dame, R. F. (ed.), Marsh-Estuarine Systems Simulation. U. of South Carolina Press, Columbus, S.C.

Kleiber, P., and T. H. Blackburn. 1978. Model of biological and diffusional processes involving hydrogen sulfide in a marine microcosm. Oikos 31:280-283.

Klein, D. A. 1977. Seasonal carbon flow and decomposer parameter relationships in a semiarid grassland soil. Ecology 58(1):184-190.

Klein, D. A., and E. M. Molise. 1975. Ecological ramifications of silver iodide nucleating agent accumulation in a semi-arid grassland environment. J. Appl. Meteorol. 14:673-680.

Klotz, R. L., J. R. Cain, and F. R. Trainor. 1976. Algal competition in an epilithic river flora. J. Phycol. 12:363-368.

Kochhar, M., U. Blum, and R. A. Reinert. 1980. Effects of O_3 and (or) fescue on ladino clover: Interactions. Can. J. Bot. 58(2):241-249.

Kormanik, P. P., W. C. Bryan, and R. C. Schultz. 1980. Procedures and equipment for staining large numbers of plant root samples for endomycorrhizal assay. Can. J. Microbiol. (in press).

Kricher, J. C., C. L. Bayer, and D. A. Martin. 1979. Effects of two Aroclor fractions on the productivity and diversity of algae from two lentic ecosystems. Int. J. Environ. Stud. 13:159-167.

Krzywicka, A., and D. Krupa. 1975. Preliminary investigations on mutual growth relations of the populations of the blue-green alga *Microcystis aeruginosa* and green algae *Monoraphidium minutum* and *Scenedesmus abundans* in bicultures. Acta Hydrobiol. 17:81-88.

Kudeyarov, V. N., and D. S. Jenkinson. 1975. The effects of biocidal treatments on metabolism in soil - VI. Fumigation with carbon disulphide. Soil Biol. Biochem. 8:375-378.

Kulkarni, J. H., J. S. Sardeshpande, and D. J. Bagyaraj. 1974. Effect of four soil-applied insecticides on symbiosis of *Rhizobium* with *Arachis hypogaea* Linn. Plant Soil 40(1):169-172.

Kurihara, Y. 1956. Dynamic aspects of the community structure of the benthic protists in bamboo container. Jpn. J. Ecol. 5:111-117.

Kurihara, Y. 1958. Analysis of the structure of microcosm, with special reference to the succession of protozoa in the bamboo container. Jpn. J. Ecol. 8:163-171.

Kurihara, Y. 1959. Synecological analysis of the biotic community in microcosm. VIII. Studies of the limiting factor in determining the distribution of mosquito larvae in the polluted water of bamboo container, with special reference to bacteria. Jpn. J. Zool. 12: 391-400.

Kurihara, Y. 1960. Dynamic aspect of the structure of microcosm, with special reference to interrelationships among biotic and abiotic factors. Jpn. J. Ecol. 10:115-120.

Kurihara, Y. 1978. Studies of "succession" in a microcosm. Sci. Rep. Tohoku Univ. Ser. 4 (Biol.) 37:151-160.

Kurihara, Y. 1978. Studies of the interaction in a microcosm. Sci. Rep. Tohoku Univ. Ser. 4 (Biol.) 37:161-178.

Kwasnik, J. F. S. 1977. Effects of Cadmium on the Predator-Prey Behavior of Fathead Minnows (*Pimephales promelas*) and Largemouth Bass (*Micropterus salmoides*) in a Model Ecosystem. Ph.D. dissertation, Purdue University.

Labeda, D. P., and M. Alexander. 1978. Effects of SO_2 and NO_2 on nitrification in soil. J. Environ. Qual. 7:523-526.

Landry, M. R. 1978. Predatory feeding behavior of a marine copepod, *Labidocera trispinosa*. Limnol. Oceanogr. 23:1103-1113.

Lange, W. 1974. Competitive exclusion among three planktonic blue-green algal species. J. Phycol. 10:411-414.

Lauff, G. H., and K. W. Cummins. 1964. A model stream for studies in lotic ecology. Ecology 45:188-191.

Le Cato, G. L. 1975. Interactions among four species of stored-product insects in corn: A multifactorial study. Ann. Entomol. Soc. of Am. 66(4):677-679.

Le Cato, G. L. 1975. Predation by red flour beetle on sawtoothed grain beetle. Environ. Entomol. 4(1):504-506.

Le Cato, G. L. 1978. Functional response of red flour beetles to density of cigarette beetles and the role of predation in population regulation. Environ. Entomol. 7(1):77-80.

Lee, A. H., P. Y. Lu, R. L. Metcalf, and E. L. Hsu. 1976. The environmental fate of three dichlorophenyl nitrophenyl ether herbicides in a rice paddy model ecosystem. J. Environ. Qual. 5: 482-486.

Leffler, J. W. 1974. The concept of ecosystem stability: Its relationship to species diversity. Assoc. Southeast Biol. Bull. 21:65-66.

Leffler, J. W. 1977. A Microcosm Approach to an Evaluation of the Diversity-Stability Hypothesis. Ph.D. dissertation, University of Georgia.

Leffler, J. W. 1978. Ecosystem responses to stress in aquatic microcosms. pp. 102-119. IN Thorp, J. H., and J. W. Gibbons (eds.), Energy and Center, Oak Ridge, TN.

Lerner, I. M., and E. R. Dempster. 1962. Indeterminism in interspecific competition. Proc. Nat. Acad. Sci. U.S.A. 48:821-826.

Lerner, I. M., and F. K. Ho. 1961. Genotype and competitive ability of *Tribolium* species. Am. Nat. 95:329-343.

Leslie, P. H. 1958. A stochastic model for studying the properties of certain biological systems by numerical methods. Biometrika 45: 16-31.

Leslie, P. H., T. Park, and D. Mertz. 1968. The effect of varying the initial numbers on the outcome of competition between two *Tribolium* species. J. Anim. Ecol. 37:9-23.

Letchworth, M. B., and U. Blum. 1977. Effects of acute ozone exposure on growth, nodulation and nitrogen content of ladino clover. Environ. Pollut. 14:303-312.

L'Heritier, P., and G. Teissier. 1937. Elimination des forms mutants dans les populations des drosophiles. Cas des Drosophiles Bar. C. R. Soc. Biol. (Paris) 124:880-882.

Li, J. L., and H. W. Li. 1979. Species-specific factors affecting predator-prey interactions of the copepod Acanthocyclops vernalis with its natural prey. Limnol. Oceanogr. 24:613-626.

Liang, C. N., and M. A. Tabatabai. 1977. Effects of trace elements on nitrogen mineralization in soils. Environ. Pollut. 12:141-147.

Lichtenstein, E. P. 1979. Fate of pesticides in a soil-plant microcosm. pp. 95-101. IN Witt, J. M., and J. W. Gillett (eds.), Terrestrial Microcosms and Environmental Chemistry. NSF/RA 79-0026. National Science Foundation, Washington, D.C.

Lichtenstein, E. P., T. W. Fuhremann, and K. R. Schulz. 1974. Translocation and metabolism of [^{14}C]phorate as affected by percolating water in a model soil-plant ecosystem. J. Agric. Food Chem. 22:991-996.

Lichtenstein, E. P., T. W. Fuhreman, K. R. Schulz, and R. F. Skrentny. 1967. Effect of detergents and inorganic salts in water on the persistence and movement of insecticides in soils. J. Econ. Entomol. 60:1714-1721.

Lichtenstein, E. P., K. R. Schulz, and T. T. Liang. 1977. Fate of fresh and aged soil residues of the insecticide (^{14}C)-N-2596 in a soil-corn-water ecosystem. J. Econ. Entomol. 70:169-175.

Lighthart, B., and H. Bond. 1976. Design and preliminary results from soil/litter microcosms. Int. J. Environ. Stud. 10:51-58.

Lighthart, B., H. Bond, and M. Ricard. 1977. Trace element research using coniferous forest soil/litter microcosms. EPA-600/3-77-091. U.S. Environmental Protection Agency, Corvallis, Ore. 51 pp.

Likens, G. E., F. H. Bormann, R. S. Pierce, J. S. Eaton, and N. M. Johnson. 1977. Biogeochemistry of a Forested Ecosystem. Springer-Verlag, New York. 146 pp.

Lin, S., B. R. Funke, and J. T. Schulz. 1972. Effects of some organophosphate and carbamate insecticides on nitrification and legume growth. Plant Soil 37:489-496.

Longstaff, B. C. 1976. The dynamics of collembolan populations: Competitive relationships in an experimental system. Can. J. Zool. 54(6):948-962.

Lu, PoYung, R. L. Metcalf, and E. M. Carlson. 1978. Environmental fate of five radiolabled coal conversion by-products evaluated in a laboratory model ecosystem. Environ. Health Perspect. 24:201-208.

Lu, PoYung, R. L. Metcalf, and L. K. Cole. 1978. The environmental fate of ^{14}C-pentachlorophenol in laboratory model ecosystems. pp. 53-63. IN Rango-Rao, K. (ed.), Pentachlorophenol: Chemistry, Pharmacology and Environmental Toxicology. Plenum Press, New York.

Lu, PoYung, R. L. Metcalf, A. S. Hirwe, and J. W. Williams. 1975. Evaluation of environmental distribution and fate of hexachlorocyclopentadiene, chlordene, heptachlor, and heptachlor epoxide in a laboratory model ecosystem. J. Agric. Food Chem. 23:967-973.

Luckinbill, L. S. 1973. Coexistence in laboratory populations of _Paramecium aurelia_ and its predator _Didinium nasutum_. Ecology 54: 1320-1327.

Luckinbill, L. S. 1974. The effects of space and enrichment on a predator-prey system. Ecology 55:1142-1147.

Luxmore, R. J., and C. L. Begovich. 1979. Simulated heavy metal fluxes in tree microcosms and a deciduous forest--A review. ISEM J. 1:48-60.

Lynch, M. 1979. Predation, competition, and zooplankton community structure: An experimental study. Limnol. Oceanogr. 24:253-272.

McClanahan, R. J. 1970. Integrated control of greenhouse whitefly on cucumbers. J. Econ. Entomol. 63:499-601.

McConnell, W. J. 1962. Productivity relations in carboy microcosms. Limnol. Oceanogr. 7:335-343.

McConnell, W. J. 1965. Relationship of herbivore growth to rate of gross photosynthesis in microcosms. Limnol. Oceanogr. 10:539-543.

McCormick, J. F., and R. B. Platt. 1962. Effects of ionizing radiation on a natural plant community. Radiat. Bot. 2:161-188.

McCormick, J. F., and R. B. Platt. 1964. Ecotypic differentiation in _Diamorpha cymosa_. Bot. Gaz. 125:271-279.

McIntire, C. D. 1968. Physiological-ecological studies of benthic algae in laboratory streams. J. Water Pollut. Control Fed. 40:1940-1952.

McIntire, C. D. 1968. Structural characteristics of benthic algal communities in laboratory streams. Ecology 49:520-537.

McIntire, C. D. 1973. Periphyton dynamics in laboratory streams: A simulation model and its implications. Ecol. Monogr. 43:399-420.

McIntire, C. D., R. L. Garrison, H. K. Phinney, and C. E. Warren. 1964. Primary production in laboratory streams. Limnol. Oceanogr. 9: 92-102.

McMillian, W. W., K. J. Starks, and M. C. Bowman. 1967. Resistance in corn to the corn earworm, Heliothis zea and the fall armyworm, Spodoptera frugiperda (Lepidoptera: Noctuidae). Part I. Larval feeding responses. Ann. Entom. Soc. Am. 60:871-873.

McMurtry, J. A., and G. T. Scriven. 1968. Studies on predator-prey interactions between Amblyseius hibisci and Oligonychus punicae: Effects of host-plant conditioning and limited quantities of an alternate food. Ann. Entomol. Soc. of Am. 61:393-397.

McQueen, D. J. 1969. Reduction of zooplankton standing stocks by predacious Cyclops bicuspidatus thomasi in Marion Lake, British Columbia. J. Fish. Res. Board Can. 26:1605-1618.

Maguire, B., Jr. 1980. Some patterns in post-closure ecosystem dynamics (failure). IN Giesy, J. P. (ed.), Microcosms in Ecological Research (in press).

Maki, A. W. 1980. Evaluation of a toxicant on structure and function of model stream communities: Correlations with natural stream effects. IN Giesy, J. P. (ed.), Microcosms in Ecological Research (in press).

Maki, A. W., and H. E. Johnson. 1976. Evaluation of a toxicant on the metabolism of model stream communities. J. Fish. Res. Board Can. 33:2740-2746.

Manning, W. J., W. A. Feder, and P. M. Papia. 1972. Influence of long-term low levels of ozone and benomyl on growth and nodulation of pinto bean plants. Phytopathology 62(5):497.

Manuel, C. Y., and G. W. Marshall. 1980. Limitations on the use of microcosms for predicting algal response to nutrient enrichment in lotic systems. IN Giesy, J. P. (ed.), Microcosms in Ecological Research (in press).

Marshall, J. S. 1969. Competition between *Daphnia* *pulex* and *D.* *magna* as modified by radiation stress. Ecol. Soc. Am. Annual Meeting, University of Vermont, August 17-22, 1969.

Marx, D. H. 1969. Antagonism of mycorrhizal fungi to root pathogenic fungi and soil bacteria. Phytopathology 59:153-163.

Marx, D. H., W. G. Morris, and J. G. Mexal. 1978. Growth and ectomycorrhizal development of loblolly pine seedlings in fumigated and nonfumigated soil infested with different fungal symbionts. For. Sci. 24:193-203.

Mauck, W. L., and D. W. Coble. 1971. Vulnerability of some fishes to northern pike (*Esox* *lucius*) predation. J. Fish. Res. Board Can. 28:957-969.

May, R. M. 1973. Stability and complexity in model ecosystems. Princeton University Press, Princeton, N.J.

Medine, A. J. 1979. The Use of Microcosms to Study Aquatic Ecosystem Dynamics--Methods and Case Studies. Ph.D. dissertation, Utah State University.

Medine, A. J., D. B. Porcella, and V. D. Adams. 1980. Heavy metal and nutrient effects on sediment oxygen demand in three-phase aquatic microcosms. IN Giesy, J. P. (ed.), Microcosms in Ecological Research (in press).

Meers, J. L. 1973. Growth of bacteria in mixed cultures. Microb. Ecol. 136-181.

Menge, J. A., E. L. V. Johnson, and V. Minassian. 1979. Effect of heat treatment and three pesticides upon the growth and reproduction of the mycorrhizal fungus *Glomus* *fasciculatus*. New Phytol. 82(2): 473-480.

Merrell, D. J. 1951. Interspecific competition between *Drosophila* *funebris* and *Drosophila* *melanogaster*. Am. Nat. 85:159-169.

Mertz, D. B., D. A. Cawthon, and T. Park. 1976. An experimental analysis of competitive indeterminacy in *Tribolium*. Proc. Nat. Acad. Sci. U.S.A. 73:1368-1372.

Mertz, D. M. 1972. The *Tribolium* model and the mathematics of population growth. Annu. Rev. Ecol. Syst. 3:51-78.

Messenger, P. S. 1964. Use of life tables in a bioclimatic study of an experimental aphid-braconid wasp host-parasite system. Ecology 45: 119-131.

Messenger, P. S., and D. C. Force. 1963. An experimental host-parasite system: *Therioaphis maculata* (Buckton)-*Praon palitans* Muesebeck (Homoptera: Aphidae: Hymenoptera: Bracomidae). Ecology 44: 532-540.

Metcalf, R. L. 1971. A model ecosystem for the evaluation of pesticide biodegradability and ecological magnification. Outlook on Agriculture 7:55-59.

Metcalf, R. L. 1977. Model ecosystem approach to insecticide degradation: A critique. Annu. Rev. Entomol. 22:241-261.

Metcalf, R. L. 1977. Model ecosystem studies of bioconcentration and biodegradation of pesticides. Environ. Sci. Res. 10:127-144.

Metcalf, R. L., L. K. Cole, S. G. Wood, D. J. Mandel, and M. L. Milbrath. 1979. Design and evaluation of a terrestrial model ecosystem for evaluation of substitute pesticide chemicals. EPA-600/3-79-004. U.S. Environmental Protection Agency, Corvallis, Ore. 20 pp.

Metcalf, R. L., I. P. Kapoor, P.-Y. Lu, C. K. Schuth, and P. Sherman. 1973. Model ecosystem studies of the environmental fate of six organochloride pesticides. Environ. Health Perspect. 4:35-44.

Metcalf, R. L., G. K. Sangha, and I. P. Kapoor. 1971. Model ecosystem for the evaluation of pesticide biodegradability and ecological magnification. Environ. Sci. Technol. 5:709-713.

Mickelson, M. J., H. Maske, and R. C. Dugdale. 1979. Nutrient-determined dominance in multispecies chemostat cultures of diatoms. Limnol. Oceanogr. 24:298-315.

Miller, R. S. 1964. Interspecies competition in laboratory populations of *Drosophila melanogaster* and *Drosophila simulans*. The Am. Nat. 98(901):221-238.

Miller, R. S. 1967. Larval competition in *Drosophila melanogaster* and *D. simulans*. Ecology 75:132-148.

Mitchell, D. 1971. Eutrophication of lake water microcosms: Phosphate versus nonphosphate detergents. Science 174:827-829.

Moore, J. A. 1952. Competition between *Drosophila melanogaster* and *Drosophila simulans*. II. The improvement of competitive ability through selection. Genetics 38:813-817.

Mortimer, C. H. 1941. The exchange of dissolved substances between mud and water in lakes. J. Ecol. 29:280-329.

Mortimer, C. H. 1942. The exchange of dissolved substances between mud and water in lakes. J. Ecol. 30:147-201.

Mosser, J. L., N. S. Fisher, and C. F. Wurster. 1972. Polychlorinated biphenyls and DDT alter species composition in mixed cultures of algae. Science 176:533-535.

Moth, J. J., and J. S. F. Barker. 1977. Interspecific competition between Drosophila melanogaster and Drosophila simulans: Effects of adult density on adult viability. Genetica 47(3):203-218.

Muller, W. A., and J. J. Lee. 1977. Biological interactions and the realized niche of Euplotes vannus from the salt marsh aufwuchs. J. Protozool. 24:523-527.

Mullin, M. M. 1979. Differential predation by the carnivorous marine copepod, Tortanus discaudatus. Limnol. Oceanogr. 24:774-777.

Mullin, M. M., and P. M. Evans. 1974. The use of a deep tank in plankton ecology. 2. Efficiency of a planktonic food chain. Limnol. Oceanogr. 19:902-911.

Murdoch, W. W., and J. R. Marks. 1973. Predation by coccinellid beetles: Experiments on switching. Ecology 54:160-167.

Murphy, P. G., and J. F. McCormick. 1971. Ecological effects of acute beta irradiation from simulated fallout particles on a natural plant community. pp. 454-481. IN Bensen, D. W., and A. H. Sparrow (eds.), Survival of Food Crops and Livestock in the Event of Nuclear War. Atomic Energy Commission Symposium Series, No. 24.

Nash, R. G., and M. L. Beall, Jr. 1979. A microagroecosystem to monitor the environmental fate of pesticides. pp. 86-94. IN Witt, J. M., and J. W. Gillett (eds.), Terrestrial Microcosms and Environmental Chemistry. NSF/RA 79-0026. National Science Foundation, Washington, D.C.

Nash, R. G., M. L. Beall, Jr., and W. G. Harris. 1977. Toxaphene and 1,1,1-trichloro-2,2-bis(p-chlorophenyl) ethane (DDT) losses from cotton in an agroecosystem chamber. J. Agric. Food Chem. 25(2): 336-341.

Neame, P. A., and C. R. Goldman. 1980. Oxygen uptake and production in sediment--Water microcosms. IN Giesy, J. P. (ed.)., Microcosms in Ecological Research (in press).

Nechols, J. R., and M. J. Tauber. 1977. Age-specific interaction between the greenhouse whitefly and Encarsia formosa: Influence of host on the parasite's oviposition and development. Environ. Entomol. 6: 143-149.

Nechols, J. R., and M. J. Tauber. 1977. Age-specific interaction between the greenhouse whitefly and Encarsia formosa: Influence of the parasite on host development. Environ. Entomol. 6:207-210.

Neill, W. E. 1972. Effects of Size-Selective Predation on Community Structure in Laboratory Aquatic Microcosms. Ph.D. dissertation, University of Texas.

Neill, W. E. 1975. Experimental studies of microcrustacean competition, community composition, and efficiency of resource utilization. Ecology 56:809-826.

Neyman, J., T. Park, and E. L. Scott. 1958. Struggle for existence. The tribolium model: Biological and statistical aspects. Genet. Syst. Yearbook 3:152-179.

Nicholson, A. J. 1954. An outline of the dynamics of animal populations. Aust. J. Zool. 2:9-65.

Nixon, S. W. 1969. A synthetic microcosm. Limnol. Oceanogr. 14:142-145.

Nixon, S. W., D. Alonso, M. E. Q. Pilson, and B. A. Buckley. 1980. Turbulent mixing in aquatic microcosms. IN Giesy, J. P. (ed.), Microcosms in Ecological Research (in press).

Nixon, S. W., C. A. Oviatt, J. N. Kremer, and K. Perez. 1979. The use of numerical models and laboratory microcosms in estuarine ecosystem analysis simulations of a winter phytoplankton bloom. pp. 165-188. IN Dame, R. F. (ed.), Marsh-Estuarine Systems Simulation. U. of South Carolina Press, Columbia, S.C.

Notini, M., B. Nagell, A. Hagstrom, and O. Grahn. 1977. An outdoor model simulating a Baltic Sea littoral ecosystem. Oikos 28:1-8.

O'Bannon, J. H., and S. Nemec. 1978. Influence of soil pesticides on vesiculararbuscular mycorrhizae in citrus soil. Nematropica 8: 56-61.

O'Brien, W. J. 1979. The predator-prey interaction of planktivorous fish and zooplankton. Am. Sci. 67:572-581.

O'Brien, W. J., D. Kettle, and H. Riessen. 1979. Helmets and invisible armor: Structures reducing predation from tactile and visual planktivores. Ecology 60:287-294.

O'Brien, W. J., and D. Schmidt. 1979. Arctic Bosmina morphology and copepod predation. Limnol. Oceanogr. 24:564-568.

O'Brien, W. J., N. A. Slade, and G. L. Vinyard. 1976. Apparent size as the determinant of prey selection by bluegill sunfish (*Lepomis macrochirus*). Ecology 57:1304-1310.

O'Brien, W. J., and G. L. Vinyard. 1979. Polymorphism and predation: The effect of invertebrate predation on the distribution of two varieties of *Daphnia carinata* in South India ponds. Limnol. Oceanogr. 23:452-460.

Odum, E. P. 1969. The strategy of ecosystem development. Science 164: 262-270.

Odum, E. P. 1971. Fundamentals of Ecology. 3rd ed. W. B. Saunders, Philadelphia. 574 pp.

Odum, H. T. 1956. Primary production in flowing waters. Limnol. Oceanogr. 1:102-117.

Odum, H. T. 1957. Trophic structure and productivity of Silver Spring, Florida. Ecol. Monogr. 27:55-112.

Odum, H. T., and C. M. Hoskin. 1957. Metabolism of a laboratory stream microcosm. Publ. Inst. Mar. Sci. Texas 4:115-133.

Odum, H. T., and C. M. Hoskin. 1958. Comparative studies on the metabolism of marine waters. Publ. Inst. Mar. Sci., Univ. of Tex. 5:16-46.

Odum, H. T., and A. Lugo. 1970. Metabolism of forest-floor microcosms. IN Odum, H. T. (ed.), Tropical Rain Forest. U.S. Atomic Energy Commission, Washington, D.C.

Odum, H. T., W. L. Siler, R. J. Beyers, and N. Armstrong. 1963. Experiments with engineering of marine ecosystems. Publ. Inst. Mar. Sci. Tex. 9:373-403.

Ollason, J. G. 1977. Freshwater microcosms in fluctuating environments. Oikos 28:262-269.

Olson, D., and D. Pimentel. 1974. Evolution of resistance in a host population to attacking parasite. Environ. Entomol. 3:621-624.

O'Neill, R. V., B. S. Ausmus, D. R. Jackson, R. I. Van Hook, P. Van Voris, C. Washburne, and A. P. Watson. 1977. Monitoring terrestrial ecosystems by analysis of nutrient export. Water, Air, and Soil Pollut. 8:271-277.

O'Neill, R. V., and J. M. Giddings. 1979. Population interactions and ecosystem function. pp. 103-123. IN Innis, G. S., and R. V. O'Neill (eds.), Systems Analysis of Ecosystems. International Cooperative Publishing House, Fairland, Md.

Ortman, E. E., and T. F. Branson. 1976. Growth pouches for studies of host plant resistance to larvae of corn rootworms. J. Econ. Entomol. 69:380-382.

Oviatt, C. A., S. W. Nixon, K. T. Perez, and B. Buckley. 1979. On the season and nature of perturbations in microcosm experiments. pp. 143-164. IN Dame, R. F. (ed.), Marsh-Estuarine Systems Simulation. U. of South Carolina Press, Columbia, S.C.

Oviatt, C. A., K. T. Perez, and S. W. Nixon. 1977. Multivariate analysis of experimental marine ecosystems. Helgol. Wiss. Meeresunters. 30: 30-46.

Owen, D. F., and R. G. Wiegert. 1976. Do consumers maximize plant fitness? OIKOS 27(3):488-492.

Palmblad, I. G. 1968. Competition in experimental populations of weeds with emphasis on the regulation of population size. Ecology 49:26-34.

Pareek, R. P., and A. C. Gaur. 1970. Effect of dichloro diphenyl trichloro-ethane (DDT) on symbiosis of Rhizobium sp. with Phaseolus aureus (green gram). Plant Soil 33:297-304.

Park, T. 1948. Experimental studies of interspecies competition. I. Competition between populations of the flour beetles, Tribolium confusum and Tribolium castaneum. Herbst. Ecol. Mono. 18:265-308.

Park, T. 1954. Experimental studies of interspecies competition. II. Temperature, humidity and competition in two species of Tribolium. Physiol. Zool. 27:177-238.

Park, T. 1957. Experimental studies of interspecies competition. II. Relation of initial species proportition to competitive outcome in populations of Tribolium. Physiol. Zool. 30:22-40.

Park, T. 1962. Beetles, competition and populations. Science 138: 1369-1375.

Park, T., P. H. Leslie, and D. B. Mertz. 1964. Genetic strains and competition in populations of Tribolium. Physiol. Zool. 37:97-162.

Park, T., and M. Lloyd. 1955. Natural selection and the outcome of competition. Am. Nat. 89:235-240.

Parr, J. F. 1974. Effects of pesticides on microorganisms in soil and water. pp. 315-340. IN Guenzi, W. D. (ed.), Pesticides in Soil and Water. Soil Science Society of America, Inc., Madison, Wisc.

Patrick, R. 1973. Use of algae, especially diatoms, in the assessment of water quality. pp. 76-95. IN Cairns, J., Jr., and K. L. Dickson (eds.), Biological Methods for the Assessment of Water Quality. ASTM Special Technical Publication 528, American Society for Testing and Materials, Philadelphia.

Patton, B. C., and M. Witkamp. 1967. Systems analysis of ^{134}cesium kinetics in terrestrial microcosms. Ecology 48:813-824.

Perez, K. T., G. M. Morrison, N. F. Lackie, C. A. Oviatt, S. W. Nixon, B. A. Buckley, and J. F Heltshe. 1977. The importance of physical and biotic scaling to the experimental simulation of a coastal marine ecosystem. Helgol. Wiss. Meeresunters. 30:144-162.

Peterman, R. M., and M. Gatto. 1978. Estimation of functional responses of predators on juvenile salmon. J. Fish Res. Board Can. 35:797-808.

Phinney, H. K., and C. D. McIntire. 1965. Effect of temperature on metabolism of periphyton communities developed in laboratory streams. Limnol. Oceanogr. 10:341-344.

Pilson, M. E. Q., C. A. Oviatt, and S. W. Nixon. 1980. Annual nutrient cycles in a marine microcosm. IN Giesy, J. P. (ed.), Microcosms in Ecological Research (in press).

Pilson, M. E. Q., G. A. Vargo, P. Gearing, and J. N. Gearing. 1977. The marine ecosystems research laboratory: A facility for the investigation of effects and fates of pollutants. IN Proc. of the 2nd National Conference, Interagency Energy/Environment R&D Program, Washington, D.C., June 6-7, 1977.

Pimentel, D. 1968. Population regulation and genetic feedback. Science 159:1432-1437.

Pimentel, D., E. H. Feinberg, P. W. Wood, and J. T. Hayes. 1965. Selection, spatial distribution, and the coexistence of competing fly species. Am. Nat. 99(905):97-109.

Pimentel, D., S. A. Levin, and D. Olson. 1978. Coevolution and the stability of exploiter-victim systems. Am. Nat. 112:119-125.

Pimentel, D., W. P. Nagel, and J. L. Madden. 1963. Space-time structure of the environment and the survival of parasite-host systems. Am. Nat. 97:141-167.

Pimentel, D., and F. A. Stone. 1968. Evolution and population ecology of parasite-host systems. Can. Entomol. 100:655-562.

Pippy, J. H. C., and G. M. Hare. 1969. Relationship of river pollution to bacterial infection in salmon (Salmo salar) and suckers (Catastomus commersoni). Trans. Am. Fish. Soc. 98:685-690.

Pomeroy, L. R., E. E. Smith, and C. M. Grant. 1965. The exchange of phosphate between estuarine water and sediment. Limnol. Oceanogr. 10:167-172.

Porcella, D. B., V. D. Adams, and P. A. Cowan. 1976. Sediment water microcosms for assessment of nutrient interactions in aquatic ecosystems. pp. 293-322. IN Middlebrooks, E., D. H. Falkenborg, and T. E. Maloney (eds.), Biostimulation and Nutrient Assessment. Ann Arbor Science, Ann Arbor.

Porcella, D. B., V. D. Adams, P. A. Cowan, S. Austrheim-Smith, and W. F. Holmes. 1975. Nutrient dynamics and gas production in aquatic ecosystems: The effects and utilization of mercury and nitrogen in sediment-water microcosms. W76-05246; OWRT-B-081-Utah(2); PRWG 121-1. Utah Water Research Lab., Logan. Office of Water Research and Technology, Washington, D.C.

Powlson, D. S., and D. S. Jenkinson. 1976. The effects of biocidal treatments on metabolism in soil II. Gamma irradiation, autoclaving, air-drying and fumigation. Soil Biol. Biochem. 8:179-188.

Press, J. W., B. R. Flaherty, and G. L. Le Cato. 1974. Interactions among Tribolium castoneum (Coleoptera: Tenebrionidae), Cadra cautella (Lepidoptera: Pyrilidae) and Xylocoris flavipes (Hemiptera: Anthrocoridae). J. Ga. Entomol. Soc. 9:101-103.

Pritchard, P. H., A. W. Bourquin, H. L. Frederickson, and T. Maziarz. 1979. System design factors affecting environmental fate studies in microcosms. pp. 251-272. IN Bourquin, A. W., and P. H. Pritchard (eds.), Microbial Degradation of Pollutants in Marine Environments. EPA-600/9-79-012.

Ramm, A. E., and D. A. Bella. 1974. Sulfide production in anaerobic microcosms. Limnol. Oceanogr. 19:110-118.

Raynal, D. J., and F. A. Bazzaz. 1975. Interference of winter annuals with Ambrosia artemesiifolia in early successional fields. Ecology 56:35-49.

Reddy, S. R. 1975. Effect of water temperature on the predatory efficiency of Gambusia affinis. Experientia 31:801-802.

Reddy, S. R., and T. J. Pandian. 1974. Effect of running water on the predatory efficiency of the larvivorous fish Gambusia affinis. Oecologia 16:253-256.

Reed, C. C. 1976. Species Diversity in Aquatic Microecosystems. Ph.D. dissertation, University of Northern Colorado.

Rees, J. T. 1979. Community development in fresh water microcosms. Hydrobiologia 63:113-128.

Reichgott, M., and L. H. Stevenson. 1977. Microbial biomass in salt marsh and microecosystem sediments. Abstr. Annu. Meet. Am. Soc. Microbiol.

Reichgott, M., and L. H. Stevenson. 1978. Microbiological and physical properties of salt marsh and microecosystem sediments. Appl. Environ. Microbiol. 36:662-667.

Reichle, D. E., R. V. O'Neill, and W. F. Harris. 1975. Principles of energy and material exchange in ecosystems. pp. 27-43. IN Van Dobben, W. H., and R. H. Lowe-McConnell (eds.), Unifying Concepts in Ecology. W. Junk, the Hague.

Reinbold, K., I. P. Kapoor, W. F. Childers, W. N. Bruce, and R. L. Metcalf. 1971. Comparative uptake and biodegradability of DDT and methoxychlor by aquatic organisms. Ill. Nat. Hist. Surv. Bull. 30:405-415.

Rennie, R. J., and E. L. Schmidt. 1977. Autecological and kinetic analysis of competition between strains of Nitrobacter in soils. Ecol. Bull. (Stockholm) 25:431-441.

Rice, E. L. 1971. Inhibition of nodulation of innoculated legumes by leaf leachates from pioneer plant species from abandoned fields. Am. J. Bot. 58:368-371.

Rice, E. L. 1974. Allelopathy. Academic Press, New York. 353 pp.

Rice, E. L. 1979. Allelopathy--an Update. Bot. Rev. 45:15-109.

Richardson, R. E. 1930. Notes on the simulation of natural aquatic condition in fresh-water by the use of small non-circulating balanced aquaria. Ecology 11:102-109.

Richmond, R. C., M. E. Gilpin, S. P. Salas, and F. J. Ayala. 1975. A search for emergent competitive phenomena: The dynamics of multispecies Drosophila systems. Ecology 56:709-714.

Riley, G. A. 1956. Factors controlling phytoplankton populations on Georges Bank. J. Mar. Res. 6:54-73.

Ringelberg, J. 1977. Properties of an aquatic microecosystem. II. Steady-state phenomena in the autotrophic subsystem. Helgol. Wiss. Meeresunters. 30:134-143.

Ringelberg, J., and K. Kersting. 1978. Properties of an aquatic microecosystem. I. General introduction to the prototypes. Arch. Hydrobiol. 83:47-68.

Robertson, A., C. W. Gehrs, B. D. Hardin, G. W. Hunt. 1974. Culturing and ecology of Diaptomus clavipes and Cyclops vernalis. EPA-660/ 3-74-006.

Rodgers, J. H., Jr., J. R. Clark, K. L. Dickson, and J. Cairns, Jr. 1980. Nontaxonomic analyses of structure and function of aufwuchs communities in lotic microcosms. IN Giesy, J. P. (ed.), Microcosms in Ecological Research (in press).

Roper, M. M., and K. C. Marshall. 1978. Effects of a clay mineral on microbial predation and parasitism of Escherichia coli. Microbial Ecol. 4:279-289.

Rose, F. L., and C. E. Cushing. 1970. Accumulation of dieldrin by benthic algae in laboratory streams. Hydrobiologia 35:481-493.

Ross-Todd, M., E. G. O'Neill, and R. V. O'Neill. 1980. Synthesis of terrestrial microcosm results. pp. 242-264. IN Harris, W. F. (ed.), Microcosms as Potential Screening Tools for Evaluating Transport and Effects of Toxic Substances: Final Report. ORNL/EPA-4, Oak Ridge National Laboratory, Oak Ridge, Tenn.

Ruhling, A., and G. Tyler. 1973. Heavy metals pollution and decomposition of spruce needle litter. Oikos 24:402-416.

Russell, G., and A. H. Fielding. 1974. The competitive properties of marine algae in culture. J. Ecol. 62:689-698.

Saakyan-Baranova, A. A. 1964. On the biology of the soft scale Coccus hesperidum L. (Homoptera: Coccoidea). Entomol. Rev. 1:135-147.

Sakai, K. I. 1961. Competitive ability in plants: Its inheritance and some related problems. pp. 245-263. IN Mechanisms in Biological Competition, Symposia of the Society of Experimental Biology XV. Academic Press, Inc., New York.

Saks, N. M., J. J. Lee, W. A. Muller, and J. H. Tietjen. 1973. Growth of salt marsh microcosms subjected to thermal stress. pp. 391-398. IN Gibbons, J. W., and R. R. Sharitz (eds.), Thermal Ecology. USAEC Technical Information Center, Oak Ridge, TN, CONF-730505.

Salt, G. 1934. Experimental studies in insect parasitism. II. Superparasitism. Proc., Royal Soc. London 114:455-476.

Salt, G. 1935. Experimental studies in insect parasitism. III. Host selection. Proc., Royal Soc. London 117:413-435.

Salt, G. W. 1967. Predation in an experimental protozoan population (Woodruffia-Paramecium). Ecol. Monogr. 37:113-144.

Salt, G. W. 1968. The feeding of Amoeba proteus on Paramecium aurelia. J. Protozool. 15:275-280.

Salt, G. W. 1969. A measure of culture-induced changes in a laboratory population of protozoa. Ecology 50:

Salt, G. W. 1974. Predator and prey densities as controls of the rate of capture by the predator Didinium nasutum. Ecology 55:434-439.

Salt, G. W. 1979. A comment on the use of the term emergent properties. Am. Nat. 113:145-148.

Salt, G. W. 1979. Density, starvation, and swimming rate in Didinium populations. Am. Nat. 113:135-143.

Samsel, G. L. 1972. The effects of temperature and radiation stress on aquatic microecosystem. Trans. Ky. Acad. Sci. 33:1-12.

Samsel, G. L., G. C. Llewellyn, and D. Fick. 1974. A preliminary study of the effects of gamma irradiation and oxygen stress on an aquatic microecosystem. Va. J. Sci. 25:169-172.

Samsel, G. L., and B. C. Parker. 1972. Nutrient factors uniting primary productivity in simulated and field antarctic microecosystems. Va. J. Sci. 23:64-71.

Sanborn, J. R., R. L. Metcalf, W. N. Bruce, and P. Y. Lu. 1975. The fate of chlordane and toxaphene in a terrestrial-aquatic model ecosystem. Environ. Entomol. 5:533-538.

Sanborn, J. R., and C.-C. Yu. 1973. The fate of dieldrin in a model ecosystem. Bull. Environ. Contam. and Toxicol. 10:340-346.

Scherff, R. H. 1973. Control of bacterial blight of soybean by Bdellovibrio bacteriovorus. Phytopathology 63:400-402.

Schillinger, J. A., and R. C. Leffel. 1964. Persistance of ladino clover, Trifolium repens. L. Agron. J. 56:7-14.

Schindler, D. W., F. A. J. Armstrong, S. K. Holmgren, and G. J. Brunskill. 1971. Eutrophication of lake 227, experimental lakes area, northwestern Ontario, by addition of phosphate and nitrate. J. Fish. Res. Board Can. 28:1763-1782.

Schlinger, E. I., and J. C. Hall. 1959. A synopsis of the biologies of three important parasites of the spotted alfalfa aphid. J. Econ. Entomol. 52:154-157.

Schlinger, E. I., and J. C. Hall. 1960. The biology, behavior, and morphology of Praon palitans Muesebeck, an internal parasite of the spotted alfalfa aphid, Therioaphis maculata (Buckton) (Hymenoptera: Braconidae, Aphidiinae). Ann. Entomol. Soc. Amer. 53:144-160.

Schlinger, E. I., and J. C. Hall. 1961. The biology, behavior, and morphology of Trioxys utilis, an internal parasite of the spotted alfalfa aphid, Therioaphis maculata (Hymenoptera: Braconidae, Aphidiinae). Ann. Entomol. Soc. Amer. 54:34-45.

Schreiber, M. M. 1967. A technique for studying weed competition in forage legume establishment. Weeds 15:1-4.

Schulz, K. R., T. W. Fuhreman, and E. P. Lichtenstein. 1976. Interactions of pesticide chemicals. effect of eptam and its antidote on the uptake and metabolism of [^{14}C]phorate in corn plants. J. Agric. Food Chem. 24:269-299.

Schuth, C. K., A. R. Isensee, E. A. Woolson, and P. C. Kearney. 1974. Distribution of C-14 and arsenic derived from C-14 cacodylic acid in an aquatic ecosystem. J. Agr. Food Chem. 22:999-1003.

Seaton, A. P. C., and J. Antonovics. 1966. Population inter-relationships. I. Heredity 22:19-33.

Sebetich, M. J. 1975. Phosphorus kinetics of freshwater microcosms. Ecology. 56:1262-1280.

Seed, M. T. 1978. Effect of pH on the nature of competition between Eichornia crassipes and Pistia stratiotes. J. Aquat. Plant Manage. 16:53-57.

Selim, K. G., S. A. Z. Mahmoud, and M. T. El-Mokadem. 1970. Effect of dieldrin and lindane on the growth and nodulation of Vicia faba. Plant Soil 33:325-329.

Shirazi, M. A. 1979. Development of scaling criteria for terrestrial microcosms. EPA-600 13-79-017. U.S. Environmental Protection Agency, Corvallis, Oregon.

Shugart, H. H., Jr., and B. G. Blaylock. 1973. The niche variation hypothesis: An experimental study with Drosophila populations. Am. Nat. 107:575579.

Sigmon, C. F., H. J. Kania, and R. J. Beyers. 1977. Reductions in biomass and diversity resulting from exposure to mercury in artificial streams. J. Fish. Res. Bd. Can. 34:493-500.

Smart, R. M., R. L. Eley, and J. M. Falco. 1978. Design of a laboratory microcosm for evaluating effects of dredged material disposal on marsh-estuarine ecosystems. Army Engineer Waterways Experiment Station, Vicksburg, Mississippi, WES-TR-D-78-52, 54 pp.

Smith, C. R., B. R. Funke, and J. T. Schulz. 1978. Effects of insecticides on acetylene reduction by alfalfa, red clover and sweetclover. Soil Biol. and Biochem. 10(6):463-466.

Smith, S. V., P. Jokiel, G. S. Key, and E. B. Guinther. 1979. Metabolic responses of shallow tropical benthic microcosm communities to perturbation. Environmental Protection Agency, EPA-600/3-79-061. 67 pp.

Smrchek, J. C. 1974. The Effects of Various Tertiary Treatment Nutrient Removal Schemes upon the Productivity of Autotrophic (Periphyton) Communities in Model Laboratory Stream Ecosystems. Ph.D. dissertation, Virginia Polytechnic Institute and State University.

Smrchek, J. C., J. Cairns, Jr., K. L. Dickson, P. H. King, C. W. Randall, J. Crowe, D. Huber, and J. W. Olver. 1976. The Effect of Various Tertiary Treatment Removal Schemes on Periphyton Communities in Model Laboratory Streams. UPI-VWRRC-BULL86, Virginia Polytechnic Institute and State University.

Snieszko, S. F. 1974. The effects of environmental stress on outbreaks of infectious diseases of fishes. J. Fish. Biol. 6:197-208.

Sodergren, A. 1973. Transport, distribution, and degradation of chlorinated hydrocarbon residues in aquatic model ecosystems. Oikos 24:30-41.

Sokal, R. R., and R. L. Sullivan. 1963. Competition between mutant and wild-type house-fly strains at varying densities. Ecology 44(2):314-322.

Sokoloff, A. 1955. Competition between sibling species of the Pseudoobscura subgroup of Drosophila. Ecol. Monogr. 25:387-409.

Solomon, H. N. 1949. The natural control of animal populations. J. Anim. Ecol. 18:1-37.

Spalding, B. P. 1977. Enzymatic activities related to the decomposition of coniferous leaf litter. Soil Sci. Soc. Am. J. 41:622-627.

Spalding, B. P. 1978. The effect of biocidal treatments on respiration and enzymatic activities of douglas-fir needle litter. Soil. Biol. Biochem. 10:537-543.

Spalding, B. P. 1979. Effects of divalent metal chlorides on respiration and extractable enzymatic activities of douglas-fir needle litter. J. Environ. Qual. 8:105-109.

Sprules, W. G. 1972. Effects of size-selective predation and food competition on high altitude zooplankton communities. Ecology 53:375-386.

Starks, K. J., and W. W. McMillian. 1967. Resistance in corn to the corn earworm and fall armyworm. Part II: Types of field resistance to the corn earworm. J. Econ. Entomol. 60:920-923.

Starr, M. P., and N. L. Baigent. 1966. Parasitic interaction of Bdellovibris bacteriovorus with other bacteria. J. Bacteriol. 91:2006-2017.

Stein, R. A. 1977. Selective predation, optimal foraging, and the predator-prey interaction between fish and crayfish. Ecology 58:1237-1253.

Stein, R. A., and J. J. Magnuson. 1976. Behavioral response of crayfish to a fish predator. Ecology 57:751-761.

Stenson, J. A. E. 1978. Differential predation by fish on two species of Chaoborus (Diptera, Chaoboridae). Oikos 31:98-101.

Stern, W. R., and C. M. Donald. 1962. The influence of leaf area and radiation on the growth of clover in swards. Aust. J. Agric. Res. 13:615-623.

Stotzky, G. 1965. Microbial respiration. pp. 1550-1572. IN Black, C. A. (ed.), Methods of Soil Analysis, Part 2, Chemical and Microbial Properties. American Society of Agronomy, Inc., Madison, Wis.

Strange, R. J. 1976. Nutrient release and community metabolism following application of herbicide to macrophytes in microcosms. J. Appl. Ecol. 13:889-897.

Streit, B. 1979. Uptake, accumulation, and release of organic pesticides by benthic invertebrates. 3. Distribution of carbon-14 atrazine and carbon-14 lindane in an experimental 3 step food chain microcosm. Arch. Hydrobiol. suppl. 55:373-400.

Strickland, J. D. H., O. Holm-Hansen, R. W. Eppley, and R. J. Linn. 1969. The use of a deep tank in plankton ecology. I. Studies of the growth and composition of phytoplankton crops at low nutrient levels. Limnol. Oceanogr. 14:23-34.

Strickler, J. R. 1977. Observation of swimming performances of planktonic copepods. Limnol. Oceanogr. 22:165-170.

Stuckey, I. H. 1962. Factors affecting persistence of ladino white clover. Crop Sci. 2:173-174.

Sugiura, K., S. Sato, M. Goto, and Y. Kurihara. 1976. Toxicity assessment using an aquatic microcosm. Chemosphere 2:113-118.

Sugiura, K., S. Sato, M. Goto, and Y. Kurihara. 1976. Effects of beta-BHC on aquatic microcosm. Chemosphere 1:39-44.

Sullivan, J. F., and G. J. Atchison. 1978. Predator-prey behavior of fathead minnows, Pimephales promelas, and largemouth bass, Micropterus salmoides, in a model ecosystem. J. Fish. Biol. 13:249-253.

Sullivan, J. F., G. J. Atchison, D. J. Kolar, and A. W. McIntosh. 1978. Changes in the predator-prey behavior of fathead minnows (Pimephales promelas) and largemouth bass (Micropterus salmoides) caused by cadmium. J. Fish. Res. Board Can. 35:446-451.

Suter, G. W. 1981. Methods for measuring effects of chemicals on terrestrial ecosystem properties. IN Hammons, Anna S. (ed.), Ecotoxicological Test Systems: Proceedings of a Series of Workshops, ORNL-5709; EPA 560/6-81-004, Oak Ridge National Laboratory.

Suter, G. W. 1981. Methods for measuring effects of chemicals on terrestrial population interaction. IN Hammons, Anna S. (ed.), Ecotoxicological Test Systems: Proceedings of a Series of Workshops, ORNL-5709; EPA 560/6-81-004, Oak Ridge National Laboratory.

Sylvester, J. R. 1972. Effect of thermal stress on predator avoidance in sockeye salmon. J. Fish. Res. Board Can. 29:601-603.

Sylvester, J. R. 1973. Effect of light on vulnerability of heat-stressed sockeye salmon to predation by coho salmon. Trans. Am. Fish. Soc. 102:139-142.

Tagatz, M. E. 1976. Effect of mirex on predator-prey interaction in an experimental estuarine ecosystem. Trans. Am. Fish. Soc. 105:546-549.

Tarrant, R. M., Jr. 1960. Choice between two sizes of forage fish by largemouth bass under aquarium conditions. Prog. Fish. Cult. 83:84.

Taub, F. B. 1969. A biological model of a freshwater community: A gnotobiotic ecosystem. Limnol. Oceanogr. 14:136-142.

Taub, F. B. 1969. A continuous gnotobiotic (species defined) ecosystem. pp. 101-120. IN Cairns, J., Jr. (ed.), The Structure and Function of Fresh-Water Microbial Communities. Research Monograph 3, Virginia Polytechnic Institute and State University, Blacksburg, Va.

Taub, F. B. 1969. Gnotobiotic models of freshwater communities. Verh. Int. Ver. Limnol. 17:485-496.

Taub, F. B. 1976. Demonstration of pollution effects in aquatic microcosms. Int. J. Environ. Stud. 10:23-33.

Taub, F. B., and M. E. Crow. 1978. Loss of a critical species in a model (laboratory) ecosystem. Verh. Int. Ver. Limnol. 20:1270-1276.

Taub, F. B., and M. E. Crow. 1980. Synthesizing aquatic microcosms. IN Giesy, J. P. (ed.), Microcosms in Ecological Research (in press).

Taub, F. B., M. E. Crow, and H. J. Hartmann. 1980. Responses of aquatic microcosms to acute mortality. IN Giesy, J. P. (ed.), Microcosms in Ecological Research (in press).

Tauber, M. J., and R. G. Helgeson. 1974. Biological control of whiteflies in greehouse crops. N.Y. Food and Life Sci. 7:13-16.

Terhaar, C. J., W. S. Ewell, S. P. Dziuba, W. W. White, and P. J. Murphy. 1977. A laboratory model for evaluating the behavior of heavy metals in an aquatic environment. Water Res. 11:101-110.

Thomas, C. L. 1978. A microcosm study of the interactions of nutrients and cadmium in aquatic systems. M.S. Thesis, University of Georgia.

Thompson, D. J. 1978. Towards a realistic predator-prey model: The effect of temperature on the functional response and life history of the damselfly, _Ischnura elegans_. J. Anim. Ecol. 47:757-767.

Tilman, D. 1977. Resource competition between planktonic algae: An experimental and theoretical approach. Ecology 58:338-348.

Tison, D. L., and A. J. Lingg. 1979. Dissolved organic matter utilization and oxygen uptake in algal bacterial microcosms. Can. J. Microbiol. 25:1315-1320.

Titman, D. 1976. Ecological competition between algae: experimental confirmation of resource-based competition theory. Science 192:463-465.

Torroja, E., and M. Almazan. 1973. Evolution of competition between Drosophila hydei and D. simulans in a cage population. Genetics 73:278-279.

Trabalka, J. R., and L. D. Eyman. 1976. Distribution of plutonium-237 in a littoral freshwater microcosm. Health Phys. 31:390-393.

Trabalka, J. R., and M. L. Frank. 1978. Trophic transfer by chironomids and distribution of plutonium-239 in simple aquatic microcosms. Health Phys. 35:492-494.

Tsuchiya, H. M., J. F. Drake, J. L. Jost, and A. G. Frederickson. 1972. Predator-prey interactions of Dictyostelium discoideum and Escherichia coli in continuous culture. J. Bacteriol. 110:1147-1153.

Tu, C. M. 1970. Effect of four organophosphorus insecticides on microbial activities in soil. Appl. Microbiol. 19:479-484.

Tu, C. M. 1977. Effects of pesticide seed treatments on Rhizobium japonicum and its symbiotic relationship with soybean. Bull. Environ. Contam. Toxicol. 18(2):190-199.

Tu, C. M. 1978. Effect of pesticides on acetylene reduction and microorganisms in a sandy loam. Soil Biol. Biochem. 10:451-456.

Tyler, G. 1976. Heavy metal pollution, phosphatase activity, and mineralization of organic phosphorus in forest soils. Soil Biol. Biochem. 8:327-332.

Uhlmann, V. D. 1969. Primary production and decomposition in micro-ecosystems with different proportions of illuminated and dark layers. Arch. Hydrobiol. 66:113-138.

Uhlmann, D. 1971. Influence of dilution, sinking and grazing rate on phytoplankton populations in hyperfertilized ponds and microecosystems. Mitt. Int. Ver. Theor. Angew. Limnol. 19:100-124.

Ullyett, G. C. 1949. Distribution of progeny by Chelonus texanus Cress. (Hymenoptera: Braconidae). Can. Entomol. 81:25-44.

Ullyett, G. C. 1949. Distribution of progeny by Cryptus inornatus Pratt (Hymenoptera: Ichneumonidae). Can. Entomol. 81:285-296.

Ullyett, G. C. 1950. Competition for food and allied phenomena in sheep-blowfly populations. Philos. Trans. R. Soc. London, Ser. B. 234:77-174.

U.S. Environmental Protection Agency. 1979. Toxic substances control act premanufacture testing of new chemical substances (OTS-050003; FRL-1069-1) Fed. Regist. 44(53):16240-16292.

Utida, S. 1950. On the equilibrium state of the interacting population of an insect and its parasite. Ecology 31:165-175.

Utida, S. 1957. Cyclic fluctuations of population density intrinsic to the host-parasite system. Ecology 38:442-449.

Utida, S. 1957. Population fluctuation, an experimental and theoretical approach. Cold Springs Harbor Symposia on Quantitative Biology 22:139-151.

Van De Vrie, M. 1962. The influence of spray chemicals on predatory and phytophagous mites on apple trees in laboratory and field trials in the netherlands. Entomophaga 3(3):243-250.

Van den Ende, P. 1973. Predator-prey interactions in continuous culture. Science 54:562-564.

Van Emden, H. F., and M. J. Way. 1973. Host plants in the population dynamics of insects. pp. 181-199. IN Van Emden, H. F. (ed.), Insect/Plant Relationships, Symposium of the R. Entomol. Soc. of London: Number Six. Blackwell Scientific Publications, Oxford.

Van Voris, P., R. V. O'Neill, H. J. Shugart, and W. R. Emanual. 1978. Functional complexity and ecosystem stability: An experimental approach. ORNL/TM-6199. Oak Ridge National Laboratory, Oak Ridge, Tenn. 120 pp.

Vaughan, G. E. 1979. Comparative vulnerability of bluegills with and without lymphocystis disease to predation by largemouth bass. Prog. Fish-Cult. 41:163-164.

Veilleux, B. G. 1979. An analysis of the predatory interaction between _Paramecium_ and _Didinium_. J. Anim. Ecol. 48:787-804.

Vinyard, G. L., and W. J. O'Brien. 1975. Dorsal light response as an index of prey preference in bluegill (_Lepomis macrochirus_). J. Fish. Res. Board Can. 32:1860-1863.

Vinyard, G. L., and W. J. O'Brien. 1976. Effects of light and turbidity on the reactive distance of bluegill (_Lepomis macrochirus_). J. Fish. Res. Board Can. 33:2845-2849.

Waide, J. B., J. E. Schindler, M. C. Waldron, J. J. Hains, S. P. Schreiner, M. L. Freedman, S. L. Benz, D. R. Pettigrew, L. A. Schissel, and P. J. Clarke. 1980. A microcosm approach to the study of biogeochemical systems: 2. Responses of aquatic laboratory microcosms to physical, chemical, and biological perturbations. IN Giesy, J. P. (ed.), Microcosms in Ecological Research (in press).

Waiss, A. C., Jr., B. G. Chan, and C. A. Elliger. 1977. Host plant resistance to insects. pp. 115-128. IN Hedin, P. A. (ed.), Host Plant Resistance to Pests. ACS Symposium Series 62. Am. Chem. Soc., Washington, D.C.

Wallace, B. 1974. Studies in intra-and-interspecific competition in Drosophila. Ecology 55:227-244.

Ward, D. V., B. L. Howes, and D. F. Ludwig. 1976. Interactive effects of predation pressure and insecticide (temefos) toxicity on populations of the marsh fiddler crab Uca pugnax. Mar. Biol. 35:119-126.

Ware, D. M. 1972. Predation by rainbow trout (Salmo gairdneri): The influence of hunger, prey density, and prey size. J. Fish. Res. Board Can. 29:1193-1201.

Ware, D. M. 1973. Risk of epibenthic prey to predation by rainbow trout (Salmo gairdneri). J. Fish. Res. Board Can. 30:787797.

Warren, C. E., and G. E. Davis. 1971. Laboratory stream research: Objectives possibilities, and constraints. Ann. Rev. Ecol. Syst. 2:111-144.

Warshaw, S. J. 1972. Effects of alewives (Alosa pseudoharengus) on the zooplankton of Lake Wononskopomuc, Conn. Limnol. Oceanogr. 17:816-825.

Waterland, L. R. 1979. Definition of terrestrial ecology bioassay protocols for environmental assessment programs. Workshop Proceedings, FR-79-342. Acurex Corp., Mountain View, Ca.

Webster, J. R. 1978. Analysis of Potassium and Calcium Dynamics in Stream Ecosystems on Three Southern Appalachian Watersheds of Contrasting Vegetation. Ph.D. dissertation, University of Georgia.

Wedemeyer, G. 1970. The role of stress in disease resistance of fishes. pp. 30-35. IN Snieszko, S. F. (ed.), A Symposium on Diseases of Fishes and Shellfishes. Amer. Fish. Soc., Washington, D.C.

Wells, L. 1970. Effects of alewife predation on zooplankton populations in Lake Michigan. Limnol. Oceanogr. 15:556-565.

Werner, E. E. 1974. The fish size, prey size, handling time relation in several sunfishes and some implications. J. Fish. Res. Board Can. 31:1531-1536.

Werner, E. E., and D. J. Hall. 1974. Optimal foraging and size selection of prey by the bluegill sunfish (Lepomis macrochirus). Ecology 55:1042-1052.

White, E. G., and C. B. Huffaker. 1969. Regulatory processes and population cyclicity in laboratory populations of Anagasta kuhniella (Zeller) (Lepidoptera: Phycitidae). I. Competition for food and predation. Res. Popul. Ecol. 11:57-83.

White, E. G., and C. B. Huffaker. 1969. Regulatory processes and population cyclicity in laboratory populations of Anagasta kuhniella (Zeller) (Lepidoptera: Phycitidae). II. Parasitism, predation, competition and protective cover. Res. Popul. Ecol. 11:150-185.

White, J., and J. L. Harper. 1970. Correlated changes in plant size and number in plant populations. J. Ecol. 58:467-485.

Whitford, L. A., G. E. Dillard, and G. J. Schumacher. 1965. An artificial stream apparatus for the study of lotic organisms. Limnol. Oceanogr. 6:423-425.

Whittaker, R. H. 1961. Experiments with radiophosphorus tracer in aquarium microcosms. Ecol. Monogr. 31:157-187.

Whittaker, R. H., and G. M. Woodwell. 1972. Evolution of natural communities. pp. 137-159. IN Wiens, J. A. (ed.), Ecosystem Structure and Function. Oregon State University Press, Corvallis, Oregon.

Whitworth, W. R., and T. H. Lane. 1969. Effects of toxicants on community metabolism in pools. Limnol. Oceanogr. 14:53-58.

Wilhm, J. L. 1970. Transfer of radioisotopes between detritus and benthic macroinvertebrates in laboratory microecosystems. Health Phys. 18:277-284.

Wilkinson, S. R., and C. F. Gross. 1964. Competition for light, soil moisture, and nutrients during ladino clover establishment in orchardgrass Sod. Agron. J. 56:389-392.

Williams, M. L., and M. Kosztarab. 1972. Morphology and systematics of the Coccidae of Virginia, with notes on their biology (Homoptera: Coccidae). Va. Polytech. Inst. and State Univ. Res. Bull. 74:215.

Wilt, G. R., M. M. Joshi, and J. Metcalf. 1973. Studies on the interactions of bacteria and nematodes. Water Resource Res. Insti., Auburn University, Bull. 10.

Windle, P. N., and E. H. Franz. 1979. The effects of insect parasitism on plant competition: Greenbugs and barley. Ecology 60(3):521-529.

Witkamp, M. 1969. Environmental effects on microbial turnover of some mineral elements. Soil Biol. Biochem. 1:167-184.

Witkamp, M. 1976. Microcosm experiments on element transfer. Int. J. Environ. Stud. 10(1):59-63.

Witkamp, M., and B. Ausmus. 1975. Effects of tree species, temperature, and soil on transfer of manganese-54 from litter to roots in a microcosm. pp. 694-699. IN Howell, F. G., J. B. Gentry, and M. H. Smith (ed.), Mineral Cycling in Southeastern Ecosystems. CONF-740513. National Technical Information Service, Springfield, Va.

Witkamp, M., and B. Baryansky. 1968. Microbial immobilization of ^{137}Cs in forest litter. Oikos 19:392-395.

Witkamp, M., and M. Frank. 1967. Cesium-137 kinetics in terrestrial microcosms. pp. 635-643. IN Nelson, D. J., and F. C. Evans (eds.), Symposium on Radioecology. USAEC Document Conf. 670503.

Witkamp, M., and M. L. Frank. 1970. Effects of temperature, rainfall and fauna on transfer of ^{137}Cs, K, Mg, and mass in consumer-decomposer microcosms. Ecology 51:465-474.

Witt, J. M., and J. W. Gillett. 1979. Terrestrial microcosms and environmental chemistry. NSF/RA 79-0026. National Science Foundation, Washington, D.C. 147 pp.

Woltering, D. M., J. L. Hedtke, and L. J. Weber. 1978. Predator-prey interactions of fishes under the influence of ammonia. Trans. Am. Fish. Soc. 107:500-504.

Wolters, W. R., and C. C. Coutant. 1976. The effect of cold shock on the vulnerability of young bluegill (_Lepomis macrochirus_) to predation. pp. 162-164. IN Esch, G. W. and R. W. McFarlane (eds.), Thermal Ecology II. CONF-750425.

Wood, P. W. 1971. Coexistence of Competing Dipteran Species *Musca domestica* L. (Muscidae) and *Phaenicia* (=*Lucilia*) *sericata* Meig. (Calliphoridae) in Laboratory Ecosystems. Ph.D. dissertation. Cornell University, Ithica, N.Y. 160 pp.

Wool, D. 1973. Size, productivity, age and competition in *Tribolium* populations subjected to long-term serial transfer. J. Anim. Ecol. 42:183-200.

Wulff, B. L. 1971. Structure and Productivity of Marine Benthic Diatom Communities in a Laboratory Model Ecosystem. Ph.D. dissertation, Oregon State University.

Yockim, R. S., A. R. Isensee, and E. A. Walker. 1980. Behavior of trifluralin in aquatic model ecosystems. Bull. Environ. Contam. Toxicol. 24:134-141.

Yocum, T. G., and T. A. Edsall. 1974. Effects of acclimation temperature and heat shock on vulnerability of fry of lake whitefish (*Coregonus clupeaformis*) to predation. J. Fish. Res. Board Can. 31:1503-1506.

Yoda, K., T. Kira, H. Ogawa, and H. Hozumi. 1963. Self-thinning in overcrowded pure stands under cultivated and natural conditions. J. Biol. Osaka City Univ. 14:107-129.

Young, A. M. 1970. Predation and abundance in populations of flour beetles. Ecology 51:602-619.

Yu, C.-C., G. M. Booth, D. J. Hanson, and J. R. Larsen. 1974. Fate of bux insecticide in a model ecosystem. Environ. Entomol. 3:975-977.

Yu, C.-C., G. M. Booth, D. J. Hanson, and J. R. Larsen. 1974. Fate of carbofuran in a model ecosystem. J. Agric. Food Chem. 22:431-434.

Yu, C.-C., G. M. Booth, D. J. Hanson, and J. R. Larsen. 1975. Fate of alachlor and propachlor in a model ecosystem. J. Agric. Food Chem. 23:877-879.

Yu, C.-C., G. M. Booth, D. J. Hanson, and J. R. Larsen. 1975. Fate of pyrazon in a model ecosystem. J. Agric. Food Chem. 23:300-311.

Yu, C.-C., G. M. Booth, and J. R. Larsen. 1975. Fate of triazine herbicide cyanazine in a model ecosystem. J. Agric. Food Chem. 23:1014-1015.

Yu, C., and J. R. Sanborn. 1975. The fate of parathion in a model ecosystem. Bull. Environ. Contam. Toxicol. 13:543-550.

Zaret, T. M. 1972. Predators, invisible prey, and the nature of polymorphism in the cladocera (Class Crustacea). Limnol. Oceanogr. 17:171-184.

Zaret, T. M. 1975. Strategies for existence of zooplankton prey in homogeneous environments. Verh. Int. Ver. Limnol. 19:1484-1489.

Zaret, T. M., and W. C. Kerfoot. 1975. Fish predation on *Bosmina longirostris*: Body-size selection versus visibility selection. Ecology 56:232-237.

APPENDIX D

SECTIONAL BIBLIOGRAPHY

AQUATIC AND TERRESTRIAL TEST SYSTEMS

3. AQUATIC TEST SYSTEMS

3.1.3 COMPETITION

Confer, J. L. 1972. Interrelations among plankton, attached algae, and the phosphorus cycle in open artificial systems. Ecol. Monogr. 42:1-23.

Fielding, A. H., and G. Russell. 1976. The effect of copper on competition between marine algae. J. Ecol. 64:871-876.

Fisher, N. S., E. J. Carpenter, C. C. Remsen, and C. F. Wurster. 1974. Effects of PCB on interspecific competition in natural and gnotobiotic phytoplankton communities in continuous and batch cultures. Microbial Ecol. 1:39-50.

Frank, P. W. 1957. Coactions in laboratory populations of two species of Daphnia. Ecology 38:510-519.

Goulden, C. E., and L. L. Hornig. 1980. Population oscillations and energy reserves in planktonic cladocera and their consequences to competition. Proc. Nat. Acad. Sci. (in press).

Hansen, S. R., and S. P. Hubbell. 1980. Single-nutrient microbial competition: Qualitative agreement between experimental and theoretically forecast outcomes. Science 207:1491-1493.

Kindig, A. 1979. Investigations for Streptomycin-Induced Algal Competitive Dominance Reversals. Experimental Report ME25, FDA Contract No. 223-76-8348, University of Washington.

Klotz, R. L., J. R. Cain, and F. R. Trainor. 1976. Algal competition in an epilithic river flora. J. Phycol. 12:363-368.

Kricher, J. R., C. L. Bayer, and D. A. Martin. 1979. Effects of two Aroclor fractions on the productivity and diversity of algae from two lentic ecosystems. Int. J. Environ. Stud. 13:159-167.

Krzywicka, A., and D. Krupa. 1975. Preliminary investigations on mutual growth relations of the populations of the blue-green alga Microcystis aeruginosa and green algae Monoraphidium minutum and Scenedesmus abundans in bicultures. Acta Hydrobiol. 17:81-88.

Lange, W. 1974. Competitive exclusion among three planktonic blue-green algal species. J. Phycol. 10:411-414.

Marshall, J. S. 1969. Competition between Daphnia pulex and D. magna as modified by radiation stress. Ecol. Soc. Amer. Annual Meeting, University of Vermont, August 17-22, 1969.

May, R. M. 1973. Stability and complexity in model ecosystems. Princeton University Press, Princeton, New Jersey.

Mickelson, M. J., H. Maske, and R. C. Dugdale. 1979. Nutrient-determined dominance in multispecies chemostat cultures of diatoms. Limnol. Oceanogr. 24:298-315.

Mosser, J. L., N. S. Fisher, and C. F. Wurster. 1972. Polychlorinated biphenyls and DDT alter species composition in mixed cultures of algae. Science 176:533-535.

Muller, W. A., and J. J. Lee. 1977. Biological interactions and the realized niche of _Euplotes_ _vannus_ from the salt marsh aufwuchs. J. Protozool. 24:523-527.

Odum, E. P. 1971. Fundamentals of ecology. 3rd ed. W. B. Saunders, Philadelphia. 574 pp.

O'Neill, R. V., and J. M. Giddings. 1979. Population interactions and ecosystem function: Phytoplankton competition and community production. IN Innis, G. S., and R. V. O'Neil (eds.), Systems Analysis of Ecosystems. International Co-Operative Publishing House, Fairland, Maryland.

Russell, G., and A. H. Fielding. 1974. The competitive properties of marine algae in culture. J. Ecol. 62:689-698.

Seed, M. T. 1978. Effect of pH on the nature of competition between _Eichornia_ _crassipes_ and _Pistia_ _stratiotes_. J. Agric. Plant Manag. 16:53-57.

Tilman, D. 1977. Resource competition between planktonic algae: An experimental and theoretical approach. Ecology 58:338-348.

Titman, D. 1976. Ecological competition between algae: Experimental confirmation of resource-based competition theory. Science 192: 463-465.

3.2.7 PREDATION

Akre, B. G., and D. M. Johnson. 1979. Switching and sigmoid functional response curves by damselfly naiads with alternative prey available. J. Animal Ecol. 48:703-720.

Allan, D. 1973. Competition and the relative abundance of two cladocerans. Ecology 54:484-498.

Anderson, R. S. 1970. Predator-prey relationships and predation rates for crustacean zooplankters from some lakes in western Canada. Can. J. Zool. 48:1229-1240.

Baker, J. A., and T. Modde. 1977. Susceptibility to predation of blacktail shiners stained with Bismarck Brown Y. Trans. Am. Fish. Soc. 106:334-338.

Barns, R. A. 1967. Differences in performance of naturally and artificially propagated sockeye salmon migrant fry, as measured with swimming and predation tests. J. Fish. Res. Board Can. 24:1117-1153.

Bethel, W. M., and J. C. Holmes. 1977. Increased vulnerability of amphipods to predation owing to altered behavior induced by larval acanthocephalans. Can. J. Zool. 55:110-115.

Bisson, P. A. 1978. Diet food selection by two sizes of rainbow trout (Salmo gairdneri) in an experimental stream. J. Fish. Res. Board Can. 35:971-975.

Brandl, Z., and C. H. Fernando. 1974. Feeding of the copepod Acanthocyclops vernalis on the cladoceran Ceriodaphnia reticulata under laboratory conditions. Can. J. Zool. 52:99-105.

Brandl, Z., and C. H. Fernando. 1978. Prey selection by the cyclopoid copepods Mesocyclops edax and Cyclops vicinus. Verh. Int. Verein. Limnol. 20:2505-2510.

Brooks, J. L., and S. I. Dodson. 1965. Predation, body size and composition of plankton. Science 150:28-35.

Coble, D. W. 1970. Vulnerability of fathead minnows infected with yellow grub to largemouth bass predation. J. Parasitol. 56:395-396.

Coble, D. W. 1973. Influence of appearance of prey and satiation of predator on food selection by northern pike (Esox lucius). J. Fish. Res. Board Can. 30:317-320.

Confer, J. L. 1971. Intrazooplankton predation by Mesocyclops edax at natural prey densities. Limnol. Oceanogr. 16:663-666.

Confer, J. L., and P. I. Blades. 1975. Omnivorous zooplankton and planktivorous fish. Limnol. Oceanogr. 20:571-579.

Confer, J. L., and P. I. Blades. 1975. Reaction distance to zooplankton by Lepomis gibbosus. Verh. Int. Verein. Limnol. 19:2493-2497.

Confer, J. L., and J. M. Cooley. 1977. Copepod instar survival and predation by zooplankton. J. Fish. Res. Board Can. 34:703-706.

Confer, J. L., G. L. Howick, M. H. Corzette, S. L. Kramer, S. Fitzgibbon, and R. Landesberg. 1978. Visual predation by planktivores. Oikos 31:27-37.

Cooke, A. S. 1971. Selective predation by newts on frog tadpoles treated with DDT. Nature 229:275-276.

Coutant, C. C. 1973. Effect of thermal shock on vulnerability of juvenile salmonids to predation. J. Fish. Res. Board Can. 30:965-973.

Coutant, C. C., D. K. Cox, and K. W. Moored, Jr. 1976. Further studies of cold shock effects on susceptibility of young channel catfish to predation. pp. 154-158. IN Esch, G. W., and R. W. McFarlane (eds.), Thermal Ecology II. ERDA Technical Information Center, Oak Ridge, TN, CONF-750425.

Coutant, C. C., H. M. Ducharme, Jr., and J. R. Fisher. 1974. Effects of cold shock on vulnerability of juvenile channel catfish (Ictalurus punctatus) and largemouth bass (Micropterus salmoides) to predation. J. Fish. Res. Board Can. 31:351-354.

Coutant, C. C., R. B. McLean, and D. L. De Angelis. 1979. Influences of physical and chemical alterations on predator-prey interactions. pp. 57-68. IN Clepper, H. (ed.), Predator-Prey Systems in Fisheries Management. Sport Fishing Inst., Washington, D.C.

Deacutis, C. F. 1978. Effect of thermal shock on predator avoidance by larvae of two fish species. Trans. Am. Fish. Soc. 107:632-635.

Dodson, S. I. 1970. Complementary feeding niches sustained by size-selective predation. Limnol. Oceanogr. 15:131-137.

Dodson, S. I. 1974. Adaptive change in plankton morphology in response to size-selective predation: A new hypothesis of cyclomorphosis. Limnol. Oceanogr. 19:721-729.

Dodson, S. I. 1974. Zooplankton competition and predation: An experimental test of the size-efficiency hypothesis. Ecology 55: 605-613.

Drenner, R. W., J. R. Strickler, and W. J. O'Brien. 1978. Capture probability: The role of zooplankter escape in the selective feeding of planktivorous fish. J. Fish. Res. Board Can. 35:1370-1373.

Eggers, D. M. 1977. The nature of prey selection by planktivorous fish. Ecology 58:46-59.

Eisler, R. 1973. Latent effects of Iranian crude oil and a chemical oil dispersant on Red Sea molluscs. Israel J. Zool. 22:97-105.

Farr, J. A. 1977. Impairment of antipredator behavior in Palaemonetes pugio by exposure to sublethal doses of parathion. Trans. Am. Fish Soc. 106:287-290.

Farr, J. A. 1978. The effect of methyl parathion on predator choice of two estuarine prey species. Trans. Am. Fish. Soc. 107:87-91.

Fitz Gerald, G. J., and M. H. A. Keenleyside. 1978. Technique for tagging small fish with I^{131} for evaluation of predator-prey relationships. J. Fish. Res. Board Can. 35:143-145.

Fitmarice, P. 1979. Selective predation on cladocera by brown trout Salmo trutta. J. Fish. Biol. 15:521-526.

Furnass, T. I. 1979. Laboratory experiments on prey selection by perch fry (Perca fluviatilis). Freshwater Biol. 9:33-44.

Galbraith, M. G., Jr. 1967. Size-selective predation on Daphnia by rainbow trout and yellow perch. Trans. Am. Fish. Soc. 96:1-10.

Gause, G. F. 1934. The Struggle for Existence. Williams and Wilkins, Baltimore.

Gause, G. F., N. P. Smaragdova, and A. A. Witt. 1936. Further studies of interaction between predators and prey. J. Anim. Ecol. 5:1-18.

Gerritsen, J. 1978. Instar-specific swimming patterns and predation of planktonic copepods. Verh. Int. Verein. Limnol. 20:2531-2536.

Gerritsen, J., and J. R. Strickler. 1977. Encounter probabilities and community structure in zooplankton: A mathematical model. J. Fish. Res. Board Can. 34:73-82.

Gilbert, J. J., and C. E. Williamson. 1978. Predator-prey behavior and its effect on rotifer survival in associations of Mesocyclops edax, Asplanchna girodi, Polyarthra vulgaris, and Keratella cochleuris. Oecologia 37:13-22.

Ginetz, R. M., and P. A. Larkin. 1975. Factors affecting rainbow trout (Salmo gairdneri) predation on migrant fry of sockeye salmon (Oncorhynchus nerka). J. Fish. Res. Board Can. 33:19-24.

Goodyear, C. P. 1972. A simple technique for detecting effects of toxicants or other stresses on a predator-prey interaction. Trans. Am. Fish. Soc. 101:367-370.

Green, J. 1967. The distribution and variation of Daphnia lumholzi (Crustacea: Cladocera) in relation to fish predation in Lake Albert, East Africa. J. Zool. 151:181-197.

Hall, D. J., W. E. Cooper, and E. E. Werner. 1970. An experimental approach to the production dynamics and structure of freshwater animal communities. Limnol. Oceanogr. 15:839-928.

Hall, D. J., S. T. Threlkeld, C. W. Burns, and P. H. Crowley. 1976. The size-efficiency hypothesis and the size structure of zooplankton communities. Annu. Rev. Ecol. Syst. 7:177-208.

Hatfield, C. T., and J. M. Anderson. 1972. Effects of two insecticides on the vulnerability of Atlantic salmon (Salmo salar) Parr to brook trout (Salvelinus fontinalis) predation. J. Fish. Res. Board Can. 29:27-29.

Herting, G. E., and A. Witt, Jr. 1967. The role of physical fitness of forage fishes in relation to their vulnerability to predation by bowfin (Amia calva). Trans. Am. Fish. Soc. 96:427-430.

Jacobs, J. 1978. Coexistence of similar zooplankton species by differential adaptation to reproduction and escape in an environment with fluctuating food and enemy densities. Part 3. Laboratory experiments. Oecologia 35:35-54.

Jacobs, J. 1978. Influence of prey size, light intensity, and alternative prey on the selectivity of plankton feeding fish. Verh. Int. Verein. Limnol. 20:2461-2466.

Jamieson, G. S., and G. G. E. Scudder. 1979. Predation in Gerris (Hemiptera): Reactive distances and locomotion rates. Oecologia 44: 13-20.

Janssen, J. 1976. Feeding modes and prey size selection in the alewife (Alosa pseudoharengus). J. Fish. Res. Board Can. 33:1972-1975.

Janssen, J. 1976. Selectivity of an artificial filter feeder and suction feeders on calanoid copepods. Am. Midl. Nat. 95:491-493.

Kania, H. J., and J. O'Hara. 1974. Behavioral alterations in a simple predator-prey system due to sublethal exposure to mercury. Trans. Am. Fish. Soc. 103:134-136.

Kerfoot, W. C. 1974. Egg-size cycle of a cladoceran. Ecology 55:1259-1270.

Kerfoot, W. C. 1975. The divergence of adjacent populations. Ecology 56:1298-1313.

Kerfoot, W. C. 1977. Competition in cladoceran communities: The cost of evolving defenses against copepod predation. Ecology 58:303-313.

Kerfoot, W. C. 1977. Implications of copepod predation. Limnol. Oceanogr. 22:316-325.

Kerfoot, W. C. 1978. Combat between predatory copepods and their prey: Cyclops, Epischura, and Bosmina. Limnol. Oceanogr. 23:1089-1102.

Kettle, D., and W. J. O'Brien. 1978. Vulnerability of Arctic zooplankton species to predation by small lake trout (Salvelinus namaycush). J. Fish. Res. Board Can. 35:1495-1500.

Kwasnik, J. F. S. 1977. Effects of Cadmium on the Predator-Prey Behavior of Fathead Minnows (Pimephales promelas) and Largemouth Bass (Micropterus salmoides) in a Model Ecosystem. Ph.D. dissertation, Purdue University.

Landry, M. R. 1978. Predatory feeding behavior of a marine copepod, Labidocera trispinosa. Limnol. Oceanogr. 23:1103-1113.

Li, J. L., and H. W. Li. 1979. Species-specific factors affecting predator-prey interactions of the copepod Acanthocyclops vernalis with its natural prey. Limnol. Oceanogr. 24:613-626.

Luckinbill, L. S. 1973. Coexistence in laboratory populations of Paramecium aurelia and its predator Didinium nasutum. Ecology 54: 1320-1327.

Luckinbill, L. S. 1974. The effects of space and enrichment on a predator-prey system. Ecology 55:1142-1147.

Lynch, M. 1979. Predation, competition, and zooplankton community structure: An experimental study. Limnol. Oceanogr. 24:253-272.

McQueen, D. J. 1969. Reduction of zooplankton standing stocks by predacious Cyclops bicuspidatus thomasi in Marion Lake, British Columbia. J. Fish. Res. Board Can. 26:1605-1618.

Mauck, W. L., and D. W. Coble. 1971. Vulnerability of some fishes to northern pike (Esox lucius) predation. J. Fish. Res. Board Can. 28:957-969.

Metcalf, R. L., G. K. Sangha, and I. P. Kapoor. 1971. Model ecosystem for the evaluation of pesticide biodegradability and ecological magnification. Environ. Sci. Technol. 5:709-713.

Mullin, M. M. 1979. Differential predation by the carnivorous marine copepod, Tortanus discaudatus. Limnol. Oceanogr. 24:774-777.

O'Brien, W. J. 1979. The predator-prey interaction of planktivorous fish and zooplankton. Amer. Sci. 67:572-581.

O'Brien, W. J., D. Kettle, and H. Riessen. 1979. Helmets and invisible armor: Structures reducing predation from tactile and visual planktivores. Ecology 60:287-294.

O'Brien, W. J., and D. Schmidt. 1979. Arctic *Bosmina* morphology and copepod predation. Limnol. Oceanogr. 24:564-568.

O'Brien, W. J., N. A. Slade, and G. L. Vinyard. 1976. Apparent size as the determinant of prey selection by bluegill sunfish (*Lepomis macrochirus*). Ecology 57:1304-1310.

O'Brien, W. J., and G. L. Vinyard. 1978. Polymorphism and predation: The effect of invertebrate predation on the distribution of two varieties of *Daphnia carinata* in South India ponds. Limnol. Oceanogr. 23:452-460.

Peterman, R. M., and M. Gatto. 1978. Estimation of functional responses of predators on juvenile salmon. J. Fish. Res. Board Can. 35:797-808.

Reddy, S. R. 1975. Effect of water temperature on the predatory efficiency of *Gambusia affinis*. Experientia 31:801-802.

Reddy, S. R., and T. J. Pandian. 1974. Effect of running water on the predatory efficiency of the larvivorous fish *Gambusia affinis*. Oecologia 16:253-256.

Robertson, A., C. W. Gehrs, B. D. Hardin, and G. W. Hunt. 1974. Culturing and ecology of *Diaptomus clavipes* and *Cyclops vernalis*. EPA-660/3-74-006.

Salt, G. W. 1967. Predation in an experimental protozoan population (*Woodruffia-Paramecium*). Ecol. Monogr. 37:113-144.

Salt, G. W. 1968. The feeding of *Amoeba proteus* on *Paramecium aurelia*. J. Protozool. 15:275-280.

Salt, G. W. 1969. A measure of culture-induced changes in a laboratory population of protozoa. Ecology 50:

Salt, G. W. 1974. Predator and prey densities as controls of the rate of capture by the predator *Didinium nasutum*. Ecology 55:434-439.

Salt, G. W. 1979. Density, starvation, and swimming rate in *Didinium* populations. Am. Nat. 113:135-143.

Sprules, W. G. 1972. Effects of size-selective predation and food competition on high altitude zooplankton communities. Ecology 53: 375-386.

Stein, R. A. 1977. Selective predation, optimal foraging, and the predator-prey interaction between fish and crayfish. Ecology 58: 1237-1253.

Stein, R. A., and J. J. Magnuson. 1976. Behavioral response of crayfish to a fish predator. Ecology 57:751-761.

Stenson, J. A. E. 1978. Differential predation by fish on two species of Chaoborus (Diptera, Chaoboridae). Oikos 31:98-101.

Strickler, J. R. 1977. Observation of swimming performances of planktonic copepods. Limnol. Oceanogr. 22:165-170.

Sullivan, J. F., and G. J. Atchison. 1978. Predator-prey behavior of fathead minnows, Pimephales promelas, and largemouth bass, Micropterus salmoides, in a model ecosystem. J. Fish. Biol. 13: 249-253.

Sullivan, J. F., G. J. Atchison, D. J. Kolar, and A. W. McIntosh. 1978. Changes in the predator-prey behavior of fathead minnows (Pimephales promelas) and largemouth bass (Micropterus salmoides) caused by cadmium. J. Fish. Res. Board Can. 35:446-451.

Sylvester, J. R. 1972. Effect of thermal stress on predator avoidance in sockeye salmon. J. Fish. Res. Board Can. 29:601-603.

Sylvester, J. R. 1973. Effect of light on vulnerability of heat-stressed sockeye salmon to predation by coho salmon. Trans. Am. Fish. Soc. 102:139-142.

Tagatz, M. E. 1976. Effect of mirex on predator-prey interaction in an experimental estuarine ecosystem. Trans. Am. Fish. Soc. 105:546-549.

Tarrant, R. M., Jr. 1960. Choice between two sizes of forage fish by largemouth bass under aquarium conditions. Prog. Fish Cult. 83:84.

Thompson, D. J. 1978. Towards a realistic predator-prey model: The effect of temperature on the functional response and life history of the damselfly, Ischnura elegans. J. Anim. Ecol. 47:757-767.

Tsuchiya, H. M., J. F. Drake, J. L. Jost, and A. G. Frederickson. 1972. Predator-prey interactions of Dictyostelium discoideum and Escherichia coli in continuous culture. J. Bacteriol. 110:1147-1153.

Van den Ende, P. 1973. Predator-prey interactions in continuous culture. Science 54:562-564.

Vaughan, G. E. 1979. Comparative vulnerability of bluegills with and without lymphocystis disease to predation by largemouth bass. Prog. Fish Cult. 41:163-164.

Veilleux, B. G. 1979. An analysis of the predatory interaction between *Paramecium* and *Didinium*. J. Anim. Ecol. 48:787-804.

Vinyard, G. L., and W. J. O'Brien. 1975. Dorsal light response as an index of prey preference in bluegill (*Lepomis macrochirus*). J. Fish. Res. Board Can. 32:1860-1863.

Vinyard, G. L., and W. J. O'Brien. 1976. Effects of light and turbidity on the reactive distance of bluegill (*Lepomis macrochirus*). J. Fish. Res. Board Can. 33:2845-2849.

Ward, D. V., B. L. Howes, and D. F. Ludwig. 1976. Interactive effects of predation pressure and insecticide (Temefos) toxicity on populations of the marsh fiddler crab *Uca pugnax*. Mar. Biol. 35: 119-126.

Ware, D. M. 1972. Predation by rainbow trout (*Salmo gairdneri*): The influence of hunger, prey density, and prey size. J. Fish. Res. Board Can. 29:1193-1201.

Ware, D. M. 1973. Risk of epibenthic prey to predation by rainbow trout (*Salmo gairdneri*). J. Fish. Res. Board Can. 30:787-797.

Warshaw, S. J. 1972. Effects of alewives (*Alosa pseudoharengus*) on the zooplankton of Lake Wononskopomuc, Connecticut. Limnol. Oceanogr. 17:816-825.

Wells, L. 1970. Effects of alewife predation on zooplankton populations in Lake Michigan. Limnol. Oceanogr. 15:556-565.

Werner, E. E. 1974. The fish size, prey size, handling time relation in several sunfishes and some implications. J. Fish. Res. Board Can. 31:1531-1536.

Werner, E. E., and D. J. Hall. 1974. Optimal foraging and size selection of prey by the bluegill sunfish (*Lepomis macrochirus*). Ecology 55: 1042-1052.

Wilt, G. R., M. M. Joshi, and J. Metcalf. 1973. Studies on the interactions of bacteria and nematodes. Water Resources Research Institute, Auburn University, Bull. 10.

Woltering, D. M., J. L. Hedtke, and L. J. Weber. 1978. Predator-prey interactions of fishes under the influence of ammonia. Trans. Am. Fish. Soc. 107:500-504.

Wolters, W. R., and C. C. Coutant. 1976. The effect of cold shock on the vulnerability of young bluegill (Lepomis macrochirus) to predation. pp. 162-164. IN Esch, G. W., and R. W. McFarlane (eds.), Thermal Ecology II. CONF-750425.

Yocum, T. G., and T. A. Edsall. 1974. Effects of acclimation temperature and heat shock on vulnerability of fry of lake whitefish (Coregonus clupeaformis) to predation. J. Fish. Res. Board Can. 31:1503-1506.

Zaret, T. M. 1972. Predators, invisible prey, and the nature of polymorphism in the cladocera (Class Crustacea). Limnol. Oceanogr. 17:171-184.

Zaret, T. M. 1975. Strategies for existence of zooplankton prey in homogeneous environments. Verh. Int. Verein. Limnol. 19:1484-1489.

Zaret, T. M., and W. C. Kerfoot. 1975. Fish predation on Bosmina longirostris: Body-size selection versus visibility selection. Ecology 56:232-237.

3.3.2 PARASITISM

Boyce, N. P., and S. B. Yamada. 1977. Effects of a parasite, Eubothrium salvelini (Cestoda: Pseudophyllidea), on the resistance of juvenile sockeye salmon, Oncorhynchus nerka, to zinc. J. Fish. Res. Board Can. 34:706-709.

Couch, J. A. 1976. Attempts to increase Baculovirus prevalence in shrimp by chemical exposure. Prog. Exp. Tumor Res. 20:304-314.

Couch, J. A., and L. Courtney. 1977. Interaction of chemical pollutants and virus in a crustacean: A novel bioassay system. Annals N.Y. Acad. Sci. 298:497-504.

Draggan, S. 1977. Interactive effect of chromium compounds and a fungal parasite on carp eggs. Bull. Environ. Contam. Toxicol. 17:653-659.

Pippy, J. H. C., and G. M. Hare. 1969. Relationship of river pollution to bacterial infection in salmon (Salmo salar) and suckers (Catastomus commersoni). Trans. Am. Fish. Soc. 98:685-690.

Snieszko, S. F. 1974. The effects of environmental stress on outbreaks of infectious diseases of fishes. J. Fish. Biol. 6:197-208.

Wedemeyer, G. 1970. The role of stress in disease resistance of fishes. pp. 30-35. IN Snieszko, S. F. (ed.), A Symposium on Diseases of Fishes and Shellfishes. Amer. Fish. Soc., Washington, D.C.

3.5.5 ECOSYSTEMS

Beyers, R. J. 1962. Relationship between temperature and the metabolism of experimental ecosystems. Science 136:980-982.

Beyers, R. J. 1963. The metabolism of twelve aquatic laboratory microecosystems. Ecol. Monogr. 33:281-306.

Bott, T. L., J. Preslan, J. Finlay, and R. Brunker. 1977. The use of flowing-water microcosms and ecosystem streams to study microbial degradation of leaf litter and nitrilotriacetic acid (NTA). IN Dev. Ind. Microbiol., Washington, D.C. 18:171-184.

Brockway, D. L., J. Hill IV, J. R. Maudsley, and R. R. Lassiter. 1979. Development, replicability and modeling of naturally derived microcosms. Int. J. Environ. Stud. 13:149-158.

Bryfogle, B. M., and W. F. McDiffett. 1979. Algal succession in laboratory microcosms as affected by an herbicide stress. Am. Midl. Nat. 101:344-354.

Cooke, G. D. 1977. Experimental aquatic laboratory ecosystems and communities. pp. 59-103. IN Cairns, J., Jr. (ed.), Aquatic Microbial Communities. Garland Publishing, New York.

Cooper, D. C. 1973. Enhancement of net primary productivity by herbivore grazing in aquatic laboratory microcosms. Limnol. Oceanogr. 18: 31-37.

Copeland, B. J. 1965. Evidence for regulation of community metabolism in a marine ecosystem. Ecology 46:563-564.

Crow, M. E., and F. B. Taub. 1979. Designing a microcosm bioassay to detect ecosystem level effects. Int. J. Environ. Stud. 13:141-147.

Cushing, C. D., and F. L. Rose. 1970. Cycling of zinc-65 by Columbia River periphyton in a closed lotic microcosm. Limnol. Oceanogr. 15:762-767.

Dudzik, M., J. Harte, A. Jassby, E. Lapan, D. Levy, and J. Rees. 1979. Some considerations in the design of aquatic microcosms for plankton studies. Int. J. Environ. Stud. 13:125-130.

Eggert, C. R., R. G. Kaley, and W. E. Gledhill. 1979. Application of a laboratory freshwater lake model in the study of linear alkylbenzene sulfonate (LAS) biodegradation. pp. 451-461. IN Bourquin, A. W., and P. H. Pritchard (eds.), Microbial Degradation of Pollutants in Marine Environments. EPA-600/9-79-012.

Ferens, M. C., and R. J. Beyers. 1972. Studies of a simple laboratory microecosystem: Effects of stress. Ecology 53:709-713.

Fraleigh, P. C. 1971. Ecological Succession in an Aquatic Microcosm and a Thermal Spring. Ph.D. dissertation, University of Georgia.

Gerhart, D. Z., S. M. Anderson, and J. Richter. 1977. Toxicity bioassays with periphyton communities: Design of experimental streams. Water Res. 11:567-570.

Giddings, J. M. 1979. Pollution studies in aquatic microcosms. Third Int. Symp. on Aquatic Pollutants, Oct. 15-17, 1979, Jekyll Island, Ga. (abstract).

Giddings, J. M. 1980. Types of aquatic microcosms and their research applications. IN Giesy, J. P. (ed.), Microcosms in Ecological Research (in press).

Giddings, J. M., and G. K. Eddlemon. 1977. The effects of microcosm size and substrate type on aquatic microcosm behavior and arsenic transport. Arch. Environ. Contam. Toxicol. 6:491-505.

Giddings, J. M., and G. K. Eddlemon. 1978. Photosynthesis/respiration ratios in aquatic microcosms under arsenic stress. Water Air Soil Pollut. 9:207-212.

Giddings, J. M., and G. K. Eddlemon. 1979. Some ecological and experimental properties of complex aquatic microcosms. Int. J. Environ. Stud. 13:119-123.

Giesy, J. P. (ed.). 1980. Symposium on Microcosms in Ecological Research. Augusta, Ga. November, 1978 (in press).

Gledhill, W. E., and V. W. Saeger. 1979. Microbial degradation in the environmental hazard evaluation process. pp. 434-442. IN Bourquin, A. W., and P. H. Pritchard (eds.), Microbial Degradation of Pollutants in Marine Environments. EPA-600/9-79-012.

Golterman, H. L. (ed.). 1976. Interactions Between Sediments and Fresh Waters. Proceedings of an International Symposium Held at Amsterdam, the Netherlands, September 6-10, 1976. Dr. W. Junk, D. V. Publishers, Wageningen, Netherlands.

Gorden, R. W. 1967. Heterotrophic Bacteria and Succession in a Simple Laboratory Aquatic Microcosm. Ph.D. dissertation, University of Georgia.

Gorden, R. W., R. J. Beyers, E. P. Odum, and R. G. Eagon. 1969. Studies of a simple laboratory microecosystem: Bacterial activities in a heterotrophic succession. Ecology 50:86-100.

Harris, W. F., B. S. Ausmus, G. K. Eddlemon, S. J. Draggan, J. M. Giddings, D. R. Jackson, R. J. Luxmoore, E. G. O'Neill, R. V. O'Neill, M. Ross-Todd, and P. Van Voris. 1980. Microcosms as potential screening tools for evaluating transport and effects of toxic substances. EPA-600/3-80-042; ORNL/EPA-600/7-79.

Harte, J., D. Levy, E. Lapan, A. Jassby, M. Dudzik, and J. Rees. 1978. Aquatic microcosms for assessment of effluent effects. Electrical Power Research Institute EA-936.

Harte, J., D. Levy, J. Rees, and E. Saegebarth. 1980. Making microcosms an effective assessment tool. IN Giesy, J. P. (ed.), Microcosms in Ecological Research (in press).

Hutchinson, G. E. 1975. A Treatise on Limnology. Vol. 1. J. Wiley and Sons, New York.

Jassby, A., M. Dudzik, J. Rees, E. Lapan, D. Levy, and J. Harte. 1977. Production cycles in aquatic microcosms. EPA-600/7-77-097.

Jassby, A., J. Rees, M. Dudzik, D. Levy, E. Lapan, and J. Harte. 1977. Trophic structure modifications by planktivorous fish in aquatic microcosms. EPA-600/7-77-096.

Jordan, M., and G. E. Likens. 1975. An organic carbon budget for an oligotrophic lake in New Hampshire, U.S.A. Verh. Int. Verein. Limnol. 19:994-1003.

Kehde, P. M., and J. L. Wilhm. 1972. The effects of grazing by snails on community structure of periphyton in laboratory streams. Am. Midl. Nat. 87:8-24.

Kelly, R. A. 1971. The Effects of Fluctuating Temperature on the Metabolism of Freshwater Microcosms. Ph.D. dissertation, University of North Carolina.

Kevern, N. R., and R. C. Ball. 1965. Primary productivity and energy relationships in artificial streams. Limnol. Oceanogr. 10:74-87.

Kurihara, Y. 1978. Studies of "Succession" in a microcosm. Sci. Rep. Tohoku Univ. Fourth Ser. (Biol.) 37:151-160.

Kurihara, Y. 1978. Studies of the interaction in a microcosm. Sci. Rep. Tohoku Univ. Fourth Ser. (Biol.) 37:161-178.

Leffler, J. W. 1977. A Microcosm Approach to an Evaluation of the Diversity-Stability Hypothesis. Ph.D. dissertation, University of Georgia.

Likens, G. E., F. H. Bormann, R. S. Pierce, J. S. Eaton, and N. M. Johnson. 1977. Biogeochemistry of a Forested Ecosystem. Springer-Verlag, New York. 146 pp.

McConnell, W. J. 1962. Productivity relations in carboy microcosms. Limnol. Oceanogr. 7:335-343.

McConnell, W. J. 1965. Relationship of herbivore growth to rate of gross photosynthesis in microcosms. Limnol. Oceanogr. 10:539-543.

McIntire, C. D. 1968. Physiological-ecological studies of benthic algae in laboratory streams. J. Water Pollut. Control Fed. 40:1940-1952.

McIntire, C. D. 1968. Structural characteristics of benthic algal communities in laboratory streams. Ecology 49:520-537.

McIntire, C. D. 1973. Periphyton dynamics in laboratory streams: A simulation model and its implications. Ecol. Monogr. 43:399-420.

McIntire, C. D., R. L. Garrison, H. K. Phinney, and C. E. Warren. 1964. Primary production in laboratory streams. Limnol. Oceanogr. 9:92-102.

Medine, A. J., D. B. Porcella, and V. D. Adams. 1980. Heavy metal and nutrient effects on sediment oxygen demand in three-phase aquatic microcosms. IN Giesy, J. P. (ed.), Microcosms in Ecological Research (in press).

Mortimer, C. H. 1941. The exchange of dissolved substances between mud and water in lakes. J. Ecol. 29:280-329.

Mortimer, C. H. 1942. The exchange of dissolved substances between mud and water in lakes. J. Ecol. 30:147-201.

Neill, W. E. 1972. Effects of Size-Selective Predation on Community Structure in Laboratory Aquatic Microcosms. Ph.D. dissertation, University of Texas.

Neill, W. E. 1975. Experimental studies of microcrustacean competition, community composition, and efficiency of resource utilization. Ecology 56:809-826.

Nixon, S. W. 1969. A synthetic microcosm. Limnol. Oceanogr. 14:142-145.

Odum, E. P. 1969. The strategy of ecosystem development. Science 164: 262-270.

Odum, H. T. 1956. Primary production in flowing waters. Limnol. Oceanogr. 1:102-117.

Odum, H. T. 1957. Trophic structure and productivity of Silver Spring, Florida. Ecol. Monogr. 27:55-112.

Odum, H. T., and C. M. Hoskin. 1958. Comparative studies on the metabolism of marine waters. Publ. Inst. Mar. Sci., University of Texas 5:16-46.

Ollason, J. G. 1977. Freshwater microcosms in fluctuating environments, including planktonic algae. Oikos 28:262-269.

Patrick, R. 1973. Use of algae, especially diatoms, in the assessment of water quality. pp. 76-95. IN Cairns, J., Jr., and K. L. Dickson (eds.), Biological Methods for the Assessment of Water Quality. ASTM Special Technical Publication 528, American Society for Testing and Materials, Philadelphia.

Phinney, H. K., and C. D. McIntire. 1965. Effect of temperature on metabolism of periphyton communities developed in laboratory streams. Limnol. Oceanogr. 10:341-344.

Pomeroy, L. R., E. E. Smith, and C. M. Grant. 1965. The exchange of phosphate between estuarine water and sediment. Limnol. Oceanogr. 10:167-172.

Porcella, D. B., V. D. Adams, and P. A. Cowan. 1976. Sediment water microcosms for assessment of nutrient interactions in aquatic ecosystems. pp. 293-322. IN Middlebrooks, J. E., D. H. Falkenborg, and T. E. Maloney (eds.), Biostimulation and Nutrient Assessment. Ann Arbor Science, Ann Arbor.

Pritchard, P. H., A. W. Bourquin, H. L. Frederickson, and T. Maziarz. 1979. System design factors affecting environmental fate studies in microcosms. pp. 251-272. IN Bourquin, A. W., and P. H. Pritchard (eds.), Microbial Degradation of Pollutants in Marine Environments. EPA-600/9-79-012.

Reed, C. C. 1976. Species Diversity in Aquatic Microecosystems. Ph.D. dissertation, University of Northern Colorado.

Reichle, D. E., R. V. O'Neill, and W. F. Harris. 1975. Principles of energy and material exchange in ecosystems. pp. 27-43. IN Van Dobben, W. H., and R. H. Lowe-McConnell (eds.), Unifying Concepts in Ecology. W. Junk, the Hague.

Riley, G. A. 1956. Factors controlling phytoplankton populations on Georges Bank. J. Mar. Res. 6:54-73.

Rodgers, J. H., Jr., J. R. Clark, K. L. Dickson, and J. Cairns, Jr. 1980. Nontaxonomic analyses of structure and function of aufwuchs communities in lotic microcosms. IN Giesy, J. P. (ed.), Microcosms in Ecological Research (in press).

Schindler, D. W., F. A. J. Armstrong, S. K. Holmgren, and G. J. Brunskill. 1971. Eutrophication of Lake 227, Experimental Lakes Area, Northwestern Ontario, by addition of phosphate and nitrate. J. Fish. Res. Board Can. 28:1763-1782.

Sugiura, K., S. Sato, M. Goto, and Y. Kurihara. 1976. Effects of beta-BHC on aquatic microcosm. Chemosphere 1:39-44.

Sugiura, K., S. Sato, M. Goto, and Y. Kurihara. 1976. Toxicity assessment using an aquatic microcosm. Chemosphere 2:113-118.

Taub, F. B. 1969. A biological model of a freshwater community: A gnotobiotic ecosystem. Limnol. Oceanogr. 14:136-142.

Taub, F. B. 1969. A continuous gnotobiotic (species defined) ecosystem. pp. 101-120. IN Cairns, J., Jr. (ed.), The Structure and Function of Fresh-Water Microbial Communities. Research Monograph 3, Virginia Polytechnic Institute and State University, Blacksburg, Va.

Taub, F. B. 1969. Gnotobiotic models of freshwater communities. Verh. Int. Verein. Limnol. 17:485-496.

Taub, F. B. 1976. Demonstration of pollution effects in aquatic microcosms. Int. J. Environ. Stud. 10:23-33.

Taub, F. B., and M. E. Crow. 1980. Synthesizing aquatic microcosms. IN Giesy, J. P. (ed.), Microcosms in Ecological Research (in press).

Taub, F. B., M. E. Crow, and H. J. Hartmann. 1980. Responses of aquatic microcosms to acute mortality. IN Giesy, J. P. (ed.), Microcosms in Ecological Research (in press).

Thomas, C. L. 1978. A Microcosm Study of the Interactions of Nutrients and Cadmium in Aquatic Systems. M.S. Thesis, University of Georgia.

Waide, J. B., J. E. Schindler, M. C. Waldron, J. J. Hains, S. P. Schreiner, M. L. Freedman, S. L. Benz, D. R. Pettigrew, L. A. Schissel, and P. J. Clarke. 1980. A microcosm approach to the study of biogeochemical systems: 2. Responses of aquatic laboratory microcosms to physical, chemical, and biological perturbations. IN Giesy, J. P. (ed.), Microcosms in Ecological Research (in press).

Warren, C. E., and G. E. Davis. 1971. Laboratory stream research: Objectives, possibilities, and constraints. Annu. Rev. Ecol. Syst. 2:111-144.

Webster, J. R. 1978. Analysis of Potassium and Calcium Dynamics in Stream Ecosystems on Three Southern Appalachian Watersheds of Contrasting Vegetation. Ph.D. dissertation, University of Georgia.

Whittaker, R. H., and G. M. Woodwell. 1972. Evolution of natural communities. pp. 137-159. IN Wiens, J. A. (ed.), Ecosystem Structure and Function. Oregon State University Press, Corvallis.

Whitworth, W. R., and T. H. Lane. 1969. Effects of toxicants on community metabolism in pools. Limnol. Oceanogr. 14:53-58.

3.7 ECOSYSTEM PROPERTIES

Abbott, W. 1966. Microcosm studies on estuarine waters. I. The replicability of microcosms. J. Water Pollut. Control Fed. 38:256-270.

Abbott, W. 1967. Microcosm studies on estuarine waters. II. The effects of single doses of nitrate and phosphate. J. Water Pollut. Control Fed. 39:113-122.

Abbott, W. 1969. High levels of nitrate and phosphate in carboy microcosm studies. J. Water Pollut. Control Fed. 14:1748-1751.

Admiraal, W. 1977. Experiments with mixed populations of benthic estuarine diatoms in laboratory microecosystems. Bot. Mar. 20:479-485.

Allen, S. D., and T. D. Brock. 1968. The adaptation of heterotrophic microcosms to different temperatures. Ecology 49:343-346.

Armitage, B. J. 1980. Effects of temperature on periphyton biomass and community composition in the Browns Ferry Experimental Channels. IN Giesy, J. P. (ed), Microcosms in Ecological Research (in press).

Atz, J. W. 1949. The balanced aquarium myth. The Aquarist 14:159-160.

Batchelder, A. R. 1975. Eutrophication of microponds. J. Environ. Qual. 4:520-526.

Beyers, R. J. 1962. Some metabolic aspects of balanced aquatic microcosms. Am. Zool. 2:391.

Beyers, R. J. 1963. A characteristic diurnal metabolic pattern in balanced microcosms. Publ. Inst. Mar. Sci., Texas 9:19-27.

Beyers, R. J. 1964. The microcosm approach to ecosystem biology. Am. Biol. Teach. 26:491-498.

Beyers, R. J. 1965. The pattern of photosynthesis and respiration in laboratory microecosystems. IN Goldman, C. R. (ed.), Primary Productivity in Aquatic Environments. Mem. Ist. Ital. Idrobial. 18:61-74.

Beyers, R. J., P. C. Fraleigh, B. Braybog, and H. Morrissett. 1968. The effects of gamma radiation on simplified microecosystems. Sav. River Ecol. Lab. Ann. Report, pp. 176-182.

Bott, T. L., K. Rogenmuser, and P. Thorne. 1978. Effects of No. 2 fuel oil, Nigerian crude oil, and used crankcase oil on benthic algal communities. J. Environ. Sci. Health, Part A 10:751-779.

Bourquin, A. W. 1977. Effects of malathion on microorganisms of an artificial salt-marsh environment. J. Environ. Qual. 6:373-378.

Bourquin, A., L. Kiefer, and S. Cassidy. 1974. Microbial response to malathion treatments in salt marsh microcosms. Abstr. Annu. Meet. Am. Soc. Microbiol.

Bourquin, A. W., P. H. Pritchard, R. Vanolinda, and J. Samela. 1979. Fate of dimilin in estuarine microcosms. Abstr. Annu. Meeting Am. Soc. Microbiol.

Bourquin, A. W., R. L. Garnas, P. H. Pritchard, F. G. Wilkes, C. R. Cripe, and N. I. Rubinstein. 1979. Interdependent microcosms for the assessment of pollutants in the marine environment. Int. J. Environ. Stud. 13:131-140.

Bruning, K., R. Lingeman, and J. Ringelberg. 1978. Properties of an aquatic microecosystem. Part 3. Development of the decomposer subsystem and the phosphorus output stability. Verh. Int. Verein. Limnol. 20:1231-1235.

Busch, D. 1978. Successional Changes Associated with Benthic Assemblages in Experimental Streams. Ph.D. dissertation, Oregon State University.

Butler, J. L. 1964. Interaction of Effects by Environmental Factors on Primary Productivity in Ponds and Microecosystems. Ph.D. dissertation, Oklahoma State University.

Cairns, J., Jr. 1979. Hazard evaluation with microcosms. Int. J. Environ. Stud. 13:95-99.

Cairns, J., K. L. Dickson, J. P. Slocomb, S. P. Almeida, and J. K. Eu. 1976. Automated pollution monitoring with microcosms. Int. J. Environ. Stud. 10:43-49.

Coats, J. R., R. L. Metcalf, and I. P. Kapoor. 1974. Metabolism of the methoxychlor isotere, dianisylneopentane, in mouse, insects, and a model ecosystem. Pestic. Biochem. Physiol. 4:201-211.

Coats, J. R., R. L. Metcalf, P. Y. Lu, D. D. Brown, J. F. Williams, and L. G. Hansen. Model ecosystem evaluation of the environmental impacts of the veterinary drugs phenothiazine, sulfamethazine, clopidiol, and diethylstilbestrol. Environ. Health Perspect. 18: 167-179.

Cook, W. L., D. Fiedler, and A. W. Bourquin. 1980. Succession of microfungi in estuarine microcosms perturbed by carbaryl, methyl parathion and pentachlorophenol. Bot. Mar. 23:129-131.

Cooke, G. D. 1967. The pattern of autotrophic succession in laboratory microcosms. Bio. Sci. 17:717-721.

Cooper, D. C., and B. J. Copeland. 1973. Responses of continuous-series estuarine microecosystems to point-source input variations. Ecol. Monogr. 43:213-236.

Cross, F. A., J. N. Willis, and J. P. Baptist. 1971. Distribution of radioactive and stable zinc in an experimental marine ecosystem. J. Fish. Res. Board. Can. 28:1783-1788.

Crouthamel, D. A. 1977. A Microcosm Approach to the Effects of Fish Predation on Aquatic Community Structure and Function. Ph.D. dissertation, University of Georgia.

Cushing, C. D., and F. L. Rose. 1970. Cycling of zinc 65 by Columbia River periphyton in a closed lotic microcosm. Limnol. Oceanogr. 15: 762-767.

Cushing, C. E., J. M. Thomas, and L. L. Eberhardt. 1974. Modelling mineral cycling by periphyton in a simulated stream system. Battelle Pacific Northwest Laboratories, CONF-740826-4. 10 pp.

Davis, G. E. 1963. Trophic Relations of Simplified Animal Communities in Laboratory Streams. Ph.D. dissertation, Oregon State University.

Davis, W. P., B. S. Hester, R. L. Yoakum, and R. G. Domey. 1977. Marine ecosystem testing units: Design for assessment of benthic organism responses to low-level pollutants. Helgol. Wiss. Meeresunters. 30: 673-681.

Di Salvo, L. H. 1971. Regenerative functions and microbial ecology of coral reefs: Labelled bacteria in a coral reef microcosm. J. Exp. Mar. Biol. Ecol. 7:123-136.

Duke, T. W., J. Willis, T. Price, and K. Fischler. 1969. Influence of environmental factors on the concentration of zinc-65 by an experimental community. Proc. 2nd Nat. Symp. Radioecol., Ann Arbor, Mich. 1967. pp. 355-362.

Elmgren, R., G. A. Vargo, J. F. Grassle, J. P. Grassle, D. R. Heinle, G. Langlois, and S. L. Vargo. 1980. Trophic interactions in experimental marine ecosystems perturbed by oil. IN Giesy, J. P. (ed.), Microcosms in Ecological Research (in press).

Evans, E. C., III. 1977. Microcosm responses to environmental perturbants. Helgol. Wiss. Meeresunters. 30:178-191.

Evans, E. C., and R. S. Henderson. 1977. Elutriator/microcosm system pilot model and test. EPA-600/3-77-093.

Everest, J. W. 1979. Predicting phosphorus movement and pesticide action in salt marshes with microecosystems. Office of Water Research and Technology W79-07006, OWRT-A-045-ALA(1). 90 pp.

Everest, J. W., and D. E. Davis. 1979. Phosphorus movement using salt marsh microecosystems. J. Environ. Qual. 8:465-468.

Ferens, M. C. 1971. The Effects of Gamma Radiation on a Laboratory Microecosystem. M.S. Thesis, University of Georgia.

Fraleigh, P. C., and P. C. Dibert. 1980. Inorganic carbon limitation during ecological succession in aquatic microcosms. IN Giesy, J. P. (ed.), Microcosms in Ecological Research (in press).

Fredrickson, H. L., A. W. Bourquin, and P. H. Pritchard. 1979. A comparative study of the fate of pentachlorophenol, methyl parathion, and carbaryl in estuarine microcosms. Abstr. Annu. Meeting Am. Soc. Microbiol. 1979.

Gallepp, G. W. 1979. Chironomid influence on phosphorus release in sediment-water microcosms. Ecology 60:547-556.

Giddings, J. M., B. T. Walton, G. K. Eddlemon, and K. G. Olson. 1979. Transport and fate of anthracene in aquatic microcosms. pp. 312-320. IN Bourquin, A. W., and P. H. Pritchard (eds.), Microbial Degradation of Pollutants in Marine Environments. Environmental Protection Agency, EPA-600/9-79-012.

Giesy, J. P., Jr. 1978. Cadmium inhibition of leaf decomposition in an aquatic microcosm. Chemosphere 7:467-475.

Goodyear, C. P., C. E. Boyd, and R. J. Beyers. 1972. Relationships between primary productivity and mosquitofish (Gambusia affinis) production in large microcosms. Limnol. Oceanogr. 17:445-450.

Gorden, R. W., and L. B. Hill. 1971. Ecology of heterotrophic aerobic bacteria of Playa Lakes and microcosms. Southwest. Nat. 15:419-428.

Guthrie, R. K., E. M. Davis, D. S. Cherry, and H. E. Murray. 1979. Biomagnification of heavy metals by organisms in a marine microcosm. Bull. Environ. Contam. Toxicol. 21:53-61.

Hagstrom, A. 1977. The fate of oil in a model ecosystem. Ambio 6: 229-231.

Hall, D. J., W. E. Cooper, and E. E. Werner. 1970. An experimental approach to the production dynamics and structure of freshwater animal communities. Limnol. Oceanogr. 15:839-928.

Heath, R. T. 1979. Holistic study of an aquatic microcosm: Theoretical and practical implications. Int. J. Environ. Stud. 13:87-93.

Heath, R. T. 1980. Are microcosms useful for ecosystem analysis? IN Giesy, J. P. (ed.), Microcosms in Ecological Research (in press).

Heinle, D. R., D. A. Flemer, R. T. Huff, S. T. Sulkin, and R. E. Ulanowicz. 1979. Effects of perturbations on estuarine microcosms. pp. 119-142. IN Dame, R. F. (ed.), Marsh-Estuarine Systems Simulation. U. of South Carolina Press, Columbus, S.C.

Henderson, R. S., S. V. Smith, and E. C. Evans. 1976. Flow-through microcosms for simulation of marine ecosystems: Development and intercomparison of open coast and bay facilities. Naval Undersea Center, San Diego, California. NUC-TP-519, 76 pp.

Hill, J., IV, H. P. Kollig, D. F. Paris, N. L. Wolfe, and R. G. Zepp. 1976. Dynamic behavior of vinyl chloride in aquatic ecosystem. Environmental Protection Agency, EPA-600/3-76-001.

Hill, J., IV, and D. B. Porcella. 1974. Component description of sediment-water microcosms. Utah State University Center for Water Resources W74-12868; OWRR-B-080-Utah; PRWG 121-122.

Hirwe, A. S., R. L. Metcalf, P. Y. Lu, and L. C. Chio. 1975. Comparative metabolism of 1,1-bis-(P-chlorophenyl)-2,2-nitropropane (Prolan) in mouse, insects, and in a model ecosystem.

Hoffman, R. W., and A. J. Horne. 1980. Onsite flume studies for assessment of effluent impacts on stream aufwuchs communities. IN Giesy, J. P. (ed.), Microcosms in Ecological Research (in press).

Howarth, R. W., and S. G. Fisher. 1976. Carbon, nitrogen and phosphorous dynamics during leaf decay in nutrient enriched stream microecosystems. Freshwater Biol. 6:221-228.

Huckabee, J. W., and B. G. Blaylock. 1976. Microcosm studies on the transfer of mercury, cadmium, and selenium from terrestrial to aquatic ecosystems. Proc. Univ. Mo. Annu. Conf. Trace Subst. Environ. Health 8:219-228.

Hueck, H. J., and D. M. M. Adema. 1968. Toxicological investigations in an artificial ecosystem. A progress report on copper toxicity towards algae and _Daphnia_. Helgol. Wiss. Meeresunters. 17:188-199.

Hura, M., E. C. Evans III, and F. G. Wood. 1976. Coastal water protection the Navy way. Environ. Sci. Technol. 10:1098-1103.

Hurlbert, S. H., J. Zedler, and D. Fairbanks. 1972. Ecosystem alteration by mosquitofish (_Gambusia affinis_) predation. Science 175:639-641.

Isensee, A. R. 1976. Variability of aquatic model ecosystem derived data. Int. J. Environ. Stud. 10:35-41.

Isensee, A. R., and G. E. Jones. 1975. Distribution of 2,3,7,8-tetrachloro-dibenzene-p-dioxin (TCDD) in aquatic model ecosystems. Environ. Sci. Technol. 9:668-672.

Isensee, A. R., P. C. Kearney, E. A. Woolson, G. E. Jones, and U. P. Williams. 1973. Distribution of alkyl arsenicals in model ecosystems. Environ. Sci. Technol. 7:841-845.

Johnson, D. L. 1978. Biological mediation of chemical speciation. Part 1. Microcosm studies of the diurnal pattern of copper species in sea water. Chemosphere 7:641-644.

Kanazawa, J., A. R. Isensee, and P. C. Kearney. 1975. Distribution of carbaryl and 3,5-xylyl methylcarbamate in an aquatic model ecosystem. J. Agric. Food Chem. 23:760-763.

Kania, H. J., and R. J. Beyers. 1970. Feedback control of light imput to a microecosystem by the system. Sav. River Ecol. Lab. Ann. Report, pp. 146-148.

Kania, H. J., and R. J. Beyers. 1974. NTA and mercury in artificial stream systems. Environmental Protection Agency, EPA-660/3-73-025.

Kania, H. J., R. L. Knight, and R. J. Beyers. 1976. Fate and biological effects of mercury introduced into artificial streams. Environmental Protection Agency, EPA-600/3-76-060.

Kapoor, I. P., R. L. Metcalf, A. S. Hirwe, P. Y. Lu, J. R. Coats, and R. F. Nystrom. 1972. Comparative metabolism of DDT, methoxychlor, and ethoxychlor in mouse, insects, and in a model ecosystem. J. Agric. Food Chem. 20:1-6.

Kapoor, I. P., R. L. Metcalf, R. F. Nystrom, and G. K. Sangha. 1970. Comparative metabolism of methoxychlor and DDT in mouse, insects, and in a model ecosystem. J. Agric. Food Chem. 18:1145-1152.

Kawabata, Z., and Y. Kurihara. 1978. Computer simulation study on the nature of the steady-state of the aquatic microcosm. Sci. Rep. Tohoku Univ. Fourth Ser. (Biol.) 37:205-218.

Kawabata, Z., and Y. Kurihara. 1978. Computer simulation study of the relationships between the total system and subsystems in the early stages of succession of the aquatic microcosm. Sci. Rep. Tohoku Univ. Fourth Ser. (Biol.) 37:179-204.

Kawabata, Z., and Y. Kurihara. 1978. Effects of the consumer on the biomass and spatial heterogeneity in the aquatic microcosm. Sci. Rep. Tohoku Univ. Fourth Ser. (Biol.) 37:219-234.

Kersting, K. 1975. The use of microsystems for the evaluation of the effects of toxicants. Hydrobiol. Bull. 9:102-108.

Kevern, N. R. 1963. Primary Productivity and Energy Relationships in Artificial Streams. Ph.D. dissertation, Michigan State University.

Kitchens, W. M. 1979. Development of a salt marsh microecosystem. Int. J. Environ. Stud. 13:109-118.

Kitchens, W. M., and B. J. Copeland. 1980. Succession in laboratory microecosystems subjected to thermal and nutrient addition. IN Giesy, J. P. (ed.), Microcosms in Ecological Research (in press).

Kitchens, W. M., R. T. Edwards, and W. U. Johnson. 1979. Development of a living salt marsh ecosystem model: A microecosystem approach. pp. 107-118. IN Dame, R. F. (ed.), Marsh-Estuarine Systems Simulation. U. of South Carolina Press, Columbus, S.C.

Kleiber, P., and T. H. Blackburn. 1978. Model of biological and diffusional processes involving hydrogen sulfide in a marine microcosm. Oikos 31:280-283.

Kurihara, Y. 1956. Dynamic aspects of the community structure of the benthic protists in bamboo container. Jap. J. Ecol. 5:111-117.

Kurihara, Y. 1958. Analysis of the structure of microcosm, with special reference to the succession of protozoa in the bamboo container. Jap. J. Ecol. 8:163-171.

Kurihara, Y. 1959. Synecological analysis of the biotic community in microcosm. VIII. Studies of the limiting factor in determining the distribution of mosquito larvae in the polluted water of bamboo container, with special reference to bacteria. Jap. J. Zool. 12: 391-400.

Kurihara, Y. 1960. Dynamic aspect of the structure of microcosm, with special reference to interrelationships among biotic and abiotic factors. Jap. J. Ecol. 10:115-120.

Lauff, G. H., and K. W. Cummins. 1964. A model stream for studies in lotic ecology. Ecology 45:188-191.

Lee, A. H., P. Y. Lu, R. L. Metcalf, and E. L. Hsu. 1976. The environmental fate of three dichlorophenyl nitrophenyl ether herbicides in a rice paddy model ecosystem. J. Environ. Qual. 5: 482-486.

Leffler, J. W. 1974. The concept of ecosystem stability: Its relationship to species diversity. Assoc. Southeast Biol. Bull. 21:65-66.

Leffler, J. W. 1978. Ecosystem responses to stress in aquatic microcosms. pp. 102-119. IN Thorp, J. H., and J. W. Gibbons (eds.), Energy and Environmental Stress in Aquatic Systems. DOE Technical Info. Center, Oak Ridge, TN.

Lu, P. Y., R. L. Metcalf, and E. M. Carlson. 1978. Environmental fate of five radiolabelled coal conversion by-products evaluated in a laboratory model ecosystem. Environ. Health Perspect. 24:201-208.

Maguire, B., Jr. 1980. Some patterns in post-closure ecosystem dynamics (failure). IN Giesy, J. P. (ed.), Microcosms in Ecological Research (in press).

Maki, A. W. 1980. Evaluation of a toxicant on structure and function of model stream communities: Correlations with natural stream effects. IN Giesy, J. P. (ed.), Microcosms in Ecological Research (in press).

Maki, A. W., and H. E. Johnson. 1976. Evaluation of a toxicant on the metabolism of model stream communities. J. Fish. Res. Board Can. 33:2740-2746.

Manuel, C. Y., and G. W. Marshall. 1980. Limitations on the use of microcosms for predicting algal response to nutrient enrichment in lotic systems. IN Giesy, J. P. (ed.), Microcosms in Ecological Research (in press).

Medine, A. J. 1979. The Use of Microcosms to Study Aquatic Ecosystem Dynamics--Methods and Case Studies. Ph.D. dissertation, Utah State University.

Metcalf, R. L. 1971. A model ecosystem for the evaluation of pesticide biodegradability and ecological magnification. Outlook Agric. 7:55-59.

Metcalf, R. L. 1977. Model ecosystem approach to insecticide degradation: A critique. Annu. Rev. Entomol. 22:241-261.

Metcalf, R. L., G. H. Sangha, and I. P. Kapoor. 1971. Model ecosystem for the evaluation of pesticide biodegradability and ecological magnification. Environ. Sci. Technol. 5:709-713.

Mitchell, D. 1971. Eutrophication of lake water microcosms: Phosphate versus nonphosphate detergents. Science 174:827-829.

Mullin, M. M., and P. M. Evans. 1974. The use of a deep tank in plankton ecology. 2. Efficiency of a planktonic food chain. Limnol. Oceanogr. 19:902-911.

Neame, P. A., and C. R. Goldman. 1980. Oxygen uptake and production in sediment--Water microcosms. IN Giesy, J. P. (ed.), Microcosms in Ecological Research (in press).

Nixon, S. W., D. Alonso, M. E. Q. Pilson, and B. A. Buckley. 1980. Turbulent mixing in aquatic microcosms. IN Giesy, J. P. (ed.), Microcosms in Ecological Research (in press).

Nixon, S. W., C. A. Oviatt, J. N. Kremer, and K. Perez. 1979. The use of numerical models and laboratory microcosms in estuarine ecosystem analysis: Simulations of a winter phytoplankton bloom. pp. 165-188. IN Dame, R. F. (ed.), Marsh-Estuarine Systems Simulation. U. of South Carolina Press, Columbia, S.C.

Notini, M., B. Nagell, A. Hagstrom, and O. Grahn. 1977. An outdoor model simulating a Baltic Sea littoral ecosystem. Oikos 28:1-8.

Odum, H. T., and C. M. Hoskin. 1957. Metabolism of a laboratory stream microcosm. Public Inst. Mar. Sci. Texas 4:115-133.

Odum, H. T., W. L. Siler, R. J. Beyers, and N. Armstrong. 1963. Experiments with engineering of marine ecosystems. Public Inst. Mar. Sci. Texas 9:373-403.

Ollason, J. G. 1977. Freshwater microcosms in fluctuating environments. Oikos 28:262-269.

Oviatt, C. A., S. W. Nixon, K. T. Perez, and B. Buckley. 1979. On the season and nature of perturbations in microcosm experiments. pp. 143-164. IN Dame, R. F. (ed.), Marsh-Estuarine Systems Simulation. U. of South Carolina Press, Columbia, S.C.

Oviatt, C. A., K. T. Perez, and S. W. Nixon. 1977. Multivariate analysis of experimental marine ecosystems. Helgol. Wiss. Meeresunters. 30: 30-46.

Perez, K. T., G. M. Morrison, N. F. Lackie, C. A. Oviatt, S. W. Nixon, B. A. Buckley, and J. F. Heltshe. 1977. The importance of physical and biotic scaling to the experimental simulation of a coastal marine ecosystem. Helgol. Wiss. Meeresunters. 30:144-162.

Pilson, M. E. Q., C. A. Oviatt, and S. W. Nixon. 1980. Annual nutrient cycles in a marine microcosm. IN Giesy, J. P. (ed.), Microcosms in Ecological Research (in press).

Pilson, M. E. Q., G. A. Vargo, P. Gearing, and J. N. Gearing. 1977. The marine ecosystems research laboratory: A facility for the investigation of effects and fates of pollutants. IN Proceedings of the 2nd National Conference, Interagency Energy/Environment R&D Program, Washington, D.C., June 6-7, 1977.

Porcella, D. B., V. D. Adams, P. A. Cowan, S. Austrheim-Smith, and W. F. Holmes. 1975. Nutrient dynamics and gas production in aquatic ecosystems: The effects and utilization of mercury and nitrogen in sediment-water microcosms. Utah Water Research Lab., Logan. Office of Water Research and Technology, Washington, D.C. W76-05246; OWRT-B-081-Utah (2); PRWG 121-1.

Ramm, A. E., and D. A. Bella. 1974. Sulfide production in anaerobic microcosms. Limnol. Oceanogr. 19:110-118.

Rees, J. T. 1979. Community development in fresh water microcosms. Hydrobiologia 63:113-128.

Reichgott, M., and L. H. Stevenson. 1977. Microbial biomass in salt marsh and microecosystem sediments. Abstr. Annu. Meet. Am. Soc. Microbiol.

Reichgott, M., and L. H. Stevenson. 1978. Microbiological and physical properties of salt marsh and microecosystem sediments. Appl. Environ. Microbiol. 36:662-667.

Reinbold, K., I. P. Kapoor, W. F. Childers, W. N. Bruce, and R. L. Metcalf. 1971. Comparative uptake and biodegradability of DDT and methoxychlor by aquatic organisms. Ill. Nat. Hist. Surv. Bull. 30:405-415.

Richardson, R. E. 1930. Notes on the simulation of natural aquatic conditions in fresh-water by the use of small non-circulating balanced aquaria. Ecology 11:102-109.

Ringelberg, J. 1977. Properties of an aquatic microecosystem. II. Steady-state phenomena in the autotrophic subsystem. Helgol. Wiss. Meeresunters. 30:134-143.

Ringelberg, J., and K. Kersting. 1978. Properties of an aquatic microecosystem. I. General introduction to the prototypes. Arch. Hydrobiol. 83:47-68.

Rose, F. L., and C. E. Cushing. 1970. Accumulation of dieldrin by benthic algae in laboratory streams. Hydrobiologia 35:481-493.

Saks, N. M., J. J. Lee, W. A. Muller, and J. H. Tietjen. 1973. Growth of salt marsh microcosms subjected to thermal stress. pp. 391-398. IN Gibbons, J. W., and R. R. Sharitz (eds.), Thermal Ecology. USAEC Technical Information Center, Oak Ridge, TN, CONF-730505.

Samsel, G. L. 1972. The effects of temperature and radiation stress on aquatic microecosystem. Trans. Ky. Acad. Sci. 33:1-12.

Samsel, G. L., G. C. Llewellyn, and D. Fick. 1974. A preliminary study of the effects of gamma irradiation and oxygen stress on an aquatic microecosystem. Va. J. Sci. 25:169-172.

Samsel, G. L., and B. C. Parker. 1972. Nutrient factors uniting primary productivity in simulated and field antarctic microecosystems. Va. J. Sci. 23:64-71.

Sanborn, J. R., R. L. Metcalf, W. N. Bruce, and P. Y. Lu. 1975. The fate of chlordane and toxaphene in a terrestrial-aquatic model ecosystem. Environ. Entomol. 5:533-538.

Sanborn, J. R., and C. C. Yu. 1973. The fate of dieldrin in a model ecosystem. Bull. Environ. Contam. Toxicol. 10:340-346.

Schuth, C. K., A. R. Isensee, E. A. Woolson, and P. C. Kearney. 1974. Distribution of C-14 and arsenic derived from C-14 cacodylic acid in an aquatic ecosystem. J. Agric. Food Chem. 22:999-1003.

Sebetich, M. J. 1975. Phosphorus kinetics of freshwater microcosms. Ecology 56:1262-1280.

Sigmon, C. F., H. J-Kania, and R. J. Beyers. 1977. Reductions in biomass and diversity resulting from exposure to mercury in artificial streams. J. Fish. Res. Board Can. 34:493-500.

Smart, R. M., R. L. Eley, and J. M. Falco. 1978. Design of a laboratory microcosm for evaluating effects of dredged material disposal on marsh-estuarine ecosystems. Army Engineer Waterways Experiment Station, Vicksburg, Mississippi, WES-TR-D-78-52, 54 pp.

Smith, S. V., P. Jokiel, G. S. Key, and E. B. Guinther. 1979. Metabolic responses of shallow tropical benthic microcosm communities to perturbation. Environmental Protection Agency, EPA-600/3-79-061. 67 pp.

Smrchek, J. C. 1974. The Effects of Various Tertiary Treatment Nutrient Removal Schemes upon the Productivity of Autotrophic (Periphyton) Communities in Model Laboratory Stream Ecosystems. Ph.D. dissertation, Virginia Polytechnic Institute and State University.

Smrchek, J. C., J. Cairns, Jr., K. L. Dickson, P. H. King, C. W. Randall, J. Crowe, D. Huber, and J. W. Olver. 1976. The effect of various tertiary treatment removal schemes on periphyton communities in model laboratory streams. UPI-VWRRC-BULL86, Virginia Polytech. Inst. & State U.

Sodergren, H. 1973. Transport, distribution, and degradation of chlorinated hydrocarbon residues in aquatic model ecosystems. Oikos 24:30-41.

Strange, R. J. 1976. Nutrient release and community metabolism following application of herbicide to macrophytes in microcosms. J. Appl. Ecol. 13:889-897.

Streit, B. 1979. Uptake, accumulation, and release of organic pesticides by benthic invertebrates. 3. Distribution of carbon-14 atrazine and carbon-14 lindane in an experimental 3 step food chain microcosm. Arch. Hydrobiol. Suppl. 55:373-400.

Strickland, J. D. H., O. Holm-Hansen, R. W. Eppley, and R. J. Linn. 1969. The use of a deep tank in plankton ecology. I. Studies of the growth and composition of phytoplankton crops at low nutrient levels. Limnol. Oceanogr. 14:23-34.

Taub, F. B., and M. E. Crow. 1978. Loss of a critical species in a model (laboratory) ecosystem. Verh. Int. Verein. Limnol. 20:1270-1276.

Terhaar, C. J., W. S. Ewell, S. P. Dzinba, W. W. White, and P. J. Murphy. 1977. A laboratory model for evaluating the behavior of heavy metals in an aquatic environment. Water Res. 11:101-110.

Tison, D. L., and A. J. Lingg. 1979. Dissolved organic matter utilization and oxygen uptake in algal bacterial microcosms. Can. J. Microbiol. 25:1315-1320.

Trabalka, J. R., and L. D. Eyman. 1976. Distribution of plutonium-237 in a littoral fresh water microcosm. Health Phys. 31:390-393.

Trabalka, J. R., and M. L. Frank. 1978. Trophic transfer by chironomids and distribution of plutonium-239 in simple aquatic microcosms. Health Phys. 35:492-494.

Uhlmann, V. D. 1969. Primary production and decomposition in micro-ecosystems with different proportions of illuminated and dark layers. Arch. Hydrobiol. 66:113-138.

Uhlmann, D. 1971. Influence of dilution, sinking and grazing rate on phytoplankton populations in hyperfertilized ponds and microecosystems. Mitt. Int. Verein. Limnol. 19:100-124.

Whitford, L. A., G. E. Dillard, and G. J. Schumacher. 1964. An artificial stream apparatus for the study of lotic organisms. Limnol. Oceanogr. 6:423-425.

Whittaker, R. H. 1961. Experiments with radiophosphorus tracer in aquarium microcosms. Ecol. Monogr. 31:157-187.

Wilhelm, J. L. 1970. Transfer of radioisotopes between detritus and benthic macroinvertebrates in laboratory microecosystems. Health Phys. 18:277-284.

Wulff, B. L. 1971. Structure and Productivity of Marine Benthic Diatom Communities in a Laboratory Model Ecosystem. Ph.D. dissertation, Oregon State University.

Yockim, R. S., A. R. Isensee, and E. A. Walker. 1980. Behavior of trifluralin in aquatic model ecosystems. Bull. Environ. Contam. Toxicol. 24:134-141.

Yu, C., G. Booth, D. I. Hansen, and J. R. Larsen. 1974. Fate of bux insecticide in a model ecosystem. Environ. Entomol. 3:975-977.

Yu, C., and J. R. Sanborn. 1975. The fate of parathion in a model ecosystem. Bull. Environ. Contam. Toxicol. 13:543-550.

4. TERRESTRIAL TEST SYSTEMS

Waterland, L. R. 1979. Definition of terrestrial ecology bioassay protocols for environmental assessment programs. Workshop Proceedings, FR-79-342. Acurex Corp., Mountain View, Ca.

4.1.1 COMPETITION

Adams, W. T., and G. T. Duncan. 1979. A maximum likelihood statistical method for analyzing frequency-dependent fitness experiments. Behav. Genet. 9:7-21.

Anderson, J. M. 1962. The enigma of soil animal species diversity. pp. 51-58. IN Murphy, P. W. (ed.), Progress in Soil Zoology. Butterworths, London.

Anderson, J. M. 1978. Competition between two unrelated species of soil Cryptostigmata (Acari) in experimental microcosms. J. Anim. Ecol. 47:787-803.

Atkinson, W. D. 1979. A field investigation of larval competition in domestic Drosophila. J. Anim. Ecol. 48:91-102.

Ayala, F. J. 1966. Reversal of dominance in competing species of Drosophila. The Am. Nat. 100(910):81-83.

Ayala, F. J. 1967. Improvement in competitive ability of two species of Drosophila. Genetics 56:542-543.

Ayala, F. J. 1969. Evolution of fitness. IV. Genetic evolution of interspecific competitive ability in Drosophila. Genetics 61:737-747.

Ayala, F. J. 1969. Experimental invalidation of the principle of competitive exclusion. Nature 224:1076-1079.

Ayala, F. J. 1970. Competition, coexistence, and evolution. pp. 121-158. IN Hecht, M. K., and W. C. Steere (eds.), Essays in Evolution and Genetics in Honor of Theodosius Dobzhansky.

Ayala, F. J. 1971. Competition between species: Frequency dependence. Science 171:820-824.

Ayala, F. J. 1972. Competition between species. Am. Sci. 60:348-357.

Ayala, F. J., M. E. Gilpin, and J. G. Ehrenfeld. 1973. Competition between species: Theoretical models and experimental tests. Theor. Popul. Biol. 4:331-356.

Barker, J. S. F., and R. N. Podger. 1970. Interspecific competition between Drosophila melanogaster and Drosophila simulans: Effects of larval density on viability, developmental period and adult body weight. Ecology 51:170-189.

Barker, J. S. F. 1971. Ecological differences and competitive interaction between Drosophila melanogaster and Drosophila simulans in small laboratory populations. Oecologia 8:139-156.

Bazzaz, F. A., and J. L. Harper. 1976. Relationship between plant weight and numbers in mixed populations of Sinapsis abla, (L.) rabenh. and Lepidium sativum. J. Appl. Ecol. 13:211-216.

Bennett, J. P., and V. C. Runeckles. 1977. Effects of low levels of ozone on plant competition. J. Appl. Ecol. 14:877-880.

Benson, J. F. 1973. The biology of Lepidoptera infesting stored products, with special reference to population dynamics. Biol. Rev. 48:1-26.

Blaylock, B. G. 1969. Effects of ionizing radiation on interspecific competition. pp. 61-67. IN Nelson, D. J., and F. C. Evans (eds.), Symposium on Radioecology. CONF-670503. U.S. Atomic Energy Commission, Washington, D.C.

Blaylock, B. G., and H. H. Shugart, Jr. 1972. The effect of radiation-induced mutations on the fitness of Drosophila populations. Genetics 72:469-474.

Boggild, O., and J. Keiding. 1958. Competition in house fly larvae. Oikos 9(1):1-25.

Budnik, M., and D. Brncic. 1974. Preadult competition between Drosophila pavani and Drosophila melanogaster, Drosophila simulans, and Drosophila willistoni. Ecology 55:657-661.

Christiansen, K. 1967. Competition between collembolan species in culture jars. Rev. Ecol. Biol. Sol. 4:439-462.

Crombie, A. C. 1945. On competition between different species of graminivorous insects. Pro. R. Soc. London, Series B--Biological Sciences 132:362-395.

Crombie, A. C. 1946. Further experiments on insect competition. Pro. R. Soc. London, Series B--Biological Sciences 133:76-109.

Culver, D. 1974. Competition between Collembola in a patchy environment. Rev. Ecol. Biol. Sol. 11(4):533-540.

Dawson, P. S. 1969. A conflict between Darwinian fitness and population fitness in Tribolium "competition" experiments. Genetics 62:413-419.

Dawson, P. S., and I. M. Lerner. 1962. Genetic variation and indeterminism in interspecific competition. Am. Natur. 96:379-380.

De Bach, P. 1966. The competitive displacement and coexistence principles. Ann. Rev. Entomol. 11:183-212.

De Benedictis, P. A. 1977. The meaning and measurement of frequency-dependent competition. Ecology 58:158-166.

De Witt, C. T. 1960. On competition. Versl. Landbouwkd. Onderz. 66.8: 1-82.

De Witt, C. T. 1971. On the modeling of competitive phenomena. pp. 269-281. IN Den Boer, P. J., and G. R. Gradwell (eds.), Proceedings of the Advanced Study Institute on Dynamics of Numbers in Populations. Centre for Agricultural Publishing and Documentation, Wageningen.

De Witt, C. T., P. G. Tow, and G. C. Ennik. 1966. Competition between legumes and grasses. Agricultural Research Report 687. Centre for Agricultural Publications and Documentation, Wageningen. 30 pp.

Fredrickson, A. G. 1977. Behavior of mixed cultures of microorganisms. Ann. Rev. Microbiol. 31:63-87.

Futuyma, D. J. 1970. Variation in genetic response to interspecific competition in laboratory populations of Drosophila. Am. Natur. 104:239-252.

Gilpin, M. E., and F. J. Ayala. 1976. Schoener's model and Drosophila competition. Theor. Popul. Biol. 9:12-14.

Gross, C. F., and R. R. Robinson. 1968. Competition between ladino clover seedlings and established orchardgrass in nutrient solution cultures. Agron. J. 60:512-514.

Harper, J. L. 1961. Approaches to the study of plant competition. pp. 1-39. IN Mechanisms in Biological Competition, Symposia of the Society for Experimental Biology XV. Academic Press, Inc., New York.

Harper, J. L. 1977. Population biology of plants. Academic Press, New York.

Harper, J. L., and I. H. McNaughton. 1962. The comparative biology of closely related species living in the same area. VII. Interference between individuals in pure and mixed populations of Papaver species. The New Phytol. 61:175-188.

Hendrick, P. W. 1972. Factors responsible for a change in interspecific competitive ability in Drosophila. Evolution 26:513-522.

Jackman, R. H., and M. C. H. Mouat. 1972. Competition between grass and clover for phosphate I. N. Z. J. Agric. Res. 15:653-666.

Jain, S. K. 1969. Comparative ecogenetics of two Avena species occurring in central California. Evol. Biol. 3:73-117.

King, C. E., and P. S. Dawson. 1972. Population biology and the Tribolium model. Evol. Biol. 5:133-227.

Le Cato, G. L. 1975. Interactions among four species of stored-product insects in corn: A multifactorial study. Ann. Entomol. Soc. of Am. 66(4):677-679.

Le Cato, G. L. 1975. Predation by red flour beetle on sawtoothed grain beetle. Environ. Entomol. 4(1):504-506.

Le Cato, G. L. 1978. Functional response of red flour beetles to density of cigarette beetles and the role of predation in population regulation. Environ. Entomol. 7(1):77-80.

Lerner, I. M., and F. K. Ho. 1961. Genotype and competitive ability of Tribolium species. Amer. Natur. 95:329-343.

Lerner, I. M., and E. R. Dempster. 1962. Indeterminism in interspecific competition. Proc. Nat. Acad. Sci. U.S.A. 48:821-826.

Leslie, P. H. 1958. A stochastic model for studying the properties of certain biological systems by numerical methods. Biometrika 45:16-31.

Leslie, P. H., T. Park, and D. Mertz. 1968. The effect of varying the initial numbers on the outcome of competition between two Tribolium species. J. Anim. Ecol. 37:9-23.

L'Heritier, P., and G. Teissier. 1937. Elimination des forms mutants dans les populations des drosophiles. Cas des drosophiles bar. C. R. Soc. Biol. (Paris) 124:880-882.

Longstaff, B. C. 1976. The dynamics of collembolan populations: Competitive relationships in an experimental system. Can. J. Zool. 54(6):948-962.

Meers, J. L. 1973. Growth of bacteria in mixed cultures. Microbiol. Ecol. pp. 136-181.

Merrell, D. J. 1951. Interspecific competition between Drosophila funebris and Drosophila melanogaster. Amer. Natur. 85:159-169.

Mertz, D. M. 1972. The Tribolium model and the mathematics of population growth. Ann. Rev. Ecol. Syst. 3:51-78.

Mertz, D. B., D. A. Cawthon, and T. Park. 1976. An experimental analysis of competitive indeterminacy in Tribolium. Proc. Nat. Acad. Sci. U.S.A. 73:1368-1372.

Miller, R. S. 1964. Interspecies competition in laboratory populations of Drosophila melanogaster and Drosophila simulans. The Am. Nat. 98(901):221-238.

Miller, R. S. 1967. Larval competition in Drosophila melanogaster and D. simulans. Ecology 75:132-148.

Moore, J. A. 1952. Competition between Drosophila melanogaster and Drosophila simulans. II. The improvement of competitive ability through selection. Genetics 38:813-817.

Moth, J. J., and J. S. F. Barker. 1977. Interspecific competition between Drosophila melanogaster and Drosophila simulans: Effects on adult density on adult viability. Genetica 47(3):203-218.

Neyman, J., T. Park, and E. L. Scott. 1958. Struggle for existence the tribolium model: Biological and statistical aspects. Gen. Syst. Yearbook 3:152-179.

Palmblad, I. G. 1968. Competition in experimental populations of weeds with emphasis on the regulation of population size. Ecology 49:26-34.

Park, T. 1948. Experimental studies of interspecies competition. I. Competition between populations of the flour beetles, Tribolium confusum and Tribolium castaneum Herbst. Ecol. Mono. 18:265-308.

Park, T. 1954. Experimental studies of interspecies competition. II. Temperature, humidity and competition in two species of Tribolium. Physiol. Zool. 27:177-238.

Park, T. 1957. Experimental studies of interspecies competition. II. Relation of initial species proportion to competitive outcome in populations of Tribolium. Physiol. Zool. 30:22-40.

Park, T. 1962. Beetles, competition and populations. Science 138:1369-1375.

Park, T., P. H. Leslie, and D. B. Mertz. 1964. Genetic strains and competition in populations of Tribolium. Physiol. Zool. 37:97-162.

Park, T., and M. Lloyd. 1955. Natural selection and the outcome of competition. Amer. Natur. 89:235-240.

Pimentel, D., E. H. Feinberg, P. W. Wood, and J. T. Hayes. 1965. Selection, spatial distribution, and the coexistence of competing fly species. The Am. Nat. 99(905):97-109.

Press, J. W., B. R. Flaherty, and G. L. Le Cato. 1974. Interactions among Tribolium castoneum (Coleoptera: Tenebrionidae), Cadra cautella (Lepidoptera: Pyrilidae) and Xylocoris flavipes (Hemiptera: Anthrocoridae). J. Ga Entomol. Soc. 9:101-103.

Raynal, D. J., and F. A. Bazzaz. 1975. Interference of winter annuals with Ambrosia artemesiifolia in early successional fields. Ecology 56:35-49.

Rennie, R. J., and E. L. Schmidt. 1977. Autecological and kinetic analysis of competition between strains of Nitrobacter in soils. Ecol. Bull. (Stockholm) 25:431-441.

Rice, E. L. 1971. Inhibition of nodulation of innoculated legumes by leaf leachates from pioneer plant species from abandoned fields. Am. J. Bot. 58:368-371.

Rice, E. L. 1974. Allelopathy. Academic Press, New York. 353 pp.

Rice, E. L. 1979. Allelopathy--An Update. Bot. Rev. 45:15-109.

Richmond, R. C., M. E. Gilpin, S. P. Salas, and F. J. Ayala. 1975. A search for emergent competitive phenomena: The dynamics of multispecies Drosophila systems. Ecology 56:709-714.

Sakai, K. I. 1961. Competitive ability in plants: Its inheritance and some related problems. pp. 245-263. IN Mechanisms in Biological Competition, Symposia of the Society of Experimental Biology XV. Academic Press, Inc., New York.

Schillinger, J. A., and R. C. Leffel. 1964. Persistence of ladino clover, Trifolium repens. L. Agron. J. 56:7-14.

Schreiber, M. M. 1967. A technique for studying weed competition in forage legume establishment. Weeds 15:1-4.

Seaton, A. P. C., and J. Antonovics. 1966. Population inter-relationships I. Heredity 22:19-33.

Shugart, H. H., Jr., and B. G. Blaylock. 1973. The niche variation hypothesis: An experimental study with Drosophila populations. Amer. Natur. 107:575-579.

Sokal, R. R., and R. L. Sullivan. 1963. Competition between mutant and wild-type house-fly strains at varying densities. Ecology 44(2): 314-322.

Sokoloff, A. 1955. Competition between sibling species of the Pseudoobscura subgroup of Drosophila. Ecol. Mon. 25:387-409.

Stern, W. R., and C. M. Donald. 1962. The influence of leaf area and radiation on the growth of clover in swards. Aust. J. Agric. Res. 13:615-623.

Stuckey, I. H. 1962. Factors affecting persistence of ladino white clover. Crop Sci. 2:173-174.

Suter, G. W. 1981. Methods for measuring effects of chemicals on terrestrial population interaction. IN Hammons, Anna S. (ed.), Ecotoxicological Test Systems: Proceedings of a Series of Workshops, ORNL-5709; EPA 560/6-81-004, Oak Ridge National Laboratory.

Torroja, E., and M. Almazan. 1973. Evolution of competiton between Drosophila hydei and D. simulans in a cage population. Genetics 73: 278-279.

Ullyett, G. C. 1950. Competition for food and allied phenomena in sheep-blowfly populations. Philos. Trans. R. Soc. London, Ser. B. 234:77-174.

Wallace, B. 1974. Studies in intra-and-interspecific competition in Drosophila. Ecology 55:227-244.

White, J., and J. L. Harper. 1970. Correlated changes in plant size and number in plant populations. J. Ecol. 58:467-485.

Wilkinson, S. R., and C. F. Gross. 1964. Competition for light, soil moisture, and nutrients during ladino clover establishment in orchardgrass sod. Agron. J. 56:389-392.

Wood, P. W. 1971. Coexistence of Competing Dipteran Species Musca domestica L. (Muscidae) and Phaenicia (Lucilia) sericata Meig. (Calliphoridae) in Laboratory Ecosystems. Ph.D. dissertation, Cornell University, Ithica, New York. 160 pp.

Wool, D. 1973. Size, productivity, age and competition in <u>Tribolium</u> populations subjected to long-term serial transfer. J. Anim. Ecol. 42:183-200.

Yoda, K., T. Kira, H. Ogawa, and H. Hozumi. 1963. Self-thinning in overcrowded pure stands under cultivated and natural conditions. J. Biol. Osaka City Univ. 14:107-129.

Young, A. M. 1970. Predation and abundance in populations of flour beetles. Ecology 51:602-619.

4.1.2 HERBIVORE--PLANT

Adams, J. B., and H. F. Van Emden. 1972. The biological properties of aphids and their host plant relationships. pp. 47-104. IN Van Emden, H. F. (ed.), Aphid Technology. Academic Press, New York.

Andison, H. 1940. The soft scale (<u>Coccus hesperidum</u>) investing holly on Vancouver Island. Proc. Entomol. Soc. B.C. 36:3-5.

Branson, T. F. 1971. Resistence of the grass tribe Maydeae to larvae of the western corn rootworm. Ann. Entomol. Soc. Amer. 64:861-863.

Capinera, J. L., and P. Barbosa. 1977. Influence of natural diet and larval density on gypsy moth, <u>Lymantria dispar</u> (Lepidoptera: Orgyiidae) egg mass characteristics. Can. Entomol. 109:1313-1318.

Chiu, C., and C. A. Kouskolekas. 1978. Laboratory rearing of tea scale. Ann. Entomol. Soc. Amer. 71:850-851.

Dickson, R. C., E. L. Laird, Jr., and G. R. Pesho. 1955. The spotted alfalfa aphid (yellow clover aphid on alfalfa). Hilgardia 24:93-118.

Dyer, M. I., and U. G. Bokhari. 1976. Plant-animal interactions: Studies of the effects of grasshoppers grazing on blue grama grass. Ecology 57:762-772.

Gilbert, L. E. 1979. Development of theory in the analysis of insect-plant interactions. pp. 117-154. IN Horn, D. J., G. R. Stairs, and R. D. Mitchell (eds.), Analysis of Ecological Systems. State U. Press, Columbus, Ohio.

Graham, H. M. 1959. Effect of temperature and humidity on the biology of <u>Therioaphis maculata</u> (Buckton). Univ. Calif. Publ. Entomol. 16: 47-80.

Hoffman, J. H., and V. C. Moran. 1977. Pre-release studies on *Tucumania tapiacola* Dyar (Lepidoptera: Pyridae), a potential biocontrol agent for jointed cactus. J. Entomol. Soc. South Afr. 40:205-209.

Hough, J. A., and D. Pimentel. 1978. Influence of haste foliage on development, survival and fecundity of the gypsy moth. Environ. Entomol. 7:97-102.

McMillian, W. W., K. J. Starks, and M. C. Bowman. 1967. Resistance in corn to the corn earworm, *Heliothis zea* and the fall armyworm, *Spodoptera frugiperda* (Lepidoptera: Noctuidae). Part I. Larval feeding responses. Ann. Entomol. Soc. Am. 60:871-873.

Ortman, E. E., and T. F. Branson. 1976. Growth pouches for studies of host plant resistance to larvae of corn rootworms. J. Econ. Entomol. 69:380-382.

Saakyan-Baranova, A. A. 1964. On the biology of the soft scale *Coccus hesperidum* L. (Homoptera: Coccoidea). Entomol. Rev. 1:135-147.

Starks, K. J., and W. W. McMillian. 1967. Resistance in corn to the corn earworm and fall armyworm. Part II: Types of field resistance to the corn earworm. J. Econ. Entomol. 60:920-923.

Van Emden, H. F., and M. J. Way. 1973. Host plants in the population dynamics of insects. pp. 181-199. IN Van Emden, H. F. (ed.), Insect/Plant Relationships, Symposium of the R. Entomol. Soc. of London: Number Six. Blackwell Scientific Publications, Oxford.

Waiss, A. C., Jr., B. G. Chan, and C. A. Elliger. 1977. Host plant resistance to insects. IN Hedin, P. A. (ed.), Host Plant Resistance to Pests, ACS Symposium Series 62. American Chemical Society, Washington, D.C.

Windle, P. N., and E. H. Franz. 1979. The effects of insect parasitism on plant competition: Greenbugs and barley. Ecology 60(3):521-529.

Williams, M. L., and M. Kosztarab. 1972. Morphology and systematics of the Coccidae of Virginia, with notes on their biology (Homoptera: Coccidae). Virg. Polyt. Inst. and State Univ. Res. Bull. 74. 215 pp.

4.1.3 PREDATOR-PREY

Bakker, K., H. J. P. Eijsackers, J. C. van Lenteren, and E. Meelis. 1972. Some models describing the distribution of eggs of the parasite *Pseudeucoila* (Hym., Cynip.) over its hosts, larvae of *Drosophila melanogaster*. Oecologia 10:29-57.

Benson, J. F. 1960. Population dynamics of *Bracon hebetor* Say (Hymenoptera: Braconidae) and *Ephestia cautella* (Walker) (Lepidoptera: Phycitidae) in a laboratory ecosystem. J. Anim. Ecol. 43:71-86.

Burnett, T. 1949. The effect of temperature on an insect host-parasite population. Ecology 30:113-134.

Burnett, T. 1960. Effects of initial densities and periods of infestation on the growth-forms of a host and parasite population. Can. J. Zool. 38:1063-1077.

Burnett, T. 1967. Aspects of the interaction between a chalcid parasite and its aleurodid host. Can. J. Zool. 45:539-578.

Burnett, T. 1970. Effect of simulated natural temperatures on an acararine predator-prey population. Physiol. Zool. 43:155-165.

Burnett, T. 1970. Effect of temperature on a greenhouse acarine predator-prey population. Can. J. Zool. 48:555-562.

Chabora, P. C., and D. Pimentel. 1970. Patterns of evolution in parasite-host systems. Ann. Entomol. Soc. Amer. 63:479-486.

Chant, D. A. 1961. An experiment in biological control of *Tetranychus telarius* (L.) (Acarina: Tetranychidae) in a greenhouse using the predacious mite *Phytoseiulus persimilis* Athias-Henriol (Phytoseiidae). Can. Entomol. 93:437-443.

Collyer, E. 1958. Some insectary experiments with predacious mites to determine their effect on the development of *Metatetranychus ulmi* (Koch) populations. Entomol. Exp. Appl. 1:138-146.

Collyer, E. 1964. The effect of an alternative food supply on the relationship between two *typhlodromus* species and *Panonychus ulmi* (Koch) (Acarina). Entomol. Exp. Appl. 7:120-124.

Cornell, H., and D. Pimentel. 1978. Switching in the parasitoid *Nasonia vitripennis* and its effects on host competition. Ecology 59:297-308.

Craig, R. B. 1978. An analysis of the predatory behavior of the loggerhead shrike. Auk 95:221-234.

Danso, S. K. A., S. O. Keya, and M. Alexander. 1975. Protoza and the decline of Rhizobium populations added to soil. Can. J. Microbiol. 21:884-895.

De Bach, P., and C. B. Huffaker. 1971. Experimental techniques for evaluation of the effectiveness of natural enemies. pp. 113-140. IN Huffaker, C. B. (ed.), Biological Control. Plenum Press, New York.

De Bach, P., and H. S. Smith. 1941. The effect of host density on the rate of reproduction of entomophagous parasites. J. Econ. Entomol. 34:741-745.

De Telegdy-Kovats, L. 1932. The growth and respiration of bacteria in sand cultures in the presence and absence of protozoa. Ann. Appl. Biol. 19:65-86.

Dickerson, W. A., et al. 1980. Arthropod Species in Culture. Entomol. Soc. of Am., Hyattsville, Md. 93 pp.

Dixon, A. F. G. 1970. Factors limiting the effectiveness of the coccinellid beetle, Adalia bipunctata (L.), as a predator of the sycamore aphid, Drepanosiphon platanoides (Schr.). J. Anim. Ecol. 39:739-751.

Doutt, R. L., and P. De Bach. 1964. Some biological control concepts and questions. Chap. 5. IN De Bach, P. (ed.), Biological Control of Insect Pests and Weeds. Reinhold Publ. Co., New York. 844 pp.

Finney, G. L., B. Puttler, and L. Dawson. 1960. Rearing of three spotted alfalfa aphid hymenopterous parasites for mass release. J. Econ. Entomol. 53(4):655-659.

Flanders, S. E. 1968. Mechanisms of population homeostasis in Anagasta ecosystems. Hilgardia 39:367-404.

Flanders, S. E., and M. E. Badgley. 1963. Prey-predator interactions in self-balanced laboratory populations. Hilgardia 35(8):145-183.

Force, D. C. 1970. Competition among four hymenopterous parasites of an endemic insect host. Ann. Entomol. Soc. of Am. 63:1675-1688.

Force, D. C. 1974. Ecology of insect host-parasitoid communities. Science 184:624-632.

Force, D. C., and P. S. Messenger. 1964. Duration of development, generation time, and longevity of three hymenopterous parasites of Therioaphis maculata, reared at various constant temperatures. Ann. of the Entomol. Soc. of Am. 57(4):405-413.

Force, D. C., and P. S. Messenger. 1964. Fecundity, reproductive rates and innate capacity for increase of three parasites of Therioaphis maculata (Buckton). Ecology 45:706-715.

Force, D. C., and P. S. Messenger. 1965. Laboratory studies of competition among three parasites of the spotted aphid Thirioaphis maculata (Buckton). Ecology 46:853-859.

Gardner, B. T. 1966. Hunger and characteristics of the prey in the hunting behavior of salticid spiders. J. Comp. Physiol. Psychol. 62(3):475-478.

Habte, M., and M. Alexander. 1975. Protozoa as agents responsible for the decline of Xanthomonas campestris in soil. Appl. Microbiol. 29(2):159-164.

Habte, M., and M. Alexander. 1977. Further evidence for the regulation of bacterial populations in soil by protozoa. Arch. Microbiol. 113: 181-183.

Habte, M., and M. Alexander. 1978. Mechanisms of persistence of low numbers of bacteria preyed upon by protozoa. Soil Biol. Biochem. 10:1-6.

Habte, M., and M. Alexander. 1978. Protozoan density and the coexistence of protozoan predators and bacterial prey. Ecology 59:140-146.

Hardman, J. M., and A. L. Turnbull. 1974. The interaction of spatial heterogeneity, predator competition and the functional response to prey density in a laboratory system of wolf spiders (Araneae: Lycosidae) and fruit flies (Diptera: Drosophilidae). J. Anim. Ecol. 43:155-171.

Harpaz, I. 1955. Bionomics of Therioaphis maculata (Buckton) in Israel. J. Econ. Entomol. 48:668-671.

Harris, R. L., and L. M. Oliver. 1979. Predation of Philonthus flavolimbatus on the horn fly. Environ. Entomol. 8:259-260.

Hassell, M. P. 1971. Parasite behavior as a factor contributing to the stability of insect host-parasite interactions. pp. 366-378. IN Den Boer, P. J., and G. R. Gradwell (eds.), Proceedings of the Advanced Study Institute on Dynamics of Numbers in Populations. Centre for Agricultural Publishing and Documentation, Wageningen.

Hassell, M. P., and C. B. Huffaker. 1969. Regulatory processes and population cyclicity in laboratory populations of Anagasta kuhniella (Zeller) (Lepidoptera: Phycitidae). III. The development of population models. Res. Popul. Ecol. 11:186-210.

Haynes, D. L., and P. Sisojevic. 1966. Predatory behavior of Philodromus rufus Walckenaer (Araneae: Thomisidae). The Can. Entomol. 98(2): 113-133.

Helgesen, R. G., and M. J. Tauber. 1974. Biological control of greenhouse whitefly, Trialeurodes vaporariorum (Aleyrodidae: Homoptera), on short-term crops by manipulating biotic and abiotic factors. The Can. Entomol. 106:1175-1188.

Helgesen, R. G., and M. J. Tauber. 1974. Pirimicarb, an aphicide nontoxic to three entomophagous arthropods. Environ. Entomol. 3:99-101.

Henis, Y., A. Ghaffar, and R. Baker. 1978. Integrated control of Rhizoctonia solani damping-off of radish: Effect of successive plantings, PCNB, and Trichoderma harzianum on pathogen and disease. Phytopathology 68:900-907.

Herbert, H. J. 1962. Influence of Typhlodromus (T.) Pyri Scheuten on the development of Bryobia arborea M. & A. populations in the greenhouse. The Can. Entomol. 94:870-873.

Holling, C. S. 1959. The components of predation as revealed by a study of small-mammal predation of the European pine sawfly. Can. Entomol. 91:293-320.

Holling, C. S. 1966. The functional response of invertebrate predators to prey density. Mem. Entomol. Soc. Can. 48:1-88.

Huffaker, C. B. 1958. Experimental studies on predation: Dispersion factors and predator-prey oscillations. Hilgardia 27(14):343-383.

Huffaker, C. B. 1971. The phenomenon of predation and its roles in nature. pp. 327-343. IN Den Boer, P. J., and G. R. Cradwell (eds.), Dynamics of Populations, Proceedings of the Advanced Study Institute on Dynamics of Numbers in Populations. Centre for Agricultural Publishing and Documentation, Wageningen.

Huffaker, C. B., and C. E. Kennett. 1956. Experimental studies on predation: Predation and cyclamen-mite populations on strawberries in California. Hilgardia 26(4):191-222.

Huffaker, C. B., C. E. Kennett, B. Matsumoto, and E. G. White. 1973. Some parameters in the role of enemies in the natural control of insect abundance. pp. 59-75. IN Southwood, T. R. E. (ed.), Insect Abundance. Blackwell Scientific Publications, Oxford.

Huffaker, C. B., P. S. Messenger, and P. De Bach. 1971. The natural enemy component in natural control and the theory of biological control. pp. 16-67. Huffaker, C. B. (ed.), Biological Control. Plenum Press, New York.

Huffaker, C. B., K. P. Shea, and S. G. Herman. 1963. Experimental studies on predation: Complex dispersion and levels of food in an acarine predator-prey interaction. Hilgardia 34(9):305-330.

Hussey, N. W., and W. J. Parr. 1965. Observations on the control of Tetranychus urticae Koch on cucumbers by the predatory mite Phytoseiulus riegeli Dosse. Entomol. Exp. Appl. 8:271-281.

McClanahan, R. J. 1970. Intergrated control of greenhouse whitefly on cucumbers. J. Econ. Entomol. 63:599-601.

McMurtry, J. A., and G. T. Scriven. 1968. Studies on predator-prey interactions between Amblyseius hibisci and Oligonychus punicae: Effects of host-plant conditioning and limited quantities of an alternate food. Ann. Entomol. Soc. of Am. 61:393-397.

Messenger, P. S. 1964. Use of life tables in a bioclimatic study of an experimental aphid-braconid wasp host-parasite system. Ecology 45: 119-131.

Messenger, P. S., and D. C. Force. 1963. An experimental host-parasite system: Therioaphis maculata (Buckton)-Praon palitans Muesebeck (Homoptera: Aphidae: Hymenoptera: Bracomidae). Ecology 44:532-540.

Murdoch, W. W., and J. R. Marks. 1973. Predation by coccinellid beetles: Experiments on switching. Ecology 54:160-167.

Nechols, J. R., and M. J. Tauber. 1977. Age-specific interaction between the greenhouse whitefly and Encarsia formosa: Influence of host on the parasite's oviposition and development. Environ. Entomol. 6:143-149.

Nechols, J. R., and M. J. Tauber. 1977. Age-specific interaction between the greenhouse whitefly and Encarsia formosa: Influence of the parasite on host development. Environ. Entomol. 6:207-210.

Olson, D., and D. Pimentel. 1974. Evolution of resistance in a host population to attacking parasite. Environ. Entomol. 3:621-624.

Pimentel, D. 1968. Population regulation and genetic feedback. Science 159:1432-1437.

Pimentel, D., S. A. Levin, and D. Olson. 1978. Coevolution and the stability of exploiter-victim systems. Am. Nat. 112:119-125.

Pimentel, D., W. P. Nagel, and J. L. Madden. 1963. Space-time structure of the environment and the survival of parasite-host systems. The Am. Nat. 97:141-167.

Pimentel, D., and F. A. Stone. 1968. Evolution and population ecology of parasite-host systems. Can. Entomol. 100:655-662.

Roper, M. M., and K. C. Marshall. 1978. Effects of a clay mineral on microbial predation and parasitism of *Escherichia coli*. Microbiol. Ecology 4:279-289.

Salt, G. 1934. Experimental studies in insect parasitism. II. Superparasitism. Proc. Royal Soc. London 114:455-476.

Salt, G. 1935. Experimental studies in insect parasitism. III. Host selection. Proc. Royal Soc. London 117:413-435.

Scherff, R. H. 1973. Control of bacterial blight of soybean by *Bdellovibrio bacteriovorus*. Phytopathology 63:400-402.

Schlinger, E. I., and J. C. Hall. 1959. A synopsis of the biologies of three important parasites of the spotted alfalfa aphid. J. Econ. Entomol. 52:154-157.

Schlinger, E. I., and J. C. Hall. 1960. The biology, behavior, and morphology of *Praon palitans* Muesebeck, an internal parasite of the spotted alfalfa aphid, *Therioaphis maculata* (Buckton) (Hymenoptera: Braconidae, Aphidiinae). Ann. Entomol. Soc. Am. 53:144-160.

Schlinger, E. I., and J. C. Hall. 1961. The biology, behavior, and morphology of *Trioxys utilis*, an internal parasite of the spotted alfalfa aphid, *Therioaphis maculata* (Hymenoptera: Braconidae, Aphidiinae). Ann. Entomol. Soc. Am. 54:34-45.

Starr, M. P., and N. L. Baigent. 1966. Parasitic interaction of *Bdellovibris bacteriovorus* with other bacteria. J. Bacteriol. 91: 2006-2017.

Tauber, M. J., and R. G. Helgeson. 1974. Biological control of whiteflies in greenhouse crops. N.Y. Food Life Sci. 7:13-16.

Ullyett, G. C. 1949. Distribution of progeny by *Cryptus inornatus* Pratt (Hymenoptera: Ichneumonidae). Can. Entomol. 81:285-296.

Ullyett, G. C. 1949. Distribution of progeny by *Chelonus texanus* Cress. (Hymenoptera: Braconidae). Can. Entomol. 81:25-44.

Utida, S. 1950. On the equilibrium state of the interacting population of an insect and its parasite. Ecology 31:165-175.

Utida, S. 1957. Cyclic fluctuations of population density intrinsic to the host-parasite system. Ecology 38:442-449.

Utida, S. 1957. Population fluctuation, an experimental and theoretical approach. Cold Springs Harbor Symposia on Quantitative Biology 22: 139-151.

Van de Vrie, M. 1962. The influence of spray chemicals on predatory and phytophagous mites on apple trees in laboratory and field trials in the Netherlands. Entomophaga 3(3):243-250.

White, E. G., and C. B. Huffaker. 1969. Regulatory processes and population cyclicity in laboratory populations of Anagasta kuhniella (Zeller) (Lepidoptera: Phycitidae). I. Competition for food and predation. Res. Popul. Ecol. 11:57-83.

White, E. G., and C. B. Huffaker. 1969. Regulatory processes and population cyclicity in laboratory populations of Anagasta kuhniella (Zeller) (Lepidoptera: Phycitidae). II. Parasitism, predation, competition and protective cover. Res. Popul. Ecol. 11:150-185.

4.1.5 SYMBIOSIS

Ambler, J. R., and J. L. Young. 1977. Techniques for determining root length infected by vesicular-arbuscular mycorrhizae. Soil Sci. Soc. Am. J. 41:551-555.

Backman, P. A., and E. M. Clark. 1977. Effect of carbofuran and other pesticides on vesicular-arbuscular mycorrhizae in peanuts. Nematropica 7:13-18.

Bird, G. W., J. R. Rich, and S. U. Glover. 1974. Increased endomycorrhizae of cotton roots in soil treated with nematocides. Phytopathol. 64:48-51.

Carlyle, R. E., and J. D. Thorpe. 1947. Some effects of ammonium and sodium 2,4-dichlorophenoxyacetates on legumes and the Rhizobium bacteria. J. Am. Soc. Agron. pp. 929-936.

Carney, J. L., H. E. Garrett, and H. G. Hedrick. 1978. Influence of air pollutant gases on oxygen uptake of pine roots with selected mycorrhizae. Phytopathology 68:1160-1163.

Ferry, B. W., M. S. Baddeleym, and D. L. Hawksworth. 1973. Air Pollution and Lichens. The Athlone Press of the University of London. 389 pp.

Fisher, D. J. 1976. Effects of some fungicides on Rhizobium trifolii and its symbiotic relationship with white clover. Pestic. Sci. 7:10-18.

Fisher, D. J., A. L. Hayes, and C. A. Jones. 1978. Effects of some surfactant fungicides on Rhizobium trifolii and its symbiotic relationship with white clover. Ann. of Appl. Biol. 90(1):73-84.

Grossbard, E. 1970. Effect of herbicides on the symbiotic relationship between Rhizobium trifolii and white clover. pp. 47-59. IN Symposium on White Clover Research, Queens Univ. of Belfast, 1969.

Guttay, A. J. R. 1976. Impact of deicing salts upon the endomycorrhizae of roadside sugar maples. Soil Sci. Soc. Amer. J. 40:952-954.

Halliday, J., and J. S. Pate. 1976. The acetylene reduction assay as a means of studying nitrogen fixation in white clover under sward and laboratory conditions. J. Brit. Grassland Soc. 31:29-35.

Hawksworth, D. L., and F. Rose. 1976. Lichens as Pollution Monitors. Edward Arnold, London. 60 pp.

Iyer, J. G., and S. A. Wilde. 1965. Effect of vapam biocide on the growth of red pine seedlings. J. Forestry 63:703-704.

Kochhar, M., U. Blum, and R. A. Reinert. 1980. Effects of O^3 and (or) fescue on ladino clover: Interactions. Can. J. Bot. 58(2):241-249.

Kormanik, P. P., W. C. Bryan, and R. C. Schultz. 1980. Procedures and equipment for staining large numbers of plant root samples for endomycorrhizal assay. Can. J. Microbiol. In press.

Kulkarni, J. H., J. S. Sardeshpande, and D. J. Bagyaraj. 1974. Effect of four soil-applied insecticides on symbiosis of Rhizobium with Arachis hypogaea Linn. Plant Soil 40(1):169-172.

Letchworth, M. B., and U. Blum. 1977. Effects of acute ozone exposure on growth, nodulation and nitrogen content of ladino clover. Environ. Pollut. 14:303-312.

Lin, S., B. R. Funke, and J. T. Schulz. 1972. Effects of some organophosphate and carbamate insecticides on nitrification and legume growth. Plant Soil 37:489-496.

Manning, W. J., W. A. Feder, and P. M. Papia. 1972. Influence of long-term low levels of ozone and benomyl on growth and nodulation of pinto bean plants. Phytopathology 62(5):497.

Marx, D. H. 1969. Antagonism of mycorrhizal fungi to root pathogenic fungi and soil bacteria. Phytopathology 59:153-163.

Marx, D. H., W. G. Morris, and J. G. Mexal. 1978. Growth and ectomycorrhizal development of loblolly pine seedlings in fumigated and nonfumigated soil infested with different fungal symbionts. Forest Sci. 24:193-203.

Menge, J. A., E. L. V. Johnson, and V. Minassian. 1979. Effect of heat treatment and three pesticides upon the growth and reproduction of the mycorrhizal fungus Glomus fasciculatus. The New Phytol. 82(2): 473-480.

O'Bannon, J. H., and S. Nemec. 1978. Influence of soil pesticides on vesicular-arbuscular mycorrhizae in citrus soil. Nematropica 8:56-61.

Pareek, R. P., and A. C. Gaur. 1970. Effect of dichloro diphenyl trichloro-ethane (DDT) on symbiosis of Rhizobium sp. with Phaseolus aureus (Green Gram). Plant Soil 33:297-304.

Selim, K. G., S. A. Z. Mahmoud, and M. T. El-Mokadem. 1970. Effect of dieldrin and lindane on the growth and nodulation of Vicia faba. Plant Soil 33:325-329.

Smith, C. R., B. R. Funke, and J. T. Schulz. 1978. Effects of insecticides on acetylene reduction by alfalfa, red clover and sweetclover. Soil Biol. and Biochem. 10(6):463-466.

Tu, C. M. 1977. Effects of pesticide seed treatments on Rhizobium japonicum and its symbiotic relationship with soybean. Bull. Environ. Contam. Toxicol. 18(2):190-199.

4.2 ECOSYSTEMS

Gillett, J. W., and J. M. Witt (eds.). 1979. Terrestrial Microcosms. Proceedings of the Workshop on Terrestrial Microcosms, Symposium on Terrestrial Microcosms and Environmental Chemistry. NSF/RA 79-0034. National Science Foundation, Washington, D.C. 35 pp.

Harris, W. F. (ed.). 1980. Microcosms as potential screening tools for evaluating transport and effects of toxic substances: Final report. ORNL/EPA-4. Oak Ridge National Laboratory, Oak Ridge, Tennessee. 382 pp.

Suter, G. W. 1981. Methods for measuring effects of chemicals or terrestrial ecosystem properties. IN Hammons, Anna S. (ed.), Ecotoxicological Test Systems: Proceedings of a Series of Workshops, ORNL-5709; EPA 560/6-81-004, Oak Ridge National Laboratory.

Witt, J. M., and J. W. Gillett. 1979. Terrestrial microcosms and environmental chemistry. NSF/RA 79-0026. National Science Foundation, Washington, D.C. 147 pp.

4.2.1 PARAMETERS

Coughtrey, P. J., C. H. Jones, M. H. Martin, and S. W. Shales. 1979. Litter accumulation in woodlands contaminated by Pb, Zn, Cd and Cu. Oecologia (Berlin) 39:51-60.

Jackson, D. R., and A. P. Watson. 1977. Disruption of nutrient pools and transport of heavy metals in a forested watershed near a lead smelter. J. Environ. Qual. 6:331-338.

4.2.2 TEST COMPONENTS

Ausmus, B. S., and E. G. O'Neill. 1978. Comparison of carbon dynamics of three microcosm substrates. Soil Biol. Biochem. 10:425-429.

Draggan, S. 1979. Effects of substrate type and arsenic dosage level on arsenic behavior in grassland microcosms. Part I: Preliminary results on ^{74}As as transport. pp. 102-110. IN Witt, J. M., and J. W. Gillett (eds.), Terrestrial Microcosms and Environmental Chemistry. NSF/RA 79-0026. National Science Foundation, Washington, D.C.

4.2.4 SIZE

Shirazi, M. A. 1979. Development of scaling criteria for terrestrial microcosms. EPA-600 13-79-017. U.S. Environmental Protection Agency, Corvallis, Oregon.

4.2.5 SYNTHETIC SYSTEMS

Anderson, R. V., D. C. Coleman, C. V. Cole, E. T. Elliott, and J. F. McClellan. 1979. The use of soil microcosms in evaluating bacteriophogic nematode response to other organisms and effects on nutrient cycling. Int. J. Environ. Studies 13:175-182.

Anderson, R. V., E. T. Elliott, J. F. McClellan, D. C. Coleman, C. V. Cole, and H. W. Hunt. 1978. Trophic interactions in soils as they affect energy and nutrient dynamics. III. Biotic interactions of bacteria, amoebae, and nematodes. Microbiol. Ecol. 4:361-371.

Atlas, R. M., D. Pramer, and R. Bartha. 1978. Assessment of pesticide effects on non-target soil microorganisms. Soil Biol. Biochem. 10: 231-239.

Bartha, R., R. P. Lanzilotta, and D. Pramer. 1967. Stability and effects of some pesticides in soil. Applied Microbiol. 15:67-75.

Bartha, R., and D. Pramer. 1965. Features of a flask and method of measuring the persistence and biological effects of pesticides in soil. Soil Sci. 100:68-70.

Beall, M. L., Jr., R. G. Nash, and P. C. Kearney. 1976. Agroecosystem--A laboratory model ecosystem to simulate field conditions for monitoring pesticides. pp. 790-793. Proc. of EPA Conf. on Environ. Modeling and Simulation. April 19-22, Cincinnati, Oh.

Bond, H., B. Lighthart, R. Shimabuku, and L. Russell. 1976. Some effects of cadmium on coniferous forest soil and litter microcosms. Soil Sci. 121(5):278-287.

Bond, H., B. Lighthart, and R. Volk. 1979. The use of soil/litter microcosms with and without added pollutants to study certain components of the decomposer community. pp. 111-123. Witt, J. M., and J. W. Gillett (eds.), Terrestrial Microcosms and Environmental Chemistry. NSF/RA 79-0026. National Science Foundation, Washington, D.C.

Cole, C. V., E. T. Elliott, H. W. Hunt, and D. C. Coleman. 1978. Trophic interactions in soils as they affect energy and nutrient dynamics. V. Phosphorus transformations. Microbiol. Ecol. 4:381-387.

Cole, L. K., and R. L. Metcalf. 1979. Predictive environmental toxicology of pesticides in the air, soil, water and biota of terrestrial model ecosystems. pp. 57-73. IN Witt, J. M., and J. W. Gillett (eds.), Terrestrial Microcosms and Environmental Chemistry. NSF/RA 79-0026 National Science Foundation, Washington, D.C.

Cole, L. K., R. L. Metcalf, and J. R. Sanborn. 1976. Environmental fate of insecticides in terrestrial model ecosystem. Int. J. Environ. Stud. 10:7-14.

Cole, L. K., J. R. Sanborn, and R. L. Metcalf. 1976. Inhibition of corn growth by aldrin and the insecticides fate in the soil, air, crop and wildlife of a terrestrial model ecosystem. Environ. Entomol. 5: 583-589.

Coleman, D. C., R. V. Anderson, C. V. Cole, E. T. Elliott, L. Woods, and M. K. Campion. 1978. Trophic interactions in soils as they affect energy and nutrient dynamics. IV. Flows of metabolic and biomass carbon. Microbiol. Ecol. 4:373-380.

Coleman, D. C., C. V. Cole, R. V. Anderson, M. Blaha, M. K. Campion, M. Clarholm, E. T. Elliott, H. W. Hunt, B. Shaefer, and J. Sinclair. 1977. An analysis of rhizosphere-saprophage interactions in terrestrial ecosystems. Ecol. Bull. (Stockholm) 25:299-309.

Coleman, D. C., C. V. Cole, H. W. Hunt, and D. A. Klein. 1978. Trophic interactions in soils as they affect energy and nutrient dynamics. I. Introduction. Microbiol. Ecol. 4:345-349.

Cullimore, D. R. 1971. Interaction between herbicides and soil micro-organisms. Residue Rev. 35:65-80.

Domsch, K. H. 1970. Effects of fungicides on microbial populations in soil. pp. 42-46. IN Pesticides in the Soil: Ecology, Degradation and Movement. Int. Symp. on Pesticides in the Soil. Michigan State University, East Lansing.

Domsch, K. H., and W. Paul. 1974. Simulation and experimental analysis of the influence of herbicides on soil nitrification. Arch. Microbiol. 97:283-301.

Elliott, E. T., C. V. Cole, D. C. Coleman, R. V. Anderson, H. W. Hunt, J. F. McClellan. 1979. Amoebal growth in soil microcosms: A model system of C,N, and P trophic dynamics. Int. J. Environ. Stud. 13:169-174.

Eno, C. F., and P. H. Everett. 1977. Effects of soil applications of 10 chlorinated hydrocarbon insecticides on soil microorganisms and the growth of stringless black valentine beans. J. Environ. Qual. 6(1):235-238.

Ghiorse, W. C., and M. Alexander. 1977. Effect of nitrogen dioxide on nitrate oxidation and nitrate-oxidizing populations in soil. Soil Biol. Biochem. 9:353-355.

Gile, J. D., and J. W. Gillett. 1979. Fate of ^{14}C-dieldrin in a simulated terrestrial ecosystem. Arch. Environ. Contam. Toxicol. 8:107-124.

Gile, J. D., and J. W. Gillett. 1979. Fate of selected fungicides in a terrestrial laboratory ecosystem. J. Agric. Food Chem. 27:1159-1164.

Gile, J. D., and J. W. Gillett. 1979. Terrestrial microcosm chamber evaluations of substitute chemicals. pp. 75-85. IN Witt, J. M., and J. W. Gillett (eds.), Terrestrial Microcosms and Environmental Chemistry. NSF/RA 79-0026. National Science Foundation, Washington, D.C.

Gillett, J. W., and J. D. Gile. 1976. Pesticide fate in terrestrial laboratory ecosystems. Int. J. Environ. Stud. 10:15-22.

Greaves, M. P., H. A. Davies, J. A. P. Marsh, and G. I. Wingfield. 1976. Herbicides and soil microorganisms. Crit. Rev. Microbiol. 5(1): 1-38.

Herzberg, M. A., D. A. Klein, and D. C. Coleman. 1978. Trophic interactions in soils as they affect energy and nutrient dynamics. II. Physiological responses of selected rhizosphere bacteria. Microbiol. Ecol. 4:351-359.

Jenkinson, D. S., and D. S. Powlson. 1976. The effects of biocidal treatments on metabolism in soil. I. Fumigation with chloroform. Soil Biol. Biochem. 8:167-177.

Johnen, B. G., and E. A. Drew. 1977. Ecological effects of pesticides on soil microorganisms. Soil Sci. 123(5):319-324.

Klein, D. A. 1977. Seasonal carbon flow and decomposer parameter relationships in a semiarid grassland soil. Ecology 58(1):184-190.

Klein, D. A., and E. M. Molise. 1975. Ecological ramifications of silver iodide nucleating agent accumulation in a semi-arid grassland environment. J. Appl. Meteorol. 14:673-680.

Kudeyarov, V. N., and D. S. Jenkinson. 1975. The effects of biocidal treatments on metabolism in soil. VI. Fumigation with carbon disulphide. Soil Biol. Biochem. 8:375-378.

Labeda, D. P., and M. Alexander. 1978. Effects of SO_2 and NO_2 on nitrification in soil. J. Environ. Qual. 7:523-526.

Lichtenstein, E. P. 1979. Fate of pesticides in a soil-plant microcosm. pp. 95-101. Witt, J. M., and J. W. Gillett (eds.), Terrestrial Microcosms and Environmental Chemistry. NSF/RA 79-0026. National Science Foundation, Washington, D.C.

Lichtenstein, E. P., T. W. Fuhremann, and K. R. Schulz. 1974. Translocation and metabolism of [^{14}C] phorate as affected by percolating water in a model soil-plant ecosystem. J. Agric. Food Chem. 22:991-996.

Lichtenstein, E. P., T. W. Fuhreman, K. R. Schulz, and R. F. Skrentny. 1967. Effect of detergents and inorganic salts in water on the persistence and movement of insecticides in soils. J. Econ. Entomol. 60:1714-1721.

Lichtenstein, E. P., K. R. Schulz, and T. T. Liang. 1977. Fate of fresh and aged soil residues of the insecticide (^{14}C)-N-2596 in a soil-corn-water ecosystem. J. Econ. Entomol. 70:169-175.

Lighthart, B., and H. Bond. 1976. Design and preliminary results from soil/litter microcosms. Int. J. Environ. Stud. 10:51-58.

Lighthart, B., H. Bond, and M. Ricard. 1977. Trace element research using coniferous forest soil/litter microcosms. EPA-600/3-77-091. U.S. Environmental Protection Agency, Corvallis, Ore. 51 pp.

Lu, Po-Yung, R. L. Metcalf, and E. M. Carlson. 1978. Environmental fate of five radiolabled coal conversion by-products evaluated in a laboratory model ecosystem. Environ. Health Perspect. 24:201-208.

Lu, Po-Yung, R. L. Metcalf, and L. K. Cole. 1978. The environmental fate of ^{14}C-pentachlorophenol in laboratory model ecosystems. pp. 53-63. IN Rango-Rao, K. (ed.), Pentachlorophenol: Chemistry, Pharmacology and Environmental Toxicology, Plenum Press, N.Y.

Lu, Po-Yung, R. L. Metcalf, A. S. Hirwe, and J. W. Williams. 1975. Evaluation of environmental distribution and fate of hexachlorocyclopentadiene, chlordene, heptachlor, and heptachlor epoxide in a laboratory model ecosystem. J. Agric. Food Chem. 23:967-973.

Metcalf, R. L. 1977. Model ecosystem approach to insecticide degradation: A critique. Ann. Rev. Entomol. 22:241-261.

Metcalf, R. L. 1977. Model ecosystem studies of bioconcentration and biodegradation of pesticides. Environ. Sci. Res. 10:127-144.

Metcalf, R. L., L. K. Cole, S. G. Wood, D. J. Mandel, and M. L. Milbrath. 1979. Design and evaluation of a terrestrial model ecosystem for evaluation of substitute pesticide chemicals. EPA-600/3-79-004. U.S. Environmental Protection Agency, Corvallis, Ore. 20 pp.

Metcalf, R. L., I. P. Kapoor, P.-Y. Lu, C. K. Schuth, and P. Sherman. 1973. Model ecosystem studies of the environmental fate of six organochloride pesticides. Environ. Health Perspect. 4:35-44.

Metcalf, R. L., G. K. Sangha, and I. P. Kapoor. 1971. Model ecosystem for the evaluation of pesticide biodegradability and ecological magnification. Environ. Sci. Tech. 5(8):709-713.

Nash, R. G., and M. L. Beall, Jr. 1979. A microagroecosystem to monitor the environmental fate of pesticides. pp. 86-94. IN Witt, J. M., and J. W. Gillett (eds.), Terrestrial Microcosms and Environmental Chemistry. NSF/RA 79-0026. National Science Foundation, Washington, D.C.

Nash, R. G., M. L. Beall, Jr., and W. G. Harris. 1977. Toxaphene and 1,1,1-trichloro-2,2-bis(p-chlorophenyl) ethane (DDT) losses from cotton in an agroecosystem chamber. J. Agric. Food Chem. 25(2): 336-341.

Odum, H. T., and A. Lugo. 1970. Metabolism of forest-floor microcosms. pp. 135-156. IN Odum, H. T. (ed.), Tropical Rain Forest. U.S. Atomic Energy Commission, Washington, D.C.

Parr, J. F. 1974. Effects of pesticides on micro-organisms in soil and water. pp. 315-340. IN Guenzi, W. D. (ed), Pesticides in Soil and Water. Soil Science Society of America, Inc., Madison, Wisc.

Patton, B. C., and M. Witkamp. 1967. Systems analysis of ^{134}cesium kinetics in terrestrial microcosms. Ecology 48:813-824.

Powlson, D. S., and D. S. Jenkinson. 1976. The effects of biocidal treatments on metabolism in soil. II. Gamma irradiation, autoclaving, air-drying and fumigation. Soil Biol. Biochem. 8:179-188.

Ruhling, A., and G. Tyler. 1973. Heavy metals pollution and decomposition of spruce needle litter. Oikos 24:402-416.

Sanborn, J. R., and C.-C. Yu. 1973. The fate of dieldrin in a model ecosystem. Bull. Environ. Contam. Toxicol. 10:340-346.

Schulz, K. R., T. W. Fuhreman, and E. P. Lichtenstein. 1976. Interactions of pesticide chemicals. Effect of eptam and its antidote on the uptake and metabolism of [^{14}C]phorate in corn plants. J. Agric. Food Chem. 24:269-299.

Spalding, B. P. 1977. Enzymatic activities related to the decomposition of coniferous leaf litter. Soil Sci. Soc. Amer. J. 41:622-627.

Spalding, B. P. 1978. The effect of biocidal treatments on respiration and enzymatic activities of douglas-fir needle litter. Soil Biol. Biochem. 10:537-543.

Spalding, B. P. 1979. Effects of divalent metal chlorides on respiration and extractable enzymatic activities of douglas-fir needle litter. J. Environ. Qual. 8:105-109.

Tu, C. M. 1970. Effect of four organophosphorus insecticides on microbial activities in soil. Appl. Microbiol. 19:479-484.

Tu, C. M. 1978. Effect of pesticides on acetylene reduction and microorganisms in a sandy loam. Soil Biol. Biochem. 10:451-456.

Witkamp, M. 1969. Environmental effects on microbial turnover of some mineral elements. Soil Biol. Biochem. 1:167-184.

Witkamp, M. 1976. Microcosm experiments on element transfer. Int. J. Environ. Stud. 10(1):59-63.

Witkamp, M., and B. Ausmus. 1975. Effects of tree species, temperature, and soil on transfer of manganese-54 from litter to roots in a microcosm. pp. 694-699. IN Howell, F. G., J. B. Gentry, and M. H. Smith (eds.), Mineral Cycling in Southeastern Ecosystems. CONF-740513. National Technical Information Service, Springfield, VA.

Witkamp, M., and B. Baryansky. 1968. Microbial immobilization of ^{137}Cs in forest litter. Oikos 19:392-395.

Witkamp, M., and M. Frank. 1967. Cesium-137 kinetics in terrestrial microcosms. pp. 635-643. IN Nelson, D. J., and F. C. Evans (eds.), Symposium on Radioecology. USAEC Document Conf. 670503.

Witkamp, M., and M. L. Frank. 1970. Effects of temperature, rainfall and fauna on transfer of ^{137}Cs, K, Mg, and mass in consumer-decomposer microcosms. Ecology 51:465-474.

Yu, C. C., G. M. Booth, D. J. Hanson, and J. R. Larsen. 1974. Fate of bux insecticide in a model ecosystem. Environ. Entomol. 3:975-977.

Yu, C. C., G. M. Booth, D. J. Hanson, and J. R. Larsen. 1974. Fate of carbofuran in a model ecosystem. J. Agric. Food Chem. 22:431-434.

Yu, C. C., G. M. Booth, D. J. Hanson, and J. R. Larsen. 1975. Fate of alachlor and propachlor in a model ecosystem. J. Agric. Food Chem. 23:877-879.

Yu, C. C., G. M. Booth, D. J. Hanson, and J. R. Larsen. 1975. Fate of pyrazon in a model ecosystem. J. Agric. Food Chem. 23:300-311.

Yu, C. C., G. M. Booth, and J. R. Larsen. 1975. Fate of triazine herbicide cyanazine in a model ecosystem. J. Agric. Food Chem. 23: 1014-1015.

4.2.6 EXCISED SYSTEMS

Ausmus, B. S., G. J. Dodson, and D. R. Jackson. 1978. Behavior of heavy metals in forest microcosms. III. Effects on litter-soil carbon metabolism. Water Air Soil Pollut. 10:19-26.

Ausmus, B. S., S. Kimbrough, D. R. Jackson, and S. Lindberg. 1979. The behaviour of hexachlorobenzene in pine forest microcosms: Transport and effects on soil processes. Environ. Pollut. 13:103-111.

Campbell, S. D. 1973. The Effect of Cobalt-60 Gamma-Rays on Terrestrial Microcosm Metabolism. Ph.D. dissertation, University of Michigan, Ann Arbor, Mich. 144 pp.

Gile, J. D., J. C. Collins, and J. W. Gillett. 1979. The soil core microcosm--A potential screening tool. EPA-600/3-79-089. U.S. Environmental Protection Agency, Corvallis, Oregon. 41 pp.

Jackson, D. R., B. S. Ausmus, and M. Levine. 1979. Effects of arsenic on nutrient dynamics of grassland microcosms and field plots. Water Air Soil Pollut. 11:13-21.

Jackson, D. R., and J. M. Hall. 1978. Extraction of nutrients from intact soil cores to assess the impact of chemical toxicants on soil. Pedobiologica 18:272-278.

Jackson, D. R., and M. Levine. 1979. Transport of arsenic in grassland microcosms and field plots. Water Air Soil Pollut. 11:3-12.

Jackson, D. R., J. J. Selvidge, and B. S. Ausmus. 1978. Behavior of heavy metals in forest microcosms. I. Transport and distribution among components. Water Air Soil Pollut. 10:3-11.

Jackson, D. R., W. J. Selvidge, and B. S. Ausmus. 1978. Behavior of heavy metals in forest microcosms. II. Effects on nutrient cycling processes. Water Air Soil Pollut. 10:13-18.

Jackson, D. R., C. D. Washburne, and B. S. Ausmus. 1977. Loss of Ca and NO_3-N (calcium, nitrate-nitrogen) from terrestrial microcosms as an indicator for assessing contaminants of soil pollution. Water Air Soil Pollut. 8(3):279-284.

McCormick, J. F., and R. B. Platt. 1962. Effects of ionizing radiation on a natural plant community. Radiat. Bot. 2:161-188.

McCormick, J. F., and R. B. Platt. 1964. Ecotypic differentiation in Diamorpha cymosa. Bot. Gaz. 125:271-279.

Murphy, P. G., and J. F. McCormick. 1971. Ecological effects of acute beta irradiation from simulated fallout particles on a natural plant community. pp. 454-481. Bensen, D. W., and A. H. Sparrow (eds.), Survival of Food Crops and Livestock in the Event of Nuclear War. Atomic Energy Commission Symposium Series, No. 24.

Ross-Todd, M., E. G. O'Neill, and R. V. O'Neill. 1980. Synthesis of terrestrial microcosm results. pp. 242-264. IN Harris, W. F. (ed.), Microcosms as Potential Screening Tools for Evaluating Transport and Effects of Toxic Substances: Final Report. ORNL/EPA-4, Oak Ridge National Laboratory, Oak Ridge, Tenn.

Van Voris, P., R. V. O'Neill, H. J. Shugart, and W. R. Emanual. 1978. Functional complexity and ecosystem stability: An experimental approach. ORNL/TM-6199. Oak Ridge National Laboratory, Oak Ridge, Tenn. 120 pp.

INDEX

Acartia 35
Acyrthosiphon pisum 107,112
Adalia bipunctata 112
Aerobacter aerogenes 31
Agroecosystem chamber 134
Algal competition 9,36
Alosa pseudoharengus 41
Amia calva 48
Amaeba proteus 33
Anisopteromalus calandrae 113
Aphelinus asychis (A. semiflavus) 111
Aphid-alfalfa, herbivory 107
Aphid-grain, herbivory 107
Aphid-parasitoid 111
Aphid-predator 112
Aphis fabae 112
Arthropod competition 102-105
Arthropod predators 110-116
ATP assay 127
Aquatic plant-herbivore 54
Avena 101
Baccharis pilularis 110,111
Baculovirus 53,54
Bdellovibrio 109
Begonia 108
Blattisocius 112
Bosmina longirostris 35,36,52
Bouteloua gracilis 109
Cactoblastis 108
Callosobruchus chinensis 113
Ceriodaphnia 35,52
    C. cornutum 42
Ceriodaphnia reticulata 40,42
Chaoborus 34,35,40
Chewing insect-plant, herbivory 108
Chrysopa 112
CO_2 efflux 126,128,132,133,135,137,139
Coccinella 112
    C. septempunctata 112
Coccus hesperidum 108
Coleus 108
Colias eurytheme 108
Community composition (terrestrial) 121
Community metabolism (terrestrial) 126
    ATP assay 127
    Chemical transformation 127
    CO_2 efflux 126,128,131,132,133,
        135,137,139

Competition
    Algal 9,36
    Terrestrial 98-105
        Drosophila 102
        Microbial 99
        Plant 101
        Triboleum 104
Coregonus clupeaformis 47
Crangonyx richmondensis 42
Criteria
    for evaluating and selecting
       models 163
    for standardized tests
       5,25,95
Cyclops 35,40,42,52
    C. bicuspidatus thomasi 36,41
    C. versalis 36
Cyprinodon variegatus 44
Daphnia galeata mendotae 40,42
    D. magna 38,39,40,42
    D. pulex 40
    D. retrocurva
Diaptomus 35,52
    D. clavipes 36
    D. oregonensis 41
    D. pallidus 40,42
Didinium nasutum 31,32,33
Dorosoma cepedianum 41
Drepanosiphon platanoides 112
Drosophila 98,102,103,104,106
    114,122
    D. melanogaster 102,103
    D. nebulosa 102
    D. pseudoobscura 102
    D. serrata 102
    D. simulans 102,103
    D. willistoni 102
Dunaliella tertiolecta 27
Ecosystem properties
    Aquatic 55-58
    Terrestrial 123
Ecosystem simulation models 16,158
Ectomycorrhizal infection 121
Emergent properties 96
Encarsia formosa 111
Endomycorrhizal infection 121
Ephesta (Anagasta) kuhniella 112
Epilachna varivestis 108

Epischura 35
Excised terrestrial systems 136-139
Exidechthis canescens 112
Fish-fish, predation 46-51
Fish-macroinvertebrates, predation 43-46
Fish-zooplankton, predation 11,37-43
Forest succession models 159
Fundulus grandis 44
Fundulus majalis 47
Gall midge-parasitoid 112
Gambusia affinis 46
Generalized multipopulation models 17,160
Glomus 121
Grain moth-parasitoid 112
Grassland core 137
Haematobia viritans 114
Heliothis zea 108
Heterospilus prosopidis 113
Holistic properties 96
Hyalella azteca 42
Hyspodamia 112
Ictalurus punctatus 47
Input-output analysis 17,162
Lagodon rhomboides 44
Lepomis cyanellus 41,48
   L. gibbosus 39,40
   L. macrochirus 38-42,47
Leptodora 34
Lichens 117
Lichtenstein microcosm 134
Litter systems 133
Loop analysis 17,161
Melaniris chagresi 38,42
Melanoplus sanguinipes 109
Menidia menidia 47
Mesocyclops 35,40,42
   M. edax 52
Metasyrphus 112
Metcalf microcosm 135
Microbe-microbe predation 109
Microbial competition 99
Microcosms
   Agroecosystem chamber 134
   Grassland core 137
   Lichtenstein 134
   Litter systems 133
   Metcalf 135
   Mixed flask cultures 10,61

Microcosms (continued)
   Odum 135
   Pelagic 13,67
   Periphyton communities 10,63
   Pond 11,70
   Sediment cores 65
      Soil cores 136
      Streams 13,71
   Terrestrial microcosm chamber 136
   Treecosm 137
   Whitcamp 135
Micropterus dolomieui 45
   M. salmoides 46
Mite-mite predation 114
Mixed flask cultures 10,61
Model ecosystems (see Microcosms)
Musca domestica 113
Muscidifurax raptor 113
Mycorrhizae 15,118,121
Nabis 112
Nasonia vitripennis 113
Neocatolaccus namezophagus 113
Neodiprion sertifler 116
Nitrogen cycle 124
Nitrogen fixation 117,124,128
Notegonus chrysoleucas 48
Notiophilus 114
Notropis venustus 49
Nutrient cycling
   Aquatic 57
   Terrestrial 124
Nutrient leaching 124-126,128,139
Oncorhynchus tshawytscha 47
   O. kisutch 47
   O. nerka 47
Orconectes propinquus 45
Oryzaephilus surinamensis 105
Outcrops 139
Palaemonetes pugio 44
Papaver 101
Paralichthys dentatus 47
Paramecium 62
   P. aurelia 31,32,33
   P. caudatum 31
Parasitism
   Aquatic 12,53
   Terrestrial 116
Pelagic microcosm 13,67
Perca flavescens 47
Periphyton communities 10,63
Peromyscus maniculatus 116

Phaenicia sericata 113
Philonthus creunatus 144
Phormia regina 113
Pimephales promelas 47
Pisolithus tinctorius 121
Plant competition 101
Plant, herbivory 54
Polyphemus 34
Pond microcosms 11,70
Praon exsoletum (P. palitans) 111
Predation
    Aquatic 11,28-53
    Terrestrial 109-116
Population genetics models 17,162
Primary productivity
    Aquatic 56
    Terrestrial 123
Pseudeucoila bochei 113
Rhizobium 109,117,123
Rhizopertha dominica 104
Rhopalomzia californica 110
Salmo gairdneri 39-42
Salvelinus namaycush 38,39
Scale-plant, herbivory 108
Schizaphis graminum 107
Sediment cores 136
Sitotroga cerealella 105
Soil cores 136

Spider-prey 114
Streams 13,71
Symbiosis
    Aquatic 55
    Lichens 117
    Mycorrhizae-plant 15,118
    Rhizobia-legume 15,117
Synthetic terrestrial systems 132-136
Syriphus 112
Terrestrial microcosm chamber 136
Testing scheme 5,25
Thalassia testudinum 44
Thalassiosira pseudonana 27
Therioaphis trifolli 107
Toxic Substances Control Act 1-4,
    55,72
Treecosm 137
Trialeurodes vaporariorum 107
Triboleum 99,104,106,122
    T. castaneum 104
    T. confusum 104
Tricoderma harizisnum 109
Trioxys complanatus
    T. utilis 111
Vertebrate predators 116
Whitefly-plant, herbivory 107
Witcamp microcosm 135
Woodruffia metabolica 33
Zabrotes subfasciatus 113